SOCIAL JUSTICE AND POLITICAL CHANGE

SOCIAL INSTITUTIONS AND SOCIAL CHANGE

An Aldine de Gruyter Series of Texts and Monographs

EDITED BY

Michael Useem • James D. Wright

SOCIAL JUSTICE AND POLITICAL CHANGE

Public Opinion in Capitalist and Post-Communist States

James R. Kluegel, David S. Mason, and Bernd Wegener

EDITORS

ALDINE DE GRUYTER

New York

About the Editors

James R. Kluegel is Professor of Sociology at the University of Illinois at Urbana-Champaign. His publications include *Beliefs About Inequality* (Aldine de Gruyter, 1986; with Eliot Smith) and numerous publications in professional journals.

David S. Mason is Professor and Head of the Department of Political Science at Butler University in Indianapolis. His publications include *Public Opinion and Political Change in Poland* (1985) and *Revolution in East-Central Europe: The Rise and Fall of Communism and the Cold War* (1992).

Bernd Wegener is Professor of Sociology at Humboldt University of Berlin. Among his recent publications are *Kritik des Prestiges* [Critique of Prestige] (Westdeutscher Verlag, 1988) and a book with H.P. Mueller on social inequality and social justice (*Soziale Ungleichheit und soziale Gerechtigkeit*, Leske und Budrich 1994).

ALDINE DE GRUYTER
A division of Walter de Gruyter, Inc.
200 Saw Mill River Road
Hawthorne, New York 10532

This publication is printed on acid free paper ∞

Library of Congress Cataloging-in-Publication Data

Social justice and political change : public opinion in capitalist and
    post communist states / James R. Kluegel, David S. Mason, and Bernd
    Wegener.
        p.   cm. — (Social institutions and social change)
    Includes bibliographical references (p.   ) and index.
    ISBN 0-202-30503-1 (cloth : acid-free paper). — ISBN
    0-202-30504-X (paper : acid-free paper)
        1. Social justice—Public opinion. 2. Post-communism.
I. Kluegel, James R. II. Mason, David S. (David Stewart), 1947– .
III. Wegener, Bernd, fl. 1977– . IV. Series.
JC578.S55   1995
303.3′72—dc20   95-8048
                                                                                          CIP

Manufactured in the United States of America

10 9 8 7 6 5 4 3 2 1

Contents

Project Participants

This book was a result of collaboration among all of the following people.

Bulgaria

Galin Gornev, Senior Research Fellow, Institute of Sociology, Academy of Sciences, Sofia.
Pepka Boyadjieva, Research Fellow, Institute of Sociology.

Czech Republic

Petr Matějů, Deputy Director, Institute of Sociology, Academy of Sciences of the Czech Republic, Prague.
Jan Hartl, Director, Centre for Empirical Research, Prague.

Estonia

Andrus Saar, Director, Saar Poll Limited, Tallinn.

Germany

Bernd Wegener, Professor of Sociology, Humboldt University, Berlin.
Pamela Davidson, Ph.D. Candidate, University of Massachusetts, Amherst.
Stefan Liebig, Lecturer in Sociology, Humboldt University, Berlin.
Susanne Steinmann, Research Assistant, University of Mannheim.

Holland

Wil Arts, Professor of Sociology, Erasmus University, Rotterdam.
Piet Hermkens, Professor of Sociology, University of Utrecht.
Peter van Wijck, Assistant Professor of Economics, Leiden University.

Hungary

Tamás Kolosi, Director of TARKI (public opinion research center), Budapest.

György Csepeli, Head of Department of Social Psychology, Institute for Sociology, Eötvös Loránd University, Budapest.

Mária Neményi, Institute of Sociology, Hungarian Academy of Sciences, Budapest.

Antal Örkény, Institute of Sociology, Eötvös Loránd University, Budapest.

Japan

Akihiro Ishikawa, Professor of Sociology, Chuo University, Tokyo.

Masaru Miyano, Professor of Sociology, Chuo University.

Poland

Witold Morawski, Professor of Sociology and Head of the Section on the Sociology of Work and Organizations, Institute of Sociology, Warsaw University.

Bogdan Cichomski, Associate Professor of Sociology and Director of the Polish General Social Survey, Institute for Social Studies, Warsaw University.

Russia

Ludmila Khakhulina, Senior Research Fellow, All Russian Center for Public Opinion Research, Moscow.

Svetlana Sydorenko, Research Fellow at the All Russian Center.

Slovenia

Vojko A. Antončič, Director, Institute of Social Sciences, Faculty of Social Sciences, University of Ljubljana.

United Kingdom

Gordon Marshall, Fellow in Sociology, Nuffield College, Oxford.

Adam Swift, Fellow in Politics and Sociology, Balliol College, Oxford.
Carole Burgoyne, Lecturer in Psychology, University of Exeter.
David Routh, Senior Lecturer in Psychology, University of Bristol.

United States

Duane Alwin, Research Scientist and Professor of Sociology, Institute for
Social Research, University of Michigan.
David S. Mason, Professor of Political Science and Head of the Department
of Political Science, Butler University, Indianapolis, Indiana.
James Kluegel, Professor of Sociology and Chair of Department of Sociology, University of Illinois, Urbana, Illinois.

Preface and Acknowledgments

This book is the first joint product of the International Social Justice Project, an international collaborative research project that involved over twenty researchers from twelve countries. Because of both the international scope of this project, and its collaborative nature, the project was a long time in genesis, development, and execution, and we are indebted to dozens of individuals and organizations for their support and assistance along the way.

The idea for a comparative public opinion survey on social justice was first hatched in 1986 by David Mason and Witold Morawski, while Mason was in Poland on a short-term research exchange sponsored by the International Research and Exchanges Board (IREX). At that time, there were very few survey instruments that had been fielded in both communist and noncommunist states, and the original idea was a comparison of justice values in those two systems. They began developing the project in the spring of 1989, when Mason held a research fellowship at Stanford University's Hoover Institution, under support by the United States Department of State, Soviet-East European Research and Training Act of 1983 (Title VIII). In developing the project, Mason benefited enormously from discussions there with Gabriel Almond of Stanford, Alex Inkeles of the Hoover Institution, and Gail Lapidus of Berkeley, as well as Samuel Barnes and Zvi Gitelman, who visited Stanford that spring.

In March 1989, the first core group of this project met in London, in conjunction with the meeting there of the International Studies Association. Participants in this meeting were Wil Arts (Holland), Masaru Miyano (Japan), Witold Morawski and Bogdan Cichomski (Poland), Veljko Rus (Yugoslavia), Duane Alwin, Jim Kluegel and David Mason (United States), Federico D'Agostino (Italy), and Feng Chujun and Yang Guansan (Peoples' Republic of China). (Italy and China later withdrew from the project.) We agreed to develop a multinational survey on popular perceptions of justice, and drew up a set of "working principles" to guide the project, which was to be genuinely collaborative, from the conceptualization and design of the survey questionnaire to the analysis and publication of the data. We agreed at that time, for example, that none of us would publish cross-national analysis of the survey data until our joint project volume—this book—was in production.

In October 1989, a second meeting was held in Dubrovnik, Yugoslavia, to discuss the concepts and design of the common questionnaire. The Dubrovnik conference was organized by Veljko Rus and Vojko Antončič of the University of Ljubljana and supported in part by the Interuniversity Conference Center in Dubrovnik. Travel expenses to this conference for some of the participants were supported by a grant from IREX. By this time, our group had expanded to include Bernd Wegener (West Germany), Galin Gornev (Bulgaria), Svetlana Sydorenko (USSR), and new participants from Yugoslavia (Vojko Antončič) and Holland (Piet Hermkens). Our East–West comparative agenda had also changed some-what, as all around us (literally) communist governments were in the process of collapsing. We had an opportunity now to do a survey on justice that was not only genuinely comparative and cross-national, but that could provide a kind of "baseline" of public opinion in the East European states as they began the difficult transition toward the market and democracy (see Chapter 1).

Beginning in the summer of 1990, the overall project was supported by funds provided by the National Council for Soviet and East European Research, which was renewed and extended in 1991 through 1993. (The council, however, is not responsible for the contents or findings of this report.) Funds from the council were especially crucial in assisting some of our colleagues in attending our collaborative meetings during that three-year period (see below), and in provid-ing seed money for the fieldwork in a number of the East European states. Bob Randolph, the executive director of the council, was extremely helpful and flex-ible as the project evolved. Stanislaw Pomorski of Rutgers University, the exter-nal reviewer for the project, also provided helpful advice and assistance.

In May 1990, Mason visited Moscow, under an exchange sponsored by IREX and the Social Science Research Council, to meet with the directors and other sociologists of the All Union Center for Public Opinion Research (now the All Russian Center) to discuss their participation in our project and the mechanism for fielding the survey in the Soviet Union.

In the months after the Dubrovnik conference, a committee of the group had designed a pretest version of the international questionnaire, and in June 1990 we met in Utrecht, Holland, to discuss this version of the questionnaire. This confer-ence was organized by Piet Hermkens and Wil Arts, and supported by the University of Utrecht and the Dutch Ministry of Social Affairs. We added two other countries to the project at this meeting, with the participation of Antal Örkény from Hungary and Gordon Marshall and Adam Swift from the United Kingdom. Ludmila Khakhulina from Russia also joined us for the first time. In September, Bernd Wegener hosted a smaller meeting in Heidelberg, where the final version of the pretest questionnaire was hammered out.

The pretest version of the questionnaire was tested in each country in the fall of 1990, and the group met in Budapest in January 1991 to discuss the results of the pretest and to adopt the final version of the questionnaire. This meeting was organized by our Hungarian colleagues, Tamás Kolosi, Antal Örkény, György Csepeli, and Mária Neményi, and hosted by Eötvös Loránd University.

The surveys were fielded in each country in the spring and fall of 1991. The group's working principles called for each country to secure primary support for the fieldwork internally, so the list of supporters of the national fieldwork is a long one: the British Social Justice Project was funded by the Economic and Social Research Council (grant number R00232421), Nuffield College, Oxford (a Norman Chester Research Fellowship), and a British Academy/Leverhulme Trust Senior Research Fellowship; in both East and West Germany, the project was funded by the Deutsche Forschungsgemeinschaft (German Research Council) under grant numbers WE 1019/1-1, WE 1019/1-2, and WE 1019/1-3; in Japan the fieldwork and data analysis were supported by the Institute of Social Science of Chuo University, a Ministry of Education grant-in-aid for scientific research, the Labor Research Center, and the Japan Securities Scholarship Foundation; in Holland, data collection was supported by the Dutch Ministry of Social Affairs; in Hungary, the survey was supported by OTKA (the National Scientific Research Fund) and TS (the Social Stratification Research Fund); in the United States, fieldwork and data archiving were supported by the National Science Foundation (SES-9023954) and the Institute for Social Research at the University of Michigan; in Bulgaria, the survey was funded by the Bulgarian Academy of Sciences; in Czechoslovakia by STEM (Center for Empirical Research) and the Czechoslovak Academy of Sciences; in Slovenia by the Ministry of Science and Technology; in Poland by the Komitet Badań Naukowych (State Committee for Scientific Research); in Russia by the Russian Federation Ministry of Labor; and in Estonia by Saar Poll, Limited.

After the collection and preliminary coding of the data, the group met in February 1992 at the Bellagio Conference Center in Italy, with the support of the Rockefeller Foundation, to discuss the first phases of data analysis and publication timetables. By this time, we had also been joined by Stefan Liebig from Germany and Carole Burgoyne from the United Kingdom, and by Petr Matějů and Jan Hartl from Czechoslovakia, where the survey had been fielded in the common time frame, despite their late entry into the project. The very difficult task of archiving and cleaning the data from twelve countries was supervised by Duane Alwin, with the assistance of David M. Klingel and Merilynn Dielman, with National Science Foundation funds (see above) generously supplemented by the University of Michigan's Institute for Social Research. After the Bellagio meeting, Andrus Saar from Estonia joined the project, and was able to field our survey in his country in early 1992.

Subsequent meetings for presentation of papers, discussion of collaborative work, and plans for a replication of the survey were held in August 1992 at the University of Michigan (organized by Duane Alwin and supported by the university's Institute for Social Research); in May 1993 in Tokyo (organized by Masaru Miyano and Akihiro Ishikawa and supported by the Institute of Social Science of Chuo University); and in May 1994 in Warsaw (organized by Bogdan Cichomski and Witold Morawski and supported by IREX and the University of Warsaw's

Institute for Social Studies). At that last meeting, we discussed replicating the 1991 survey in the postcommunist states.

We thank Robert Robinson of Indiana University for his very helpful comments and suggestions on the entire manuscript. Each of the three editors of this volume would also like to thank the people and institutions that facilitated their work on this project. Jim Kluegel received generous support for travel and other research costs during the design and implementation of this study from the Department of Sociology and the Liberal Arts and Sciences College at the University of Illinois at Urbana-Champaign. The time provided by a sabbatical leave and by a fellowship through the Cultural Values and Ethics program was invaluable for data analysis and writing.

David Mason would like to thank Butler University for its generous support for a sabbatical leave in 1988–1989, for release time in 1989–1990, for travel support, and for administrative support for project coordination. Marta Goertemiller, the secretary for the Department of Political Science, assisted in numerous ways with the administration, coordination and publications of this project. Lori Jancik was enormously helpful as student research and administrative assistant for the project.

Bernd Wegener gratefully acknowledges extensive funding by the German Research Council (Deutsche Forschungsgemeinschaft) as well as substantial support from the Department of Sociology of the University of Heidelberg.

Finally, we would like to thank our families for their patience, forebearing, and moral support throughout this project: Sharon, Dana, and Melanie Mason; and Kathleen, Alan, and Leah Kluegel.

James Kluegel, Urbana
David Mason, Indianapolis
Bernd Wegener, Berlin

1

The International Social Justice Project

James R. Kluegel, David S. Mason, and Bernd Wegener

The struggle over economic and political justice has, of course, been a central force in human history. In recent times, wars and revolutions have been fought in the name of democracy as political justice, and in the name of market versus socialist justice in the economic realm. Correspondingly, economic and political justice long has been the subject of scholarly analysis—by theologians, philosophers, and historians, and in recent times by social scientists. Until recently, however, analysis and debate about economic and political justice did not involve research on the views of the common person. Scholars often made assumptions about what common people think is fair (see Chapter 2), but for the most part they argued for the justice of economic or political institutions on rational or moral grounds.

In the past few decades the study of what and how the common person thinks about economic and political justice has burgeoned, especially in the United States. Psychological theories of distributive justice have been formulated, refined, and tested in the laboratory on a quite sizable population of college students. Through in-depth interviews and extensive surveys, political scientists and sociologists have probed how the general American public evaluates the justice of its economic and political systems. It may fairly be said that we know quite a bit about economic and political justice in the American mind (for broad overviews of justice research, see Cohen 1986; Greenberg and Cohen 1982; Scherer 1992).

In contrast, we know very little in any systematic, international comparative perspective about justice beliefs and norms. In addition to studies of the United States, there are single-country studies that give some insight into justice beliefs and norms in certain Western European countries, most especially England, and a few studies offering comparisons of two countries (Törnblom 1992). Following the revolution of 1989, we are beginning to see the publication of research on justice beliefs in Eastern European nations, especially in the former Soviet Union and Russia (Finifter and Mickiewicz 1992; Duch 1993; Miller, Reisinger, and Hesli 1993). Until quite recently, however, we have had no truly comparative studies, i.e., studies that employ common methods of data collection and, within the limits of translation, identical data collection instruments.

1

The lack of comparative study of popular justice norms and beliefs is due to more than parochialism. Like the weather, it is easy to talk about doing truly comparative research, but it has been hard to do anything about it. Until quite recently, the obstacles facing scholars wishing to mount a comparative study involving original data collection have been serious. Not the least of these has been communication, both in terms of language and technology.

Figuratively and literally, the walls limiting international comparative study are coming down (cf. Kohn 1989a). The worldwide availability of electronic mail and fax machines has made communication possible among teams of scholars from virtually all industrialized nations. International exchanges that took weeks by mail and were prohibitively expensive by phone may now be done in minutes by electronic mail or cheaply by fax. English has become the universal language of scholars, markedly reducing the investment in language training once required to do comparative work. In the case of Eastern and Central Europe, walls barring cooperation among scholars have literally been taken down.

In this improved climate for international comparative research, the International Social Justice Project (ISJP) was born. Nearly forty social scientists from twelve countries have participated at some point in the design, resource procurement, implementation, and analysis phases of the ISJP. This book reports the first analysis results from this project.

PROJECT GOALS

Our goals are both descriptive and theoretical. On the descriptive side of the ISJP agenda, we sought to generate a comparative picture of popular perceptions of economic and political justice in advanced industrialized nations. The ISJP includes surveys of people from five of the world's most influential capitalist democracies—Germany (both former East and West), Great Britain, Japan, the Netherlands, and the United States. It also includes surveys of people from countries comprising the large majority of the population of Central and Eastern Europe—Bulgaria, (former) Czechoslovakia, Estonia, Hungary, Poland, Russia, and Slovenia.

It is popularly said that timing is everything. We indeed were fortunate to begin this study in the year prior to the revolutions of 1989. We were able to use the new intellectual freedom in the former communist-controlled nations to field the same questionnaire in eight postcommunist countries (including the former East Germany), getting our survey into the field circa the summer of 1991. Thus we set as one of our goals to provide baseline data for the study of social change in this region. Our results give us a picture of what may be called "justice in transition."

Our results also give us a comparative picture of popular views of justice in the major capitalist democracies. Although there has been much more research on popular justice norms and beliefs in capitalist democracies than in postcommunist countries, the ISJP is only one of two studies to field a common questionnaire about economic and political justice in several capitalist democracies. The International Social Survey Program (ISSP) contained modules on the related topic of beliefs about inequality in its 1987 and 1992 surveys.[1]

In Kohn's typology of comparative research, most of the chapters in this book fall in the category he calls "nation as context" studies:

> In such research, one is primarily interested in testing the generality of findings and interpretations about how certain social institutions operate or about how certain aspects of social structure impinge on personality. (1989a:21)

The object of such research, as in much of the research presented in this book, is to see if similar processes hold in diverse nations. We agree with the goal articulated by Przeworski and Teune (1970) of ultimately "replacing the names of nations with the names of variables" in analyses of comparative data. We also agree, however, with Kohn's (1989a) assessment that we have much to learn from nations as context analyses before we are ready to do so. This assessment applies especially to the study of popular perceptions of economic and political justice where theory and research has been developed largely in the American and British contexts.

Our research is not motivated by a single, overarching theory or theoretical perspective on public opinion about economic and political justice. The scholars involved in this project bring to bear different theories and perspectives in analyzing justice beliefs. Some project scholars test social science theory that seeks to explain the origins of the justice norms and beliefs held by the public, while others are interested in theory that concerns the consequences of justice norms and beliefs. Instead of being motivated by a single broadly encompassing theory, the question areas and the specific items used were chosen to measure justice concepts central to testing hypotheses drawn from the current major theories and perspectives on justice norms and beliefs.

We shall say more about the specific contributions of project scholars in the subsequent chapter overview section. Here, however, it is useful to place the ISJP in the broader context of justice studies.

An important distinction in the large and varied body of justice theory and research is between empirical or descriptive studies, on the one hand, and normative studies on the other (Bell and Schokkaert 1992; Scherer 1992). Roughly speaking, empirical justice theory and research concerns the "what is" dimension, attempting to explain how people in fact evaluate economic and political justice. Normative studies concern the "what ought to be" dimension, making moral and rational arguments for the ideal justice of particular economic and political principles and institutions. The ISJP, of course, falls within the empirical-studies grouping. Nevertheless, the design of our study was importantly informed by normative theory. We employed questions eliciting popular justice evaluations that at least roughly correspond to key justice criteria elaborated and discussed by normative justice scholars. Borrowing from Swift et al. in this volume (Chapter 2) we assess "what the people think" about such normative justice concepts as entitlement, equality of opportunity, and desert. In other words, we study the general public as "normative theorists," examining their justice norms or beliefs about "what ought to be."

Another important distinction among justice scholars involves the level of justice evaluation. Following Brickman, Folger, Goode, and Schul (1981) we may distinguish between theory and research concerning criteria (a) used in the evaluation of justice or rewards received by individuals and small groups, or *microjustice,* and (b) used to evaluate the aggregate or societal level fairness of the reward distribution, or *macrojustice.* The ISJP was designed to address research questions at both levels and indeed, then, to permit analysis of the correspondence between levels. A particular strength of this study is the ability to examine microjustice evaluations in the real world. Our study also follows the call to develop a cross-national and cross-cultural scope for the social psychology of justice evaluation (Törnblom 1992; cf. Bond 1988).

We have included in the ISJP survey numerous *macrojustice* questions concerning economic and political orders in the ideal (normative justice) and in fact (existential justice). These questions permit examination of people's views of what a just society should be and their assessments of how just their societies are in fact. As discussed by David Mason (Chapter 3), popular views of justice play an important role in postcommunist countries as they struggle to put in place new political and economic orders. More generally, analysis of responses to macrojustice questions speaks to issues concerning the legitimation of political and stratification orders that are central in political and sociological theory (Arts and van der Veen 1992). As readers shall see, several chapters in this volume test hypotheses drawn from theories of the legitimation process.

DATA

To avoid confounding country differences with differences in data collection procedures, we attempted to employ standardized procedures in all countries. We sought to have a personal (face-to-face) interview using the exact same questionnaire given to a representative national sample from each country, to be given to persons eighteen and older. With only a few exceptions this is what we achieved. All samples were drawn as stratified probability samples. Funding considerations led to using a computer-aided self-administered interview procedure in the Netherlands, and to telephone interviews in the United States. The lower age limit varies by a couple of years among our countries. The sampling and inter-viewing was carried out by leading academic or commercial survey research organizations in all nations but Japan.[2]

With the exception of Japan (at 52%) the response rates achieved are good (at 70% or higher in all other countries), and equal or better than rates commonly achieved by the best survey research organizations in the respective countries. Checks of sociodemographic characteristics (age, education, occupation, income, etc.) of the respondents in each sample show that each survey closely matches the demographic profile expected on the basis of census or other large-scale survey data for the respective countries (see Table 5.1 in Chapter 5 for a profile of sociodemographic characteristics for each of the ISJP countries). This also holds in general for Japan, where the response rate is lower than we desired. The respondents in our Japanese sample have slightly higher incomes on average and are slightly more likely to be self-employed than the average Japanese citizen. However, these deviations are not large enough to warrant more than some caution about generalizing analyses of the Japanese data.

Further information about sampling and other data collection procedures is presented in the Appendix.

MEASUREMENT

The equivalence of measurement is a key issue in international comparative research (Kuechler 1987). Although it is also important regarding "objective" states such as education and social status (cf. Erikson and Goldthorpe 1992), it is an especially important issue regarding "subjective" states. It is never possible to establish the exact equivalence of measurement between or among countries. However, we took three important steps to achieve as closely equivalent mea-surement as is possible.

First, with only a few minor exceptions all countries employed the identical questionnaire: the same in length, question order, and response formats.[3] (Addi-tional, country-specific questions, if any, were asked after those of the common questionnaire.) The original questionnaire was written in English and translated into the principal language of each country. (In Czechoslovakia the questionnaire was translated into both Czech and Slovak, and in Estonia it was translated into both Estonian and Russian.) Iterative back-translation of the questionnaire to English was performed to validate the translation into English. Second, as much as possible we used questions and question-asking formats of known validity in international comparative research. Some questions were taken verbatim or with slight modification from the ISSP and other respected international comparative studies of the recent past. We employed questions and coding schemes developed in other major comparative projects—such as the CASMIN project coding of education (Erikson and Goldthorpe 1992) and the ISCO coding of occupations (see the Appendix). Third, the translation was carried out or overseen by social scientists with extensive survey research experience within their own countries, and extensive experience in translating measures developed in English for use in their countries.

We also recognize that survey research procedures well established in the West are only now becoming standard in certain of our postcommunist nations. Although much progress has been made in recent years, sampling, interviewing, and other key aspects of the survey process are subject to problems due to inexperience and other factors perhaps not present in the West (cf. Hahn 1993). Correspondingly, the analyses we present here avoid emphasizing small differences in marginal frequencies among countries. On the other hand, we are confident that the research design guidelines followed in each country permit valid inferences about large-scale differences between individual nations and categories of nations, such as Western European vs. Eastern European nations or capitalist vs. postcommunist nations. At the very least we should keep in mind that what we offer here is based on interviews of fifty minutes or longer with over seventeen thousand persons, selected to be as representative of each nation's citizenry as possible. This is a far better basis for inferring what the common person believes and how they may differ in their beliefs than taking readings from popular media or using anecdotal evidence of various kinds, as (often for the simple lack of survey data) has been the primary method employed in much prior research on certain postcommunist nations.

CHAPTER OVERVIEW

The four major sections of this book correspond to major divisions that prevail within the empirical literature on economic and political justice beliefs. At the most general level, this literature is divided by a focus on one of two questions: (1) What do justice beliefs explain? (2) How do we explain justice beliefs? Research concerning the former question generally examines the political and economic significance of justice beliefs, and often is addressed to political actors, policymakers, and others concerned with social policy as well as scholars of social change. The literature addressing the second question is predominantly the product of academic-based, or "basic" researchers testing social science theory within the fields of psychology, political science, and sociology.

Although the respective audiences for research answering these two questions are often composed of different people, this book includes chapters that address both of them. In part this simply reflects that the ISJP brought together social scientists with interests corresponding to each of the two major questions about justice beliefs. However, we also believe that including both kinds of work is of intellectual value. Research seeking to explain justice beliefs tends to focus on a narrowly defined issue or problem, often testing one or a few hypotheses about the determinants of justice beliefs. It is sometimes difficult to see the broader significance or implications of findings from such research. Work that addresses what justice beliefs explain usually takes a broader-brush approach, and thus helps one see the larger significance and implications of work that addresses what explains justice beliefs.

All of the chapters in Part I address the "What do justice beliefs explain?" question, or the "So what?" question. What, in broader perspective, is the significance of the findings of the ISJP? Swift et al. (Chapter 2) pose the question of significance directly in the title of their chapter, "Distributive Justice: Does It Matter What the People Think?" They break this large question down into its constituent smaller ones—questions concerning the coherency of public opinion about justice, the relationship between attitudes and behavior, and the relevancy of research on popular beliefs to reasoned, scholarly statements about justice. Special attention is given to the question of why political theory, as in the work of such political philosophers as Rawls and Walzer, should pay attention to what surveys such as the ISJP tell us about what the people think. This paper takes into account a major shift in normative justice theory according to which justice is not a metaphysical but a political issue (Rawls 1993; Rorty 1990).

Mason (Chapter 3) examines the implications of the economic and political justice beliefs of the publics of postcommunist nations for economic and political change during the current transition era. Mason begins by discussing important sociopolitical characteristics of the postcommunist nations at the time of our survey (ca. 1991), which provide important context for interpreting the findings for these countries presented in other chapters. He provides a broad-sweep view of public opinion relevant to the goal of developing both democratic political institutions and a capitalist economy. Mason stresses that the ISJP data, and those from other studies, show that postcommunist countries occupy a kind of "ideological limbo," where old political and economic ideologies have been rejected, but new ones have yet to take hold. Also of major importance to the political climate prevailing in these countries, Mason's analysis shows that at the practical (as opposed to the ideological) level, the population of postcommunist nations embraces both capitalism and socialism, desiring to achieve the higher living standard of the former without relinquishing the economic security of the latter. He further shows that the political situation is complicated by the fact that the politically active minorities in these countries are much more promarket and antisocialist than the rest of the populations.

Complementing the focus of Mason on justice beliefs relevant to the central economic concerns of postcommunist nations, Kluegel and Miyano (Chapter 4) examine the relevance of justice beliefs to one of the central economic issues in capitalist democracies: welfare state policies. Kluegel and Miyano propose that the effects of status and justice beliefs on support for government intervention to

reduce inequalities differ among countries according to differences in the structure of their welfare state programs, and according to cultural differences involving collectivist vs. individualist orientations. They show that respondents in all of
the five ISJP capitalist nations share a similar level of majority opposition to
government intervention placing an upper limit on income. They also show that
support for an upper limit is, with a few exceptions, affected by status and justice
beliefs in the same way in all countries. On the other hand, support for government intervention to ensure minimums (guaranteed jobs and minimum standards
of living) differs markedly among these countries. Consistent with their thesis,
effects of status and justice beliefs on support for government-ensured minimums
substantially differ among countries.

Chapters in Parts II, III, and IV address the "How do we explain justice
beliefs?" question, testing hypotheses drawn from different theoretical perspectives. These three sections are formed according to two divisions within the
research literature on justice beliefs. Research addressing the explanations of
justice beliefs has for the most part examined either macrojustice or microjustice
beliefs. As discussed earlier, macrojustice beliefs are those referring to justice at
the societal level, and microjustice beliefs have individual-level or personal-level
justice as their referent. Put roughly, microjustice beliefs concern how fairly a
single individual is treated, and macrojustice beliefs concern how fairly people in
general are treated. The chapters of Part II in major part test hypotheses drawn
from microjustice theory.

In Chapter 5, Alwin et al. examine perceptions of personal income in the
twelve countries of the ISJP, focusing especially on how people evaluate "deserved" or "fair" personal income. They call upon equity and status value theory
to formulate an explanation of perceived deserved income. Among other hypotheses, they predict that the link between income received and income deserved
will be strongest under conditions of high system legitimacy. Consistent with this
hypothesis, Alwin et al. find that although actual personal income (existential
income) substantially predicts deserved personal income (fair income) in all
countries, the link between existential and perceived fair income is much stronger in Western capitalist democracies (and Japan) than in postcommunist countries. In contrast, perceived family need (the discrepancy between actual family
income and that which a person perceives her or his household needs) more
strongly influences perceived income desert in postcommunist countries than in
the West. Art, Hermkens, and van Wijck (Chapter 6) call on equity and framing
theory to develop and test a model of how people evaluate the justice of the
income distribution. Although their ultimate focus is a macrojustice evaluation,
they approach it from principles of microjustice theory. Arts et al. call attention
to Homan's proposition that in a stable system "what is" comes to be evaluated as
"what ought to be." They show that the correlation between the perceived actual
and evaluated fair income for occupations is substantial higher in the stable
systems of the West than in the unstable systems of postcommunist nations. An

attempt to explicitly link microjustice with macrojustice considerations is undertaken in Chapter 7 by Wegener and Steinmann. Building on Guillermina Jasso's formal framework of justice psychophysics, the authors pose the question whether the psychophysical statements are general enough as to be valid across different social, political and national conditions. Comparing the populations of the two now-united parts of Germany, Wegener and Steinmann model the effects of sociostructural factors, comparison processes, and what they call microjustice and macrojustice forces on satisfaction with income and one's standard of living, or material satisfaction. Results of their analyses show that microjustice processes are strongly influential in both (former) East and West Germany. However, they also demonstrate the need for extending the psychophysical formulations in order to make them work "in the real world."

Scholarship on macrojustice beliefs may be divided according to a primary emphasis on ideology versus social structural factors as determinants of justice beliefs. As a rough generalization, scholars emphasizing ideology have underscored the influence of common socialization—as shaped by political and economic elites or "culture"—on the justice beliefs that prevail in a specific nation or specific kinds of nations. In contrast, those emphasizing structural factors underscore the more universal. In particular, they point to the common influence across nations of socioeconomic position, gender, and like factors that define relative social and economic interests. In this view, country-level (aggregate) differences in justice beliefs are the product of "compositional" differences among countries, i.e., the different distributions of education, occupation, income, age, and so on that are found among countries.

The Chapters in Part III in important part address the ideological level of justice belief determination. Kluegel et al. (Chapter 8) examine existential (as opposed to normative) justice beliefs, analyzing the balance of social versus individualist explanations of poverty and wealth in all of the ISJP nations. They test hypotheses drawn from perspectives that differ in how much and what kind of effect they propose that elite-shaped ideology has on how people account for the rich and the poor in their respective countries. The results of this chapter, as do those reported by Kluegel and Matějů (Chapter 9), best support a "split consciousness" interpretation of the influence of ideology and "rational" interests. Kluegel and Matějů test the generality of a finding in U.S. and British research concerning adherence to egalitarian and inegalitarian principles of distributive justice. Specifically, they examine whether the pattern of simultaneous adherence to both egalitarian and inegalitarian principles present in the United States and Great Britain also holds among the other capitalist and postcommunist nations of the ISJP. They find that dual adherence to both egalitarian and inegalitarian sentiment not only holds in postcommunist as well as capitalist nations, but is even more pronounced among the populations of Central and Eastern Europe.

Chapters 8 and 9 emphasize the political-ideological level of determination of justice. Wegener and Liebig in Chapter 10 call our attention to the cultural dimension. In particular, they contrast "primary" and "secondary" justice ideologies. They contrast primary justice ideologies, rooted in normative, i.e., cultural causes, with secondary justice ideologies based on rational calculation that importantly derives from one's structural location, and particularly from one's economic class. Wegener and Liebig contrast East and West Germany with the United States, arguing that (1) egalitarian-statism is the primary ideology in Germany, while self-interested individualism is the secondary ideology, and (2) the reverse holds in the United States. They trace the difference in primary ideologies in each country to the two different variants of the Protestant religion that have historically prevailed in them—Lutheran doctrine in Germany, Calvinist doctrine in the United States.

The final two papers of this book share a focus on how the social structural positions people occupy shape their justice beliefs. In Chapter 11, Wegener and Liebig apply theory expounded by Mary Douglas to generate hypotheses about the differential effects among (former) East and West Germans of structural positions on four justice "cosmologies." They find that East-West differences in justice cosmologies can in major part be explained by differences between the regions in the distribution of structural positions. In general, their analyses show that structural positions have the same effect in each country, with the important exception of age. The young in East Germany are markedly less likely to support egalitarianism than are the old. In West Germany there are less pronounced, but still statistically significant differences such that younger people are somewhat more egalitarian than older people. This points to an important role for generational socialization net of structural factors.

Davidson, Steinmann, and Wegener (Chapter 12) examine gender differences in justice beliefs in two capitalist and two postcommunist countries. This paper addresses the controversy about differences between men and women in moral consciousness. Davidson and Steinmann contrast a normative approach to gender differences in justice evaluations with a rational approach. The normative approach accounts for gender differences in justice beliefs by appeal to gender differences in interpersonal values, proposing that women, for example, place more value on interpersonal harmony and solidarity and therefore prefer equality as a criteria for distributive justice more so than do men, who give greater emphasis to equity. The rational approach underscores differences in the structural positions held by men and women and their differential experience with injustice. Their results do not admit to a simple explanation exclusively in terms of either the normative or rational approaches.

COMMON FINDINGS

In planning this book, ISJP participants specified certain broad topic areas of interest to them, but no effort was made to prescribe theoretical emphases or analysis techniques. We thought it best to capitalize on the various strengths among the project colleagues, rather than force people to all march to the same drummer. Each chapter is a quite independent product. As a result the reader will notice that there are some seeming inconsistencies among chapters in conceptualization and measurement. For example, Kluegel et al. (Chapter 8) take a set of questions to be indicative of "social explanations" of poverty. Wegener and Liebig (Chapter 11) use a subset of these items to measure what they call "fatalism." However, these inconsistencies in the end are overshadowed by the much larger consistency and complementarity of the findings that emerge.

Because each chapter ends with its own conclusions, a formal conclusions chapter in this volume would be redundant. Nevertheless, it is useful here to note a few common findings that emerge across all the chapters.

First, we see across countries and regions that factor structures for economic justice items are strongly similar. The tale of this common factor structure begins in Chapter 4 and continues through Chapters 8 to 12. On the "ideal justice" side, the story is one of two major factor complexes. Although they are variably named in different chapters, they are broadly defined by sentiment in support of equality on the one hand vs. sentiment in support of inequality on the other hand. Norms of strict equality and of need, and attitudes toward government policy regarding inequality, form parts of the "equality complex," while notions of market justice, inegalitarianism, and individualism are subsumed in the "inequality complex." On the "existential justice" side, Chapter 8 demonstrates that items measuring poverty and wealth have the same basic factor structure in all twelve countries of the ISJP. The existence of common measurement structures across countries offers strong evidence of the equivalence of measurement on key constructs.[4]

Second, several chapters underscore the duality of thinking about economic justice that prevails in all industrialized societies. In Chapter 3, we see that postcommunist countries are struggling with this duality in the form of embracing market justice beliefs and norms, but steadfastly holding to the egalitarian past in the form of government guarantees against the effects of markets. Yet in many ways this egalitarian-inegalitarian duality clearly exists in the mature capitalist democracies as well. It is found as well in explanations of the justice of "what is"—as seen in Chapter 8, in the simultaneous expression of individualist and social explanations of poverty. Chapters in this volume offer different, but not necessarily competing views of what is responsible for this fundamental duality.

Third, in spite of large differences on average between the citizens of capitalist and postcommunist countries in many micro-and macrojustice sentiments and beliefs, there are common effects of sociostructural and social-psychological factors on justice beliefs across all countries. However, we see in several chapters that when we control or "adjust" for distributional differences in socioeconomic status and social psychological variables significant differences among countries remain. This underscores the need for a multilevel approach to understanding popular justice evaluations, bringing to bear historical and cultural factors, as well as the structural and social psychological.

As with many first results, the chapters in this book often pose as many new questions as ones they answer. This is perhaps especially so for analyses of the postcommunist countries, where the newness of the opportunity to do such research and the rapid political and economic change taking place pose numerous questions. We hope that our colleagues find the answers to questions we have provided of value, and that they will be motivated by these chapters to answer the new questions our research presents.

NOTES

1.   However, these modules are only fifteen minutes in length and give little to no coverage to important areas of beliefs that are covered in the ISJP; e.g., the ISSP does not contain questions on the range of economic justice norms, beliefs about existential justice such as those concerning poverty and wealth, and the area of political justice entirely. Japan was not among the countries fielding the ISSP survey in either of these years.

2.   In Japan interviews were carried out by students under the supervision of Professor Masaru Miyano of Chuo University in Tokyo.

3.   Space considerations prohibit us from including a copy of the entire questionnaire. However, information about the questionnaire or any other information about project methods can be obtained from any of the editors of this book. A copy of the codebook containing question wordings and response frequencies may be acquired from ICPSR at the University of Michigan or from the Zentralarchiv in Cologne, Germany. See also the Appendix.

4.   At the same time, we recognize the need to further research questions of equivalence of measurement, making use of new tools and new disciplinary perspectives (Alwin et al. 1994).

I

JUSTICE IN POLITICAL PERSPECTIVE

2

Distributive Justice: Does It Matter
What the People Think?[1]

Adam Swift, Gordon Marshall, Carole Burgoyne,
and David Routh

The International Social Justice Project (ISJP) is the first comprehensive sociological survey of popular beliefs about distributive justice. Based on a common
research design and interview schedule, developed and fielded by colleagues
working in twelve democratic capitalist and former state socialist societies, the
study investigates attitudes toward a number of economic and political issues that
are central to debates about social justice. In this chapter we report some early
findings from three of the national surveys.[2]

The new project is entering an already crowded academic arena. Indeed,
interest in justice issues is such that the field boasts its own international journal,
and supports a sizeable industry in textbooks and student readers.[3] Fortunately,
the political theorist David Miller has recently distilled the principal findings
from the extensive literature into a pair of influential review articles (Miller 1991,
1992), and these provide a useful context for introducing this latest contribution
to the debate.

In the first of these essays, Miller examines the various theories of justice
currently on offer, charting the differences between monolithic and pluralistic
accounts; rights-based, meritorian, and egalitarian perspectives; and analyses
rooted in the Aristotelian, Hegelian, and feminist traditions. However, sociologists will probably be more interested in his second article, an overview of what
is now a substantial field of empirical research into public perceptions of distributive justice. Miller here uses the heuristic device of comparing justice in small-
group contexts with justice across whole societies, on the one hand, and beliefs
about justice (what people say is fair or just) with actual behavior (what they do
when asked to allocate valuable resources) on the other. Much of the relevant
work fits easily into the conceptual space defined by these twin dimensions of
micro versus macro and attitudes versus behavior. Social psychologists have
focused on behavior at the microlevel, exploring the factors that influence people

to distribute rewards according to one criterion rather than another, at least in experimental situations involving small groups. By contrast, sociologists most commonly investigate popular judgments about the fairness of the distribution of resources across whole societies, normally by means of sample surveys. In their case it is beliefs about macrolevel distributions that are the focus of attention.

One of Miller's objectives in bringing together these diverse literatures is to identify unresolved problems and possible directions for future inquiry. In this regard his articles raise three issues of some consequence for a study such as ours. The first is the possibility that the opinions of ordinary people, who are not used to thinking systematically about the often complex questions of justice, will be ill considered and therefore contradictory. Lack of appropriate cognitive sophistication on the part of respondents might well result in largely unstructured data that are difficult if not impossible to interpret. Miller himself is not unduly worried by this prospect, merely observing that "provided there are consistent general trends in popular belief, a minority who give random or contradictory responses will appear simply as 'noise' to be discounted" (1992:557). The question then arises of whether or not our own data satisfy the condition in question. Is there a discernible pattern to commonsense beliefs about social justice—or is popular opinion just so much attitudinal "noise"?

Miller also considers the further worry that there is in any case little to be gained by exploring what people think about social justice since expressed beliefs have an indeterminate relationship to how individuals actually behave. Thus, responses to an attitude survey might be shaped to reflect socially acceptable opinion, while behavior is steered in a quite different direction by self-interest or any one of a large number of contextual constraints. Miller gives scant attention to this problem, merely observing that the researcher must be cautious in the inferences drawn from any particular study, and should look for convergence in findings arrived at in different ways (1992:557–58). As coauthors of a cross-national survey of attitudes perhaps we need to confront the issue more directly. Do popular beliefs about distributive justice in fact shed any light on social behavior?

Finally, in placing the philosophical material summarized in the earlier of his articles alongside the subsequent review of empirical findings, Miller is led naturally to pose the question of the relationship between the two. How does political theory relate to commonsense understandings of moral notions like justice? Arguably, the whole corpus of empirical research on popular beliefs about distributive justice might be limited in its significance simply because public opinions are one thing, while a coherent theory of social justice is quite another. Miller's own view is that "the theorist should welcome evidence of firmly and consistently held beliefs about justice as data against which prospective theories of justice may be tested" (1992:556). However, as he also observes (1992:555), almost without exception political theorists of justice have failed to consider the bearing that empirical findings might have on their formulations.

Quite reasonably, therefore, the skeptical thinker might well ask why he or she should look to the ISJP for guidance in theoretical constructions. Of what possible relevance are our survey results for solving the complex philosophical problems of justice?

In short, Miller's articles raise three important issues of principle about research into popular attitudes toward social justice, in terms of which we might assess the findings from our own particular study: Are beliefs organized in a more or less consistent fashion? How important are beliefs for understanding behavior? and What is the relationship between empirical research and normative theory?

POLITICAL PHILOSOPHY AND POPULAR BELIEFS

On the face of it there would seem to be no clear reason for political philosophers to pay attention to the findings of empirical research such as ours. Arguably, the justification of moral principles simply occupies a different logical space from the description and explanation of the moral principles to which people actually subscribe. Empirical research cannot contribute to political-theoretical debate since the philosophical task of justification remains immune from whatever one might discover about the justice beliefs current in any particular society.

Moreover, since the philosopher's reasons for endorsing a particular view are invariably rather complicated and have taken a great deal of thought to assemble, it would be surprising if ordinary people, not necessarily less intelligent but in all probability having devoted less time to the exercise of that intelligence, arrived at similarly measured conclusions. This was certainly the view of one of the anonymous referees who was asked to comment upon Marshall's 1990 request for funding for the ISJP from the Economic and Social Research Council:

> Surveys of popular opinion on these topics seem to me of little academic value. The great debate about justice that has been in progress since the time of Plato has thrown up many difficulties. But we will not be helped in the least in the resolution of these difficulties by a knowledge of the quirks of public opinion. Justice is, one might almost say, a semi-technical notion. It is the topic discussed by Plato in the *Republic*, by Aquinas in *Summa Theologia*, and by Mill in *Utilitarianism*: there are obvious continuities between views of these very different thinkers. Someone who knows nothing of this material is hardly in a position to contribute to the resolution of our problems. It would seem therefore a waste of time to survey the views of people who are not in a position to judge the issues.

From this perspective, there is no problem in concluding that people are simply wrong in advocating distributive principles that more careful thought, or perhaps even superior moral sense, would lead them to disavow.

These positions may be contrasted with that of Miller himself, whom we have already observed suggesting that empirical beliefs can be regarded as "data" against which theories of justice may be "tested." According to him, and citing the work of John Rawls and Michael Walzer in support,

> few contemporary political theorists would wish to draw such a sharp line between common opinion and theoretical truth. Most would claim in one way or another to incorporate and systematize existing beliefs about justice in their theoretical constructions. (1992:556)

In an apparently similar vein, Jon Elster has argued that "theories of justice need empirical foundations" (1992:192), and that these might be provided by studies of the ways in which institutions allocate the scarce resources at their disposal.

Clearly, there are deep and complex philosophical issues at stake here, and it is not our aim to provide a definitive treatment of the matter. For purposes of clarification, however, it seems to us helpful to distinguish three ways in which empirical research into the normative beliefs held by lay social actors might be thought important to political philosophy. In increasing order of strength, they are first, that such beliefs, and knowledge of their causal determinants, provide food for thought; second, that they constitute feasibility constraints on the realization of the philosophically justifiable distribution; and third, that they are constitutive of that distribution itself.

The first, so weak as to be uncontroversial, is simply that knowing others think differently gives the philosopher, or at least the philosopher with a proper sense of humility and fallibility, grounds for caution. As Elster puts it, "the knowledge that others hold or practice very different conceptions should make him scrutinize his own opinions with extra care" (1992:193). Thus, Elster (1995) has quite rightly suggested that Frolich and Oppenheimer's (1992) finding that truncated utilitarianism—maximizing total welfare subject to a floor constraint on individual welfare—is overwhelmingly the most popular distribution actually chosen by people in a situation simulating Rawls's veil of ignorance, gives the philosopher reason to accord it more careful consideration than it has received hitherto. On this account, the philosopher may still end up rejecting popular opinion, but it will at least have been treated with appropriate respect.

If descriptive studies can play this cautionary role, then research into the factors that explain why people believe what they do about distributive justice can and should be similarly thought-provoking. For example, where sociological research reveals that people are inclined to favor principles that correspond to their self-interest, then philosophers whose own views seem to reflect this process should think again. Of course, they may come to the same conclusions: as Elster (1995) acknowledges, correlations of this kind are not sufficient to invalidate arguments. But one does not have time to question all of one's intuitions equally carefully, and empirical research of an explanatory kind can help the philosopher identify those most worthy of suspicion.

Descriptive and explanatory empirical research can, then, be helpful for the normative project—but this role remains merely external. There is no suggestion here that what other people think, or even why they think it, can do more than give the philosopher reason cautiously to reconsider his or her own arguments and intuitions. The second reason why empirical research might be of interest to the political theorist continues to adopt this external attitude, but holds that lay beliefs matter insofar as they constitute the causal field that confronts his or her attempts to guide action. In the first place, conceptions of justice that fail sufficiently to correspond to ordinary thinking are doomed to failure, however sound they may be in philosophical terms, for, as John Dunn observes, "if historical agents are to be provided with reasons for acting, they must be furnished with reasons which are reasons for *them*" (1980:247; italics in original). But as well as ensuring that one's arguments are presented in such a way that they can actually motivate those to whom they are addressed, there is the separate point that it may be strategically justified to compromise with opponents for the sake of achieving on balance better outcomes than would be achieved by insisting on pure truth. The bounds of political possibility are to a great extent set by popular opinion, so that judging what can be done politically requires knowledge of that opinion. Add to this the claim that it makes little sense to advocate that which it is impossible to achieve, or that the responsible theorist should worry about the set of feasible outcomes given the status quo, and one has a variety of moral arguments for taking lay beliefs into account when constructing one's normative theory. We need not regard those beliefs as making any difference to the truth about justice, for our conclusion may well be simply that justice is unattainable and will be so while popular opinion remains as it is, but we will have reason to take them into account when offering prescriptions here and now.

The third argument as to why popular beliefs might bear on political philosophies of justice is much stronger. The idea here is that the right answer in politics, in this case the distributive principles that are justified for the society in question, may be internally related to lay beliefs themselves. Where the second argument regards those beliefs merely as constraints upon the feasibility of achieving a just society, and the justification of principles of justice as occurring quite independently of popular beliefs,[4] this third argument claims that at least part of the answer to the question of how goods should be distributed is to be found by looking at the way that people think that they ought to be distributed. Some recent work in political philosophy has taken a turn in this direction, and since it would seem potentially to accord considerable significance to our research, it is worth examining in some detail.

There would seem to be two versions of the claim that empirical beliefs have a constitutive role to play in the justificatory project. On the one hand, there is the antifoundationalist (one might say antiphilosophical) stance, simply rejecting the idea that there is anything else to which one might appeal other than a society's "shared meanings" or "shared understandings." By contrast, on the other hand, there is the position that holds that there are good (quite possibly "foundational") moral reasons why we should respect the opinions and judgments of our fellow citizens. On this second view, it is not that there is no other way to arrive at normative principles than by what Richard Rorty calls "a historico-sociological description of the way we live now" (1990:287), but rather that we have normative reason to accord moral weight to the beliefs of relevant others.

We need say little about the first, antifoundationalist version of this claim, other than to make clear that some of the influential theorists who can look as if they hold such a position do not in fact do so. It is Rorty who is its most explicit advocate, but in a paper that attributes the stance to Rawls: the latter's claim that his theory of justice is political and not metaphysical is taken to show how liberal democracy can get along without philosophical presuppositions, requiring "only history and sociology" (Rorty 1990:284). Properly understood, however, Rawls' claim is that we should take seriously "certain fundamental ideas seen as implicit in the public political culture of a democratic society" (1993:13–14), not simply because they represent "the way we live now," but rather because we have reason to value a society that is publicly justifiable to its members. Putting a complex argument as concisely as possible, what Rawls actually argues is that it is valuable if people live in a society where coercion is not used, except in ways that are publicly justifiable; the importance of public justifiability leads the political theorist to "society's main institutions, and their accepted forms of interpretation. . .seen as a fund of implicitly shared ideas and principles" (ibid.); the idea of society as a fair scheme of cooperation between free and equal citizens is such an idea, which is articulated by Rawls in terms of the imaginative construct of the "original position"; and from that device of representation emerges a substantive theory of distributive justice (see Mulhall and Swift 1992:167–205).

In other words, Rawls gives a constitutive role to the ideas shared by his fellow citizens for independently justified moral reasons, not because those shared ideas are all there are. If we ask why it matters that society be publicly justifiable, and hence why political philosophy should take seriously those shared ideas, the answer is in terms of what he calls "the liberal principle of legitimacy." As he puts it,

> our exercise of political power is fully proper only when it is exercised in accordance with a constitution the essentials of which all citizens as free and equal may reasonably be expected to endorse in the light of principles and ideals acceptable to their common human reason. (1993:137)

Rawls is thus led to espouse a methodology constraining him to the working up of ideas latent in our public political culture by his distinctively liberal (and we might say foundational) understanding of the proper relation between the individual and the state. On this view, the political philosopher has moral reason to care not about truth as such, but about truth that can be justified publicly.

Although sometimes presenting his position in antifoundationalist terms, Walzer too can most charitably be read as premising his attention to shared social meanings on a more fundamental normative claim. On his account of the proper relation between philosophy and democracy (Walzer 1981), it is a democratic respect for lay beliefs that requires the philosopher to accord them moral weight. If one understands politics and political theory as in the business of responding to citizens' wills, then what matters is not so much the independent philosophical validity ("rightness") of citizens' beliefs, but the fact that they are theirs. In *Spheres of Justice* (Walzer 1983:314, 320), he puts the point slightly differently, claiming that what guides his approach is "a decent respect for the opinions of mankind," and grounding this respect in the claim that it is as culture-producing creatures that we are one another's equals. Just as Rawls's methodological concern with what people think relies ultimately on a foundational claim about freedom and equality, and the constraints this puts on how the state can treat its citizens, so Walzer's insistence on the importance of respecting shared social meanings builds upon a foundational claim about the sense in which people are equal. Even Rorty, who is most keen to deny the need for foundations, presents himself as asserting the priority of democracy to philosophy, which suggests that he too can plausibly be read as arguing the democratic case for heeding the beliefs of his fellow citizens.[5]

Whatever the reason for giving moral weight to shared ideas or meanings, there remains the question of how these relate to empirical research of the kind that we are undertaking, under the auspices of the international project. To what extent are the things that Rawls and Walzer would have political philosophers consider really empirical people's empirical beliefs about distributive justice? The answer, in our view, is very little, since their methodological injunctions leave a great deal of room for philosophical maneuver.

In Walzer's case, it is crucial to his argument that he can distinguish between the "social meaning" of a good, and "the opinions that people currently have about how it should be distributed." That is why he can defend his methodology as consistent with radical social criticism. He knows, for example, that many of his fellow Americans think it quite proper for health care to be on sale in the market, and his argument against this view (Walzer 1983:86–90) in fact relies upon a claim about "the distributive logic of the practice of medicine" and the inconsistency involved in a society's permitting a market whilst simultaneously recognizing health care to be a need, evidenced by the use of communal funds to finance research, build hospitals, underwrite the treatment of the very old, and so on. As Georgia Warnke puts it, "social meaning is not a matter of the opinion individuals may have about goods, institutions and practices; it is a matter of the goods, institutions and practices themselves about which individuals have opinions" (1992:18). Walzer's "decent respect for the opinions of mankind" turns out to have little to do with what social scientists usually regard as public opinion.

Where Walzer claims to be providing a reading of the way we understand particular goods in our society, Rawls's text is that much vaguer thing he calls "the public political culture," so that he is even further from relying on a claim about the specific importance of the way ordinary people think about distributive questions. Insofar as his explicit project is to seek those deeper bases of agreement that underlie our superficial but real disagreements (most generally the apparent conflict between freedom and equality), Rawls is less concerned with what people believe now than with what they might come to believe after due reflection and having accepted the condition of public justifiability; that is, on Rawls's account, after they have followed him into and out of the thought experiment of the original position. While knowledge of others' intuitions about justice can perhaps help in the process of reaching reflective equilibrium, by providing food for thought as discussed above, it is clear that he at least takes his commitment to public justifiability to be consistent with conclusions that are a long way from the beliefs of most Americans. This is most obvious in the case of desert, to which Rawls is notoriously hostile, but which the great majority of U.S. citizens endorse.[6]

Does Rawls fail to follow through on his own methodological injunctions? Miller (1994) has recently argued that fulfilling the Rawlsian commitment to public justifiability requires greater attention to empirical evidence than is paid by Rawls himself. While it is possible to distinguish between what people now believe about justice and that which can be justified using only commonly accepted modes of argument, it is implausible to think that the two will differ radically. For these kinds of argument are going to be just the familiar correction of empirical error, of faulty inference, of the distorting effect of self-interest, which cannot be expected to lead to beliefs that contrast markedly with those already current. If we really care about producing a theory that can be justified to all citizens, then we have to know what those citizens currently believe, and our conclusions can only be those beliefs corrected in commonsensical ways.

It is not obvious to us, however, that restricting the philosopher to the publicly justifiable correction of popular opinion entails that his conclusions will be similar in content to that opinion, as Miller seems to suggest, for it is at least possible that that opinion itself rests upon faulty inference of the kind that can be demonstrated publicly. We can grant that a theory of justice should be understood as bringing out "the deep structure of a set of everyday beliefs which, on the surface, are to some degree ambiguous, confused, contradictory" (Miller 1994:177) but still insist that this may lead us a long way from the content of mass empirical opinion. There is, for example, no reason in principle why appeal to the commonsensical requirement of logical consistency could not bring about a major shift in what the majority thinks about justice. Empirical opinion about distributive justice is respected, on this view, in the sense that arguments must be presented as publicly justifiable corrections to it, but any plausible account of what "public justification" amounts to will leave the philosopher plenty of room to argue against public opinion as that is conventionally understood.

Perhaps the best way to illustrate this point, and to remind the reader of the various positions we have surveyed, is to consider the most glaring case of a discrepancy between lay beliefs about justice on the one hand, and those endorsed by professional political philosophers on the other. As several theorists have recently noted—and something we have already glanced at in passing—it is on the question of desert that "much of the recent theorizing about justice appears to be out step with popular opinion" (Miller 1991:372). According to Samuel Scheffler (1992), for example, it is the rejection by contemporary philosophical liberalism of traditional notions of desert and responsibility that remain widely held in the general population that goes at least some way toward explaining the failure of liberalism as a concrete political program. William Galston (1991:159–62) too has argued that Rawls's account of justice, despite the way it presents itself, fails to provide the most plausible description of the shared understanding of America's public culture, since there is in the contemporary United States a broad consensus that, among other things, regards desert as a proper basis of distribution, and ability, effort, and self-denial as the bases of desert. Again this is thought to have political implications, since the inadequacies of Rawls's dangerously one-sided reconstruction of the liberal tradition "are mirrored in the national electoral disasters of contemporary liberalism" (Galston 1991:162).

On the first of our three possibilities, this discrepancy between public and professional opinion is no more than a reason for the philosopher to think again, and to check his or her arguments. Respect for lay beliefs might perhaps lead to a reconsideration of intuitions, or a look at the variables with which the rejection of desert commonly correlates, in order to consider whether they might explain the philosophical position in a way that competes with its validity. For Galston, the matter should end here, for his view is not only that the Rawlsian analysis fails to fit public opinion but also that it "does violence to a reasonable account of the 'moral point of view'" (1991:159). Let us suppose, however, that, having reconsidered, the philosopher continues to reject that traditional thinking about responsibility and agency that underlies the belief in desert. Scheffler (1992:319), indeed, is keen to make clear his own view that liberals may well be right to be skeptical of such thinking. This leaves the more interesting second and third reasons to take such (*ex hypothesi* mistaken) opinion into account. On one, the people may be wrong about desert, but are ignored at the cost of political isolation and inconsequence. On the other, the popular affirmation of desert helps to justify distributions that accord with its requirements.

Taking the latter first, no position we have discussed holds that distributions in accordance with traditional desert claims are just simply because people think they are. The theorist who would have us pay greatest attention to empirical opinion is Miller, who argues that taking public justifiability seriously implies that justice can only be popular opinion corrected by commonly accepted modes of reasoning. But how should we apply that claim to this case? It is at least arguable that the philosophers' rejection of traditional desert claims, or at least some of them, itself depends only upon the identification of faulty inference and empirical error. The idea that we cannot deserve things on the basis of attributes for which we are not responsible is reasonably commonsensical, and the claim that at least some of our talents are ours by luck is similarly uncontroversial. So while some of contemporary liberalism's hostility to desert may not survive the filter of public justification—that component which, in denying even that we deserve to be rewarded for our efforts, perhaps does rest upon a controversial claim about human agency—it is not obvious that all of it does so.[7]

In the case of desert, then, it seems that even the philosopher limited to the task of the publicly justifiable correction of popular opinion may, *pace* Miller, argue for a position that differs radically from it. The demands of public justifiability may rule out certain kinds of philosophical argument, and what the people think may enter into the process of justification formally, as it were, in that the philosopher must understand, and present, himself or herself to be systematizing and bringing out the deep structure latent within popular beliefs. But the extent of the ambiguity, confusion, and inconsistency in those beliefs is sufficient to leave a great deal of work to be done, work that may well lead to conclusions differing markedly in content even from empirical public opinion understood as those beliefs that research shows to be regularly and consensually endorsed by the vast majority of ordinary people.

Clearly there is a great deal more to be said on the interdependent questions of what public justification really amounts to and whether we should indeed care that our theory satisfies its demands.[8] Leaving behind such complexities, let us turn finally to the alternative, strategic suggestion that arguing the truth about desert where this conflicts with popular opinion may produce, indeed has produced, suboptimal political outcomes. Here it seems plausible to distinguish between the role of the philosopher, who can properly transcend such consequentialist considerations, and that of the political actor, who, on some views at least, is irrevocably caught up in them.[9] While it is a nice question for a political party, say, whether it should include in its manifesto commitments to policies that it believes just but unpopular, or perhaps go to the other extreme and argue for what it knows to be unjust in one sphere in order to gain the power to bring about justice in others, the philosopher might claim that such problems are not his or hers. It would be a very strict form of consequentialism that required the philosopher to desist from seeking or even promulgating truth. While one can imagine scientific cases where the consequences of knowing or publishing truths were so likely to be so harmful that the scientist might, on balance, have reason to desist from their pursuit or publication, it seems less plausible that the same should apply to moral truths.

That said, philosophers may wish to defend their philosophizing on the consequentialist ground that arguing for the moral truth is likely, in the long run, to bring about better outcomes than would be achieved by not doing so. Rather than taking the feasible set as given, it might be thought it is precisely the task of the philosopher to change that set, by changing the content of those popular beliefs that do so much to determine it. From this perspective, the finding that most people mistakenly believe in conventional desert claims does not even give one reason of a consequentialist kind to pander to that opinion.

In our current context, two points in particular are worthy of comment. First, notice that this view relies upon an empirical prediction about the extent to which arguing for the truth will have the effect of bringing others to believe it. And this means, again but for a different reason, that the philosopher must pay attention to the findings of empirical research, both descriptive and explanatory. For what beliefs can plausibly be changed to depends both on what they currently are and on the causal processes that determine their formation. The philosopher must know both from where it is that the strategy of change is to start and worry about the causal factors that play a role in determining the efficacy of any such strategy. As Dunn puts it:

> How far the "subjective motivational set" of a historical agent can be stretched is an explicitly historically contingent matter. What is certain is that it cannot be stretched further than it can be stretched . . . . (All theories of action must take men not so much as they are but as it is still causally true that they can or could be.) If political edification is to be a theoretically coherent activity, it must work upon (as well as with) the material furnished by history. (1980:247)

If the lesson from social science is that people's beliefs are not readily susceptible to rational moral argument, but depend rather on other causal factors, then this particular defense of the philosopher's disregard of empirical opinion will be unsustainable. Perhaps, for example, people would not stop believing in traditional notions of desert even when their mistake was pointed out to them. What is needed, on this view, is a research program that tries to identify the efficacy of good reasons in the formation of people's beliefs.

Second, in presenting the strategic reason to attend to lay beliefs about distributive justice, we have tacitly assumed that such beliefs really are part of the causal field that is to be confronted and negotiated. But this is only the case if what people believe about justice makes a difference to what they do. Unlike the constitutive accounts, which give moral weight to citizens' beliefs or what can be justified to them simply in virtue of their being believed or justified, the strategic perspective only gives one reason to care about what the people think if what they think influences their actions. If people do not act to support (or resist) what they believe to be just (or unjust), then there can be little reason, from this perspective, to take their declared views into account. That is why, on at least one of our three reasons for examining what the people think, the issues raised by Miller are closely related. What the people think is only of (strategic) normative significance if it makes a difference to their behavior.

WHAT THE PEOPLE THINK

This conclusion brings us back to the first of the issues raised by Miller in his reviews. What in fact do the people think? Is there a discernible pattern to empirical beliefs about distributive justice?

In addressing this question we present evidence from three countries—Britain, the United States, and (what was) West Germany—chosen simply because they represent rather different types of capitalist class societies. Britain offers a good example of a society having a social structure rooted in social class relationships that also form a prominent theme in popular debates about social justice in that country. By contrast, it is usually claimed that class relationships in the United States have been overlain by a dominant ideology of liberal individualism, and that this is reflected in commonsense beliefs about inequality in America. West Germany may be described as a class society that, at least in the postwar period, has managed class conflicts by means of a corporatist bargaining structure enjoying widespread popular appeal. In this context, however, we are less interested in the details of any cross-national differences than in whether—and to a lesser extent how—popular beliefs about social justice are socially structured within particular nation-states.

The results of our analysis are shown in the tables below. Our investigative procedure was as follows. First, we identified those questions that had been asked in all three countries, and were thought to represent normative justice beliefs; that is, judgments about how various resources ought to be allocated in the interests of fairness.[10] These items (which are described in full in Table 2.1) were then explored using factor analysis, with the aim of identifying more general justice attitudes that might underlie the responses to individual items. This approach to the study of attitudes was pursued in order to minimize any idiosyncrasies due to the wording of individual questions. Despite the careful design and piloting of the surveys, we cannot discount the possibility that some items are of uncertain reliability, notably to the extent that they have different connotations in each of the countries. Rather than concentrate attention on single indicators, or on small differences in gross percentage distributions, it makes sense to look for patterns among a large number of different attitude items. These can then be used to construct a variety of scales with which to explore the distribution of beliefs across particular populations.

Separate factor analyses were therefore carried out on the matrix of polychoric correlations associated with each data set.[11] These correlations were estimated by means of PRELIS, with pairwise deletion of missing cases and of "don't knows." Next, principal-component analysis and scree tests were used to obtain an initial estimate of the number of factors to rotate. Principal factor analysis was then used to explore potential solutions above and below these estimates, with both orthogonal and oblique rotation. These analyses suggested that six

Table 2.1. Attitude Items Used in the Analysis[a]

PROFITS:	It is all right if businessmen make good profits because everybody benefits in the end.
PAIDRESP:	People would not want to take extra responsibility at work unless they were paid extra for it.

How much influence should each of the following factors have in determining the level of pay for an employee:

PAYEDUC:	The employee's level of education.
PAYCON:	Unpleasant working conditions, such as dirty, noisy, or strenuous work.
PAYEFF:	The employee's individual effort.
PAYRESP:	The responsibility held by the employee on the job.
PAYLENG:	The length of service with the employer.
PAYSIZE:	The size of the family the employee supports.
PAYSEX:	Being a man and not a woman.
GVTSOL:	The government should guarantee everyone a minimum standard of living.
GVTLIMIT:	The government should place an upper limit on the amount of money any one person can make.
EQSHARE:	The fairest way of distributing wealth and income would be to give everyone equal shares.
WEALTHEQ:	It's fair if people have more money or wealth, but only if there are equal opportunities.
KEEPEARN:	People are entitled to keep what they have earned—even if this means some people will be wealthier than others.
WKHARD:	People who work hard deserve to earn more than those who do not.
BEQUEST:	People are entitled to pass on their wealth to their children.
IGETNEED:	The most important thing is that people get what they need even if this means transferring money from those who have earned more than they need.
LUCKIQ:	It is simply luck if some people are more intelligent or skillful than others, so they don't deserve to earn more money.
OCCHIGH:	It is just that people in some occupations are rewarded more highly than people in other ones.
EDAFFORD:	It is just that those who can afford it obtain better education for their children.
INCEFFRT:	There is an incentive for individual effort only if differences in income are large enough.

Three patients are admitted to a hospital at the same time, all suffering from a form of heart disease requiring surgery. However the limited resources of the hospital allow only one heart operation each month. All three cases are equally urgent. The patient who is treated first will have a better chance of survival. What would be your view of each of the following decisions:

HOSUSFUL:	The decision is made by judging the usefulness of each patient to society at large.
HOSPAY:	The patient who can afford to pay the most is treated first.
HOSFAM:	The patient supporting the largest family is treated first.
HOSLOTT:	The decision about which patient goes first is made by a lottery.
HOSRULES:	The decision is made by following the rules of the hospital, whatever they may be.

(continued)

Table 2.1. (Continued)

A small firm has a flat to rent. Three of its employees want the flat. A selection has to be made. What would be your view of the following decisions:

APTUSFUL: The decision is made by judging the usefulness of each employee to the firm.
APTINC: The employee with the lowest income gets the flat.
APTFAM: The employee supporting the largest family gets the flat.
APTLOTT: The decision about who gets the flat is made by a lottery.
APTSELF: The decision is left to the three employees themselves, and whatever they may decide.

a Items were coded as described in Alwin, Klingel and Dielman (1993).

(Britain) or seven (United States, Germany) factors would represent the data adequately, with almost identical results for orthogonal and oblique rotations.

Three factors were sufficiently similar and interpretable across countries to suggest that they were tapping the same underlying dimensions. We therefore resorted to some well-known psychometric procedures for item analysis and the construction of summative scales. We eliminated variables with low communalities and variables involved in poorly defined factors (for example, doubletons). The three factors of primary interest exhibited considerable stability as the number of variables was reduced from 31 to 22. Now four-factor solutions were obtained for each country and these are shown in Tables 2.2, 2.3, and 2.4. These factors accounted for between 33 and 40% of the variance after rotation.

One of the factors comprises items that justify inequalities in the distribution of income and wealth, for example, the view that people who work hard deserve to earn more than those who do not, that they are entitled to keep legitimate earnings even if this creates inequality, and then to pass on their wealth to their children. (These are factors 1, 2, and 4 in the three tables respectively.) A second factor is readily interpretable in terms of attitudes to equality, loading on items that state that the fairest way of distributing wealth would be to give everyone equal shares, that particularly intelligent or skillful people don't deserve more money since this is merely a matter of luck, and that governments should place a ceiling on incomes (factor 2 in Table 2.2 and factor 1 in Tables 2.3 and 2.4). Finally, there is a common factor measuring beliefs about need, as expressed in the items dealing with the allocation of housing and health care (factor 4 in Table 2.2, 3 in Table 2.3, and 2 in Table 2.4). These factors were therefore used to create the final, country-specific scales representing beliefs about justified inequalities, equal outcomes, and need. The individual items used in scale construction are indicated by asterisks in Tables 2.2–2.4, and resulted from the process of optimizing Cronbach's alpha. The distributions and reliabilities of the scales are shown in Table 2.5. Bearing in mind the number of items, the indices of reliability (Cronbach's alpha) are generally satisfactory, with the possible excep-

Table 2.2. Factor Analysis, West Germany (Factor Loadings >.3×1000) *a*

	F1	F2	F3	F4	h²×1000*b*
KEEPEARN	607*	−451*			662
WKHARD	570*	−344*	−442		654
PROFITS	556*				350
EDAFFORD	531*				309
BEQUEST	504*				358
INCEFFRT	500*				257
OCCHIGH	434*				199
PAIDRESP	426*				256
APTUSFUL	380*		323		316
EQSHARE		766*			618
GVTLIMIT		628*			433
LUCKIQ		476*			233
WEALTHEQ	452*	−471*			433
PAYSEX		387*	362		319
PAYSIZE		302*			177
HOSPAY			783		652
HOSUSFUL			611		468
IGETNEED			−426		257
GVTSOL			−409		239
APTFAM				807*	674
HOSFAM				699*	513
APTINC				674*	482
Eigenvalue	2.617	2.154	2.061	2.027	
Explained variance (%)	11.90	9.79	9.37	9.21	(40.27)

a Asterisks indicate items used in scale construction.
b Communalities.

tion of the justified inequalities scale for the United States, which should therefore be treated with caution in the analysis. In the case of scales based upon four or more items, it was possible to use LISREL 7 to check whether the sets of items were consistent with a congeneric measurement model. The results indicated good consistency and are shown in Table 2.6 in terms of an adjusted goodness-of-fit index (AGFI)—taking account of degrees of freedom—and a coefficient of determination for all the scale items jointly.

These scales were then used in analyzing the data. We examined the relationships between scale scores and a number of other social characteristics that one might expect (on the basis of previous research) to be associated with justice beliefs; namely, social class, educational attainment, class identity, party identification, and finally sex.[12] We conducted preliminary analyses of variance in

Table 2.3. Factor Analysis, Britain (Factor Loadings >.3×1000) [a]

	F1	F2	F3	F4	$h^2 \times 1000$ [b]
EQSHARE	643*				448
GVTLIMIT	566*				368
PAYSIZE	530*				327
GVTSOL	464*				430
LUCKIQ	442*				212
PAYSEX	370*				260
IGETNEED					159
BEQUEST		624*			474
WKHARD		616*			449
KEEPEARN	−436*	503*			454
EDAFFORD		435*		341	320
PAIDRESP		433*			203
OCCHIGH		416*			224
INCEFFRT		342*			134
WEALTHEQ					127
APTFAM			789*		679
HOSFAM			594*	307	455
APTINC			583*		361
HOSUSFUL				579	368
HOSPAY				523	293
APTUSFUL				410	212
PROFITS				351	197
Eigenvalue	2.119	1.946	1.575	1.513	
Explained variance (%)	9.63	8.85	7.16	6.88	(32.51)

[a] Asterisks indicate items used in scale construction.

[b] Communalities.

order to identify main effects and interactions. Next, multiple-classification analysis (MCA) was used, with the interacting variables replaced by composite variables where necessary. MCA is basically a form of multiple regression in which categorical predictors are represented as dummy variables. Two sets of results are reported: unadjusted (without controls) and adjusted (with controls). The unadjusted coefficient (eta) is a multiple correlation. The adjusted coefficient (beta) is the partial multiple correlation. The coefficient shown for 'all variables' is the unsquared multiple-correlation coefficient (Andrews, Morgan, Sonquist, and Klein 1973; Retherford and Choe 1993:69–92).

Tables 2.7 to 2.14 summarize our findings. For the equality scale, there were significant main effects for sex, education, and party identification in West Germany; for all variables in Britain (with an interaction between education and class); and for all but sex in the United States. For the inequality scale, there were

Table 2.4. Factor Analysis, United States (Factor Loadings >.3×1000) [a]

	F1	F2	F3	F4	h²×1000 [b]
GVTLIMIT	646*				443
EQSHARE	644*				478
KEEPEARN	−578*			417*	524
PAYSIZE	543*				343
PAYSEX	520*				414
LUCKIQ	486*				255
GVTSOL	483*				385
WEALTHEQ	−344				182
APTFAM		892*			851
APTINC		644*			431
HOSFAM		457	423		391
IGETNEED					125
HOSPAY			646		432
APTUSFUL			493		271
HOSUSFUL			455		236
PROFITS			341		182
BEQUEST	−326			531*	398
WKHARD	−311			459*	334
EDAFFORD				417*	223
PAIDRESP				374*	153
OCCHIGH				364*	186
INCEFFRT				304*	102
Eigenvalue	2.626	1.732	1.571	1.408	
% Explained variance (%)	11.9	7.9	7.1	6.4	(33.35)

[a] Asterisks indicate items used in scale construction.
[b] Communalities.

Table 2.5. Observed Index Distributions and Reliabilities

Index	Min	Max	Mean	Std. dev.	Cronbach's alpha*100
W. Germany					
Equal outcomes	11	40	30.98	4.96	69
Justified inequality	10	47	22.07	5.87	72
Need	03	12	6.71	2.19	72
Britain					
Equal outcomes	08	33	23.00	4.48	63
Justified inequality	07	30	14.45	3.77	58
Need	03	12	7.37	2.04	69
United States					
Equal outcomes	12	33	25.68	4.70	67
Justified inequality	07	34	13.92	3.77	45
Need	02	08	5.34	1.59	75

Table 2.6. Congeneric Measurement Model (ULS estimation)

	AGFI	Coefficient of determination
W. Germany		
Equal outcomes	.954	.826
Justified inequality	.952	.841
Britain		
Equal outcomes	.955	.731
Justified inequality	.955	.732
United States		
Equal outcomes	.959	.780
Justified inequality	.934	.658

Table 2.7. West Germany: MCA Analysis [a]

Predictor variables	n	Unadjusted equality score	Eta	Adjusted equality score	Beta
Grand mean: 31.53					
Sex			.08		.07*
Male	482	31.86		31.83	
Female	393	31.13		31.16	
Education			.18		.13**
Low	365	30.59		30.86	
Medium	291	31.90		31.73	
High	219	32.61		32.38	
Class			.15		.07
Salariat	308	32.16		31.58	
Rout. clerical	185	31.95		31.93	
P. bourgeoisie	69	31.47		31.19	
Super/skilled	148	31.18		31.66	
Workers	165	30.22		31.02	
Class identity			.13		.03
Working class	198	30.38		31.23	
Middle class	677	31.87		31.62	
Political party			.24		.21***
Left	441	30.47		30.57	
Center	98	33.39		33.14	
Right	336	32.38		32.33	
All vars.					.304

[a] Equality scale: effects of sex, education, class, class identity, and political party. In this and subsequent tables, a high score indicates disagreement with the principle measured by the scale, and a low score agreement with the principle.
* p < .05.   ** p < .01.   *** p < .001.

Table 2.8. West Germany: MCA Analysis[a]

Predictor variables	n	Unadjusted inequality score	Eta	Adjusted inequality score	Beta
Grand mean: 21.43					
Sex			.16		.16***
Male	477	20.57		20.57	
Female	390	22.43		22.44	
Education			.10		.12***
Low	359	20.94		20.82	
Medium	291	21.22		21.30	
High	217	22.44		22.54	
Class			.13		.09
Salariat	301	22.01		21.82	
Rout. clerical	186	21.35		21.30	
P. bourgeoisie	71	19.00		19.75	
Superv/skilled	148	21.22		21.64	
Workers	161	21.56		21.30	
Class identity			.04		.03
Working class	197	21.85		21.78	
Middle class	670	21.28		21.30	
Political party			.32		.32***
Left	432	23.36		23.29	
Center	94	20.33		20.16	
Right	341	19.24		19.37	
All vars.					.394

[a] Inequality scale: effects of sex, education, class, class identity, and political party.
* $p < .05$.   ** $p < .01$.   *** $p < .001$.

significant main effects in West Germany for sex, education and party identification; and in the United States for sex, education, and class identity/party identification. The results for Britain were more complex, since there were interactions between party identification, class, and class identity. We decided, therefore, to look at the effects of the other variables separately for each party identification, and created a composite variable for class and class identity. While the grand mean shows that those who identify with parties on the left are less in favor of inequality than are those who identify with parties in the political center or on the right, other significant effects were found for education (left), class/class identity (center), and sex (right). For the need scale, class/class identity was significant in West Germany, and class/party identification in the United States, while for Britain there were no significant associations when all the variables were entered into the analysis.

Table 2.9.   West Germany: MCA Analysis[a]

Predictor variables	n	Unadjusted need score	Eta	Adjusted need score	Beta
Grand mean: 6.67					
Sex			.03		.03
Male	501	6.72		6.73	
Female	428	6.61		6.60	
Education			.05		.07
Low	381	6.65		6.61	
Medium	309	6.57		6.55	
High	239	6.83		6.91	
Class/identity			.15		.05**
W/c salariat	51	6.49		6.45	
W/c rout. cler.	32	6.09		6.16	
W/c p. bourge	8	6.25		6.25	
W/c supervis.	82	6.67		6.06	
W/c workers	90	6.73		6.74	
M/c salariat	274	6.55		6.46	
M/c rout. cler.	164	6.86		6.93	
M/c p. bourge	64	7.67		7.72	
M/c supervis.	76	6.60		6.62	
M/c workers	88	6.31		6.41	
Political party			.04		.05
Left	458	6.75		6.77	
Center	102	6.72		6.69	
Right	369	6.56		6.54	
All vars.					.176

[a] Need scale: effects of sex, education, class/class identity, and political party. w/c, working class; m/c, middle/upper class.

** $p < .01$.

So much for our research procedure. What then do these results suggest about commonsense views of justice in each of the three societies? It appears from our analysis that there is indeed a definite structure to popular justice beliefs. There is no reason to suspect this is simply an artefact of our technique. For example, a comparison of the items in the questionnaire and the factors tells against significant ordering effects, and the pattern of the responses themselves does not show systematic favoring of the merely socially acceptable. Rather, our results point toward respondents articulating established attitudes to distributive justice, although rather broad ones; namely, those of equality of outcome, justified inequalities, and need. These general orientations gloss the more nuanced philosophical distinctions between, for example, entitlement, merit, and the need for incentives, as different ways in which inequalities might be justified. But there seems little

Table 2.10. Britain: MCA Analysis[a]

Predictor variables	n	Unadjusted equality score	Eta	Adjusted equality score	Beta
Grand Mean: 23.00					
Sex			.14		.12**
Male	359	23.72		23.57	
Female	449	22.42		22.54	
Education/class			.39		.26***
Low/salariat	43	23.27		22.94	
Low/r. clerical	45	21.91		22.23	
Low/p. bourge	32	23.81		23.14	
Low/supervis.	79	21.53		22.12	
Low/workers	172	20.75		21.50	
Med/salariat	42	25.54		24.92	
Med/r. clerical	68	23.57		23.47	
Med/p. bourge	21	25.33		24.39	
Med/supervis.	40	21.72		22.04	
Med/workers	46	22.52		22.70	
High/salariat	152	24.71		24.18	
High/r. clerical	23	25.04		23.37	
High/p. bourge	14	24.14		23.85	
High/supervis.	16	26.75		25.76	
High/workers	15	23.81		23.19	
Class id.			.30		.11**
Working class	460	21.84		22.56	
Middle class	348	24.53		23.58	
Party			.36		.25***
Left	271	20.97		21.56	
Center	134	22.61		22.70	
Right	403	24.49		24.07	
All vars.					.491

[a] Equality scale: Effects of sex, class/education, class identification and political party.
** $p < .01$.   *** $p < .001$.

doubt that ordinary people deploy multiple criteria in making justice judgments, giving prominence to considerations of need in the allocation of scarce health care and housing; recognizing that inequalities in wealth and income may be justified on grounds of merit, entitlement, or incentives; and making separate judgments with respect to a guaranteed minimum standard of living and some restrictions on the maximum income available to any one individual.

Moreover, these judgments are associated with differences in social class, educational attainment, class identity, and political identification, as well as sex, in ways consonant with the findings of previous research. Thus, for example, where there are significant social class differences in normative judgments about

Table 2.11. Britain: MCA Analysis[a]

Predictor variables	n	Unadjusted inequality score	Eta	Adjusted inequality score	Beta
		Party: Left			
Grand mean: 15.10					
Sex			.01		.04
Male	128	15.05		14.95	
Female	138	15.14		15.24	
Education			.35		.28**
Low	160	14.15		14.27	
Medium	54	15.28		15.54	
High	52	17.84		17.19	
Class/class id.			.35		.22
W/c salariat	27	15.74		14.7	
M/c salariat	25	15.08		14.94	
W/c r.clerical	10	15.20		14.96	
M/c r. clerical	52	14.09		14.51	
W/c p. bourge	91	14.9		15.44	
M/c p. bourge	31	18.48		16.97	
W/c supervisors	5	13.8		14.04	
M/c supervisors	3	13.33		12.82	
W/c workers	10	14.10		14.45	
M/c workers	12	12.58		13.13	
All vars.					.407.

Predictor variables	n	Unadjusted inequality score	Eta	Adjusted inequality score	Beta
		Party: Center			
Grand mean: 14.89					
Sex			.13		.06
Male	47	14.21		14.57	
Female	88	15.25		15.06	
Education			.29		.22
Low	58	13.78		14.04	
Medium	39	15.1		15.09	
High	38	16.37		15.98	
Class/class id.			.43		.36*
W/c salariat	20	16.45		15.90	
M/c salariat	11	13.09		13.05	
W/c r.clerical	5	12.00		12.66	
M/c r. clerical	17	14.00		14.51	
W/c p. bourge	32	14.47		14.99	
M/c p. bourge	27	15.67		15.08	

(continued)

Table 2.11. (Continued)

Predictor variables	n	Unadjusted inequality score	Eta	Adjusted inequality score	Beta
W/c supervisors	7	17.14		16.94	
M/c supervisors	7	18.00		17.67	
W/c workers	6	12.00		11.95	
M/c workers	3	11.67		12.51	
All vars.					.467

Predictor variables	n	Unadjusted inequality score	Eta	Adjusted inequality score	Beta
		Party: Right			
Grand mean: 13.45					
Sex			.12		.14*
Male	179	13.04		12.99	
Female	213	13.51		13.86	
Education			.13		.11
Low	138	12.92		13.00	
Medium	122	13.74		13.76	
High	132	13.77		13.66	
Class/Class id.			.20		.19
W/c salariat	32	14.50		14.67	
M/c salariat	32	14.00		13.76	
W/c r.clerical	17	13.12		13.59	
M/c r. clerical	27	13.34		13.61	
W/c p. bourge	50	13.06		13.20	
M/c p. bourge	96	13.78		13.74	
W/c supervisors	56	13.74		13.33	
M/c supervisors	25	11.64		11.77	
W/c workers	21	13.15		13.26	
M/c workers	36	13.07		13.07	
All vars.					.259

[a] Inequality scale: Effects of sex, class/education, class identification and political party.
* $p < .05$.   ** $p < .01$.

justice, it tends to be members of the less privileged working classes who are most in favor of equality, whereas the salariat and (traditionally conservative) petite bourgeoisie are less sympathetic to this outcome. Similarly, where class identity is a salient factor, working-class identifiers are more in favor of equal outcomes than are middle-class identifiers. Those with the lowest levels of educational attainment are significantly more likely to favor equality as a distributive principle. Women are more in favor of equal outcomes than are men. They are

Table 2.12. USA: MCA Analysis[a]

Predictor variables	n	Unadjusted equality score	Eta	Adjusted equality score	Beta
Grand mean: 26.27					
Sex			.09		.06
Male	379	26.71		26.57	
Female	427	25.88		26.00	
Education			.30		.20***
Low	75	22.25		23.40	
Medium	195	25.75		26.26	
High	536	27.02		26.68	.16***
Class			.27		
Salariat	359	27.30		26.88	
Rout. clerical	171	25.74		25.81	
P. bourgeoisie	56	27.14		26.85	
Skilled	100	26.02		26.29	
Unskilled	120	23.74		24.82	.14***
Class identity			.24		
Working class	220	24.47		25.20	
Middle/upper	586	26.94		26.67	
Political party			.18		.16***
Democrat	246	25.02		25.14	
Republican	560	26.82		26.77	
All vars.					.417

[a] Equality scale: effects of sex, education, class, class identity, and political party.
*** $p < .001$.

also less inclined to accept justifications of inequality. Differences that reflect political inclination also accord with theoretical expectations. Those who align themselves with parties on the left are most in favor of equality and least supportive of principles justifying inequalities.

In sum, in each of the three rather different societies under investigation, people organize their normative judgments about justice around established and coherent principles of justice. Furthermore, different groups in the various populations endorse these criteria to varying degrees, and in ways consistent with the evidence of previous studies. Justice judgments are clearly neither arbitrary nor random. Doubtless there are some respondents whose views are ill-considered and therefore inconsistent—although, as we have argued elsewhere (Burgoyne, Swift, and Marshall 1993), strictly contradictory responses are hard to detect, especially where complex attitudinal items are concerned, because of the possibilities for contextualized reasoning. But it seems that, even though there is a good deal of "noise" not captured even by our very general orientations, we find

Table 2.13. USA: MCA Analysis[a]

Predictor variables	n	Unadjusted inequality score	Eta	Adjusted inequality score	Beta
Grand mean: 13.92					
Sex			.09		.08**
Male	585	13.56		13.61	
Female	692	14.22		14.19	
Education			.09		.08*
Low	160	13.35		13.42	
Medium	355	13.63		13.64	
High	762	14.18		14.16	
Class			.09		.07
Salariat	500	14.26		14.17	
Rout. clerical	264	14.00		13.91	
P. bourgoisie	86	13.96		14.16	
Skilled	177	13.51		13.71	
Unskilled	250	13.43		13.50	
Class id/party			.10		.11**
Dem./w/c	262	13.81		14.07	
Dem./m/c	453	14.28		14.20	
Rep./w/c	146	14.31		14.48	
Rep./m/c	416	13.47		13.33	
All vars.					.172

[a] Inequality scale: effects of sex, education, class, and class identity/party.
** $p < .01$.   *** $p < .001$.

underneath it clear and interpretable patterns in the different countries under consideration.

ATTITUDES AND ACTIONS

Even if it is conceded that more or less consistent general trends appear in popular beliefs, and that these beliefs are structured in sociologically meaningful ways across populations, it might still be argued that commonsense opinions about social justice do not matter. If attitudes have no implications for behavior, it is not obvious either that they are worthy of sociological attention, or that they are of normative interest to those who might regard them (along the lines discussed earlier) as part of the causal field with which political actors have to engage. This observation brings us to the third and final issue raised by Miller's reviews of the literature on distributive justice.

The long-running attitudes versus action controversy, a debate that has taken

Table 2.14. USA: MCA Analysis[a]

Predictor variables	n	Unadjusted need score	Eta	Adjusted need score	Beta
Grand Mean: 5.35					
Sex			.04		.03
Male	590	5.42		5.41	
Female	705	5.29		5.30	
Education			.06		.06
Low	170	5.20		5.20	
Medium	359	5.47		5.50	
High	766	5.33		5.31	
Class/party			.13		.13*
Dem./salariat	262	5.18		5.20	
Dem./r. cler.	148	5.21		5.21	
Dem./p. bourg	39	5.54		5.57	
Dem./skilled	107	5.64		5.62	
Dem./unskilled	172	5.37		5.37	
Rep./salariat	240	5.46		5.47	
Rep./r. cler	127	5.54		5.55	
Rep./p. bourg	47	5.68		5.64	
Rep./skilled	71	5.29		5.24	
Rep./unskilled	82	4.88		4.87	
Class identity			.01		.01
Working class	415	5.33		5.33	
Middle class	880	5.36		5.36	
All vars.					.143

[a] Need scale: effects of sex, education, class/party, and class identity.
* $p < .05$.

place mostly among social psychologists, has culminated (after some six decades of research) in "general agreement that attitude, no matter how assessed, is only one of the factors that influence behavior" (Ajzen and Fishbein 1980:26). However, this is as far as the consensus goes, since there is then widespread disagreement, both about where attitudes stand in this list of factors and how they relate to the many other variables in the equation. After reviewing six decades of exhaustive research, Richard Eiser can therefore do little more than conclude that "attitudes, in short have behavioural implications," but that "the question of which specific behaviours are implied by a particular attitude, however, will depend on circumstances, and is therefore an empirical one" (1986:82)[13]

Our own view, which is informed more by sociological than social-psychological literature, is that this issue is indeed an empirical matter—but certain generalizations are possible. Of course, every particular instance of social action is determined by a unique set of circumstances, a slight change in any one of which might result in a different outcome. Social scientists, however, are interested in probabilities—in patterns of action and regularities of behavior. The sociological and psychological evidence suggests to us that attitudes do not determine behavior, but they do provide relatively enduring predispositions to action, albeit leading to different behavioral outcomes in different concrete circumstances.

The well-known ideal-types of "orientations to work" are a good example. These are contrasting attitudes to employment expressed in answers to questions about job satisfaction, identification with the enterprise, and the centrality of paid labor as an interest in life. Such attitudes derive from the ordering by workers of their wants and expectations relative to the conditions of their employment. One classic study of these orientations (Goldthorpe, Lockwood, Bechhofer, and Platt 1968) distinguishes the basically instrumental, bureaucratic, and solidaristic types, explaining the behavior of particular groups of industrial workers in terms of the degree to which the different orientations are salient, given the resources available to actors in particular industrial situations. Thus, for example, employees who seek primarily extrinsic satisfactions from work (in other words who are motivated mainly toward the maximization of their wages) may recognize their tasks as monotonous and boring, but nevertheless express considerable satisfaction with their jobs. This apparent paradox is explained by the workers' primary definition of work as a means to an end that is itself extrinsic to the work situation (that is, acquiring the high income necessary to support a valued life-style). Consequently, they have a largely calculative involvement with their employing organizations, expressed in attitudes of indifference toward relative deprivation in terms of job satisfaction. This attitude routinely results in workers behaving in an appropriately economistic way, for certain purposes and in particular contexts, as for example in their relationships with trade unions (which may be supported vigorously but only to the extent that they promise a means of economic betterment). Where workers bring characteristically instrumental attitudes to their employment, union activities are unlikely to be defined as an opportunity for expressing the wider ideals and objectives of class solidarity and advancement, but rather as an additional means of satisfying the workers' basically economistic wants and expectations. The pattern of trade union behavior—in the form of attendance at meetings or support for particular strikes—tends therefore to reflect the instrumental orientation of members to their employment generally.

Such action orientations seem to be what many social psychologists have in mind when they discuss the behavioral implications of attitudes. Thus Milton Rokeach describes an attitude as "a relatively enduring organization of beliefs around an object or situation predisposing one to respond in some preferential manner" (1976:112). Of course, while attitudes are salient and stable predispositions to act in certain ways, they are not fixed or unalterable. They can, for example, be molded and focused by formal organizations such as trade unions or political parties.

A convenient illustration of our argument is offered by the pay-bargaining strategies of different class organizations in postwar Sweden (Olsson 1989).[14] Interestingly enough, from our point of view, these are informed by competing conceptions of distributive justice. For example, since 1951 the main blue-collar union constellation (LO) has pursued a solidaristic or broadly egalitarian wage policy, with primary emphasis being placed on decreasing wage differentials across the whole labor market. This strategy was underpinned by the so-called Rhen-Meidner model, which postulated that standardized wages and the raising of low incomes would accelerate structural change in the economy by forcing inefficient companies to improve productivity (in order to meet demands for increased wages) in the long run. In return the union should take responsibility for keeping pay rises to levels below the annual increase in GDP. The LO was thus opposed to wage levels being determined by the market, and in its policy documents after 1965 particularly emphasized the improvement of low incomes together with the reduction of pay differentials, especially in relation to white-collar workers.

By contrast, the white-collar union grouping (TCO) endorsed a pay policy in which wages were heavily differentiated, the aim being to raise salaries relative to the wages of blue-collar workers. TCO policy aimed at securing equal pay for equal work among members, but with a strong emphasis on the differentiation of wages according to such criteria as the productivity of the employee, his or her responsibility for personnel, and job and merit evaluations. Until the 1970s, TCO policy documents showed considerable sympathy for market forces in the determination of wages, and scarcely mentioned the issue of low wages. Although a more solidaristic strategy was adopted in the 1970s, inasmuch as improvements for those on low incomes was admitted as a policy objective, the emphasis remained on differentiating salaries (mainly according to the productivity of employees). In this respect TCO policy was quite different from that of the LO.

The SACO/SR white-collar grouping, which organizes mostly highly qualified technicians and university-educated employees in the public sector, was opposed to the solidaristic wages policy and favored an "incomes policy" focused on differentiation of rewards according to the level of difficulty of work tasks and the educational credentials, experience, leadership, responsibility, and initiative of employees. Finally, the dominant employers' organization in the private sector (SAF) stressed the importance of market forces in setting wage levels, with management being free to determine the remuneration of each employee according to his or her contribution to the production process as a whole. Historically, SAF has been opposed to solidaristic wages policies, and has argued for greater differentiation of wages by rewarding individual achievement.

With some simplification, therefore, we might say that the four major class organizations in the workplace pursued justice in the setting of wage levels, but defined this to varying degrees in terms of equality, desert (based either on productivity or expertise), and what we might call the functional inequality of the market. These principles reflected the attitudes (and, one might add, the interests) of members themselves. Survey evidence suggests that support for nondifferentiation of wages was strongest among members of the LO, while those belonging to either of the white-collar groupings were the most enthusiastic proponents of differentiation according to desert, defined either in terms of responsibility or educational attainment. In short, as Anders Olsson concludes from his review of the evidence, "the opinions of the members of each organization tend to be reflected in the organization's wage policy" (1989:165).

Conversely, however, the different union leaders succeeded at various times in modifying the goals of their organizations in order to maintain their bargaining power. In the case of the LO, for example, the solidaristic wages policy can be seen as part of a leadership strategy for collective action. Olsson suggests that

> In order to counter the comparably more powerful employers, the workers have to develop a collective strategy of conflict which not only aggregates the individual resources of the members of the organization, but also overcomes the individuality of those resources by defining a collective identity. The formation of such an identity deflates the standards according to which the costs of collective action are subjectively estimated. The solidaristic wage policy can be seen as such a principle, it is not only a wage policy, it is also an integral part of LO's entire strategy of conflict, a rallying principle. (1989:142–43)

At a certain point, however, this strategic function of the wages policy made it necessary for the LO leadership to moderate the egalitarian objectives of the union. For although in general more favorable to the reduction of income differentials, the LO membership had always embraced skilled workers who were somewhat more inclined to support differentiating principles, many of whom thought that, by the 1980s, the process of equalizing wages had gone too far. In order to maintain union solidarity, a series of reports and documents redefined the balance of wages policy within the union, and secured acceptance among unskilled members of the principle of different wages for different jobs as a legitimate basis for calculating just rewards, within the overall objective of obtaining improvements for those worst off. For example, according to Olsson,

> The 1981 report could look back at a decade of diminishing wage differentials. In it LO says that the solidaristic wage policy in practice has come to mean a reduction of existing wage differentials. It asserts that this is not the principal idea behind the wage policy. Instead a lot more consideration has to be taken to the content of different jobs. The solidaristic wage policy means, in this rendition, that wages should be fair and just when the aggregated demands of jobs are considered. (1989:143)

Later policy statements divided the goals of the solidaristic wages policy clearly into two: equality and justice. The former aimed at decreasing wage differentials across the whole labor market whereas the latter stated that LO members were to be paid different wages for different jobs.

Similarly, in order to encourage satisfaction with the various unions among their members during the hostile economic environment of the 1980s, leaders scaled down the expectations of the rank and file so that the comparison with actual outcomes in the wage rounds could more favorably be made. Union leaders appreciated that where achievements seem to match popular demands, members are less inclined to express dissatisfaction with the bargaining committee, and less likely therefore to elect new leaders or join rival organizations.

This example illustrates both sides of our argument. Popular demands for (say) more equal outcomes in the distribution of pay were expressed as collective action in support of a solidaristic wages policy: behavior corresponded to attitudes. However, where that collective action had consequences that threatened the perceived interests of at least some members of the organization (or the interest of the organization itself in securing its own future), then class representatives were able to modify the original attitudes. The union leaders themselves seem to have shared our own view that attitudes are an important influence on, or provide a potential for, particular courses of action—and for that very reason shaped them to suit the collective purpose.[15]

CONCLUSION

We have already made clear our view that the relationship between attitude and behavior is far from determinate: many factors can intervene between predispositions to act and the actions to which people are predisposed. Similarly, our claim that attitudes can be changed should not be confused with the view that this is easily done. This point is particularly important, given that the issue of the malleability of popular attitudes to distributive justice arose also in the philosophical section of our paper: the philosopher concerned to defend his or her philosophizing on consequentialist grounds might well appeal to the possibility of changing what people think about distributive issues, and hence the bounds of political possibility.

We suggested there that what was really needed was research into the efficacy of good reasons in forming people's attitudes—efficacy relative to factors (such as self-interest) with which those reasons might compete. Even the social scientist, doubtless suspicious of the idea that reasons can straightforwardly be distinguished as good or bad, can perhaps acknowledge the value of research into the processes by which people's attitudes change. Clearly, cross-sectional data of the kind provided by our survey cannot help, and we do not pretend that research instruments that might produce the relevant evidence are readily to hand.

If this research program itself sounds utopian, it would be foolish to deny that much of our discussion can be taken to reveal the gap that exists between philosophers and social scientists. It is notable, indeed, that the concrete example invoked to support our claims that attitudes to justice make a difference to what people do, and that they can be changed, is drawn from a world very different from that apparently implicit in what we might think of as a philosophical worldview. The example refers to the concrete process of bargaining between conflicting groups, groups that act in a manner consonant with self-interest in at least two different ways. In the first place, the individual members of the various union organizations seem to endorse conceptions of justice that suit their definitions of their interests as individuals: that is surely a plausible explanation for why blue-collar workers are more favorable to equality than are white collar. Furthermore, where the leaders of organizations sought to alter their members' distributive beliefs, this was apparently motivated by a strategic concern to preserve unity and hence the organizational capacity to realize what they took to be the group's collective self-interest. This picture of people whose apparently moral beliefs closely aligned with their conceptions of self-interest, and who are subject to influences that mold those beliefs further to achieve strategic objectives, takes us a long way from the philosophical ideal of securing reasonable or rational agreement on justice as something like impartiality.

We do not, of course, wish to deny that a sense of justice *can* motivate people to do things that conflict with their interests narrowly construed. Jon Elster (1989b:203–16) is surely right to think that universal suffrage and the rise of the welfare state cannot be explained by appeal to egoistic considerations alone. Our point is simply that the world of the social scientist can look a rather different place from that constructed in the philosophical mental experiment, and that philosophers may be professionally predisposed to overrate the explanatory significance of good reasons, and hence to overestimate the likelihood of reasoned consensus.

Speculation of this kind takes us far beyond the concerns of the paper. Our intention has been simply to confront as best we can the three issues raised by David Miller—issues that call for nothing less than a justification of the international project in which we have been involved. It is fortunate, then, and we hope not just a rationalization of our collective self-interest that we are able to conclude that what the people think about distributive justice does indeed matter.

NOTES

1. Grateful thanks are due to Geoff Evans, John H. Goldthorpe, Anthony Heath, David Miller, and Stefan Svallfors, all of whom offered helpful comments on an earlier draft of this paper.
2. The British study was supported by the Economic and Social Research Council

(grant number R000232421) and a British Academy/Leverhulme Trust Senior Research Fellowship.
3. For useful overviews with comprehensive bibliographies, see Ronald L. Cohen (1986) and Klaus R. Scherer (1992). The journal in question is *Social Justice Research* (first published in 1987).

4. It is important to be clear that even if one's attitude to popular opinion were of this second, merely strategic kind, it is likely that one would find some congruence between one's own beliefs and the lay beliefs prevalent in one's society. This is because, first, any plausible account of moral justification requires some kind of fit between that which is justified and one's moral intuitions; and, second, one is likely to share at least some of those intuitions with at least some lay members of one's society. What one concludes to be morally desirable, as an individual, is for these reasons likely to overlap to some extent with what one's fellow members think, even if one has not intentionally paid any attention to what they think in forming that view, but on the contrary regards their opinions solely as environmental constraints on the achievement of the independently and individually justified ideal.

5. Notice that this democratic way of putting the case is at least prima facie different from the claim discussed in the literature on the paradox of democracy. It is one thing to make the democratic case for respecting the views of one's fellow citizens about justice even where they are mistaken, but apparently another to regard those views as constitutive of justice itself. See Richard Wollheim (1962) and, for a recent contribution that provides a full bibliography on this issue, David Estlund (1989).

6. The (mainly American) evidence on desert is summarized by Miller (1992:560–70). See also Kluegel and Matěju (Chapter 9), who find that the level of endorsement of desert and equity principles is high in both capitalist and postcommunist societies, and also rather uniform across socioeconomic and demographic statuses within these countries. (Note in addition, findings presented in Chapters 5 and 10.)

7. On another interpretation of Rawls's strategy, his aim is not explicitly publicly to justify the claim that desert claims are unfounded, but rather to indicate how a conception of justice the implication of which is to deny such claims can publicly be justified. This interpretation shares some features with that reading of Rawls offered by Joshua Cohen (1993:277–81). Since Rawls (1993:226) accepts that conceptions of justice other than justice as fairness may meet the requirement of public justifiability, things are more complicated than can adequately be discussed here.

8. What of the philosopher who believes that conventional desert claims are mistaken but who accepts that this cannot be demonstrated in publicly acceptable ways—that it relies on controversial but valid forms of argument? Presumably he or she can, in private life as it were, preach and seek to persuade others of the truth, but, on the position presented here, cannot consider this part of a conception of *justice* and argue that it should be enforced by the state (because on this view it is a condition of a distribution's being just and enforceable that it be publicly justifiable). It is a nice issue, but one that cannot be explored here, precisely how this differs from the view that we should respect the democratic will even where it is mistaken.

9. The classic treatment of this issue is to be found in Max Weber's two essays on "Science as a Vocation" and "Politics as a Vocation" (Weber 1948).

10. We are, of course, aware that fairness is only one particular way of thinking about

justice (and can be contrasted with, for example, entitlement). Our use of the two interchangeably here simply reflects common usage. On the different conceptions of social justice, see Gordon Marshall and Adam Swift (1993).

11. In preliminary analyses, it was found that when common scales were created based on the pooled data (rather than each data set separately), the country variable captured a large portion of the variance. For this reason, and because of the variations in the content of the dimensions across countries, it was decided to tailor to individual countries. Nuances of cross-national variation are not the issue in the present paper.

12. In the tables, class is coded to five Goldthorpe classes: salariat; routine clerical; petite bourgeoisie and farmers; supervisors of manual workers and skilled manual workers; semi-/unskilled workers and agricultural laborers. Education categories are low (CASMIN category 1), medium (CASMIN category 2), and high (CASMIN category 3) (see the Appendix). Party identification is coded Republican and Democrat (United States); Labour, Liberal Democrat, and Conservative (left, center, and right, respectively, for the United Kingdom); and, for West Germany, left (Die Grunen/GAL, Bundnis 90, PDS, SPD), center (FDP), and right (CDU/CSU, DSU, NPD, Republikaner). Note that we are here remaining deliberately agnostic about issues of causation. On the one hand, our data provide no basis for attributing causal priority to justice beliefs, vis-à-vis other attitudes such as party preference. On the other, we do not wish to endorse any particular theory of how social characteristics such as education and sex come to influence justice attitudes.

13. For a useful summary of the major contributions to the debate, together with a discussion of the unresolved issues, see Eiser and van der Pligt (1988:20–44).

14. For a similar account, identifying the same processes in the Norwegian wage-bargaining system, see Geir Hogsnes (1989), and, for a more general discussion, see Jon Elster (1989a:215–47).

15. It is perhaps worth noting here, if only in passing, that the leadership of the British Labour Party seems to have taken a similar view in establishing its Commission for Social Justice (Institute for Public Policy Research 1993).

3

Justice, Socialism, and Participation in the Postcommunist States

David S. Mason

The former communist states succeeded in one revolution: the overthrow or replacement of the Communist party governments. Now they are attempting another, with the effort to simultaneously develop democratic political institutions and capitalist economies. The task is a complex and difficult one, even from a strictly theoretical point of view: the new governments must wrestle with the details of writing constitutions, fostering interest groups and political parties, reforming the legal system, privatizing industry and agriculture, establishing a banking system, freeing prices, and many other tasks. But these technical problems are made much more difficult by the political environment and cultural context. During the long and stressful economic transition, these fragile new governments must elicit popular support, or at least acquiescence, for the paths they have chosen. In almost all of the postcommunist states, this is proving to be the most difficult task of all. If these governments are going to succeed in their efforts, they will need some degree of support for market-oriented reform, and some degree of trust from the population. Without these, the reforms will fail or the governments will collapse, or both.

Popular support for the new political and economic regimes is dependent in large measure on popular perceptions that the new economic and political institutions are just ones, or at least more just than those of the communist era. Justice has figured prominently in the ideologies and political claims of both the old regimes and the new ones. The communist governments claimed legitimacy, especially in their early years, from their efforts to eliminate injustice based on property ownership. Many citizens of those countries recognized and appreciated the broader social and economic equality achieved by those governments, even if they objected to other policies. As the Russian dissident historian Roy Medvedev argued in the 1970s: "[T]hese countries have removed many injustices from the previous social systems. Yet, in many cases, fresh social, economic and other injustices have taken the place of the old injustices" (1977:19). The revolutions of 1989–1991 were a reaction to these new injustices, and the new postcommunist governments of Eastern Europe staked their claim to legitimacy on their efforts to eradicate the injustices of the old system, and to create new regimes that were rooted, especially, in political justice.

This chapter, then, looks at the popular perceptions of justice in the postcommunist states, focusing on attitudes toward the new political and economic institutions and ideas. While the focus is on the postcommunist states of Russia, Estonia, Poland, Hungary, Czechoslovakia, Bulgaria, Slovenia, and the former East Germany, comparisons will be made to the Western countries in the sample. After reviewing the social and political contexts of each postcommunist country at the time the survey was fielded, we will look first at people's sense of injustice in each country, then in turn at popular attitudes toward the market and socialism, and toward politics and the political system; and at the relationships between economic attitudes and political attitudes, and the implications of this relationship for political stability and economic reform in the region.

THE SOCIOPOLITICAL CONTEXT FOR THE SURVEY

In all of the postcommunist states, our survey was conducted in a period of considerable political and economic flux, and even of turmoil. In 1990 and 1991 all of these countries suffered dramatic declines in GNP and industrial production, high rates of inflation, and rapid increases in unemployment (see Table 3.1). A brief sketch of the political-economic situation in each country at the time the survey was conducted will provide a context for understanding some of the issues confronting each country.

Germany. Fieldwork was begun in April 1991 in both eastern and western Germany, just six months after the formal reunification of the country. This was a heady time for many people in the east, who had just experienced one of the quickest, most peaceful, and most dramatic transformations in modern history: the collapse of the Berlin Wall in November 1989, free elections in East Germany in March 1990, unification in October, and all-German elections in December. A government-created agency, Treuhand, had been established to manage the social and economic integration of the two economies and charged to sell off the east's state-owned enterprises. The excitement of all of this frenetic change was tempered by a sharp decline in eastern industrial production, and a rapid rise in unemployment in the region, to almost 12% of the work force by the end of 1991.

Slovenia. The survey fieldwork was begun in June 1991 in Slovenia, Bulgaria, Czechoslovakia and Poland. Slovenia, one of Yugoslavia's six constituent republics, had begun to move away from the parent state in 1990 after multiparty

Table 3.1   Economic Indicators for Postcommunist States[a]

	Bulgaria	Czechoslovakia	Estonia	Eastern Germany	Hungary	Poland	Russia[b]	Slovenia[c]
Population, 1992 (million)	8.9	15.7	1.6	16.0[g]	10.3	38.4	149.5	2.0
GDP, PPE ($US billions, 1991)	36.4	108.9		95.6	60.1	162.7		21.0
GDP per capita ($US)	4100	6900		5870	5700	4300		10,700
GNP real growth rate (%)								
1990	−6	−3		−15	−6	−9	−2 to −5	−6
1991	−22	−15	−13	−30	−7	−5	−9	−10
Consumer goods inflation rate (%)								
1990	100	9	17	1[d]	30	250	14	164
1991	420	52	200	11[e]	34	60	89	15–20
Unemployment rate (%)								
1990	2	0.8		3[f]	1.7	6.1	1–2	16
1991	10	6.7	0.1	11	8.0	11.4		10
Industrial production growth rate (%)								
1990	−15	−3		−50	−8	−23	−2	−11
1991		−22	−9	−30	−20	−14	−8	−12

[a] Sources: CIA, *The World Factbook 1991 and 1992* (Washington, D.C., 1991, 1992) and *Europa World Yearbook 1993*.
[b] 1990 figures are for entire Soviet Union.
[c] 1990 figures are for entire Yugoslavia.
[d] Data for 1989.
[e] Data for 1992.
[f] Data for first half of 1990.
[g] Figure for 1990.

elections led to the formation of a noncommunist government. Our survey was begun in Slovenia just as the country's parliament declared independence from Yugoslavia and the Serb-dominated federal government sent troops into Slovenia to try to prevent the breakaway. The fieldwork was suspended and resumed later in the summer after a cease-fire had taken place. After that point, Slovenia seemed relatively safe and isolated from the continuing conflicts in Croatia and Bosnia. But the combination of the conflicts, the reduction of ties with Serbia, and the dislocations of the economic transition contributed to a steep economic decline in Slovenia, where the population was accustomed to unusually high standards of living.

Bulgaria. Bulgaria's revolution was not quite as dramatic or as complete as those in some of the other states of the region. Historically the country had close cultural and political ties to Russia, and Bulgaria had remained one of the Soviet Union's most faithful allies in the postwar period. Soon after the collapse of the Berlin Wall at the end of 1989, a coalition of opposition groups formed the Union of Democratic Forces, which negotiated with the collapsing communist government for free elections the following year. The Bulgarian Socialist party, the former Communist party, won those elections but a second set of elections in October 1991 was a virtual stalemate between the UDF and the BSP, with the former managing to form a government only through a coalition with a small party that represented Bulgaria's sizable Turkish minority. This unstable arrangement did not bode well for decisive government action on the economy, which was the worst in Europe in 1991 when output declined by 23%, inflation exceeded 500%, and unemployment grew sevenfold (Marer 1993:92).

Czechoslovakia. Czechoslovakia held its first free elections in June 1990, and the big winners were the Civic Forum and the Public Against Violence, the two umbrella groups that had led the velvet revolution of November 1989. These groups were more like social movements than political parties, however, and both soon split into numerous factions. The government initiated a large-scale economic liberalization program in January 1991, which led to rapid price increases in the first half of the year, but a slowing of inflation after that point. The country's economic problems of growing inflation and unemployment and declining production and growth, typical of the region, were compounded by increasing tensions between the Czech and Slovak components of the federation. The Slovak leader, Vladimir Meciar, criticized the free-market reforms of the federal government and pushed for formal separation and independence for Slovakia, which finally occurred in January 1993.

Poland. Poland had led the way for the revolutions in the rest of Eastern Europe. Worker-led strikes in 1988 had forced the communist government to relegalize Solidarity (the independent trade union that had flourished for sixteen months in 1980–1981 before being banned under martial law) and to allow partially free elections. In the June 1989 elections, Solidarity won virtually every seat available to it, and by August a Solidarity supporter had formed the first noncommunist government to emerge from a communist party state. The next year Solidarity leader Lech Walesa was elected president of Poland. But while Poles overwhelmingly rejected the communists, they were not so united on what they *did* want. In the first totally free parliamentary elections in October 1991, voter turnout was just 40%, and the vote was divided among some thirty parties, none with more than 12%. In January 1990 the government had introduced a program of "shock therapy" to rapidly liberalize and marketize the economy, but the weak and unstable succession of governments was unable to push through key elements of the program. While hyperinflation (reaching 800% in 1990) was reduced, it was still over 60% in 1991, and unemployment grew steadily, exceeding 10% in mid-1991.

Hungary. Hungary's survey was fielded in July 1991. By this time, Hungary had proceeded as far along the path of democratization and marketization as any country in the region. Indeed, even before 1989 Hungary was well ahead of the rest of the bloc in terms of economic decentralization, having first implemented some such changes as early as 1968. In 1989, Hungary's revolution was not as dramatic as those in Czechoslovakia or East Germany, having been initiated and managed mostly from above by a reformist element within the Communist party. Nevertheless, the country's parliamentary elections of March 1990 were the first completely free elections in Eastern Europe. The election was a major victory for center-right parties favoring market reforms: a coalition government was formed by the Hungarian Democratic Forum, which favored evolutionary change under the slogan of a "compassionate transition." The economic dislocations of Hungary's more gradual transition were not as great as those in Czechoslovakia or Poland, but were nonetheless a source of political tension in a country that in past years had been one of the most successful of the bloc economies.

Russia. Russia's survey was fielded in October and November 1991, during one of the most turbulent periods in modern Russian history. In the spring and summer of 1991 Soviet party leader and President Mikhail Gorbachev was trying to negotiate an agreement among the Soviet Union's fifteen component republics to keep the country from flying apart. In the midst of this, in August a hard-line group representing the party, the army, and the KGB attempted to oust Gorbachev from power. Russian President Boris Yeltsin managed to rally opposition to the coup and face down the plotters. But in the following months, the country's fragmentation accelerated. By the end of the year, Gorbachev had resigned and retired, and the Soviet Union was dissolved and was replaced by a very loose confederation (the Commonwealth of Independent States) eventually including eleven of the former Soviet republics. The political collapse was accompanied by a virtual economic collapse in Russia and the other successor states as domestic production and foreign trade plummeted, and inflation exceeded 100% in 1991. The biggest economic shocks were still ahead though, as in January 1992 President Yeltsin's government initiated Polish-style economic shock therapy, including freeing most prices, which sent inflation even higher.

Estonia. Estonia, which joined our project late, fielded its survey in February and March 1992. Estonia was one of the three small Baltic states (along with Lithuania and Latvia) that had been absorbed by the Soviet Union (and thus became one of its "republics") in 1940. These three states, the last to join the USSR, also became the first to leave, with formal declarations of independence in early 1990. Their independence was not fully secured, however, until after the August 1991 coup attempt in Moscow and the extension of diplomatic recognition by several European states and the United States. Estonia had one of the highest standards of living in the USSR, but these suffered greatly in 1991–1992 as the country distanced itself from its former trade partners and moved toward a market economy. Political problems were inflamed by continuing tensions between the Estonian majority and a large (30%) Russian minority.

LIFE SATISFACTION

Given past conditions and present turmoil, it is not surprising that the levels of life satisfaction in the postcommunist states are significantly lower than in the Western states, with average satisfaction highest in the Western democracies and lowest in the former Soviet states, with Eastern Europe (and Japan) in between (see Table 3.2). The satisfaction levels correspond closely to the overall stan-

Table 3.2. Satisfaction with Life as a Whole, Average By Country

Country	Mean score[a]
United States	5.77
United Kingdom	5.66
West Germany	5.61
Holland	5.59
East Germany	5.09
Slovenia	5.03
Czechoslovakia	4.76
Poland	4.65
Japan	4.63
Hungary	4.50
Bulgaria	4.26
Estonia	4.14
Russia	3.70

[a] High scores indicate greater satisfaction. Question: All things considered, how satisfied are you with your life as a whole? [7-point scale from "completely satisfied" (7) to "completely dissatisfied" (1).]

dards of living in these areas (except for the anomalous situation of Japan). And for the postcommunist states, satisfaction with one's own standard of living is the strongest determinant of overall life satisfaction, showing a stronger correlation (.59) than income, self-perceived social standing, age, sex, or education (for detailed discussions of *income* satisfaction, see Chapters 5 and 7 of this volume).

It is difficult to know from these data if people's sense of satisfaction or dissatisfaction is due primarily to the accumulated experiences of the past, under communism, or to the more recent experiences in the transition to democracy and capitalism. Our survey did, however, ask a series of questions that explored the past, asking, How often have you personally experienced injustice [in your life] because of the following factors [each asked separately]: your religious beliefs, your sex, your social background, your age, a lack of money, the part of the country you are from, your political beliefs, and your race or ethnic group?

In all of the postcommunist states, the overwhelming majority responded "never" to each of these questions. And an index consisting of the sum of positive responses across all eight of these dimensions found no significant difference between the postcommunist and the capitalist states. On average, respondents in the postcommunist states gave only *one* positive response (very often, often, or sometimes) across all eight of these questions.[1] Comparing the capitalist and postcommunist states on each of these dimensions, one still sees only small differences between the two populations. While people in the post-communist states have in the past experienced injustice more often because of political beliefs, lack of money, and religious beliefs, they have experienced injustice *less* often than respondents in the capitalist states due to their race, region, age, social background, and gender (see Figure 3.1).

It is not surprising that people in the former communist states had experienced greater injustice because of their political and religious beliefs. But it is surprising how small are the differences on those dimensions from the democratic states, and that those in the communist states apparently experienced less injustice than those in the Western states in so many other facets of their lives. Since these questionnaire items were phrased in a way that asked about injustice "in their lives," it should be tapping past experiences (i.e., during the communist period) as well as present-day ones, and so these questions reveal a remarkably low sense of oppression or repression by most people in the postcommunist states. This raises the question of why there were revolutions in these countries, or where the source of such apparent dissatisfaction was. This will be discussed further later in this chapter, but the basic answer is that in these revolutions, as in most revolutions in history, a relatively small proportion of the population actually participated in the revolt, and the overwhelming majority of the population remained passive or even apathetic. As we will see below, it is disproportionately those people who *did* experience injustice who took political action; but most people neither experienced such injustice nor participated much politically.

Figure 3.1 also shows that respondents in the postcommunist states reported

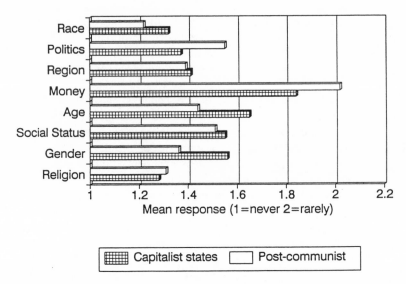

Figure 3.1. Experiences of injustice (by category) in capitalist and postcommunist states.

"lack of money" as a source of injustice far more than any other category, including political or religious beliefs. This points to the prevalence of economic issues and economic dissatisfaction in the postcommunist states, and we will see below that economic issues continued to dominate these societies and public consciousness in the transitions from communism. While repression of political and religious freedom was indisputably a problem in the communist countries, these forms of oppression probably affected far fewer people than the more widespread economic problems. At least one can infer from the data in Figure 3.1 that people in those countries *perceived* economic problems as predominant. And when political legitimacy is at stake, popular perceptions are more important even than the reality of the situation. As M. S. Weatherford (1989:226) argues, "legitimacy is unambiguously at issue when revolution is in the offing, and revolutions are almost always essentially about economic grievances."

ATTITUDES TOWARD SOCIALISM AND THE MARKET

In the aftermath of the democratic revolutions of 1989, citizens in the post-communist states demonstrate a remarkable ambivalence toward the theory and practice of socialism. Having just overturned the communist system, with its authoritarianism, centralization, and inefficiencies, most people are hostile to the

Table 3.3.   Views about Socialism, by Country[a]

Country	Very much in favor	Somewhat in favor	Neither for nor against	Somewhat against	Totally against
Bulgaria	8.1	16.1	24.2	19.2	32.4
Czechoslovakia	2.4	12.4	34.8	24.1	26.3
East Germany	1.6	16.6	39.2	27.6	14.9
Estonia	2.3	18.5	26.1	18.2	35.0
Poland	1.8	9.2	43.2	20.2	25.7
Russia	9.6	17.0	29.7	21.4	22.2
Slovenia	4.8	16.2	46.0	15.5	17.5

[a] Question: People have different views about socialism. Based on your experience in [country name] of socialism, would you say that you are very much in favor, somewhat in favor, neither for nor against, somewhat against, or totally against socialism?.

idea, at least, of socialism. When asked about their views on socialism, fewer than a quarter of respondents in each of eight postcommunist states expressed support for that path (see Table 3.3), while the overwhelming majority in each country agreed with the statement that "a free market economy is essential to our economic development" (see Table 5.4 in Chapter 5). Such substantial support for a new course in the economic sphere would seem to bode well for the transformational policies of the new governments in these countries.

Once one gets away from the ideologically loaded terms of *socialism* and *market*, however, this seeming consensus begins to disappear. When respondents were asked more specific questions, they tended to support important policies and values associated with the state socialist regimes they have left behind. This is perhaps most evident in widespread egalitarianism, support for a strong role for the government in the economy, and deep skepticism about a distributive system based more on merit than on need.

Egalitarianism

The radical egalitarianism of early communism in the Soviet Union was soon replaced by a more meritocratic ideology and incentive system in the Stalin period, in both Russia and Eastern Europe. Nevertheless, there remained a strong egalitarianism in the communist ideology, and both wages and incomes were less highly differentiated in the communist countries than in the Western capitalist ones (see, for example, Bergson 1989). Surveys conducted in East Europe, and especially in Poland, before 1989 showed a high degree of social and economic egalitarianism in the populations (Mason 1985:62–66).

As the East European countries move toward free enterprise and the market, economic inequality will grow sharply as the governments relax restrictions on wages and wealth and abandon their commitment to full employment. A major task of the new governments is to convince their populations to accept greater economic inequality in the society. This may be difficult, given the prevailing attitudes. When asked about the *differences* in incomes people have in their countries, the overwhelming majority in each of the East European states assert that such differences are too large. These feelings are particularly strong in Bulgaria, Hungary, and Slovenia, where 60% or more think that income differences are *much* too large. *Preferred* income differences are much less in the postcommunist states than in the developed capitalist countries. Respondents in the survey were asked to postulate a "just and fair" income for the managing director of a large corporation and for an unskilled factory worker. In the eight postcommunist states (including Eastern Germany), the average ratios between these two salaries (the first divided by the second) were uniformly smaller than in the capitalist states. The median postulated income differential in the capitalist states was 4.0 (the higher income should be 4 times larger than the smaller), compared to just 2.5 in the postcommunist ones.

While most people do not favor total income equality, many do. When asked about the fairest way of distributing wealth and income, 20–30% in each country (except Estonia) favored giving everyone equal shares. These figures may seem high for such a radically egalitarian position, but the level of support for this position was similar to that of the capitalist states (see Table 5.5 in Chapter 5). What the postcommunist populations do favor is guaranteed jobs and, to a lesser extent, ceilings on income, imposed by the government: a solution not too different than that which prevailed under the communist regimes. The preference for guaranteed jobs is overwhelming with 56% (Estonia) to 84% (Eastern Germany) *strongly* agreeing that "the government should provide a job for everyone who wants one." Smaller but still sizable percentages in each country agree (strongly or somewhat) that "the government should place an upper limit on the amount of money any one person can make." Support for this latter position is strongest in Slovenia (60%), East Germany (60%), and Hungary (58%), but considerable in the other states as well: Poland (47%), Bulgaria (42%), Russia (34%) Estonia (32%), and Czechoslovakia (30%) (see Table 5.4 in Chapter 5). As we will see below, this reflects a strong preference in the East European states for governmental solutions to economic and social problems in the region.

Need vs. Merit

This strand of economic egalitarianism is linked to a popular conception of justice that calls for rewards to be distributed on the basis of need as much as (or more than) merit or desert. This seems to be at least partly a legacy of the communist period, when the state guaranteed jobs and provided a whole host of entitlements, including national minimum wages and retirement benefits, heavy subsidies of food, housing, utilities and vacations, and generous maternity leaves. While many East Europeans complained about shortages of consumer goods and a standard of living lower than that in the West, they also became accustomed to these benefits provided by the state.

This concern about people's needs is indicated by substantial agreement with the proposition that "people [should] get what they need, even if this means allocating money from those who have earned more than they need." As seen in Table 5.5 in Chapter 5, a majority or a plurality of respondents in all the East European countries (except Bulgaria) agreed (strongly or somewhat) with this proposition. Lower-income people are somewhat more likely to agree with this statement, but support for the principle remains substantial across income groups in most cases. In Poland, for example, 66% of respondents in the bottom income quartile agree, but so do 48% of those in the top quartile. (Below, we will investigate in more detail the sources of support for this and other "socialist" principles.)

This emphasis on need over merit is also evident in another question on which of a number of factors should influence the level of pay for an employee. When asked about "the size of the family the employee supports," a clear majority of respondents in every postcommunist country (except Czechoslovakia) felt that this should have "a great deal" or "some" influence in determining salary. The average level of support for this proposition was 57% in the former communist countries, compared to 48% in the developed capitalist countries. The *highest* level of support for this proposition, however, came from Western Germany (73%). As we will see elsewhere, attitudes and values in the East European countries often are closer to those in Western Germany, with its "social market" system, than to the other capitalist states.[2]

The Role of the State

With their revolutions, the East European countries left behind systems in which the state and party dominated the economy and most other aspects of society. The state provided jobs and housing, set prices and wages, owned industries, schools, and farms (in most countries), and subsidized basic necessities. The omnipresence and omnipotence of the state aggravated many people, and contributed to the revolutionary ferment. But many people also came to rely on the benefits provided by the state. Under the communist systems, the people may not have had freedom or affluence, but they did have basic economic security. The current reforms promise to deliver the former, but threaten the latter.

Our survey asked three main questions on the role of the government in the economy: whether the government should (1) guarantee everyone a minimum standard of living, (2) place upper limits on income, and (3) provide a job for everyone who wants one. On all three questions, there was strong support in all of the postcommunist countries, and for the issues of guaranteed jobs and standard of living, it was almost universal (see Table 5.4 in Chapter 5). As is evident from the table, there was substantial support for these principles from the capitalist countries as well. But respondents in the East European countries were, overall, much more supportive of this strong government role than were those in the Western countries. When responses to these three questions were averaged at the individual level, and then by country, support for statism was strongest in Eastern Germany, followed in order by Hungary, Slovenia, Bulgaria, Poland, Russia, Japan, Estonia, Czechoslovakia, West Germany, the United Kingdom, Holland, and the United States. Americans, indeed, were *much* less supportive of strong government than any other country in this sample.

Support for Principles of Socialism: Summary Measures

On all three principles—equality, need, and role of the state—East Central Europeans generally lean toward a more egalitarian and statist system than do people in West Europe, Japan, or the United States. To make more systematic cross-national comparisons, and to allow a more systematic examination of the determinants of these attitudes, a single summary measure of prosocialist orientations was derived from six attitudinal questions from the survey, including the questions above tapping attitudes toward equality, need, and the government role in the economy.[3] The average scores on this index, by country, are indicated in Figure 3.2. The absolute value of this index is not in itself very meaningful. What is notable here is the ranking of the countries. As before, the postcommunist countries score higher in socialist orientations than do the capitalist countries. The only exception to this division is Japan, which is closer to the postcommunist states than to the Western capitalist ones. As we have seen before, the United States is a distant outlier on this scale. Values and attitudes in the East European countries are much closer to those in West Europe (especially Germany) and Japan than they are to those in the United States. If this is the case, the West European and Japanese models of economic and social development, involving a greater emphasis on community and government activism, might be more appropriate for the postcommunist states than the more individualistic and laissez-faire approach in the United States.

For and against Reform: Determinants of Attitudes

So far we have looked only at national averages of attitudes toward issues relevant to the economic reforms. But in assessing the likely success of the market-oriented reforms in the postcommunist states, it is necessary to look at who supports and who opposes these reforms. It would be helpful for the market-

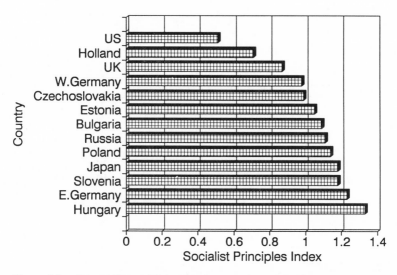

Figure 3.2. Support for socialist principles by country. Note: Highest numbers
indicate strongest support for socialist principles. Index is based on the
average of *z*-scores of responses on six questions tapping support for socialist principles (all 4- or 5-point Likert scales):

—level of pay for an employee should be based on "the size of the family the
employee supports."

—"the government should guarantee everyone a minimum standard of living."

—"the government should place an upper limit on the amount of money any one
person can make."

—"the government should provide a job for everyone who wants one."

—"the fairest way of distributing wealth and income would be to give everyone
equal shares."

—"the most important thing is that people get what they need, even if this means
allocating money from those who have earned more than they need."

Pairwise differences of .13 or more are significant at the .01 level (Scheffe
criterion).

oriented governments, of course, if a majority of the population supported the
kinds of policies they are implementing. As we have seen above, however, that is
not likely to be the case. Most people in these countries still have a basically
egalitarian and statist orientation that works against the laissez-faire and decen-
tralizing reforms being implemented or contemplated in each of the postcommunist states. But even in the absence of a consensus behind the reforms, the
governments might be able to push through the reforms if the proponents of the
reforms remained politically active and the opponents were not.

In all of the East European countries except Estonia, the strongest determinant
by far of prosocialist attitudes is education (see Table 3.4). In most countries,

Table 3.4. Multiple Regression Analysis of Index of Socialist Values
(Standardized Regression Coefficients—Beta)

Country	Education	Income	Sex	Social status	Age	R^2	Listwise N
Bulgaria	−.28***	−.10**	.12***	−.10***	.04	.16	1182
E. Germany	−.18***	−.07*	.05	−.06	.05	.07	950
Hungary	−.36***	−.08*	.06	−.09**	−.03	.20	935
Poland	−.35***	−.14***	.06**	−.08**	−.04	.21	1496
Russia	−.15***	−.12***	.12***	−.02	.06*	.09	1347
Slovenia	−.30***	−.13***	.09**	−.03	−.05	.15	1179
Czechoslovakia	−.31***	−.05	.11***	−.09**	.04	.16	1111
Estonia	−.10**	−.14***	.06	−.12**	.02	.08	794
Postcommunist states	−.27***	−.11***	.08***	.08***	.01	.14	9001
Capitalist states	−.12***	−.15***	.09***	−.12***	−.07***	.09	5734

a Variables: Education (based on Casmin categories); income: family income in 20-tiles;
sex; social status—self perceived; age. R^2 is significant at .001 level for all countries.
*$p < .05$.   **$p < .01$.   ***$p < .001$.

income and sex are the next most important. Those with low education and incomes, and women, are more supportive of socialist principles than others. As is evident from Figure 3.3, there is a steady decline in support for socialist principles from those with low education to those with higher educations. Across all of the East European countries, the correlation coefficient between the socialism index and educational level is −.33.

The strong negative relationship between education and support for socialism is not surprising and, in fact, prevails in the Western countries as well ($r = −.19$). In the postcommunist countries, however, it is particularly strong and reflects a real and perplexing division within those societies. The governments of these countries are pursuing nonegalitarian reforms and are supported in that effort by the more highly educated minority in those societies, who, as it happens, also have the most to gain from such reforms. Indeed, in many of these countries, the new governments are dominated by the highly educated, as the revolutions swept into power intellectuals who had previously opposed the communist system.

In the East European countries as elsewhere, education is related to income, so support for socialist principles is also related to income in those countries ($r = −.23$). In Poland, for example, 58% of those in the bottom quartile of family incomes score high in support of socialist principles, while among those in the upper quartile, only 24% do. Thus we see what could be a politically dangerous situation in the postcommunist countries, where the governments and a relatively

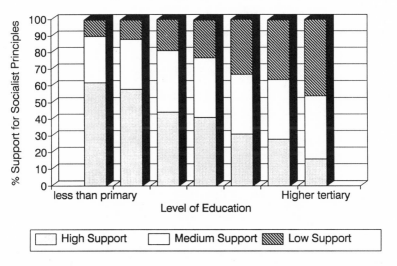

Figure 3.3. Support for socialist principles by educational level.

small educated elite favor the implementation of a market-based economy and more meritocratic society, while most of the poor and less-educated population, who will most directly feel the bite of these reforms, remain supportive of many of the social and economic principles of the old regimes. While almost everyone seems committed to the *democratic* aspects of the reform process, there are sharp divisions over the economic ones.

ECONOMIC VALUES AND POLITICAL PARTICIPATION

It may seem paradoxical that there should be such divisions between leaders and led in societies that have just undergone paroxysms of revolution, participation, and democratization. In East Germany, Czechoslovakia, and elsewhere, hundreds of thousands of people participated in demonstrations that brought down the communist governments, and voter turnout was high in the first competitive elections in each of these countries in the following year. But on closer examination, it is clear that political activity in the East European countries remained limited, even during the revolutionary ferment. Most people in all countries voted in the early elections, but were not otherwise active politically in even a minimal way. Our survey asked respondents if they had ever participated in any of ten variants of political action, ranging from writing a newspaper or signing a petition to joining a wildcat strike or blocking traffic (all questions used in the *Political Action* study—see Barnes, Kaase, et al. 1979). As Table 3.5

Table 3.5.   Political Action by Country (Percentage in
Each Country Reporting Protest Activities)[a]

Country	Number of protest activities		
	None	1–3	4–10
Eastern Germany	17	66	17
Czechoslovakia	34	49	17
Bulgaria	48	43	9
Slovenia	66	29	5
Russia	67	29	4
Estonia	69	28	3
Poland	72	23	5
Hungary	84	15	1

[a] Questions: "have you ever done any of these things over an
issue that was important to you: signed a petition; joined a
boycott; attended a protest demonstration or rally; attended
a public meeting; joined in an unofficial (wildcat) strike;
blocked traffic; written to a newspaper; written to your
(member of the national/federal legislature); refused to
pay rent, rates or taxes; occupied a building or property in
protest."

shows, there is wide variation across countries here, with the incidence of protest
high in those countries where the governments were brought down by people
power (East Germany, Czechoslovakia, Bulgaria) and low in those where the
transition was more evolutionary (Poland) or managed by the political elite
(Hungary). But what is remarkable here is the lack of political activity of any
kind in most of the countries: in the pooled sample, 58% of those in the postcommunist states had participated in *none* of ten forms of political action, compared
with just 25% reporting such low levels of political activity in the capitalist
states.[4] In all of the postcommunist states, most people (three quarters or more)
voted in the first free or semifree parliamentary elections in 1989–1991, but apart
from that, there was very little political activity.

In most of the postcommunist states, less than a third of the respondents
expressed even minimal political interest through "sympathizing with a particular
[political] party." Only in Eastern Germany, which had by this time been inte-
grated into the fully formed political structure of the West, did a majority of
respondents (53%) express such affiliation. In part, this reluctance to identify
with political parties was due to the weak structure and development of party
systems throughout the region. In both Poland and Hungary, for example, there
were dozens of political parties and groups vying for parliamentary office in the
first series of elections, including the semiserious Beer Lovers Party in Poland.

This may have been bewildering to many potential voters, but the lack of effective party organizations effectively excluded much of the population from political participation and influence.

In the United States and other Western countries, socioeconomic status, and especially education, is the most important determinant of voting and other forms of political participation (see Erikson, Luttbeg and Tedin 1991:8–9). In the postcommunist states, our survey also showed a linear relationship between educational level and both voting and political activity. In the capitalist countries in our survey, regression analysis showed education to be by far the most important determinant of political action (see Table 3.6). In the postcommunist states, education was also important, but the *major* determinant of political action was past experience of political injustice. The relationship works in both directions. Thus, those who have been politically active are more likely to have experienced political persecution, which as we have seen above is a relatively small part of the population.[5] The vast majority of the population in the postcommunist states, on the other hand, were more concerned with economic issues and economic injustice than with politics, and were not as active politically.

Political participation translates into political influence. Studies in the United States and other Western countries have shown that the economically advantaged groups in society tend to be more politically active and that the well-off, therefore, "tend to benefit more from governmental policies because they have greater influence on such policies" (Verba, Nie, and Kim 1987:5; also Verba, Schlozman, Brady, and Nie 1993). In the emerging democracies of Eastern Europe, it is also the case that political participation is disproportionately exercised by those in higher socioeconomic categories and by people who have experienced political injustice more so than economic deprivation. Perhaps this is not surprising in

Table 3.6. Determinants of Political Action in Capitalist and Postcommunist States (Standardized Regression Coefficients—Beta)

Independent variable	Postcommunist states	Capitalist
Satisfaction with income	−.03*	−.05***
Experienced injustice for political beliefs	.22***	.12***
Age	−.11***	−.01
Sex	−.07***	−.07***
Self-perceived social standing	.05***	.03**
Education	.16***	.27***
Satisfaction with life	.06***	.04***
Income (in deciles)	.02*	.06***
Index of overall experience of injustice	.04**	.14***
R^2	.16***	.15***

*$p < .05$.   **$p < .01$.   ***$p < .001$.

that the revolutions of 1989 (like most revolutions) were led by intellectuals and
other dissidents who were the main targets of political repression under communism. But if these are also the people who are leading the political and economic
transitions in these societies, as seems to be the case, their interests, needs, and
political agendas are likely to be quite different than that of the population as a
whole. What Sidney Verba and his colleagues say about the United States also
has relevance in the emerging democracies of Eastern Europe: "If those who take
part and those who do not were similar on all politically relevant dimensions,
then substantial inequalities in participation would pose no threat to the democratic principles of equal protection of interests. As our analysis has demonstrated, this is hardly the case" (Verba et al. 1993:314).

While studies of the United States by Verba and others have found significant
demographic differences between those who are politically active and those who
are not, they have usually found minimal differences in the political *attitudes* of
the two groups. In the postcommunist states, on the other hand, the demographic
differences are reinforced by significant attitudinal differences in areas important
in the transition. Those people who *were* more active, for example, tended to be
less supportive of socialist principles. In every East European country, the level
of support for socialist principles declines as the level of political activity increases (see Figure 3.4).[6] This supports the evidence above that the more politically active and involved are more committed to the market-oriented reforms
than the less active, and are less supportive of socialism and socialist principles.[7]

There is both good news and bad news in this for the reforming governments
in Eastern Europe. The good news is that the people opposed to or skeptical

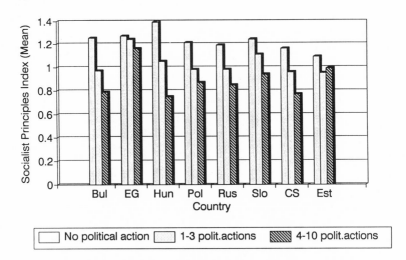

Figure 3.4.   Support for socialism by level of political activity.

about the market-oriented reforms are not likely to express this opposition in political action. There is a kind of "silent majority" in the postcommunist countries of people who are not committed to the reforms, but will not speak out or vote against them, thus allowing the reformist governments to pursue the difficult transitional policies without substantial opposition. In the early years of the transition, there were few political parties or organizations in the East European countries that attempted to mobilize this potential opposition. In part this was due to lingering resentment of the communists, and a popular suspicion that organized groups that oppose the liberalizing reforms must be communists. Indeed, there are still communist or protocommunist groups or parties in each of these countries, but these are quite small, and they may not always be any more prosocialist than the rest of the population. In all three countries (Bulgaria, Czechoslovakia, and Slovenia) where our survey asked about former communist party membership, support for socialist principles was *lower* among those reporting such membership than among those who said they never belonged to the communist party. Here, as we have seen on other indicators, potential opposition to liberalizing reforms is much broader and deeper in the population than is support for hard-line groups.

The bad news for the reforming governments is the possibility that this opposition to the reforms *might* become mobilized and politically active. The silent majority can be safely ignored as long as it stays silent. But if the transitional period becomes too painful or too long, the skepticism about the principles of the reform will be reinforced by very real economic hardship. The combination of these circumstances could very well lead to popular upheaval (e.g., strikes or demonstrations) or simply to electoral defeat for the reforming governments and the accession to power of governments committed to reversing the tide of marketization, or even of democratization. There are indicators of this outcome already with the strong electoral showing of newly revived postcommunist parties in Lithuania, Poland, and Hungary, and of antidemocratic forces in Russia.

POLITICAL DISTRUST AND DISAFFECTION

The populations of the postcommunist states express a surprisingly high degree of frustration, futility, and alienation, especially from the political system. In all of these countries a third or more agree with the statement that "there is no point arguing about social justice since it is impossible to change things" (see Table 3.7). These high feelings of futility may be understandable in Russia or Estonia, where democracy and independence were still uncertain at the time of the survey. But it is quite astounding to see almost half of the population expressing this opinion in Poland, Hungary, and Slovenia, where they had just effected some of the most dramatic political transformations in history. It suggests once

Table 3.7. Feelings of Futility, by Country (Percentage Agreeing That "It Is Impossible to Change Things")[a]

Country	Agree (strongly/somewhat)	Neither agree or disagree	Disagree (strongly/somewhat)
Bulgaria	47.0	11.2	41.8
Eastern Germany	37.7	10.9	51.4
Hungary	47.8	21.1	31.1
Poland	53.9	17.7	28.4
Russia	53.1	9.6	37.2
Slovenia	44.6	9.3	46.2
Czechoslovakia	38.9	17.3	43.8
Estonia	70.9	13.1	16.0
Average for post-communist states[b]	49.1	13.6	37.3
Average for capitalist states[b]	28.7	15.5	55.8

[a] Questionnaire item:"There is no point arguing about social justice since it is impossible to change things."

[b] Average at individual level across countries.

again that the democratization of these societies was viewed with some mixed feelings in the face of continuing and deepening economic and social problems.

This generalized sense of futility is reflected in high levels of political disaffection and distrust in the postcommunist states. One would expect there to be a certain honeymoon for the fledgling democratic governments in these countries, with popular trust and expectations high, at least for the *political* systems, if not for the economic ones. But the postcommunist societies have even higher levels of political distrust and alienation than the established democratic ones. Responding to a standard question on how often the national government is run for the benefit of all of the people, between 20 and 44% in the East European countries said "rarely" or "never," figures comparable to or even higher than most Western countries (see Table 5.6 in Chapter 5). Similar levels of distrust were expressed on a second standard survey question asking how often you can trust the national government to do what is right. An index of political distrust, made up of the means of these two question,[8] shows distrust to be highest in Japan, Poland, Russia and Estonia, and lowest in Holland, the United States, Slovenia, and Czechoslovakia (see Figure 3.5).[9] For the more stable and long-standing democracies like Japan and the United Kingdom (where disaffection is also high), such attitudes may not be particularly dangerous, and may simply mean trouble for the existing government or ruling party. In the fledgling democracies, high levels of distrust make it harder for the government to accomplish big changes, and may even threaten the permanence of democratic institutions.

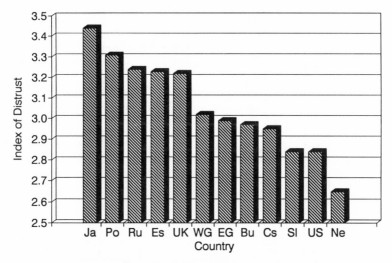

Figure 3.5.   Index of political distrust ranked by country.

Note: The higher the index, the higher the political distrust. The Index of Distrust, calculated at the individual level, is the mean response on two 5-point scaled questions: (1) How much of the time do you think you can trust the [federal] government in [capital city] to do what is right? [never–very often] (2) How much of the time do you think the [federal] government in [capital city] is run for the benefit of all the people? [never–very often] Pairwise differences of .15 or more are significant at the .01 level (Scheffe criterion).

What accounts for the high levels of distrust of government in the new postcommunist states? Most studies have shown that in the West trust in government and voting patterns are based more on people's assessment of the *national* situation rather than their own personal financial one. Thus political support is more "sociotropic" than it is egocentric (Clarke and Kornberg 1989; Kiewiet 1983; and Elliott and Zuk 1989). In the East European countries, this also seems to be the case. While our survey asked few questions about the future, one question did ask for the respondent's assessment of whether over the next five years, the percentage of poor people in their country would increase or decrease. In all of the East European countries, a majority of the respondents (from 62% in East Germany to 89% in Russia) thought poverty would increase. This variable turns out to be a strong predictor of political disaffection, in most countries more so than age, education, income, or the level of individual satisfaction with one's income or life (see Table 3.8). As is apparent from that table, these egocentric factors do play a role, but not as strong as the sociotropic factor of expectations that poverty will increase. It should be noted that family income, which was originally included in this regression analysis, had a statistically significant role in only one of the eight countries (Poland).

Table 3.8. Multiple Regression Analysis of Index of Political Distrust (Standardized Regression Coefficient—Beta)[a]

Country	Future Poverty	Life Satisf.	Socialism Index	Income Satisf.	Education	Age	Social Class	R^2	N
Czecho-Slovakia	-.20***	-.11***	.21***	-.09**	-.11***	-.05	-.01	.16	1,184
Slovenia	-.15***	-.07**	.08**	-.14***	.03	-.08**	-.03	.07	1,374
Russia	-.08**	-.08**	.00	-.06*	-.09***	-.09***	-.05	.04	1,731
Poland	-.19***	-.13***	.06	-.08**	-.11***	-.13***	.09***	.14	1,541
Estonia	-.08**	-.18***	.11***	-.05	.04	-.09**	-.22***	.15	999
E Germany	-.10***	-.05	.15***	-.19***	.03	-.14***	.11***	.14	1,018
Bulgaria	-.13***	-.06*	.09***	-.07**	-.16***	-.03	-.08**	.09	1,404
Post-Comm. States	-.13***	-.11***	.08***	-.10***	-.06***	-.07***	-.05***	.08	10,255
Capitalist States	-.10***	-.05***	.15***	-.16***	-.01	-.09***	-.14***	.14	7,129

[a] Questions: Future poverty—Will percentage of poor increase? Life and income satisfaction—How satisfied with life/income? Socialism index—index of support for socialist principles. Education. Age. Social class—Self-identified social standing. R^2 is significant at .001 level for all countries.

* $p < .05$. ** $p < .01$. *** $p < .001$.

As indicated in the last line in Table 3.8, the capitalist states show an opposite tendency: the egocentric factors of income satisfaction and self-perceived social standing weigh more heavily on political distrust than the sociotropic factor of "future poverty." This seems to contradict earlier evidence noted above (see note 9) and suggests once again the less individualistic orientations of populations in the postcommunist states.

This again points to the economic bases of political support and legitimacy in these countries and the close ties between economic and political stability. Economic concerns, whether they be macrolevel (concern over growth of poverty) or microlevel (concern over one's own standard of living), loom large in the explanation of political satisfaction or dissatisfaction. This is also consistent with our finding that many people continue to cling to the social and economic safety nets that were provided by the socialist systems.

THE POLITICS OF ECONOMIC REFORM: RESHAPING CULTURE AND IDEOLOGY

The evidence above points to the deep social and political obstacles to the transition to market democracies in East Central Europe. It is unlikely that the governments of the region will be able to work against this political culture: either the governments will have to change or the culture will. Given the overwhelming consensus among both the postcommunist political elites and Western financial institutions that they should push ahead with the reforms, the governments will not lightly change their market-oriented strategies. What they need to do, in that case, is to work on reshaping popular values and political culture. As Kent Jennings points out, "if we want to change perceptions of unfairness, one fundamental route is to change value systems first—no small task" (1991:199). [See Chapter 10 in this volume for a discussion of the cultural dimensions of dominant ideologies.]

This is normally the task of the political socialization process, which often takes a generation or more to effect substantial changes in values or culture. But in the postcommunist states, the political culture seems particularly fluid and malleable in this transitional period, so perhaps these governments will be able to bring the populations around to their point of view more quickly.

There are those who argue that changes in popular orientations are already beginning to take place, and that a shift in favor of the market and capitalism will accelerate as the economic reforms begin to improve the economies and deliver jobs, wealth, and consumer goods. Indeed, most of the postcommunist states show some shifts away from the radical egalitarianism and hostility to private enterprise that characterized the communist and early postcommunist period. As we have seen, however, in 1991, two years after the revolutions in most cases, attitudes remained much more egalitarian and statist than in the Western countries. And in the few cases where questionnaire items from our 1991 survey have been replicated subsequently, there does not appear to be much overall change in attitudes on key economic and political issues.

In Poland, for example, a survey conducted in 1992 and 1993, one and two years after our survey, included a number of questions asked the previous year.[10] This period was one in which industrial production was beginning to recover for the first time since the introduction of shock therapy in January 1990, and inflation was beginning to moderate—though unemployment was continuing to grow. In this context, one sees a surprising change in the response to our question (reported in Table 3.3) about views about socialism (see Table 3.9).[11] One sees a slight increase both in those in favor of socialism and those "somewhat against" it. But there is a marked decline in those "totally against" socialism as well as an increase in the ambivalent responses of "neither for nor against" and "don't know." As noted in our discussion above, *socialism* is an ideologically loaded term that evokes hostility from many survivors of the communist years. But in Poland, at least, much of that visceral hostility ("totally against") seems to have evaporated within a remarkably short period of time. In this respect, at least, capitalism seems not to have won over many adherents, even as it was starting to generate some successes.

On other questions, too, one sees growing concern with the effects of the economic reforms. One question asked in our survey, and repeated in Poland in 1992, asked about "differences in peoples' incomes in Poland." In 1991, 44% thought such differences were "much too large" and 17% thought they were somewhat or much too small. In 1992, these figures were 52 and 8%, respectively, showing substantial increases in those concerned about the growing gap between wealthy and poor in Poland.

In our 1991 survey, we had also asked respondents about the role of govern-

Table 3.9. Views About Socialism in Poland, 1991–1993 (%)[a]

Response	1991	1992	1993
Very much in favor	1.6	2.7	1.8
Somewhat in favor	8.5	8.6	10.4
Neither for nor against	39.9	45.6	51.9
Somewhat against	18.7	18.7	15.9
Totally against	23.7	15.6	13.0
Don't know	7.6	8.8	7.0

[a] Sources: 1991 figures are ISJP data. 1992 and 1993 figures from *Polish General Social Surveys, 1992–1993: Cumulative Codebook* (Warsaw: Institute for Social Studies, University of Warsaw, 1993), p. 120.

ment in the economy, including whether the government should provide a job for everyone who wanted one. As seen above, there was overwhelming support for this proposition throughout Eastern Europe, including 88% of the respondents in Poland. In 1992, the level of overall support in Poland for this same proposition was almost identical (89%), though there was a substantial drop in those who *strongly* agreed with that statement (from 66 to 49%).[12]

Poland was the first country in the region to introduce economic shock therapy and was the first to begin to recover from the traumas of the initial shock. In some ways then, Poland is a harbinger of the course of the transition in many of the other postcommunist states. As we have seen, though, attitudes in the country remain egalitarian and statist, with much of the population concerned about and affected by the social and economic dislocations of economic transformation. By 1992, at least, there do not seem to have been major changes in the political culture that would indicate the population becoming more accepting of the market-oriented changes than they had been the previous year.

Ideology and Value Inconsistency

Attitudes are malleable, however, and may change more substantially over the longer run. The ideologies of the postcommunist populations seem particularly subject to change. As we have seen above, citizens of the postcommunist states are remarkably nonideological in their orientations. As seen in Table 3.3, in most of the East European countries, the most frequent reaction to socialism is "neither for nor against." Much of the opposition to socialism seems to be to the political aspects of the communist system rather than to the socialist aspects of the ideology. For example, even among those who professed to be "totally against" socialism in the postcommunist states, over 25%, on average, also scored high on our index of support for socialist principles.

Even during the communist period, the formal ideology of communism never took hold very well in any country, even after years of socialization. Studies of both the Soviet Union and Poland, for example, showed how shallow the commitment to Marxism -Leninism was and, indeed, how little real *knowledge* most people had of basic ideological principles (see, for example, Shlapentokh 1986; Mason 1985). Of course, political knowledge and ideological commitment are also weak in the United States and other Western countries (Kinder and Sears 1985; Converse 1964). But in the communist states, where political socialization was so much more uniform, centralized, and intense, it was somewhat surprising how little the ideological principles had taken hold.

In the present environment, the postcommunist states are also in a kind of postideological limbo. The old ideology has been rejected, but a new one has not yet taken hold. Even the left-right and conservative-liberal political distinctions, which are fairly well understood in the capitalist countries, have been set loose from their bearings in the postcommunist states. In Russia, for example, a conservative is thought of as one who is more sympathetic to the old (communist) order than to the new (capitalist) reforms. Our survey asked respondents to identify themselves on a 10-point scale of left to right. In the capitalist countries, this variable was predictably negatively correlated with our socialism index ($r =$ $-.21$). In the postcommunist countries overall, the correlation was substantially weaker ($-.10$) and in Russia, the correlation was *positive* ($.12$) meaning that people who identified themselves on the right were more likely to support the socialist principles than were those on the left. Thus the traditional notions of left and right have been thoroughly scrambled.

This seems to be due, in part, to the tendency of much of the postcommunist populations to favor *both* capitalism and socialism; to achieve the higher standard of living of the former without relinquishing the economic security of the latter. On many important issues, most people hold what appear to be mutually contradictory views. Two questions, for example, tap different sides of the merit vs. need criteria: (1) people are entitled to keep what they have earned—even if this means some people will be wealthier than others; and (2) the most important thing is that people get what they need, even if this means allocating money from those who have earned more than they need. On these two questions, from 34% (Bulgaria) to 86% (East Germany) agreed with *both* propositions, and 20% or more in each country *strongly* agreed with both propositions.

Of course, such inconsistency is also characteristic of Western populations, but in our survey it is much stronger in the East European countries than the others (for more detailed discussion of this phenomenon, see Chapters 5, 8, and 9 of this volume). One would expect, for example, a negative correlation between these two variables. That is the case in most countries, but the correlation is much weaker in most of the postcommunist countries ($-.06$ to $-.09$) than in the capitalist ones ($-.10$ to $-.21$); becomes statistically insignificant in some (Bulgaria); and actually turns *positive* in East Germany.

What stands out in all of this is the prevalence of hard economic issues. At this point, most of the citizens of Eastern Europe seem less interested in either ideology or politics, and more interested in their own economic fate and that of their country. They favor liberalizing economic reforms, if that will bring them a better standard of living. But they are reluctant to change a system that will mean less security and more inequality.

The predominance of these economic concerns is apparent from the survey questions tapping materialism and postmaterialism. Using the standard 4-item index (Inglehart 1979:330), we asked respondents to rank "four possible political goals": maintain order in the country, give people more say in the decisions of government, fight rising prices, and protect freedom of speech. The first and third of these are considered "materialist" values; the second and fourth, "postmaterialist" ones. People who ranked the materialist values in both first and

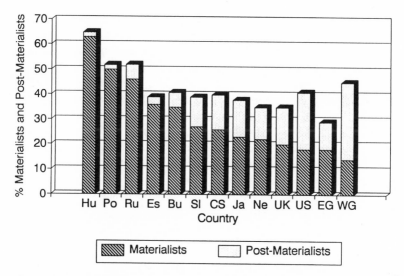

Figure 3.6. Materialists and postmaterialists by country (%).

Note: Materialists and postmaterialists include only those who were "pure," selecting materialist (or postmaterialist) values as *both* the most important and second most important values. The question reads as follows: "I will read a list of four possible political goals. Suppose you had to choose among these. Which would be most important to you? And what would be the second most important? 1. Maintain order in the country; 2. give people more say in the decisions of government; 3. fight rising prices; 4. protect freedom of speech."

second place are considered "pure materialists"; the same for the postmaterialist values. Others are considered "mixed."

As shown in Figure 3.6, materialist values predominate over postmaterialist ones in all of the East European countries. Only in East Germany, which had already been brought under the protective social system of West Germany, were materialist values as low as in the capitalist states. As Ron Inglehart and others have suggested, these values are closely related to the standard of living and to economic security in each country. Thus, as the standard of living improved in a country, one should see increased incidence of postmaterialist values over time. As a country's economy improves, each succeeding generation should demonstrate a higher incidence of postmaterialism. Indeed, in this survey, as in surveys analyzed by Inglehart, postmaterialism declines with age in every country.

On the other hand, our results seem to contradict Inglehart's assumption that such values reflect intergenerational change and the standard of living experienced by people a generation *earlier.* If this were the case, one would expect a higher incidence of postmaterialism in these countries now than ten years earlier.

But in most of the East European countries the percentage of postmaterialists is very low indeed, and is almost nonexistent in Poland, Hungary, and Estonia. Inglehart (1990:442) reports a survey conducted in Poland in 1980 in which 10–20% of the respondents were classified as postmaterialists, depending on age. Our survey shows only 1–5% (by age group) as postmaterialists. Surely this difference reflects the calamitous state of the Polish economy *at present* rather than any dramatic decline in the standard of living a generation earlier.[13]

When these questions on values were asked again in Poland in 1992, the results were almost unchanged from 1991. By far the largest numbers gave priority to "maintaining order in the country" (45%) or "fighting rising prices" (37%). In 1992, as in our 1991 survey, hardly any Poles could be classified as pure postmaterialists, that is, more concerned with issues of free speech and participation than order or inflation.

FAVORED FUTURES IN EAST CENTRAL EUROPE

As one might expect from the above analysis, citizens of the postcommunist states are divided on what kind of future they favor for their countries. In every country but Czechoslovakia, the largest number favor "a more democratic type of socialism" than either the kind of socialism they had before or a free-market economy (see Table 3.10) but in no country did a majority favor any of the four choices presented. This is consistent with other surveys, which have found that people in Hungary, Poland, and Czechoslovakia favor emulating German or

Table 3.10.   Favored Systems in East Central Europe, by Country (%)[a]

Country	Former type of socialism	Democratic socialism	Free Market	Specific national solution
Bulgaria	5.5	37.6	32.6	24.3
Poland	2.8	38.3	35.4	23.5
Russia	15.3	33.8	14.9	36.1
Slovenia	4.0	46.4	34.6	15.0
Czechoslovakia	2.8	35.5	35.6	26.1
Estonia	2.3	37.0	17.4	43.3

[a] Questionnaire item: "There are many views about the future development of [country name, e.g., Polish] society. Which one of these alternatives comes closest to your own preference? (1) A socialist society along the lines of what we have already experienced in [country]. (2) A more democratic type of socialism as found in some countries in the West. (3) A free-market economy that is essentially nonsocialist as found in some other countries in the West. (4) A specific [country name, e.g., Polish] solution unique to the country.

Swedish society more than that of the United States (Rose 1992). It is also consistent with many of our findings that attitudes toward the economy and the role of the state in East Central Europe are closer to those in Western Europe and Japan than to those in the United States.

As we found earlier with the sources of support and opposition to socialist principles, the politically active segments of the population are much more supportive of a free-market future than the inactive. Across all of the postcommunist states, a free-market solution was favored by 43% of the most politically active (four or more types of political action), compared to just 25% of the large majority of respondents reporting no political actions. In this latter group, by far the largest number (39%) favored a democratic socialist solution, followed by 28% favoring a uniquely national solution.

It is also clear from our survey that young people provide the primary source of support for a free-market solution across postcommunist states. Support for a free-market solution declines steadily from 36% of those under 27 years of age to just 21% of those over 65, and this relationship holds for each of the countries separately as well. It is understandable that young people, more risk-taking, individualistic, and Westernized, would be more attracted to a free-market system that promised wealth to the ambitious and prosperity to the nation. It is also understandable, however, that older people, more dependent on the state and more concerned about present-day economic security than future riches, would be more reluctant to abandon totally the system of guarantees and benefits provided by the state.

The age differences on these issues raises the possibility of conflict between the generations on the future of these countries, with older people favoring a commitment to some kind of socialism and the young pressing for a more thoroughgoing market economy. On the other hand, it raises the possibility that over time, an increasingly larger segment of the population will be brought over to the market alternative, as the older generations are replaced by the younger, both in the society at large and in the leadership. The fact that the current leadership in these countries *is* rather young, and the politically active are more committed to the market, means that in the short run, at least, the market approach will predominate. The question is, Will this predominance prevail as older segments of the population reenter the political arena, and as the toll of the market erodes support for capitalism even among the young?

IMPLICATIONS FOR ECONOMIC REFORM AND POLITICAL STABILITY

These survey results suggest some measure of caution and concern regarding the possibilities of a successful transition to market democracy in the former communist countries. In all of these countries, there remains a high degree of commitment to the old system of social welfare, and considerable distrust of the current political system and economic reforms. These concerns are based mostly on economic factors rather than ideological ones; or perhaps one can say as Karl Mannheim did, that to the extent most people do have an ideology, it is bound up with their own existing life situation. Most people in Eastern Europe are experiencing the economic transition as a traumatic one, with layoffs, plant closings, inflation, and declines in real incomes. While they look forward to the economic opportunities presented by capitalism, and hope for a more affluent consumer society in the future, they are feeling the economic pinch now.

The people that are the most skeptical about the reforms, and most reluctant to let go of the past, are typically older, less educated, and less politically active. In some ways, these are the people who have been left behind ("the losers") in the economic transition, which is being managed and supported by those who are younger, highly educated, and more politically active ("the winners"). Because they have not been very active politically, they do not pose an immediate threat to the political system, and can therefore fairly safely be ignored by the new political elite. But if the economy deteriorates too sharply, or for too long, they are likely to be activated, as seems to have happened already in a number of the postcommunist states.[14]

Perhaps the biggest factor working against the new governments is time. In order for the reforms to be successful, the governments need *either* to effect a fairly rapid economic turnaround, thus defusing discontent, *or* effect a change in popular values that will allow people to accept the inequality, unemployment, and reduced economic security of democratic capitalism. Both of these tasks will take a long time. Some economists predict that it will take a generation to effect a stable economic transition, and many political theorists suggest a similar time frame for the consolidation of political democracy (see, for example, Schmitter 1988). But it may take just as long to inculcate a new set of values in the population. Political values and ideologies are developed in part through the process of political socialization, which itself is a lengthy generation-consuming process. So there is not a quick or easy solution here either.

Thirty years ago David Apter pointed to the tendency of political leaders to rely on social scientists, particularly in what he called early-development communities. This seems to be the case now in the postcommunist states, where the ideology of socialism has been replaced by the functional criteria of the social scientists, who have emerged in important roles throughout the region. But, as Apter (1964:26) pointed out, social science does not well perform the functions of identity and solidarity, which ideology does, and in such situations "recourse will be had to ideology in its most dogmatic forms" as people search for such identity and solidarity. This is also a potentially dangerous scenario for much of East Central Europe. As economic conditions decline, people become frustrated, and the formerly unifying institutions and ideals disappear, people may search for scapegoats and drift toward radical political movements. Such phenomena are already growing in the region with the emergence of anti-Semitism and virulent and sometimes violent nationalism—with Bosnian Serbs and Muslims, Czechs and Slovaks, Estonians and Russians, Armenians and Azerbaijanis blaming each other for past and present economic woes and other grievances.

Some of the countries of the region have a better chance than others of making the successful transition. Slovenia and the Czech Republic, for example, exhibit relatively low levels of support for socialism, high support for the market, a low sense of political alienation and high incidence of postmaterialist values. Thus these countries seem better positioned to push ahead with market reforms while maintaining popular political support. Russia and Poland are at the opposite ends of almost all of these spectra, suggesting a rougher ride.

This might also suggest that some countries are more suited for a rapid transition through shock therapy while others are more suited to an evolutionary transition. The Czech Republic and Slovenia, with higher degrees of political support and market-oriented values, may be ready to make the "leap to the market," sustaining large-scale but short-term difficulties for the sake of longer-term growth and prosperity. Countries like Poland and Russia, without either the political support or the value orientations, may have to settle for the gradualist approach. This will afford the time to build political coalitions on behalf of the reforms, to mollify those constituencies who feel left out, and to provide for those who will be most adversely affected by the reforms. Such consensus- and coalition-building will take time, and will involve compromises. Thus the reforms may have to be delayed. But the costs in terms of growth and production may be offset by gains in social harmony and political stability.

NOTES

*Portions of this chapter are drawn from my article, "Attitudes towards the Market and Political Participation in the Post-Communist States," *Slavic Review* 54:2 (Summer 1995).

1.   This index was created by counting the number of positive responses ("very often," "often," or "sometimes") on the five-point scale offered on each of the eight questions. For the pooled group of respondents in all of the postcommunist states, the average of this index was 1.14; for the capitalist states, 1.11. A t-test revealed no significant difference (at the .05 Level) between these group means.

2.   In another survey in which people in Hungary, Poland, and Czechoslovakia were asked what sort of society they would like their country to emulate, the majority named Germany or Sweden. The United States ranked third, with an average of 18% (Rose 1992:16).

3.   The variables in this index are listed in Figure 3.2. The index was created by averaging the z-scores of these six variables (since some of them used 5-point scales and some of them 4-point) and then subtracting that number from 1 in order to make high numbers indicate positive support for socialist principles. The items on this scale were entered into a principal-components factor analysis and all items were found to load on

only one factor, providing evidence of a unidimensional scale. Using the SPSS "reliability" procedure, the items in the index produced a reliability coefficient (Cronbach's alpha) of .63.

It should be noted that this "socialist principles" index does *not* include variables tapping support for state ownership of property or industry, an important component of socialism. While such questions were originally included in pretest versions of our questionnaire, and were asked in some of our countries, they were excluded from the common core of questions in the cross-national survey. Thus, this index taps sentiment toward important elements of socialism, but does not include all dimensions of that concept.

4.   The *Political Action* study found similarly low levels of political inactivity in five Western countries (Barnes, Kaase, et al. 1979:550).

5.   In the pooled sample of postcommunist states, of the most politically active (reporting four or more variants of political action), 60% had experienced injustice because of their political views; of those with *no* political activity, only 17% experienced that kind of injustice.

6.   The same relationship holds for the direct question on support for socialism, "based on your experience in [country name] of socialism." The percentage of those somewhat or totally against socialism rises from 39% of those with no political activity to 51% of those with minimal activity to 62% of those reporting substantial activity (four or more types of political action).

7.   A study of citizen and elite attitudes in several post-Soviet states found similar elite-mass cleavages on market orientations (Miller, Hesli, and Reisinger 1993).

8.   Across all countries in the survey, these two variables are correlated at .69.

9.   Hungary is not included in this analysis because the two questions in the distrust index were not asked in that country. Another measure of political distrust using other variables, however, showed Hungary to have the highest level of distrust of any country in the survey.

10.   National representative sample surveys of about 2000 households conducted in 1992 and 1993 as part of the Polish General Social Survey. *Polish General Social Surveys 1992–1993: Cumulative Codebook* (Institute for Social Studies, University of Warsaw, 1993), Bogdan Cichomski, Director and Principal Investigator.

11.   The 1991 figures reported in Table 3.9 differ slightly from those reported in Table 3.3 because they include the "don't know" responses.

12.   There is a similar pattern in Hungary, with the 1992 ISSP survey showing three-quarters of the population still agreeing with this proposition, but a much smaller percentage (50%, compared to 80% in 1991) *strongly* agreeing.

13.   Harold Clarke (1991) in examining the Inglehart studies and the Eurobarometer studies, found that the postmaterialism index was very sensitive to short-term changes in economic conditions and that economic adversity did cause a decline in postmaterialists.

14.   Samuel Huntington (1991) argues that the lack of democratic experience and the uncertainty of economic success cast doubt on the ultimate success of many of these democratic conversions. Similarly, T. R. Gurr (1991) points out that there is no systematic evidence that the introduction of democracy is likely to lead to burgeoning economic growth.

4

Justice Beliefs and Support for the Welfare State in Advanced Capitalism

James R. Kluegel and Masaru Miyano

Welfare state policies importantly shape the stratification orders that prevail in advanced capitalist societies. In some measure welfare state policies promote the redistribution of income, but equally as important they equalize access to nonincome benefits such as health care and family support services. As put by Esping-Andersen (1990), they function as "decommodifiers," promoting the life chances of those who for various reasons are temporarily or permanently unable to participate in the market.

A large body of work seeks to explain differences among capitalist countries in adherence to welfare state policies (Ashford 1986; Eisenstadt and Ahimeir 1985; Esping-Andersen 1990; Flora 1986; Flora and Heidenheimer 1981; Jansson 1988; Mommsen 1981; Wilensky 1975; Wilensky, Luebert, Hahn, and Jamieson 1985). For the most part this work has studied the influence of political, demographic, and other social structural factors on the welfare state policies of different nations. There are three important reasons for believing that public opinion about the welfare state also is a key factor shaping the welfare state policies of different nations.

First, prior research (Coughlin 1980; Smith 1989; Taylor-Gooby 1989) has shown that support for welfare state policy correlates strongly with the actual ranking of capitalist democracies in the extent of welfare state services provided. Second, though public opinion may not have been influential at the time when many of the modern welfare states were formed, in the current age of opinion polling and political "framing" (Iyengar 1990; Tversky and Kahneman 1981) it has assumed a much more central place in the policy formation process. Third, of course, there is backlash. Backlash has been strongest in the least developed welfare states (Esping-Andersen 1990), and correspondingly strongest in countries with the lowest levels of support for key aspects of the welfare state expressed in opinion polls (Page and Young 1989). Although it may be possible to establish welfare state programs in the absence of support, it is difficult to sustain them over the long run in the face of unsympathetic public opinion—especially in periods of economic stagnation or decline.

In this chapter we present research examining the bases of differential support for the welfare state in public opinion among five advanced capitalist countries: Great Britain, (former) West Germany, Japan, the Netherlands, and the United States. Specifically, we seek to advance our understanding of how sociodemographic factors and justice beliefs shape the public's evaluation of the welfare state. We focus on the more comparable level of public support of government intervention in general to protect people against the wide range of inequalities of life chances produced by the market, rather than on attitudes toward nation-specific welfare state programs.

THEORY AND HYPOTHESES

We propose that support for government intervention to reduce inequalities is the product of three major factors: (1) objective and subjective status, (2) justice beliefs, and (3) the interaction between the structural and cultural differences among countries, on the one hand, and status and justice beliefs on the other hand. In particular, we propose that the effects of status and justice beliefs differ among countries according to differences in certain structural characteristics of their welfare state programs, and according to cultural differences in prevailing collectivist versus individualist orientations. To borrow from statistical terminology, below we first develop a set of hypotheses about the "main effects" of status and justice beliefs. These are hypothesized relationships about the effects of status and justice beliefs expected to hold equally in all of these countries if support for government intervention to reduce inequality was determined by their shared advanced capitalist economies *alone*. We then develop hypotheses about the "interactions"—specifically, hypotheses about differences among countries in the effects of status characteristics and justice beliefs on support for government intervention to reduce economic inequality.

Objective and Subjective Status

In all capitalist nations, welfare state policies tend to differentially benefit and cost groups defined by their socioeconomic and demographic statuses. Groups differ not only in terms of who currently benefits, but who expects to benefit in the near and more distant future. Clearly income defines who pays and who benefits in the short and long runs. Education functions in this way as well, in that apart from their on-average higher income, the higher educated generally may expect to benefit less from welfare state policies than persons with lower education levels. In sum,

Hypothesis 1: *The higher the socioeconomic status the greater the opposition to welfare state policies.*

Class position may shape support for the welfare state apart from its correlation with education level and income. Classes differ in how well they are cushioned from the vagaries of the market. Managerial and professional workers typically are better able to avoid loss of income due to illness or family responsibilities, have lower rates of unemployment, and better provision for private old-age pensions that result from the nature of their work or contractual relationships with private or government organizations. In contrast, unskilled workers may be totally dependent on government-provided resources to cope with higher levels of risk of unemployment, job-related illness, and family needs that result in absence from work.

Other job characteristics potentially shape justice beliefs or may directly affect support for welfare state policy. Wilensky (1975) proposes that self-employment experience encourages greater opposition to government intervention to reduce inequalities. Union membership may encourage support for such intervention by channeling diffuse dissatisfactions into demands for welfare state policies to protect workers from market vagaries (Fenwick and Olson 1986). In sum, we expect to find

Hypothesis 2: *Managerial, professional, and self-employed workers will be more opposed to government intervention to reduce inequalities than others; union members, however, will be more supportive of such government intervention.*

Age and gender also affect the ability to shield oneself from the negative effects of market nonparticipation.

Hypothesis 3: *On life-cycle grounds, one might expect that both the young and the old will be more supportive of government intervention to reduce inequalities.*

Younger workers run greater risk of unemployment due to lack of seniority and in general lack accumulated savings or other resources that cushion the impact of market fluctuations. Retirees, of course, currently are out of the market, and many are dependent on welfare state services. Other older workers may anticipate being outside the market soon. In general, women have lower rates of continuous participation in the market due to gender norms that make them principally responsible for "unwaged care-giving" (Taylor-Gooby 1991). This and other sources of women's disadvantage in the marketplace (including occupational segregation and direct discrimination in pay rates) make them more dependent on welfare state policies, and thus,

Hypothesis 4:   *We anticipate that women are more supportive of government intervention to reduce inequalities than are men.*

Perceived, i.e., subjective, status may also affect welfare state support. Effects of subjective status may reflect the influence of a number of specific objective status characteristics that are not reflected in gross measures such as occupation category, education, and income. In this regard, class perceptions, and perhaps especially working-class identification, may play a role. Analyses of macrolevel factors shaping differential employment of welfare state policies have stressed the role of working-class parties and politics (Weir, Orloff, and Skocpol 1988; Wilensky et al. 1985). Correspondingly, one might expect to find parallel effects on the microlevel that

Hypothesis 5:   *Working-class identifiers more strongly support government intervention to reduce inequalities than do middle-class identifiers.*

Paralleling class, we need also consider perceived status position. Wegener (1987) calls attention to the influence of perceived status on the perceived legitimacy of social inequality. Specifically, we anticipate that

Hypothesis 6:   *The higher the perceived rank in the status hierarchy, the greater the perceived legitimacy of the stratification order (i.e., the greater the existential justice), and the less the support for government intervention to reduce inequalities.*

Justice Beliefs

Support for government intervention to reduce inequalities may be shaped by both normative and existential justice beliefs. On the normative side, the preferences for certain criteria of economic justice have logical implications for the public evaluation of the welfare state. A large literature on distributive justice (Alwin 1992a) has identified the three principles of equality, need, and equity (merit) as widely applied justice criteria.

Hypothesis 7:   *On a continuum from choosing equality alone to choosing equity alone as one's criteria for evaluating economic justice, we would expect persons on the equality side of the spectrum to be more supportive of welfare state policy than those on the equity side.*

In addition to these three principles, the evaluation of economic justice involves "market justice" norms (Lane 1986). Equity (merit)—that rewards should be proportional to effort—is central, but market justice norms go beyond it to justify economic inequality by appeal to other criteria. Corresponding to its historical roots in liberal or laissez-faire ideology, market justice norms also include appeals to ideas of long-run benefit and entitlement (Cohen 1986; Nozick 1974). The former justifies the inequality created by allowing individuals to pursue unrestricted profit on the grounds of collective improvement in well-being over the long run. The latter idea, entitlement, advances the justice of private ownership, again by appeal to collective benefits from the market and the overall fairness of the market as a distributive agent (cf. DiQuattro 1986).

Hypothesis 8: *To the degree that one endorses market justice, we expect that person to oppose welfare state policy.*

To the extent that the economic order is functioning as it should—i.e., that existential justice holds—people may oppose welfare state policies, especially those which have redistributive consequences. Commitment to "success ideology" (Wilensky 1975) has been proposed as important in accounting for differential support of the welfare state. In summary form, success ideology holds that opportunity is widely and equally available (existential justice holds), and that therefore individuals are personally responsible for their own economic fates (Kluegel and Smith 1986). By implication, societal-level economic inequality is fair, and therefore redistribution is unfair.

Hypothesis 9: *Subscribing to success ideology encourages opposition to government intervention to reduce inequalities.*

Country Differences

Assertions about how much justice beliefs account for country differences run the continuum from those who propose a strong role (Castles 1978; Feagin 1975; Rimlinger 1971) to minimalists (Weir et al. 1988; Wilensky 1975; Wilensky et al. 1985). On one end of this continuum, Rimlinger (1971) strongly emphasizes differences in national values and their consequences for the different courses of welfare state development. In particular, he contrasts the laissez-faire liberal values of self-help and economic individualism that have historically prevailed in the United States with the patriarchal social values historically dominant in Germany. On the other end of the continuum, Wilensky (1975; Wilensky et al. 1985) has proposed that national differences in justice beliefs account very little or not at all for the differences among nations in support for the welfare state.

Until recently, with the exception of Wilensky's work, assertions about the role of justice beliefs have been made without reference to empirical data on country differences in justice beliefs or in their effects. Wilensky's argument from public opinion data suffers from acknowledged serious limitations (Wilensky et al. 1985); he relies on comparisons drawn from numerous methodologically noncomparable studies, done over a wide time span, employing differently worded questions, and with major differences in the samples employed. In addition, this argument implicitly assumes that justice beliefs affect support for the welfare state in the same way in different countries. Thus even were we to grant his assertion that relevant public opinion is essentially the same across countries, his conclusion of a minimal influence must be viewed as highly tentative.

Smith (1989) uses International Social Survey Program (ISSP) data to contrast justice beliefs in six capitalist democracies (and Hungary). The findings he presents give some support to Wilensky's assertion that beliefs about justice do not differ much on average among capitalist democracies. Specifically, the 1987 ISSP data show that average endorsement of market justice beliefs (equity and the value of profits) is roughly equal in Australia, Great Britain, West Germany, Italy, and the United States (endorsement of market justice beliefs is lower in the Netherlands). These data do not permit country comparisons in adherence to norms of equality or need as distributive justice criteria. Though one question in this survey—concerning the perceived opportunity to improve one's standard of living—suggests that there may be important country differences, the 1987 ISSP contains no questions that permit a direct assessment of country differences in beliefs about existential justice. *As does Wilensky, Smith implicitly assumes that justice beliefs affect support for government intervention to reduce inequalities the same way in all nations—an assumption we propose is in error.*

We contend that the effects of status and justice beliefs on support for government intervention to reduce inequalities differ among countries along two dimensions: (1) by characteristics of the welfare state programs found in these countries, and (2) by cultural differences in collectivist versus individualist orientation. Below we discuss the implications of these differences for effects of sociodemographic status and justice beliefs and how the five countries in this study differ along these two dimensions.

The three-category grouping recently advanced by Esping-Andersen (1990) is representative of the major classification criteria used in most schema. It points to important characteristics of different welfare states that may affect how sociodemographic status and justice beliefs influence the public's evaluation of government intervention to reduce inequalities:

1.   The liberal category "in which means-tested assistance, modest universal transfers, or modest social-insurance plans predominate. Benefits cater mainly to a clientele of low-income, usually working-class, state dependents. . . . Entitlement rules are therefore strict and often associated with stigma; benefits are typically modest" (1990:26)

2. The conservative, corporatist category, where "the liberal obsession with market efficiency and commodification was never preeminent and, as such, the granting of social rights was hardly ever a seriously contested issue. What predominated was the preservation of status differentials; rights, therefore, were attached to class and status" (1990:27)

3. The social democratic category "in which the principles of universalism and decommidification of social rights were extended also to the new middle classes. . . . Rather than tolerate a dualism between state and market, between working and middle class, the social democrats pursued a welfare state that would promote an equality of highest standards, not an equality of minimal needs that was pursued elsewhere. . . . [This model] constructs an essentially universal solidarity in favor of the welfare state. All benefit, all are dependent; and all presumably will feel obliged to pay" (1990:28).

Esping-Andersen's classification underscores the importance of two characteristics of different welfare state programs: (1) the degree to which the poor are visible and stigmatized recipients of government aid, and (2) the degree to which the welfare state provides equal benefits to all, i.e., its inclusiveness or universality. Wilensky (1975) suggests that both of these characteristics of a nation's welfare state programs affect support for the welfare state in general—but he does not clearly specify how this effect is manifested. We propose that it is shown in differences among nations in how justice beliefs and how sociodemographic status effect support for government intervention to reduce inequalities.

First, *in nations where the poor are visible and stigmatized recipients of government aid we expect to find that success ideology will have stronger effects on support for the welfare state than in nations where aid to the poor is not singled out.* When aid to the poor is made visible by the relative size of expenditures on it, or through political attention, an identity will be drawn between the welfare state as a whole and aid to the poor. In turn then, the individual responsibility tenets of the success ideology may become more salient in the public's evaluation of government efforts to reduce inequalities. Subscribers to success ideology come to see economic redistribution as handouts to the "undeserving poor." Second, *the greater the inclusiveness of a nation's welfare programs, the weaker the effects of sociodemographic variables on support for government intervention to reduce inequalities.* In other words, the larger the number of groups in a nation who benefit from welfare state programs in some tangible and salient way—or alternatively, the fewer the number of groups who are excluded from such benefit—the less likely it is that people will come to oppose government intervention to reduce inequalities.

Among the five countries in this study, the United States clearly defines the high end of the distribution of visibility and stigmatization of government aid to the poor (Esping-Andersen 1990; Feagin 1975). It also defines the low end of the distribution of inclusiveness or universality of nations' welfare state programs (Esping-Andersen 1990). Correspondingly, we expect to find that the effects of sociodemographic status and justice beliefs will be strongest in the United States.

The percentage of means-tested poor relief relative to total social expenditures is roughly the same in Germany, Japan, and the Netherlands, and markedly lower than that in the United States (Esping-Andersen 1990). If we take this as indicative of the visibility of government aid to the poor, then we expect to find that justice beliefs will less strongly influence support for government intervention to reduce inequalities in all three of these countries than in the United States. Universalism is higher in all three countries, but in the Netherlands it is substantially higher on average than in Germany, and in turn it is higher in Germany than in Japan (Esping-Andersen 1990). This gives the prediction that socioeconomic status most strongly affects support for the welfare state in the United States, followed in strength of effect (from strongest to weakest) by Japan, Germany, and the Netherlands, where differences among sociodemographic groups in this support are expected to be the smallest.

Although the relative percentage of means-tested poor relief in Great Britain is low, in recent times it is likely a poor indicator of the visibility of poor relief. The relative expenditure on poor relief (social assistance) has grown rapidly in recent years, and it also has been a time of conservative national political leadership encouraging liberal values such as personal responsibility for economic outcomes (Golding and Middleton 1982). Arguably these events have elevated the visibility of poor relief to a status similar to that in the United States, and correspondingly we would expect to find similar effects of justice beliefs in Great Britain and the United States. Great Britain ranks close to Germany in the universalism of its programs, and correspondingly we expect similar effects of sociodemographic status.

Differences among countries in the collectivist vs. individualist orientation of their cultures may shape support for government intervention to reduce inequalities through differences among countries in the average level of endorsement of egalitarian norms. The citizens of countries with historically collectivist cultures may endorse norms of equality or need more often than those from historically individualist cultures. Differences in collectivist vs. individualist orientation may also lead to country differences in how justice beliefs shape support for the welfare state. In particular, in historically individualist countries, those who hold individuals responsible for poor economic outcomes may feel freer to oppose government support for the poor. In collectivist societies, even if one holds the poor responsible as individuals for their fate, it will go against prevailing cultural norms to deny them government aid.

Among our countries Japan may be placed on the collectivist end of the spectrum (Abercrombie, Hill, and Turner 1986; Hofstede 1984), while the United States and Great Britain occupy the individualist end (Abercrombie et al. 1986; Rimlinger 1971). Accordingly, we expect that the effect of success ideology on support for government intervention to reduce inequalities is more muted—i.e., weaker—in Japan than in the United States or Great Britain.

Hypothesis 10: *Summing up, we expect the following orderings of the size of effects (from largest to smallest) of sociodemographic status and justice beliefs, respectively, on support for government intervention to reduce inequalities:*

Sociodemographic status	Success ideology
1. United States	1. United States and Great Britain
2. Japan	2. Germany and the Netherlands
3. Germany and Great Britain	3. Japan
4. The Netherlands	

DATA

In addition to the International Social Justice Project (ISJP) data for five capitalist countries, we analyze data from the 1987 ISSP. We restrict our use of the ISSP data to the four countries also in the ISJP (West Germany, Great Britain, the Netherlands, and the United States). Running parallel analyses with these independent data sources gives us a check on the reliability of results, and permits us to examine the effects of some variables measured in one study but not in the other.[1]

SUPPORT FOR GOVERNMENT INTERVENTION TO REDUCE INEQUALITIES

Table 4.1 arrays means and correlations among the responses to three questions from the ISJP and two questions from the ISSP that concern government interventions to reduce inequalities. The questions from the ISJP are worded as follows:

1. The government should guarantee everyone a minimum standard of living (SOL).
2. The government should provide a job for everyone who wants one (JOB).
3. The government should place an upper limit on the amount of money any one person can make (LIMIT).

The questions from the ISSP are

1. The government should provide everyone with a guaranteed basic income (MINIMUM).

Table 4.1. Mean Support for and Correlations among Government Intervention to Reduce Inequality Items—by Country, Data from ISJP and ISSP

	ISJP 1991				
	Great Britain	*West Germany*	*Japan*	*Netherlands*	*United States*
Minimum standard of living—SOL	4.16	4.28	4.35	4.01	3.29
Guaranteed Job—JOB	3.73	3.90	4.46	3.37	3.09
Government minimums	3.94	4.10	4.41	3.69	3.19
Limit Incomes—LIMIT	2.74	2.55	2.86	2.52	1.82

	ISSP 1987			
	Great Britain	*West Germany*	*Netherlands*	*United States*
Minimum Income—MINIMUM	3.51	3.37	3.20	2.64
Guaranteed Job—JOB	3.56	4.01	3.87	3.27
Government minimums	3.53	3.69	3.53	2.94

	ISJP 1991				
Correlation	*Great Britain*	*West Germany*	*Japan*	*Netherlands*	*United States*
SOL with JOB	0.49	0.28	0.21	0.28	0.45
SOL with LIMIT	0.29	0.18	0.16	0.16	0.30
JOB with LIMIT	0.35	0.28	0.16	0.32	0.30

	ISSP 1987			
Correlation	*Great Britain*	*West Germany*	*Netherlands*	*United States*
MINIMUM with JOB	0.53	0.49	0.27	0.55

2. The government should provide a job for everyone who wants one (JOB).[2]

In both surveys the response format is "strongly agree, agree, neither agree nor disagree, disagree, strongly disagree"—coded from 5 to 1, respectively, so that a high score indicates a more liberal response.

The first two questions in each survey concern support for government action to place a lower limit on the range of inequality that results from the normal operation of a capitalist economy; what may be called Government Minimums.

Three observations may be made from a comparison of means for these questions among countries. First, with the exception of the Netherlands, the corresponding country means for the identically worded question in each survey—question 2 (JOB)—are very close in value.[3] Second, though the absolute values are higher in the ISJP data, country means for the minimum income questions (SOL and MINIMUM) in each question stand in the same order in each survey. Third, these two questions show the same overall pattern, indicating as previously underscored (Smith 1989; Taylor-Gooby 1989) that the level of popular support for Government Minimums is much lower in the United States than in the three Western European countries. Interestingly, the ISJP data show that support for Government Minimums is substantially higher in Japan than in Western Europe, and especially higher than in the United States.[4]

Question 3 (LIMIT) in the ISJP involves support for redistribution by limiting income at the top of the distribution. Though providing a lower limit on the bottom of the economic distribution of necessity involves redistribution away from others, it may be achieved without limiting the top. Put another way, people may evaluate lower limits and upper limits differently—supporting a lower limit but opposing an upper one. As shown in Table 4.1, this is the case. The correlation between Government Minimums and Limit Incomes ranges from .20 in Japan to .37 in Great Britain.

In all countries the absolute level of support for an upper limit on income is lower than that for a lower limit. As with the lower limit, support for an upper limit is markedly lower in the United States than in the Western European countries and Japan. Japan and Great Britain show relatively equal and higher support for an upper limit than found in West Germany or the Netherlands.[5]

In addition, we see from the correlations in Table 4.1 that in all countries the correlation between the two Government Minimums questions (SOL with JOB) is larger than the correlations between the Government Minimums questions and the question concerning support for an upper limit on income (SOL with LIMIT, and JOB with LIMIT). In light of this pattern, for subsequent analyses we create an average of the two Government Minimums questions in the respective surveys, but conduct separate analyses of the question concerning an upper limit on income.

Finally, we see in Table 4.1 that the values and country pattern of correlations between the two Government Minimums questions are virtually the same in each survey. This plus the above similarity of means argues that we may assume we are measuring very much the same thing in both surveys.

OBJECTIVE AND SUBJECTIVE STATUS

To test Hypotheses 1 through 6 and part of Hypothesis 10, we conducted the series of regressions reported in Table 4.2. Age is represented by three categori-

Table 4.2. Coefficients (Unstandardized) from Regressions of Government Minimums and Government Limit Income on Sociodemographic Variables—Separately by Country, from the ISJP and ISSP Data.

ISJP 1991

Government Minimums

	Great Britain	West Germany	Japan	Netherlands	United States
Age < 30	0.242*	0.203*	−0.091	0.034	0.445*
Age 31–45	0.274*	0.079	−0.011	0.217*	0.203*
Age 46–59	0.127	0.021	−0.161*	0.162	0.088
Gender (1 = male)	−0.212*	−0.203*	−0.113*	−0.171*	−0.312*
Education	−0.057*	−0.015	0.003	0.020	−0.075*
Income Need	−0.078*	−0.098*	−0.033	−0.106*	−0.189*
Investment	−0.294*	−0.024	0.038	—	−0.269*
Social Standing	−0.033*	−0.049*	0.036*	0.047*	−0.007
Working Class	0.287*	0.091	0.101	0.238*	0.070
Salariat	−0.222*	0.101	−0.056	−0.032	−0.214*
Petit Bourgeois	−0.328*	−0.196*	−0.098	−0.028	−0.392*
R^2	0.17	0.05	0.02	0.04	0.12

Government Limit Income

	Great Britain	West Germany	Japan	Netherlands	United States
Age <30	−0.171	0.062	0.133	−0.454*	0.029
Age 31–45	0.076	−0.135	0.257	−0.281*	−0.054
Age 46–59	0.104	−0.233*	0.106	−0.136	−0.145
Gender (1 = male)	−0.271*	−0.083	−0.707*	−0.215*	−0.148*
Education	−0.025	−0.091*	−0.205*	−0.024	−0.096*
Income Need	−0.135*	−0.137*	−0.032	−0.050	−0.064
Investment	−0.070	−0.246*	0.270*	—	−0.230*
Social Standing	−0.086*	−0.116*	0.019	−0.058*	0.013
Working Class	0.348*	0.244*	0.093	0.299*	0.152*
Salariat	−0.164	0.149	−0.002	−0.037	−0.132
Petit Bourgeois	−0.171	−0.047	−0.021	−0.228	−0.343*
R^2	0.08	0.07	0.10	0.03	0.06

(*continued*)

Table 4.2. (Continued)

ISSP 1987

Government Minimums

	Great Britain	West Germany	Netherlands	United States
Age < 30	0.318*	0.182*	−0.132	0.199*
Age 31–45	0.265*	0.070	0.081	0.243*
Age 46–59	0.188	0.164*	0.037	0.179*
Gender (1 = male)	−0.082	−0.088	−0.005	−0.147*
Education (standardized)	−0.099*	−0.059	−0.033	−0.143*
Income (standardized)	−0.211*	−0.201*	−0.159*	−0.253*
Social Standing	−0.088*	−0.053*	−0.063*	−0.059*
Union	0.375*	0.232*	0.124*	0.334*
Professional-Managerial	−0.311*	−0.009	−0.071	0.019
Self-Employed	−0.274*	0.064	−0.116	−0.276*
R^2	0.18	0.08	0.10	0.15

*$p < .05$.

cal variables for four categories: (1) less than 30 years, (2) 30 to 45 years, (3) 46 to 59 years, and (4) 60 and older. This permits an assessment of the nonlinear pattern predicted in Hypothesis 3. In the ISJP data Education is measured in Casmin levels (see the Appendix), i.e., in seven categories from less than primary education to higher tertiary (König et al. 1988). In the ISSP data, Education is measured in years. As a result of different question wordings, years are grouped differently among countries, so we computed a standardized education score within each country (with mean of zero and standard deviation of 1). In both datasets, Social Standing is measured on a ten-category scale with 1 low and 10 high. Union membership is available in the ISSP data only, and is a categorical variable with 1 indicating that someone currently is or has been a member of a labor union. A measure of Working Class identification is employed in analyses of ISJP data only. It is given a value of 1 if a respondent identifies with the working class (we also include in this category the small number of respondents identifying with the lower class) or not.[6] Income is measured in categories formed from the monetary units of each country in the ISSP. To make it comparable we transform it to a standardized variable with a mean of zero and standard deviation of 1 within each country. Income is represented in two comparable measures in the ISJP. Income Need is based on the respondent's assessment of whether her or his family income is "much less than that needed," "somewhat less than that needed," "about what is needed," "somewhat more than needed," or "much more than needed"—on a scale from 1 to 5. This measure allows us to assess the effects of income in subjectively comparable terms. Income Investment is a categorical (0, 1) variable indicating whether (1) or not (0) a respondent received income from any investments.[7] We employ this because it provides an indication of perceived benefit from a market economy. Persons with income from investments in addition to earnings from a job are less dependent on market vagaries than those who depend solely on earnings. To test for objective class effects we employ two categorical variables in each set of data. The ISSP data permit only a crude categorization of respondents into Professional and Managerial occupations (0, 1 = professional or managerial occupations) and the Self-Employed (0, 1 = self-employed, not in professional or managerial occupations). In the ISJP data we used procedures developed by Goldthorpe (1987) to create two categories indicating managerial-professional and self-employment status; specifically Salariat and Petite Bourgeois categorical (0, 1) variables.[8]

Looking first at the regressions for Government Minimums run with ISJP data, we observe some support for Hypothesis 10. Effects of sociodemographic status clearly are weaker in the Netherlands than in the United States and Great Britain. This is shown both in the substantially lower value of R^2 for the Netherlands than for the United States or Great Britain, and in the values of individual regression coefficients. The effect of Social Standing in the Netherlands is opposite the expectation—indicating that support for Government Minimums increases with an increase in perceived Social Standing. Significant effects of Income Need and Working Class identification, of the expected sign, are present in the Netherlands, but "objective" class and status effects—through the variables Education, Salariat, and Petite Bourgeois—are not significant.

Inconsistent with Hypothesis 10, the effects of sociodemographic status on support for Government Minimums are equally weak in Germany as in the Netherlands, and weaker still in Japan. Also contrary to our expectations, the effects of sociodemographic variables are much stronger in Great Britain than in West Germany, and even a little stronger than in the United States.[9] Although perceived status and class—Social Standing and Working Class identification—have significant effects in Great Britain that are absent in the United States, overall these two countries have a nearly identical profile of differences among sociodemographic groups in support for Government Minimums.

Regressions for Government Minimums run in the ISSP data confirm the findings from the ISJP analyses. The anomalous effect of Social Standing in the Netherlands in the ISJP does not hold in the ISSP data—in each of the four countries increases in perceived Social Standing lead to decreased support for Government Minimums, as predicted. However, the other patterns noted above do hold. In addition to the lack of significant effects of objective class on support for Government Minimums, we also see that the effect of Union Membership, though statistically significant, is weaker than in either Great Britain or the United States (where the effects are essentially equal).

Looking next at the regressions for Government Limit Income, we see a somewhat different picture. Great Britain, West Germany, and the United States share much the same profile of effects of sociodemographic status. Opposition to an upper limit on income predictably increases with increases in objective and subjective status, and support is higher among those who identify with the working class. In the Netherlands, we see no statistically significant effects of objective status or class, but subjective status has effects in the predicted direction. Interestingly, we also see a large age effect in the Netherlands such that younger cohorts, especially persons 30 years old and under, more strongly oppose a government-imposed upper limit on incomes than persons 60 years or older. In Japan, support for Government Limit Income is most strongly shaped by two variables. There is a large gender difference, such that women are markedly more likely to support limiting income than are men, and opposition increases substantially with increasing education.

In sum, the regressions in Table 4.2 consistently support our hypotheses about objective and subjective class and status effects (specifically, Hypotheses 1, 2, 5, and 6). They also support Hypothesis 10, with some modification. The effects of socioeconomic status on support for Government Minimums are much the same in the United States and Great Britain, and Great Britain, West Germany and the United States show largely the same pattern of socioeconomic status effects on Government Limit Income. In Japan and the Netherlands the effects of class and status on support for the welfare state are consistently weaker than in the other three countries. Hypotheses 3 and 4—about age and gender effects—do not fare as well. Hypothesis 3 does not hold, in that age effects do not follow a pattern consistent with a life-cycle interpretation. They are weak or absent in Japan and the Netherlands, and in the other three countries they follow a pattern such that younger cohorts, particularly persons 45 and younger, are more supportive of Government Minimums than older cohorts (especially persons 60 and older). Age group differences in Government Limit Income are present in the Netherlands only, and follow a pattern where support increases with age. Gender has a significant partial effect in all countries in the ISJP data, such that women are more supportive of both Government Minimums and Government Limit Income than are men. However, in the ISSP data this difference is statistically significant in the United States only.[10]

EFFECTS OF JUSTICE BELIEFS

Table 4.3 arrays the means for individual items and composites used to measure justice beliefs relevant to welfare state support for our five countries. Four

Table 4.3.   Means for Justice Beliefs—by Country, ISJP Data[a]

	Great Britain	West Germany	Japan	Netherlands	United States
Poverty—Individual	3.15	3.20	3.86	3.16	3.44
Wealth—Individual	3.63	3.61	3.67	3.76	3.77
Poverty Social	3.36	3.09	2.89	3.07	3.28
Wealth Negative	3.62	3.32	3.36	3.42	3.58
Success Ideology	−0.08	0.19	0.61	0.21	0.18
Work Hard	4.52	4.51	4.38	4.34	4.58
Keep Earnings	4.05	4.30	3.83	4.19	4.45
Profits	2.89	3.11	3.52	3.01	3.08
Market Justice	3.82	3.97	3.90	3.84	4.04
Need	2.36	3.72	3.44	2.02	2.71
Equality	2.46	2.22	3.11	2.18	2.11
Egalitarianism	2.40	2.97	3.26	2.10	2.40

[a] Note: See text for item wordings and details of index construction.

indices—Poverty-Individual, Wealth-Individual, Poverty-Social and Wealth-Negative—are used to examine the effects of success ideology or existential justice beliefs on support for the welfare state. (These indices follow from factor analyses presented in Chapter 8).[11] They indicate the degree to which individuals are held responsible for economic outcomes, and the perceived influence of social factors on economic success or failure. We form a composite measure of Success Ideology by first calculating the average of Poverty-Individual and Wealth-Individual, and then subtracting from it the average of Poverty-Social and Wealth-Negative. A high score on this composite indicates that one strongly attributes success and failure to good characteristics of individuals. Market Justice is an average of three items concerning principles of justice that support inequality in capitalist societies. In particular, it combines support for equity (Work Hard), entitlement (Keep Earnings), and the idea that profits serve the general, or long-run benefit of all (Profits).[12] Support for Need is indicated by endorsement of the principle that workers should be paid according to the size of the family they support. Support for Equality is indicated by endorsement of the principle that income and wealth should be distributed in "equal shares." An average for these two items was calculated as a composite measure of Egalitarianism (scored so that a high value indicates greater egalitarianism).[13]

   The means for these measures (Table 4.3) provide some support for Wilensky's assertion that public opinion relevant to support for the welfare state is essentially the same in capitalist countries, but there also are some potentially consequential differences. The most consistent of these concern Japan, where the public on average is simultaneously both more conservative and more liberal than the publics of Western capitalist countries. The Japanese are more conservative in their higher average level of endorsement of Success Ideology than in all other countries.[14] They are more liberal in that the mean level of Egalitarianism also is higher in Japan than in the other four capitalist countries. West Germans, though, are more egalitarian than the British and the Americans (who have equal means on Egalitarianism), who in turn are more egalitarian than the Dutch.[15]

Table 4.4 gives the regression coefficients for the effects of justice beliefs on Government Minimums and Government Limit Income. Though the coefficients for the effects of the sociodemographic variables in Table 4.2 are not shown, the results in Table 4.4 are from regressions including these variables and justice beliefs. These results speak to the merits of Hypotheses 7, 8, and 9 and part of Hypothesis 10.

The results clearly support Hypothesis 7 (concerning success ideology) and Hypothesis 9 (concerning egalitarianism) for support of both Government Minimums and Government Limit Income. In all countries but Japan, adherence to success ideology lowers support for Government Minimums and Government Limit Income. In all countries, more egalitarian respondents give more support to Government Minimums and Government Limit Income. Hypothesis 8 holds for Government Limit Income, but not for Government Minimums. Market Justice

Table 4.4.   Coefficients (Unstandardized) from Regressions of Government Minimums and Government Limit Income on Justice Beliefs—by Country, ISJP Data[a]

	Great Britain	West Germany	Japan	Netherlands	United States
	Government Minimums				
Success Ideology	−0.210*	−0.115*	−0.014	−0.271*	−0.338*
Market Justice	−0.081*	0.131*	0.045	−0.016	−0.043
Egalitarianism	0.281*	0.208*	0.158*	0.208*	0.412*
R^2	0.30	0.12	0.07	0.15	0.30
	Government Limit Income				
Success Ideology	−0.166*	−0.209*	−0.207*	−0.276*	−0.202*
Market Justice	−0.401*	−0.123*	−0.088*	−0.410*	−0.169*
Egalitarianism	0.350*	0.450*	0.305*	0.279*	0.327*
R^2	0.20	0.21	0.16	0.18	0.18

[a] Note: Regression equations also include sociodemographic variables (Table 2). See the text for definitions of the justice beliefs variables.

*p < .05.

has little to no statistically significant partial effect on Government Minimums (and in the case of West Germany an effect opposite that predicted).

With some modification Hypothesis 10 holds for Government Minimums. Consistent with this hypothesis, the effects of Success Ideology and Egalitarianism are strongest in the United States and weakest in Japan. In Japan, in fact, there is no statistically significant effect of Success Ideology on Government Minimums. Also consistent with Hypothesis 10, justice beliefs have a stronger influence in Great Britain than in West Germany. However, the predicted weaker effect of justice beliefs in the Netherlands than in Great Britain does not hold. Rather, the total effects of justice beliefs in each country are nearly equal. In general, the effects of justice beliefs are stronger in the United States than they are in Great Britain, where they equal those in the Netherlands. The effects of justice beliefs on Government Minimums are stronger in the Netherlands than in West Germany, whose effects in turn are stronger than in Japan.

Hypothesis 10 does not hold at all for Government Limit Income. Market Justice more strongly affects support for Government Limit Income in Great Britain and the Netherlands than in the other three countries. The effect of Egalitarianism is slightly higher in Germany than elsewhere. There are no other statistically significant differences between countries in the effects of Success Ideology, Market Justice, and Egalitarianism.

COUNTRY DIFFERENCES REVISITED

The results to this point establish important facts about individual or microlevel differences in support for government intervention to ameliorate the affects of market economies in each of our five capitalist countries. But what of their macrolevel implications? Specifically, to what extent do our findings to this point help account for the aggregate differences in public support for the welfare state? Put another way, how much of differences in country means of Government Minimums and Government Limit Income (Table 4.1) can we explain on the basis of our regression results?

The regression results in Tables 4.3 and 4.5 potentially speak to macrolevel differences in two ways. First, macrolevel differences in support for the welfare state may result from differences between countries in the effects of sociodemographic variables and justice beliefs. Second, we can use these regression results to estimate how much of the mean differences in support for the welfare state may be explained by differences between these countries in composition, that is, in their distributions of sociodemographic variables and of justice beliefs.

As we have clearly seen there are consistent country differences in the effects of sociodemographic variables and justice beliefs on Government Minimums. Because the zero point for most of our variables is arbitrary, we cannot obtain a

Table 4.5. "Adjusted Means" Estimated Using U.S. Regression Equations—ISJP Data

	Great Britain	West Germany	Japan	Netherlands	United States
	Government Minimums				
Adjusted for differences in sociodemographic variables	3.35	3.25	3.14	3.13	(3.19)
Percentage of Observed Difference	21.3	6.6	−4.1	−12.0	
Adjusted for differences in justice beliefs	3.35	3.44	3.41	3.04	(3.19)
Percentage of observed difference	21.3	30.9	18.0	−30.0	
	Government Limit Income				
Adjusted for differences in sociodemographic variables	1.99	1.93	1.72	1.85	(1.82)
Percentage of observed difference	18.5	15.1	−8.2	4.3	
Adjusted for differences in justice beliefs	1.98	2.08	1.98	1.74	(1.82)
Percentage of observed difference	17.4	35.6	15.4	−11.1	

reliable estimate of the size of mean differences in Government Minimums due to differences between countries in the effects of variables (Jones and Kelley 1984). Instead, we will simply discuss the implications of these differences for understanding country differences in the level of public support of Government Minimums in the Conclusions section of this chapter.

Here we limit attention to estimating the effects of composition differences. In particular we estimate how much of the difference between the United States and other countries in the mean for Government Minimums and Government Limit Income may be attributed to (1) differences between the United States and other countries in the distributions of sociodemographic characteristics, and (2) differences between the United States and other countries in the distributions of justice beliefs.[16] We focus on the United States because of its status as a welfare state laggard. Table 4.5 gives "adjusted means," specifically the predicted mean for the United States if it had first the same distribution of sociodemographic variables and second the same distribution of justice beliefs as each of the other four welfare states in turn.[17] The difference between these predicted means and the actual mean for the United States (Table 4.1) tells us how much of the difference between the United States and each of the other four countries is due to compositional differences in sociodemographic status or justice beliefs.

As can be seen in Table 4.5, the only nontrivial change in the mean for Government Minimums occurs when the sociodemographic distribution for Great Britain is applied to the regression coefficients for the United States. This reflects the more "working-class" nature of the distribution of status and class characteristics in Great Britain than in the United States—in Great Britain, a higher percentage gives a working class identification, there is a lower average level of education, and a smaller percentage holds jobs in the Salariat category. Sociodemographic composition differences account for small amounts of the differences in support for Government Limit Income between the United States and Great Britain, West Germany, and Japan. The gaps between the United States and Great Britain in support for an upper limit on income, and between the United States and West Germany would decrease by roughly 18 and 15% if compositional differences in sociodemographic characteristics were removed; the gap between the United States and Japan would *increase* by 8%.

Compositional differences in justice beliefs add little or nothing over sociodemographic variables to accounting for the mean differences in Government Minimums or Government Limit Income between Great Britain and the United States and between the Netherlands and the United States. This is not surprising, however, in light of the lack of mean differences in justice beliefs among these countries (Table 4.3). Compositional differences in justice beliefs do account for nontrivial amounts of the differences between the United States and West Germany, and the United States and Japan. This reflects the higher level of Egalitarianism in West Germany and Japan then in the United States. The effect of greater Egalitarianism in Japan is countered somewhat by the fact that the Japanese also have a higher average level of endorsement of Success Ideology than do Americans (Table 4.3).

CONCLUSIONS

In one respect Wilensky seems correct in his assertion that public opinion about justice accounts for little of the aggregate differences among nations in support for the welfare state. All of the capitalist countries in this study share a similar aggregate- and individual-level profile regarding support for the most visibly redistributive kind of government intervention, placing an upper limit on incomes. It is generally opposed by the populations of all five countries, and especially by the American public. The profile of differences among sociodemographic groups generally is the same in the United States, Great Britain, and West Germany. The effects of sociodemographic status on support for an upper limit in Japan and the Netherlands do differ from the effects in the other three countries. However, the effects of justice beliefs on support for an upper limit on income in Japan and the Netherlands match closely the results for the other three countries.

Our results argue that Wilensky is wrong, however, in another critical respect: in the area of support for Government Minimums. Though the five countries in the ISJP have a similar justice belief profile as he claimed, his implicit assumption of a common influence of justice beliefs does not hold. As he claims, all capitalist countries may produce a similar profile of justice beliefs, but he erred in not recognizing that they differ in the implications of these beliefs for support of the welfare state. That they so differ argues that justice beliefs do shape aggregate differences in support for the welfare state.

The "action," one might say, is found in public support for Government Minimums. Two countries are noteworthy: Japan for its especially high level of public support and the United States, once again, for its especially low level of support. Our results show a clear ordering among countries of "class and status consciousness" regarding support for Government Minimums. Sociodemographic divisions are largest in Great Britain, followed by the United States, and then by West Germany. In West Germany it seems to be status consciousness only. The Netherlands' public is substantially less status and class conscious regarding Government Minimums than the other Western capitalist publics. In Japan sociodemographic divisions in support for Government Minimums virtually are nonexistent.

The ordering is different for what might be termed "justice consciousness." The strongest effects of justice beliefs are found in the United States, followed by Great Britain and the Netherlands—where the effects are equal. Justice consciousness is somewhat weaker in West Germany, due principally to a weaker effect of Success Ideology. Justice consciousness is weakest in Japan, due to a weaker effect of Egalitarianism, and to the complete absence of effect of Success Ideology.

We have seen that only a small part of the lower level of support for Government Minimums and Government Limit Income is due to composition differences in sociodemographic status and justice beliefs between the United States and other countries. To understand why the American public is a laggard in support for the welfare state we have to look to other factors. The regression results in Table 4.4 point toward one explanation: the above-noted greater "justice consciousness" in the United States. The greater justice consciousness in the United States in part may be due to the strongly means-tested quality of visible programs in the American welfare state. One also may point to features of the American political system in general that make public debate over the welfare state highly politicized, thus underscoring the relevance of justice beliefs. On the other hand, one might point to factors that override the influence of justice beliefs in other countries that have no influence in the United States.

One strong implication of our results is that the Japanese and the Dutch have higher levels of support for the welfare state than expected on the basis of their sociodemographic and justice belief profiles. In Japan and the Netherlands cultural or structural factors appear to over-ride the influence of sociodemographic status and justice beliefs on Government Minimums found in the other advanced capitalist countries, and especially the "liberal" ones. In the Japanese case, collectivism may play an important role. In particular, it seems that the sense of responsibility for supporting even the "undeserving" beneficiaries of the welfare state is uniformly accepted.[18] As we have seen, although the level of Success Ideology in Japan—and especially the individualistic attribution of poverty—is highest among our five nations, it is of no consequence for Government Minimums because Success Ideology has no significant effect.[19] In contrast, in the highly individualistic American culture, denying the "undeserving" minimum supports—as indicated by the strong effect of Success Ideology—is much more acceptable.

That sociodemographic factors have only weak effects in the Netherlands argues for our proposition that the inclusiveness of the welfare state structure mutes the self-interest calculations reflected in the stronger effects of sociodemographic variables in the less inclusive Western capitalist countries in our study. Also consistent with a proposed "inclusiveness effect," we have seen that in West Germany, with an inclusiveness level substantially higher than the United States, self-interest calculations have a substantially weaker impact.

The "positive" effects of muted self-interest calculations in the Netherlands, however, are offset to a significant degree by the presence in the Netherlands of "negative" effects of justice beliefs of the same size as in Great Britain. In West Germany, however, the positive effects of muted self-interest are joined by a positive effect of justice beliefs in the form of a higher level of support for need than found in other countries, and offset less by a negative effect of Success Ideology.

Finally, we note that our findings argue that the United States and Great Britain present the most fertile grounds in public opinion for political battles over welfare state policy. The stronger dissensus about Government Minimums in the United States and Great Britain provides grounds for volatile political battles over sustaining existing welfare state programs or establishing new areas of government intervention to ameliorate the effects of inequality—depending upon, for example, such factors as the ability of parties to build upon latent working-class support for Government Minimums or class differentials in voter turn-out for elections. We may also understand the proneness of these countries to welfare backlash in this context.

NOTES

1. The sample sizes for each country are ISJP: (1) Great Britain, 1,319; (2) West Germany, 1,837; (3) Japan, 777; (4) the Netherlands, 1,783,; and (5) the United States, 1,414. ISSP: (1) Great Britain, 1,212; (2) West Germany, 1,397; (3) the Netherlands, 1,638; and (5) the U.S.A., 1,564.

2. In the 1987 ISSP, three additional questions were asked that concern typical

welfare state benefits. Specifically, questions were asked concerning (1) government responsibility to reduce income differences between the rich and poor, (2) government providing more chances for children from poor families to go to the university, and (3) government providing a decent standard of living for the unemployed. The two ISSP items we employ correlate strongly with these three—the average correlations across the four countries vary from .37 to .53. A one-factor solution to the five items fits in each country. Thus, we may conclude that the two "government minimums" items we analyze—government provides jobs and government provides basic or minimum income—represent more generalized support for welfare state activities.

3. The ISJP Netherlands survey underrepresents persons in the 60 years and older category. This, however, does not account for the substantially lower mean support for "guaranteed job" in the ISJP compared to the ISSP. Applying the percentage distribution for age categories in the ISSP to the ISJP data yields the following "adjusted means" for the measures of welfare state support: minimum standard of living = 3.97; Guaranteed job = 3.35; Government minimums = 3.66; Limit incomes = 2.54. Because these adjusted means and the adjusted means for the ISJP sociodemographic variables differ only trivially from the unadjusted ones, for simplicity we do not apply age weights to the data for the Netherlands in our analyses.

4. The Scheffe test for post hoc mean comparisons indicates that the difference between means of government minimums for all pairwise comparisons of countries is statistically significant in the ISJP (at the .05 level). It also indicates in the ISSP that mean government minimums is significantly lower in the United States than in the other three countries, and that mean support for government minimums is higher in West Germany than in the other three countries.

5. The Scheffe test for post hoc mean comparisons indicates that the level of support for government limit incomes does not differ significantly between Japan and Great Britain, and between West Germany and the Netherlands. The level of support of government limit incomes is significantly higher in Japan and Great Britain than in the other three countries. It is significantly lower in the United States than all of the other four countries.

6. Though a measure of subjective class identification is available in the ISSP data, the question and response format used varies markedly among countries, prohibiting constructing a comparable measure across countries.

7. Respondents in the Netherlands were not asked whether or not they received income from investments, and this variable is excluded from analyses of data from the Netherlands.

8. We code these variables to include persons not currently in the labor force so the excluded category in our regression analyses is a heterogeneous one—made up of workers in other occupations as well as students, and others who have never worked. Those currently not in the labor force, but who have worked previously are coded according to their last job before leaving the labor force.

9. We have explicitly tested for the significance of differences between regression coefficients. We do not report these results here because of space considerations. When we claim that the effect of a variable is stronger or weaker in one country than another the reader may assume that the difference between relevant regression coefficients also is statistically significant.

10. If we were to employ a statistical significance level of .10 rather that .05, the

effects of Gender would be significant in West Germany and Great Britain in the ISSP data as well as the ISJP. It is probably best to conclude that in all countries but the United States there is a weak to moderate effect of Gender on Government Minimums support in the predicted direction.

11. Poverty-Individual is the average score on items attributing poverty to "lack of effort by the poor themselves" and "loose morals and drunkenness." Wealth-Individual is the average score on items attributing wealth to "ability or talent" and "hard work." Poverty-Social is the average score on items attributing poverty to "lack of equal opportunity" and "failure of the economic system." Wealth-Negative is the average score on items attributing wealth to "having the right connections," "dishonesty," and "the economic system allows them to take unfair advantage." The response format for all items is a 5-point scale from "very often" (5) to "never" (1).

12. The specific items are "People who work hard deserve to earn more than those who do not" (Work Hard). "People are entitled to keep what they have earned—even if this means that some people will be wealthier than others" (Keep Earnings). "It is alright if businessmen make good profits because everyone benefits in the end" (Profits). The response format for these items is a 5-point scale from "strongly agree" (5) to "strongly disagree" (1).

13. Support for Need is indicated by responses (on a four point scale from "a great deal" to "none") to "please tell me how much influence each of these factors should have in determining the level of pay for an employee. . .the size of the family the employee supports." Support for Equality is indicated by responses (on a 5-point scale from "strongly agree" to "strongly disagree") to "the fairest way of distributing wealth and income would be to give everyone equal shares."

14. The Scheffe test for post hoc mean comparisons indicates that the mean of Success Ideology for Japan is significantly larger than that for the other four countries (at the .05 level). It also indicates that the mean of Success Ideology for Great Britain is significantly smaller than that for the other four countries (at the .05 level). The means for West Germany, the Netherlands, and the United States do not significantly differ from one another.

15. The Scheffe test for post hoc mean comparisons indicates that the mean of Egalitarianism in the Netherlands is significantly lower than that in each of the other four countries, and that the mean for Japan is statistically higher than in each of the other countries. It also shows that mean Egalitarianism in West Germany is significantly higher than in Great Britain and the United States.

16. We use regression equations from the ISJP only because the measures of sociodemographic status are more comparable than those for the ISSP. Also, of course, we have a broader range of justice beliefs measures in the ISJP.

17. Following a procedure recommended by Kelley and Evans (1992), we generated these adjusted means by obtaining predicted values using the equations for the United States for every individual respondent in each of the other four countries. We then calculated the means of these predicted values.

18. Hamilton and Sanders (1992) report a parallel finding concerning crime. Japanese citizens are more likely to assign individual responsibility for crime between strangers than U.S. citizens. Japanese citizens, however, also are more favorably disposed than U.S. citizens to rehabilitation and restitution as components of punishment. U.S. citizens are

more disposed to retribution and incapacitation as rationales for punishment. Hamilton and Sanders conclude that "the responsible actor in Japan is a contextual actor, such that the appropriate sanctions are those that reintegrate the wrongdoer and restore relationships, whereas the responsible actor in the United States is an individual to be isolated and punished by wrongdoing" (1992:183). Also in this regard, Hye (1987) stresses the importance of what he calls the "family state ideology" in shaping the development of the contemporary Japanese welfare state. The family state ideal depicted "all of Japanese society as a great family, stretching from the father figure Emperor at the top to the individual family below" (1987:246).

19.   Though the lack of effect could also result from a lack of meaning of Success Ideology in Japan, keep in mind that it does have an effect on Government Limit Income equaling that in the other four countries.

II
MICROJUSTICE

5

Comparative Referential Structures, System Legitimacy, and Justice Sentiments: An International Comparison[1]

Duane F. Alwin, Galin Gornev and Ludmila Khakhulina
with the collaboration of Vojko Antončič, Wil Arts,
Bogdan Cichomski and Piet Hermkens

INTRODUCTION

This chapter examines the implications of societal transformations, and consequent disruptions in system legitimacy for the social-psychological principles used in arriving at assessments of economic justice. Data from the ISJP are used to test several hypotheses, based on theories of justice evaluation, regarding the determinants of justice perceptions. We present data on national differences in a range of beliefs about economic inequality, developing the concept of *economic system legitimacy*, analyzing data from all twelve countries. Differences on this dimension between the populations of countries in Central and Eastern Europe and those of the West are examined in both indicators reflecting *macro*perceptions of social inequality and *micro*perceptions of family needs and morale with respect to income receipts and standard of living. We examine the extent to which these national differences translate into macrolevel beliefs regarding principles of just distribution and support for economic distributive systems. As we will show, in Eastern Europe there is considerable ideological inconsistency, given the lack of support for the legitimacy of the current system of distributive justice. Despite the favorability to markets and the overwhelming rejection of socialism, and where guaranteed minimum and maximum income policies are still popular, social stratification and social inequality are becoming increasingly desirable. By focusing on the differential predictability in perceptions of justice across nations, we can examine the extent to which principles of justice evaluation vary by the nature of differences in perceived system legitimacy.

BACKGROUND

The relationship between social inequality and social justice has long been an important area of debate among scholars in a variety of national settings (see Hochschild 1981; Kluegel and Smith 1986; Lane 1986; Rutkevich 1987; Zaslavskaya 1986; see also Parts 3 & 4 of this volume). The importance of this linkage is perhaps nowhere more evident than in the processes of social transformation currently being experienced in the postcommunist societies of Eastern and Central Europe and the former Soviet Union. Indeed, the rapid fall of the communist regimes in these countries accentuated the awareness among social scientists of the paucity of a unified theory of social change capable of explaining in a convincing and systematic way the immense variety of new "social facts" involving the relationship between inequalities and the sense of social justice.

In the course of the last several decades preceding their historical breakdown, most of the communist regimes successfully formed the image of relatively broad legitimizing support whose coupling with the military power of the Soviet Union ensured their longevity (see, e.g., Pakulski 1990). This level of system legitimacy rivalled, if not exceeded, the level of perceived legitimacy in Western market economies, although the East European leaders faced more serious difficulties in legitimizing their rule than their Western counterparts. Even during the very beginning of the "tender revolutions" in these nations, the ruling elites in that part of the world appeared to be self-confident and powerful enough to preserve the status quo for another several years. This is why the unusual ease of the disintegration of several of these regimes in 1989 was staggering, not only for their citizens, but for most foreign observers as well.

The overwhelming majority of social scientists was also taken by surprise and proved to be unprepared to uncover the logic hidden behind the seeming ease of the delegitimation of these social systems. Their inability to explain what seemed to be an international process of "crisis infection" is quite understandable as far as the main lines of theoretical reasoning capable of dealing with social integration/disintegration. In the case of the prevalent Marxist scheme of class struggle, for example, the empirical realities seem to be utterly discordant with the theoretical concepts designed to meaningfully organize them. The demarcation lines within the real present-day social conflicts do not correspond to the dogmatically postulated class taxonomies of the theory, and for this reason it is hardly possible to identify the essence of the conflicting interests. And the explanations of functionalism are no more of an efficient theoretical tool, since it is equally impossible within this framework to explain the rapid transition from relatively high levels of social integration to new forms of social polarization (see Lockwood 1992).

THEORY AND HYPOTHESES

What has become increasingly evident in the social transformations under way in the postcommunist nations is that no sociological theory, of which we are aware, either adequately predicted the direction and momentum of the social changes now under way, or has been able to explain the subjective responses of individual and collective actors. Even those theories dealing explicitly with the concepts of "legitimation" processes (e.g., Habermas 1975) failed to provide an explanatory apparatus that would go beyond the general outlines of what may be commonly understood as a historical evolution of society from "traditional" to "modern" capitalist or market-based society. Of course, Habermas (1975) and other "legitimation" theorists cannot be held accountable for this theoretical failure, as their focus has been on the development of "late" capitalism and not communist systems. But even such modernization theories are hopelessly inadequate in both their understanding of the structural mechanisms of social transformation and their specification of processes of individual adaptation to change.

This general lack of adequate macrolevel theory to explain processes of system-level change, occasioned by the political and economic transformations now underway in these societies, may be disappointing for social scientists at one level, but it presents new opportunities at another.

In particular, it affords the opportunity to apply some theories of the "middle range" to this situation, theories that are deeply rooted in the more recent traditions of social psychology, which focus on the individual and her/his link to the social environment s/he inhabits. Specifically, we propose that the application of a theoretical framework of current theorizing about justice evaluations to the social transformations now being experienced in Central and Eastern Europe, as well as the established market economies of the Western democracies, represents an alternative, worthy of at least some attention and some efforts aimed at empirical verification.

There is considerable empirical evidence from sociology and social psychology that in modern industrially developed societies, the concept of *social justice* is critical to understanding social behavior in many situations. There are several assumptions on which this assertion is based. First, what we will here refer to as "justice theory," a set of ideas (stated more explicitly below) loosely derived from social exchange (Homans 1974) and status-value theories (Berger, Zelditch, Anderson, and Cohen 1972), postulates that social stability depends inherently on intersubjective belief systems, or ideologies, which provide a framework of legitimation to social mechanisms of distribution. For present purposes we assume that what people *perceive* as real in social life is real in its consequences (Thomas 1966), not only because of the inevitability of "self-fulfilling prophecies," but because of the powerful stabilizing nature of belief systems that justify existential realities (see Sennett and Cobb 1973). Second, theories of social justice assume a kind of "structural determinism," which specifies that, in particular, perceptions of social inequality, its nature, and causes have real consequences for attitudes, beliefs, and behavior. In this sense, ideologies and even justice sentiments are potentially linked to structurally organized positions. Third, the theory assumes that perceptually based beliefs about inequality are significant features in the development of sentiments about the acceptability or justice of social inequality. And finally, justice theory assumes that such beliefs are in part rooted in referential structures activated in at least two domains, *microlevel* domains (such as the family and workplace) and *macrolevel* domains (based on cultural beliefs or structural contingencies).

THE PERCEPTION OF JUSTICE

Perceptions of "what is just" are, by definition, *subjective*; and given that persons use different points of comparison for making justice evaluations, justice perceptions are inherently *relative*. To borrow the phrasing of Walster, Berscheid, and Walster (1973), *justice is in the eye of the beholder*. Theoretically, however, even though perceptions of justice are subjective, they are also no doubt organized around certain *reference standards*, and therefore have a degree of commonality and predictability. Such referential standards are rooted in social-structural conditions (e.g., membership in groups, positional location, social relationships, market rates of exchange), and we can assume that the linkage between objective social inequalities and evaluations of justice are affected by social expectations shaped by those structural conditions (see Chapter 11, this volume). At the same time, the subjective element of perceptions of social inequality may have less to do with objective social facts, but ideologies or value systems regarding social justice that coexist with the structural conditions in which they are anchored (see Chapter 11, this volume). Given that behavior is often strongly conditioned by "what is perceived" rather than "what actually exists," the subjective domain is clearly important in understanding the social transformations in the postcommunist societies, as well as the more stable capitalist democracies of the West.

There is strong justification, therefore, for the study of *subjective* aspects of social inequality, focusing specifically on the problem of justice. Here we define *justice* as a subjective sentiment concerning "what is deserved" or "what is fair," attached to the comparison between social rewards and expectations—expectations based on existential criteria and/or principles of justice. Such comparisons may refer to either the individual level or the macrosocial level. In this paper we focus on the determinants of perceptions of what is just in the economic domain, and ultimately focus on the factors linked to "principles of justice" that determine perceptions of the income believed to be deserved from one's job.

REFERENTIAL STRUCTURES AND THE
CONCEPT OF LEGITIMACY

The key theoretical element we wish to articulate in this chapter in an effort to understand variations in justice sentiments involves the role of referential structures and belief systems (see Berger et al. 1972). Specifically, we focus on the role of referential structures in the formation and maintenance of justice sentiments, the effect of system change on perceptions of legitimacy rooted in these referential structures, and ultimately the influences of such perceptions on "what is deserved." Referential structures are conceived of here as systems of beliefs about existential realities of how rewards are distributed in the system of inequality and on what basis (see Shepelak and Alwin 1986). Of course, there is no necessary relationship between ideology and belief systems on the one hand and the nature of social inequality indicated by such referential structures on the other. What people get and what they think they deserve may be quite far apart, and there may be no reason to believe that existential considerations, or the sense that "what is" determines "what ought to be," should prevail. In their recent monograph on the role of political beliefs and ideology in the transition to a market economy in Hungary, for example, Csepeli and Örkèny describe a situation where the relationship of mutual support between the economy and ideology "was never fully attained in any Eastern European socialist society" (1992b:15–16). The failure of the state-socialist ideology to efficiently satisfy the needs defined by modern reality may thus be read as the potential for "inconsistent" belief systems to coexist with socioeconomic and sociopolitical realities.

We would suggest that the proposition be extended to all social systems. We would note that substantial differences may exist between the subjective attitudes and beliefs of mass publics with the economic and political realities confronting them. On the other hand, the level of systemwide legitimacy provides a structural link between system-level success and subjective beliefs. It seems that the critical theoretical question in this regard has to do with the conditions under which subjective aspects of social circumstances are molded by social system and social structure. In this paper we address the question, What is deserved? at the subjective level, seeking to understand the determinants of the answers to that question given by our respondents.

PERCEPTIONS OF JUSTICE OF INCOME DISTRIBUTIONS

Research findings show that people do evaluate income distributions in terms of notions of justice. Not only do they distinguish just from unjust allotments of income, they also distinguish degrees of injustice. Jasso (1978) suggests that the justice evaluation of income apportionments is a function of "actual income" and "just income," a function that can be specified as the natural logarithm of the ratio of actual to just income. In this formulation *just income* is simply the amount of income expected to be just, based on both existential and nonexistential considerations. While there is little question that measurements of justice sentiments (e.g., assessments of material satisfaction) depend on *both* these components—just and actual income—the actual level of predictability is relatively low. Alwin (1987 1992b) shows that in nationally representative samples of the United States, scarcely more than 20 percent of the variance can be accounted for in measures of satisfaction with income and standard of living. This is not bad when one considers the quality of such types of self-report measures; on the other hand, it seems evident that other factors must be involved in predicting justice sentiments.

It is Jasso's (1978) view that her specification of the justice evaluation function is consistent with both "status value" and "equity" formulations of justice (see also Alwin 1987). In status value theory, due to Berger et al. (1972), a situation is described as unjust if the income of a particular person differs from the income of his or her counterpart in a referential structure. In equity theory, a situation is deemed unjust if the input/outcome ratios of two or more persons differ. If one assumes that the most relevant referential comparison a person can make and does make is a comparison to people of equal inputs, then the two theories can be shown to converge (see Alwin 1987). In this chapter we focus solely on the denominator of the "justice evaluation function," namely the just income component.

WHAT IS DESERVED?

What is deserved, from individual and/or societal perspectives, is a function of several factors. First, from the point of view of *status value theory* it can be argued that because of structural patterns/tendencies, the individual comes to accept the realities of the distributive processes that affect his/her life. Several discussions of distributive justice have recognized the principle that the *ought* is determined in the long run by the *is* (Heider 1958:235; Homans 1974:250; Berger et al. 1972:139). Presumably these expectations are based on normative principles regarding what one can legitimately claim on the basis of market mechanisms. However, as Blau has noted, "not all existing practices reflect justice; some are unjust by prevailing moral standards, and the fact that they are expected to continue to exist does not make them just" (1971:58–59).) Thus, while one can expect *job deserts* to reflect in part the existing level of income, we also expect several idiosyncratic *nonexistential* criteria also to play a role. It is the latter that is suggested by equity theory, particularly perceptions of need, norms of equality, and other "utopian" principles (see, e.g., Rawls 1971).

Later in the chapter we examine national differences in the predictability of *deserved job income* Our general hypothesis is that system-level legitimation processes help govern the factors that members of society consider to be just, and a disruption of these mechanisms of legitimation alters the subjective determination of the rules of distributive justice. Our model for *deserved job income* contains two categories of predictors, one category associated with existential factors and one linked to nonexistential factors. In the absence of any detailed information about rates of exchange and referential structures governing the distribution of income to job positions in organizations, we simply take reported job income as a meaningful proxy for existential standards. Job income is, in fact, what exists, and the extent to which this is a factor in determining what is just should reflect this component of justice evaluations. A second existential factor involves *perceived social injustice*, that is, the global perception of systemwide injustice, which we hypothesize will impinge upon the individual's perception of what s/he is due. In this case our measures of this concept refer specifically to factors involved in setting rates of job pay. The second category contains two factors associated with nonexistential criteria of justice evaluations. The first of these specifies the *criterion of need*, and in the present analysis we base this concept in the family, so that levels of perceived family need are thought to determine job deserts. The second of these specifies the *norm of equality*, that is, the sense that income differences in society should be made more equal, and that individual excesses should be restrained. There are potentially other variables, both microlevel and macrolevel variables that can be used to predict deserved job income, and we make no claim that we have exhausted this set here. For example, there is good reason to entertain the role of a number of sociodemographic determinants of justice sentiments (see, e.g., Wegener and Steinmann, Chapter 7 in this volume). Our model to this point is based on strong predictions of the theoretical literature in the study of distributive justice and the role of *justice principles* in shaping a person's sense of material well-being.

HYPOTHESIZED COUNTRY DIFFERENCES

We hypothesize that *existential* considerations are universally important in the development of expectations of deserved levels of reward, i.e., what is deserved depends on what is. However, we argue that such effects are highest under conditions of high levels of system-level legitimacy. Thus, we expect that the linkage between levels of income received and perceptions of what is a deserved income will be strongest in the Western capitalist economies, such as those in the United States, the Netherlands, Great Britain, Japan, and West Germany, and that those economies in the postcommunist countries undergoing transformation will show much less predictability of deserved income from existential factors.

In addition, we hypothesize that considerations of nonexistential principles of justice, specifically considerations based on *need* and *equality*, will play a much greater role in judgments about job income deserts under conditions of low system legitimacy. Thus, while we expect that existential considerations—what is determines what ought to be—will play a much more important role in stable economic systems, we expect assessments of need to play a much more important role in the Eastern European countries studied here. We do not, however, expect that norms of equality are at all prevalent in the postcommunist countries, despite ideological traditions to the contrary. The emergence of a new ideology of inequality seems to have gained a considerable foothold in that part of the world, even as there is such an ideology inherent in the Western capitalist countries. Where we do expect the value of *equality* to hold greatest sway is the *welfare capitalist* economies of Europe, particularly West Germany, Great Britain, and the Netherlands (see Esping-Andersen 1990). Finally, we expect that to the extent individuals perceive the social and economic system in which they live to be a just one, they will be less likely to want to change their particular income allocation. But where they do perceive injustices in the system, we hypothesize, they will favor redistributive efforts, and we expect that they would perceive themselves, if such were the case, to be worthy recipients of such policies. Thus, we hypothesize that beliefs about the extent to which the social/economic system is working toward just outcomes will be related to perceptions of the level of income they deserve.

DATA AND METHODS

This study relies on data from twelve countries participating in the International Social Justice Project (ISJP). The ISJP surveys were driven by several related theoretical perspectives—primarily social-psychological theories of justice evaluation (e.g., Berger et al. 1972; Jasso 1980; Alwin 1987), and sociological/political theories of mass belief systems (e.g., Parkin 1971; Hochschild 1981; Kluegel and Smith 1986; Lane 1986). The principal focus of this chapter is on perceptions of justice in the economic realm. Within this realm, we sought to measure public perceptions of Who gets what and how? and Who should get what and how? The focus thus was on both *existential beliefs* and *justice principles*—the *is* and the *ought*—and the comparison and evaluation of the relationship between what is and what ought to be.

The methodological characteristics of the twelve surveys are described by Alwin, Klingel, and Dielman (1993)—see the Appendix for a brief summary of this document—which provides basic information on the auspices of the study in each country, the nature of the population, methods of sampling, mode of administration, field implementation information, completion rates, and respondent sample sizes. In Table 1 we provide some of the sociodemographic information

Table 5.1. Descriptive Information for ISJP Survey (%)

Items	Bulgaria	East Germany	West Germany	Hungary	Japan	Netherlands	Poland	Great Britain	United States	Russia	Slovenia	Czechoslovakia	Estonia
Sex													
Male	47.5	45.8	50.2	47.7	46.6	53.3	45.1	43.7	44.3	45.3	43.9	47.1	40.6
Female	52.5	54.2	49.8	52.3	53.4	46.7	54.9	56.3	55.7	54.7	56.1	52.9	59.4
N	1,404	1,019	1,837	1,000	777	1,783	1,542	1,319	1,414	1,732	1,371	1,177	1,000
Cohort													
Pre-1935	28.3	26.1	30.0	33.0	34.4	12.6	31.2	32.5	25.5	23.6	20.9	28.4	27.7
1935–44	17.5	19.5	14.2	18.7	19.6	14.8	14.3	12.7	14.0	15.1	17.4	16.1	15.8
1945–54	21.4	19.0	19.0	19.0	22.3	29.4	22.3	18.1	22.2	19.2	20.6	21.3	18.8
1955–64	21.1	22.6	22.6	15.8	15.6	29.6	20.4	20.7	25.1	23.3	22.4	20.0	21.8
1965 and later	11.8	12.8	14.2	13.5	8.2	13.6	11.8	16.0	13.2	18.9	18.7	14.2	15.9
N	1,405	1,018	1,823	1,000	777	1,783	1,542	1,310	1,414	1,732	1,361	1,173	1,000
Employment status													
Full-time	55.4	44.9	39.9	49.0	56.9	45.4	50.0	39.3	57.3	63.2	60.8	56.1	60.7
Part-time	3.0	4.6	7.2	1.6	9.4	15.5	2.7	13.1	9.8	2.0	1.1	3.4	4.6
Unemployed[a]	41.6	50.4	52.9	49.4	33.7	39.0	47.4	47.5	32.9	34.7	38.1	40.5	34.7
N	1,403	1,017	1,813	1,000	777	1,744	1,539	1,319	1,390	1,717	1,374	1,180	1,000
Education													
Primary	10.0	31.1	42.3	43.4	18.5	26.4	61.4	45.2	14.5	23.1	63.0	52.7	27.0
Intermediate	21.7	50.7	30.0	23.7	14.3	20.3	14.4	27.0	27.7	35.1	17.1	8.0	30.0
Secondary	34.9	6.4	10.9	20.5	45.6	26.8	10.0	4.6	31.7	18.3	9.3	26.2	23.6
Tertiary	33.4	11.8	16.8	12.4	21.6	26.6	14.2	23.3	26.2	23.5	10.6	13.2	19.4
N	1,380	1,000	1,739	1,000	769	1,600	1,540	1,306	1,424	1,724	1,364	1,181	1,000

[a] Unemployed includes all other categories.

for each of these countries pertinent to the present study, specifically univariate distributions by country for sex, birth cohort, employment status, and educational level. As the data in Table 5.1 indicate, in some countries unusually high levels of "nonemployment" results in attrition of the sample for purposes of the present analysis, as we focus ultimately on the justice principles involved in the determination of the perceived justice of job income.[2] In all countries this excludes at least one-third of respondents, but in the two Germanies, Hungary, Poland, and Great Britain this excludes roughly one-half. However, our initial presentation of results and the development of the concept of "perceived legitimacy" includes data from all respondents, regardless of job status.

In most of the tables that follow, the actual questions employed from the ISJP are included in the table notes, along with the recoding used for presentation purposes. Thus, we can avoid any detailed rendering of those questions here. However, for purposes of the regression analysis (presented in Table 5.7) we have developed several predictor variables, some of which we have constructed as composites from individual items. Here we briefly summarize the variables involved in the regression analysis. *Actual job income* is measured as reported job income. *Deserved job income* is measured in terms of responses to the following two questions: Do you think you were paid much less than you deserved, somewhat less than you deserved, about what you deserved, somewhat more than you deserved, or much more than you deserved? (For those not responding "about what they deserved") What income do you feel you deserved from your (job/business)? *Perceived family need* is measured as the difference between reported household income and the response to the following two questions: Would you say your total (household) income is much less than you need, somewhat less than you need, about what you need, somewhat more than you need, or much more than you need? (For those not responding "about what you need") What income do you feel (you/your household) need(s)?

The measure of the ideology of *equality* is based on responses to the three following questions: Compared to other people in (country), would you say your present income for your job or business is far above average, somewhat above average, about average, somewhat below average, or far below average? Compared to people with the *same level of education or training* as yourself, do you think your present salary or wage is far above average, somewhat above average, about average, somewhat below average, or far below average? Compared to people with *similar jobs*, would you say that your present pay is far above average, somewhat above average, or far below average? For this purpose the three items are averaged and scaled so that a high score reflects above average self-perceptions relative to key referential comparisons. The assumption is that, net of other factors, the individual's perception that s/he is making more than others reflects his/her perception of benefits of inequality (on whatever criteria s/he perceives this inequality is based), and to this extent, this indicator measures the effect of the desire for equality in perceptions of deserved income. In other words, to the extent that the principle of equality operates on the individual's perceptions, this factor will have negative effects on what income is believed to be deserved.

The measure of *perceived social injustice* was obtained by obtaining the departure from "ought" and "is" for several questions regarding the *principles of pay* used in the country of interest. The questions were as follows: Please tell me how much influence each of these factors *should have* (*actually have*) in determining the level of pay for an employee: a great deal, some, not much, or none. The measure reported here uses responses for four items: the employee's level of education, the employee's individual effort, the responsibility held by the employee on the job, the length of service with the employer. Scores for these items were averaged and scaled so that a high score represents the notion that the criteria have/should have greater influence. Thus, the higher this score, the more the individual perceives there to be macrolevel injustices in the determination of pay.

In the following analysis we present descriptive univariate information on the main measures of perceptions of justice used in this study, formulating our concept of *system legitimacy*. We then assess the predictability of *perceptions of justice* within each country separately, using multiple-regression procedures. The data we use are unweighted, but we think the weighted figures will not change the observed differences in any nontrivial way. Nonetheless, one should enter into the following comparisons with caution, given the preliminary nature of the results.

One of the critical methodological steps in analyzing cross-national differences is the substitution of macrolevel concepts of "country names" (see Przeworski and Teune 1970). In the ISJP study, countries were explicitly selected to fit into a priori categories, and for purposes of comparison the study explicitly included several postcommunist, along with several Western democratic capitalist nations. We classify the nations selected for this survey according to the following scheme:

- *Postcommunist societies*—Bulgaria, Czechoslovakia, Hungary, Poland, Russia, Slovenia, East Germany, and Estonia[3]
- *Welfare capitalist and/or mixed economies*—West Germany, Great Britain, and the Netherlands
- *Nonwelfare capitalist societies*—Japan and the United States.

With respect to the differentiation between welfare capitalist and nonwelfare capitalist, this classification is consistent with Esping-Andersen's (1990) discussion (see also Wegener and Liebig, Chapter 11 in this volume).

RESULTS

In this section we present a detailed examination of univariate distributions by country on aspects of beliefs that are relevant to our concept of *system legitimacy*. We first present data relating to perceptions of beliefs about economic inequality, both macrolevel beliefs and microlevel perceptions of well-being. Then we examine perceptions of the importance of various justice principles and perceptions of the political system. If we consider these two dimensions of legitimacy—the political and the economic—we can develop an empirical framework for differentiating these countries in terms of perceptions of system legitimacy, which can then be used as a basis for evaluating our hypotheses.

Economic Legitimacy

The principal focus of the ISJP survey was on beliefs about economic inequality—the extent of inequality, its sources, the extent of equality of opportunity, the extent to which the system of economic distribution is perceived to give people what they need, the extent to which the system rewards various sorts of contributions, among other things. The ISJP questionnaire included a number of other questions that measure beliefs about the economic system: (a) whether the respondent believes there are too few or too many income differences, (b) whether people have equal opportunities to get ahead, (c) whether people get what they need, and (d) whether various aspects of individual contributions (e.g., effort and skill) are rewarded in the system of income distribution.

These indicators reflect a clear pattern of cross-national variation. Although there are some important exceptions, respondents in the postcommunist countries generally put little confidence in their economic systems, whereas in the capitalist and mixed economies there is a much higher level of support. There seems to be little doubt that there is more frustration with the economic conditions in the postcommunist countries, with respondents in some of these countries expressing considerable sentiment in favor of the view that income differences are "much too large," there are fewer perceived "equal opportunities" to get ahead, there is the perception that people do not get what they need, and the view that effort and skill are not adequately rewarded.

For purposes of comparison we calculated an *index of economic system legitimacy* based on the combination of these five indicators, shown in Table 5.2. The rank-order of countries on this dimension coincides nearly perfectly with our a priori theoretical assumptions about the legitimacy of the social orders in the countries in this study. There are several shortcomings to any fine-grained interpretation of these rankings, but we argue that the differences in the socioeconomic environmental contexts suggested by this index reflect a valid assessment of the referential structures persons use to evaluate justice.[4]

Table 5.2.　Beliefs About Economic Inequality

Question:[a]	Income diffs too large (%)	Equal opps to get ahead (%)	People get what need (%)	Effort is rewarded (%)	Skill is rewarded (%)	Economic system legitimacy rank order
Postcommunist						
Bulgaria	80.1	16.8	5.9	13.4	10.4	13
Czechoslovakia	34.7	36.9	9.5	13.7	14.6	8
Hungary	61.2	17.6	12.5	33.2	14.5	11
Poland	47.7	26.6	9.3	17.4	19.3	10
Russia	38.9	23.7	4.4	21.8	19.6	9
Slovenia	71.1	43.7	37.7	43.4	42.7	7
East Germany	22.6	24.8	41.0	39.5	53.5	5
Estonia	43.9	16.7	2.1	14.1	6.2	12
Welfare capitalist						
West Germany	32.5	54.6	54.0	71.4	75.4	1
Great Britain	41.2	42.4	25.9	48.1	57.4	6
Netherlands	33.4	45.8	63.5	49.1	53.6	3
Capitalist						
Japan	39.4	40.7	73.8	48.3	62.6	4
U.S.	28.4	65.9	40.6	71.4	75.2	2

[a] Income diffs too large: percentage responding "much too large" to "What do you think about the *differences* in income people have in (country)? Are the differences much too large, somewhat too large, about right, somewhat too small, or much too small?"

Equal opps to get ahead: percentage responding "strongly agree" and "somewhat agree" to "Please tell me how much you agree or disagree to the following statement. In (country) people have equal opportunities to get ahead. Strongly agree, somewhat agree, neither agree or disagree, somewhat disagree, strongly disagree."

People get what need: percentage responding "strongly agree" and "somewhat agree" to "In (country), people get what they need. Strongly agree, somewhat agree, neither agree or disagree, somewhat disagree, strongly disagree."

Effort is rewarded: percentage responding "strongly agree" and "somewhat agree" to "In (country), people get rewarded for their effort. Strongly agree, somewhat agree, neither agree or disagree, somewhat disagree, strongly disagree."

Skill is rewarded: percentage responding "strongly agree" and "somewhat agree" to "In (Country), people get rewarded for their intelligence and skill. Strongly agree, somewhat agree, neither agree or disagree, somewhat disagree, strongly disagree."

This conceptualization of a major gulf between the mass publics of Eastern Europe and those of the West is supported not only by indicators reflecting *macro*perceptions of income differences, equalities of opportunity, the satisfaction of need, and the social recognition of "contributions" (effort and skill), but by *micro*perceptions of one's *just desserts*, the satisfaction of family needs, and morale with respect to income receipts and standard of living. These results are given in Table 5.3. These figures indicate unambiguously that mass publics in the

Table 5.3. Economic Needs, Deserts, and Economic Satisfaction

Question:[a]	Income < than need (%)	Earn < than deserve (%)	Below equals in pay (%)	Dissat. with income (%)	Dissat. with st. living (%)	Rank order
Postcommunist						
Bulgaria	95.8%	41.9%	45.9%	64.8%	44.0%	13
Czechoslovakia	71.0	28.8	41.6	46.0	35.4	7
Hungary	76.4	49.3	38.2	58.5	42.0	9
Poland	84.5	48.7	41.0	64.1	34.0	10
Russia	89.5	33.4	37.0	73.7	65.4	11
Slovenia	68.6	36.5	52.7	53.8	31.2	8
East Germany	43.2	41.8	36.3	61.8	26.7	6
Estonia	90.2	35.7	50.4	62.4	50.1	12
Welfare capitalist						
West Germany	25.6	11.0	27.9	26.0	11.5	1
Great Britain	50.0	14.5	34.3	37.4	18.1	3
Netherlands	25.3	11.5	35.5	20.2	12.7	2
Capitalist						
Japan	49.3	14.1	41.6	38.4	19.0	5
U.S.	50.4	16.3	36.2	26.1	13.1	4

[a] Income < than need: percentage responding "less than deserve" to "Would you say your total (household) income is much less than you *need*, somewhat less than you need, about what you need, somewhat more than you need, or much more than you need?"

Earn < than deserve: percentage responding "much less than deserve" to "Do you think you were paid much less than you deserved, somewhat less than you deserved, about what you deserved, somewhat more than you deserved, or much more than you deserved?"

Below equals in pay: percentage responding "somewhat below" and "far below" average to "Compared with people with the *same level of education or training* as yourself, do you think your (present) salary or wage was far above average, somewhat above average, about average, somewhat below average, or far below average?"

Dissat. with income: percentage responding "dissatisfied" to "Please indicate how satisfied or dissatisfied you are with some different things in your life today using the scale on this card. If you are completely *dissatisfied* with the item I mention, you would say 'one.' If you are completely *satisfied*, you would say 'seven.' If you are neither satisfied or dissatisfied, you would say 'four'. (You may use any number from one to seven.) How satisfied are you with your income?"

Dissat. with st. living: percentage responding "dissatisfied" to "How satisfied are you with your standard of living?"

postcommunist countries overwhelmingly believe they have less income than they need—96 percent in Bulgaria, 92 percent in Russia, 84 percent in Poland, etc.—whereas in the capitalist countries the figures are much lower. Still, 50 percent of the publics in Great Britain, the United States, and Japan respond that they have less income than they need, whereas in West Germany and the Netherlands it is some 25 percent. The same patterns exist for persons' perceptions that they earn less than they deserve in their job and that they are below their equals in pay. Similarly, reports of satisfaction with income and standard of living correspond to the general differentiation in economic system legitimacy noted above.

These national differences correspond in systematic ways to macrolevel beliefs regarding *support for economic distributive systems*, although there seems to be considerable ideological inconsistency in Eastern Europe. There guaranteed minimum and maximum income policies are still popular, despite the favorability to markets and the overwhelming rejection of socialism. At the same time there are some increases in support for social stratification and social inequality, specifically the rejection of the principle of "equal shares" and support for passing wealth across generations. These figures are shown in Table 5.4 and 5.5.

These results indicate that the mass publics in the postcommunist countries of Eastern Europe express strong support for free markets and overwhelmingly reject socialism (see Table 5.4). This is somewhat inconsistent with their support for "economic socialism," such as support for a minimum income standard, employment for everyone, an upper limit on personal income (Table 5.4), and some modest endorsement of the equal-shares principle of income distribution, although in this latter respect the postcommunist countries are only marginally different from capitalist societies.

In addition to the focus on the economic domain, the ISJP also assessed several aspects of political beliefs. Table 5.6 presents figures regarding the extent of political alienation and satisfaction with the political system in each of the twelve nations. These results reveal a pattern that is somewhat consistent with the ranking of countries on economic system legitimacy, although there are some important exceptions. In general, respondents in the postcommunist countries are much more likely to express a sense of political alienation with respect to standard measures of *trust in government* and *political satisfaction*, whereas in western capitalist countries the perceived legitimacy of the political system is much higher. Japan and Great Britain represent important exceptions to this pattern in the West, whereas Slovenia is the exception among the postcommunist countries.

System Legitimacy and Deserved Income

As indicated in the foregoing we can evaluate the relative role of *existential* and *nonexistential* factors in judgments about deserved income within each of the countries in the ISJP survey. In Table 5.7 we present the results of the regression of respondent's level of *deserved income* on *actual income* (our measure of existential factors), *perceived social injustice*, and the two nonexistential factors: perceptions of *family need*, and perceptions of economic well-being relative to others, which we take as a reflection of the operation of *norms of equality*. These results provide strong support for the hypotheses advanced above, namely, that

Table 5.4.   Support for economic distributive systems (%)

Question:[a]	Minumum standard	Upper limit	Job for everyone	Free market	Favor socialism
Postcommunist					
Bulgaria	80.1	42.3	74.3	68.7	24.2
Czechoslovakia	69.9	29.8	61.6	82.9	14.8
Hungary	81.0	57.8	79.9	—[b]	—[b]
Poland	54.5	47.4	65.6	72.5	11.0
Russia	64.1	34.2	77.5	70.5	26.6
Slovenia	71.9	60.2	69.3	94.4	21.0
East Germany	80.2	60.0	84.3	—[b]	18.2
Estonia	80.0	32.3	56.4	73.0	20.8
Welfare capitalist					
West Germany	57.1	32.2	45.6		
Great Britain	50.2	38.6	37.3		
Netherlands	43.6	31.8	24.8		
Capitalist					
Japan	60.6	35.9	66.1		
U.S.	27.0	16.8	29.5		

[a] Minimum standard: percentage responding "strongly agree" to "Now I am going to read some statements that have been made about the role of government in (country). Using one of the phrases on this card, please tell me how much you agree or disagree with each statement. The government should guarantee everyone a minimum standard of living. Strongly agree, somewhat agree, neither agree nor disagree, somewhat disagree, strongly disagree."

Upper limit: percentage responding "strongly agree" and "somewhat agree" to "The government should place an upper limit on the amount of money any one person can make. Strongly agree, somewhat agree, neither agree nor disagree, somewhat disagree, strongly disagree."

Job for everyone: percentage responding "strongly agree" to "The government should provide a job for everyone who wants one. Strongly agree, somewhat agree, neither agree nor disagree, somewhat disagree, strongly disagree."

Free market: percentage responding "agree" to: "Please tell me how much you agree or disagree with the following statement. A free market economy is essential to our economic development. Strongly agree, somewhat agree, neither agree nor disagree, somewhat disagree, strongly disagree."

Favor socialism: percentage responding "agree" to "People have different views about socialism. Based on your experience in (country) of socialism, would you say that you are very much in favor, somewhat in favor, neither for nor against, somewhat against, or totally against socialism."

[b] Question not asked in Hungary and/or East Germany.

both existential and nonexistential considerations generally play a strong role in the development of judgments about deserved income.

The regressions in Table 5.7 show that "what is" is strongly linked to "what ought to be," in that *job income* strongly predicts *job desserts* in every country. We hypothesized that existential considerations would play a strong role in the

Table 5.5.   Principles of Just Distribution (%)

Question:[a]	Equal shares	Equal opportunity	Get what need	Work hard	Pass on wealth
Postcommunist					
Bulgaria	26.1	56.0	34.4	88.5	89.6
Czechoslovakia	19.7	33.8	44.8	63.7	78.6
Hungary	22.9	40.3	64.8	87.4	93.6
Poland	19.6	23.8	55.8	57.6	77.4
Russia	31.8	46.7	46.8	70.3	88.2
Slovenia	31.2	47.7	54.6	73.9	92.5
East Germany	24.0	37.0	85.3	80.3	37.0
Estonia	11.4	36.0	48.5	79.6	91.7
Welfare capitalist					
West Germany	21.6	36.8	76.6	62.6	37.9
Great Britain	29.6	23.2	49.0	59.9	62.9
Netherlands	18.3	31.0	46.7	50.6	71.9
Capitalist					
Japan	39.3	20.8	33.1	53.2	48.8
U.S.	19.2	42.6	45.4	70.8	83.5

[a] Equal shares: percentage responding "strongly agree" and "somewhat agree" to "The fairest way of distributing wealth and income would be to give everyone equal shares. Strongly agree, somewhat agree, neither agree nor disagree, somewhat disagree, strongly disagree."

Equal opportunity: percentage responding "strongly agree" to "It's fair if people have more money or wealth, but only if there are equal opportunities. Strongly agree, somewhat agree, neither agree nor disagree, somewhat disagree, strongly disagree."

Get what need: percentage responding "strongly agree" and "somewhat agree" to "The most important thing is that people get what they need, even if this means allocating money from those who have earned more than they need. Strongly agree, somewhat agree, neither agree nor disagree, somewhat disagree, strongly disagree."

Work hard: percentage responding "strongly agree" to: "People who work hard deserve to earn more than those who do not. Strongly agree, somewhat agree, neither agree nor disagree, somewhat disagree, strongly disagree."

Pass on wealth: percentage responding "strongly agree" to "People are entitled to pass on their wealth to their children. Strongly agree, somewhat agree, neither agree nor disagree, somewhat disagree, strongly disagree."

development of judgments about levels of deserved income, and this is confirmed in these results. The results provide strong support for the role of existential factors in virtually all countries, but there is considerable variation in the magnitude of the effects. The weakest effects, as predicted on the basis of our concept of system-level legitimacy, are in the postcommunist systems of Eastern and Central Europe and the former republics of the Soviet Union. The strongest effects are clearly in the Western capitalist democracies, again consistent with

Table 5.6.   Beliefs About the Political System

Question:[a]	Officials don't care (%)	Voters real choice (%)	Trust the govt. (%)	Govt. helps all (%)	Dissat. political system (%)	Political system legitimacy rank order
Postcommunist						
Bulgaria	46.7	51.1	32.8	33.6	67.1	7
Czechoslovakia	34.3	49.4	29.2	29.8	40.2	4
Hungary	39.0	9.3	—[b]	—[b]	47.7	10
Poland	40.8	24.6	19.4	22.2	42.9	9
Russia	43.0	20.4	25.7	22.8	78.2	11
Slovenia	45.0	43.4	32.3	41.0	41.1	4
East Germany	28.5	39.4	22.8	30.1	40.1	4
Estonia	56.7	16.0	20.8	24.2	57.7	12
Welfare capitalist						
West Germany	29.4	31.8	22.5	30.7	35.2	6
Great Britain	23.9	23.7	20.7	20.1	46.6	8
Netherlands	18.5	34.8	36.3	47.8	29.7	1
Capitalist						
Japan	47.7	23.8	17.6	17.5	50.1	13
U.S.	21.6	24.8	29.4	28.5	27.8	2

[a] Officials don't care: percentage responding "strongly agree" to "For each of the following statements, please tell me how much you agree or disagree. Public officials don't care much what people like me think. Strongly agree, somewhat agree, neither agree nor disagree, somewhat disagree, strongly disagree."

Voters real choice: percentage responding "strongly agree" to "In elections in this country, voters have a real choice. Strongly agree, somewhat agree, neither agree nor disagree, somewhat disagree, strongly disagree."

Trust the Govt.: percentage responding "very often" and "often" to "How much of the time do you think you can trust the (federal) government in (country/capital city) to do what is right? Very often, often, sometimes, rarely, or never?"

Govt. helps all: percentage responding "very often" and "often" to "How much of the time do you the the (federal) government in (capital city/country) is run for the benefit of all the people? Very often, often, sometimes, rarely, or never?"

Dissat. political system: percentage responding "dissatisfied" to "How satisfied are you with the political system in (country)?"

[b] Question not asked in Hungary.

our predictions. Indeed, the linkage between job deserts and job income is so strong in these five Western countries that it seems hardly possible that any other factors could contribute to variation in perceptions of justice.

We also hypothesized that level of perceived family need would play a much stronger role in Eastern European countries than in the West, and strong support is given for this hypothesis. Perceptions of family need strongly predict deserved

Table 5.7. Regression of Job Deserts on Job Income, Family Needs, Referential Comparisons, and Perceived Social Injustice: Employed Persons Age 18+[a]

	Listwise N	Job income	Family need	Refer. comp.	Perceived injustice	R^2
Postcommunist						
Bulgaria	587	.277***	.359***	−.046	.038	.195
Czechoslovakia	616	.576***	.371***	−.020	.019	.486
Hungary	451	.678***	.212***	−.014	.037	.506
Poland	714	.647***	.274***	−.020	.061*	.521
Russia	829	.503***	.288***	.027	.024	.328
Slovenia	490	.464***	.237***	.115**	.107*	.318
East Germany	429	.592***	.085*	−.099*	.088*	.299
Estonia	432	.184***	.304***	−.067	.006	.116
Welfare Capitalist						
West Germany	582	.995***	.089***	−.118***	.018	.868
Great Britain	532	.984***	.107***	−.115***	−.019	.864
Netherlands	712	.874***	.122***	−.084***	.052*	.684
Capitalist						
U.S.	802	.939***	.184***	−.011	.021	.820
Japan	259	.877***	.103**	−.066	.025	.710

[a] Coefficients are in standard form.
*$p < .05$.   **$p < .01$.   ***$p < .001$.

income in all of the postcommunist countries, save East Germany, and only weakly predict deserved income in the capitalist countries. It is important to note, however, that despite the range of predictability between countries, the effects of this variable are significant in all cases. The East German case, which strongly resembles other countries in the West in the magnitude of the effects of family need on job deserts, can perhaps best be explained as an effect of reunification, in that changes in the allocation of economic resources with reunification brought at least temporary satisfaction of family needs, apparent in our 1991 survey. But even the economic recession in Germany since then may not have increased the importance of family need for perceptions of job deserts (see Wegener and Steinmann, Chapter 7 in this volume, for a somewhat different interpretation). We hypothesized that the *principle of equality* would play some role in perceptions of justice. We reasoned that this principle would come into play to the extent that people perceived they earn more than other people, to whom they are comparable in certain respects. We suggested that norms of equality would not be at all prevalent in the postcommunist countries, despite ideological traditions to the contrary, suggesting that the emergence of a new ideology of inequality seems to have gained a considerable foothold in that part of the world. We suggested that the value of *equality* would be most prominent in the *welfare capitalist* economies of Europe, particularly West Germany, Great Britain, and the Netherlands, where inequality is considerably less than in the United States, for example, and welfare traditions are much stronger (see Esping-Andersen 1990). The results in Table 5.7, in fact, bear out this hypothesis, as this variable has a negative effect, net of other factors, on what people say they deserve in income from their jobs, *only* in the welfare capitalist countries (Great Britain, the Netherlands, and East and West Germany). It has a positive effect in Slovenia, which is the only case in which this occurs. Apparently, Slovenia is the only country among those considered here in which the message from the Biblical "parable of the talents" (Matthew 13:12: "For whosoever hath, to him shall be given, and he shall have more abundance; but whosoever hath not, from him shall be taken away even that he hath") is taken seriously. There it appears that those who believe they are relatively advantaged with respect to comparable others also believe they deserve even more!

Our hypotheses about the connection between perceptions of deserved income and macrolevel *beliefs about social injustice* in factors affecting job pay are not borne out, as there is little predictive role of this variable in our equations for deserved job income. This measure generally shows inconsistent and relatively weak effects, although it plays a minor role in Poland, Slovenia, East Germany and the Netherlands. Overall, there is little support for the role of macrolevel beliefs about injustice in shaping microlevel perceptions of justice.

Finally, let us address the general question of the predictability of perceptions of justice sentiments. It can be seen from the *coefficients of determination* (R^2) in Table 5.7 that, on the whole, justice sentiments are predictable, although this clearly varies from country to country. They are least predictable in Bulgaria and Estonia, where the R^2 are relatively low—in the .1 to .2 range. This is due primarily to the failure of existential factors to play any role in shaping justice sentiments in these national contexts. The perception of family need in both of these countries plays an important role, while among the strongest in the table, the systems of allocating job income existent in those countries bears little relationship to perceptions of just income. The relatively low R^2 in these two cases is completely consistent with our assessment of the ranks of Estonia and Bulgaria on our concept of *economic system legitimacy* discussed with respect to Table 5.2. The pattern of R^2 in these equations for the remaining postcommunist countries is also consistent with the classification at which we arrived in our ranking of countries with regard to this index. The R^2 for these countries range from .3 to .5, again due to the relatively weaker role of existential factors in these countries. These patterns lie in sharp contrast to the level of predictability of job deserts in the Western democracies, where the R^2 range from .7 to .9, and where, as noted above, existential factors play a very strong role in shaping justice sentiments and perceptions of *economic system legitimacy* is very high.

CONCLUSIONS

The findings reported here from the ISJP indicate, not surprisingly, that there is a substantial gulf between Eastern postcommunist and Western democratic capitalist countries in terms of perceptions of system-level economic and political legitimacy. This result is supported not only by indicators reflecting *macro*perceptions of income differences, equalities of opportunity, the satisfaction of need, and the social recognition of contributions (effort and skill), but by *micro*perceptions of one's *just deserts*, the satisfaction of family needs, and morale with respect to income receipts and standard of living. These national differences translate to some extent into macrolevel beliefs regarding principles of just distribution and support for economic distributive systems, although as we have noted, there seems to be some ideological inconsistency in Eastern Europe. Despite the growing favorability to markets and the overwhelming rejection of socialism, there is considerable support for guaranteed minimum and maximum income policies. At the same time, support for social stratification and social inequality are increasingly desirable, as indicated by the rejection of the principle of equal shares and support for passing wealth across generations.

In an effort to understand these patterns, the analyses reported here explored the applicability of *theories of justice evaluation* to the understanding of national differences in perceived legitimacy. We hypothesized that existential considerations would play a much stronger role in the development of judgments about levels of deserved income in Western capitalist democracies, where systems of beliefs regarding economic legitimacy strongly reinforce the allocation of job income. Our results provide strong support for the role of existential factors in virtually all countries, with the strongest effects appearing in Western democracies, consistent with our predictions. We also hypothesized that level of perceived family need would play a role in shaping perceptions of job deserts, but a much stronger one in Eastern European countries than in the West, and strong support is given for this hypothesis. Perceptions of family need strongly predict deserved income in seven of eight postcommunist countries and only weakly predicts deserved income in the capitalist countries. The exception in the former category is East Germany, where we reasoned that the effects of reunification had already changed the perception of family need as relevant to job income.

Our hypotheses about the connection between perceptions of deserved income and macrolevel beliefs about social injustice are not borne out, as there is little predictive role of our measure of perceptions of system-level injustices in the allocation of pay in our equations for deserved job income. These results do not, however, form the basis for a conclusion that macrolevel beliefs are not connected to microlevel evaluations of justice. There are at least two possibilities that can be used to explain this finding. First, we may not have adequately measured the macrolevel dimensions that impinge on perceived job deserts. Further exploration of other potential indicators is needed. Second, the connection between macro- and microlevels may be indirect, via some other aspects of social experience. Specifically, there may be interactions between belief systems and positions in the social structure, e.g., social class and individual resources. Further work is necessary to clarify the nature of the micro-/macrojustice linkage.

We conclude that not only are justice sentiments predictable, in the sense that we can achieve nonzero coefficients of determination for our measures of perceptions of deserved job income, but that the pattern of effects is highly predictable as well. We developed several cross-national predictions for the nature of the linkages of justice principles to justice sentiments, using an application of the concept of *referential structures* to the evaluation of system legitimacy. The fact that virtually all of our predictions were borne out, coupled with the high levels of consistency shown in these results within clusters of countries defined by our classification schema, suggests a promising future for "middle-range" theories of justice evaluation for achieving an understanding of the processes of social transformation currently being experienced in the postcommunist societies of Central and Eastern Europe and the former Soviet Union. These results also bode well for the success of the deployment of a research strategy of cross-national comparison through the replication of sample surveys for the ultimate purpose of monitoring these processes.

NOTES

1. This is a revision of a paper presented at the Fourth International Social Justice Conference, held in Trier, Germany, July 1–4, 1993. We acknowledge the assistance of David Klingel and Xiaohe Xu in conducting the data analysis reported here. Bernd Wegener provided a valuable critical reading of a previous version of the paper, for which we are grateful.

2. In this table the Unemployed category includes those persons who are unemployed, as well as those engaged in Temporary work, those identifying themselves as Housewives, those who were Retired/disabled, and those who were Full-time students. The education categories included in this table are based on the CASMIN scheme, developed by König, Lüttinger, and Müller (1988). Here the Primary category refers to general primary formal education or less, including those having basic vocational training; the Intermediate category includes medium levels of vocational training and formal education; the Secondary category includes those completing secondary schooling, including *Abitur* and *Maturitas*; and the Tertiary category includes those having postsecondary schooling.

3. Note that, while Germany was unified while we were conducting our study, separate surveys were conducted in East and West Germany, and we present the data here under the labels of West Germany and the former East Germany.

4. See Cichomski (1992) for an alternative approach.

6

Justice Evaluation of Income Distribution in East and West[1]

Wil Arts, Piet Hermkens, and Peter van Wijck

1. INTRODUCTION

Recent state-of-the-art reports concerning international comparative research (Kohn 1989b; Oyen 1990) direct our attention to two important lacunae: comparative research often lacks theoretical content, and the geographical scope of comparative research is generally confined to the study of countries in Western Europe and North America. One of the aims of the International Social Justice Project (ISJP) was to close both gaps by furnishing explanatory theories on perceptions of justice and subsequently subjecting those theories to comparable survey data from countries in the East [(former) communist states] and the West (capitalist states). The main assumption underlying this project was that there are not only differences between East and West in perceptions of justice, but also that these differences are entrenched in habitual and customary ways of perception.

This paper is an attempt to acquire an understanding of the choice of justice principles that are used as standards in judging the apportionment of incomes, and the formation of judgments regarding the distribution of income. We focus on the question whether these principles and judgments are formed in a similar way in the East and in the West. We will, therefore, first present a theoretical model of justice evaluation in Section 2.[2] This theoretical modeling approach means that a variable-oriented research strategy, in which generality is given precedence over complexity, is preferred to a case-oriented strategy, in which a comprehensive examination of cases is given preference over generality (cf. Ragin 1987, Ch. 4). An important feature of this strategy is the central goal of parsimony. An explanation citing only a few variables is preferred to one citing many. At the core of the model lies the assumption that certain psychological regularities always and everywhere underlie the evaluation of the distribution of income, whereas the exact formulations of the principles and judgments of jus-

131

tice depend on contextual factors, which are not always and everywhere the same, and on individual specific characteristics (see Chapter 7 of this volume). Some authors (e.g., Törnblom 1992) suppose that justice principles and judgments are contingent and multiplicit and therefore difficult to capture in a theoretical model. We have to realize, however, that whenever there is contingency and multiplicity we still have to look for the unity of an underlying regularity. Therefore, model building remains the solution to the problem.

The survey data used to test the hypotheses of the model stem from the ISJP and are described in Section 3. Since we focused on the question whether these principles and judgments are formed in a similar way in the East and in the West, we have estimated separate models for the East and the West. The estimation results appear in Section 4. Finally, in Section 5 we state our conclusions.

2. THEORETICAL FRAMEWORK

In most social-psychological and sociological theories of justice it is assumed that individuals consider a particular apportionment or distribution of income just if this allotment or distribution complies with the principle(s) of justice to which they adhere. Some social-psychologists and sociologists (i.e., Walster, Berscheid, and Walster 1973; Homans 1974; Lerner 1977; Moore 1978) have postulated a basic "justice motive" that will *eventually* determine the choice of justice principles and the passing of justice judgments. They agree that this motive can be reduced to a feeling of entitlement that people share, which in its most primitive form, is a perceived right to expect outcomes that are equivalent or proportional to inputs. They disagree, however, about whether this motive is part of human nature as it has developed during biological and cultural co-evolution or whether it is due to being socialized into a moral atmosphere shaped by historical developments. Obviously, people can assess entitlements in very different ways using the notion of proportionality. Any of the main principles of justice proposed in the literature (Deutsch 1975; Sampson 1975; Miller 1976; Leventhal 1976; Schwinger 1980a), be it equity (income should be proportional to achievements), equality (income should be equally divided), or need (income should be proportional to necessities), can be derived from specific types of assessments of entitlements (cf. Scherer 1992:3–4).

In spite of the universality of the justice motive and the proportionality rule, individual assessments of entitlement are therefore to a large degree variable. They depend not only on a common justice motive but also inter alia on the individual's characteristics (such as social background, motivations, and experience) and on contextual factors (such as the social, political, and economic context and the prevailing ideology).

To find a satisfactory solution for the problem at hand, we need a theoretical model that offers the opportunity to ascertain both the universal and the variable aspects of the choice of justice principles and the passing of justice judgments regarding the allotment and distribution of income. Using insights from equity and framing theories, we will try to build a model that specifies the cognitive and social mechanisms at the root of justice evaluation. In Section 2.1 we will especially pay attention to the cognitive structure of justice evaluation. In Section 2.2 we will highlight the effects of motivational factors and situational framing on the choice of justice principles and the passing of justice judgments in the East and the West.

2.1   The Cognitive Structure of Justice Evaluation

The fundamental idea underlying equity theory is that people consider the distribution of outcomes in an (exchange) situation to be equitable if and only if the outcomes are distributed to individuals in proportion to their inputs. More specifically, the individuals in a 2-person case are rewarded equitably if and only if the following equation holds (cf. Adams 1965:281):

$$O_1^e/O_2^e = I_1^e/I_2^e. \tag{1}$$

The subscripts of the variables O (outcome) and I (input) refer to individuals 1 and 2. The superscript e indicates that the variables originate from equity theory. It goes without saying that an individual is assumed to experience injustice if and only if he/she perceives a discrepancy in output/input ratios of 1 and 2. More generally, the individuals in an n-person case are rewarded equitably if and only if:

$$O_i^e = (O_{tot}^e/I_{tot}^e)I_i^e, \tag{1'}$$

where the subscript tot indicates that the concerning variable is obtained by summing over the n individuals. This paper concentrates on the case in which an individual's outcome corresponds with his/her income.

According to equity theory, an individual's input is assumed to be a weighted sum of "outcome relevant characteristics" (cf. Adams 1965; Jasso 1983). To emphasize that these characteristics are microphenomena, i.e., they concern individuals rather than social aggregates, they will be dubbed *microcharacteristics*. In the presence of m microcharacteristics, individual i's input is given by

$$I_i^e = \sum_{k=1}^{m} \alpha_k^e K_{ki}. \tag{2}$$

In fact, I_i^e is the inner product of a vector with weighing coefficients (α_k^e) and a vector with the micro-characteristics of individual i (K_{ki}). To emphasize that the α_k^es express the weight that ought to be attached to the corresponding micro-characteristics, the vector α^e might be called a *microprinciple*. By applying the vector α^e, a judge can assess the amount of income that is just for an individual characterized by certain microcharacteristics, given the total amount of income to be distributed over a population.[3]

The income O_i^e deemed just for an individual i can serve as a reference for the justice evaluation of the income O_i^a that i actually receives. Evidently, i's income is too high if $O_i^a > O_i^e$, while i's income is too low if $O_i^a < O_i^e$. Jasso (1978) has suggested that the justice evaluation E_i regarding the income received by individual i is a logarithmic function of the ratio of actual to just income of individual i:

$$E_i = \ln(O_i^a/O_i^e). \tag{3}$$

Jasso argues that Equation (3) yields a justice evaluation in meaningful justice units and quantifies the human experience by which deficiency is felt more keenly than excess. The justice evaluation score associated with an individual who earns exactly his or her just earnings would be zero, which is the logarithm of one. Zero represents the point of justice, and a person receiving that amount would be considered justly rewarded. When actual earnings exceed just earnings, the ratio O_i^a/O_i^e is larger than unity and its logarithm is a positive number, indicating unjust overreward. When just earnings exceed actual earnings, the ratio is a proper fraction and its logarithm is a negative number, indicating unjust underreward (Jasso 1978:1414).[4]

It is important to note that E_i in Equation (3) not only depends on the *distribution* of income, but also on the *total sum* of income that is being distributed. Where $O_{tot}^e > O_{tot}^a$, there is the possibility that all individuals are considered to be underrewarded; where $O_{tot}^e < O_{tot}^a$ there is the possibility that all individuals are considered to be overrewarded. In order to isolate the distributional aspect, the influence of different sum totals would have to be eliminated. This elimination is obtained by the following equation:

$$E_i = \ln[(O_i^a/O_{tot}^a)/(O_i^e/O_{tot}^e)]. \tag{3'}$$

In fact, Equation (3') yields an evaluation of i's income share. $E_i = 0$, if i receives an equitable share; $E_i > 0$ if i receives a share that is considered too large; and $E_i < 0$ if i receives a share that is considered too small. Clearly, (3') effectively amounts to (3) if $O_{tot}^e = O_{tot}^a$. From now on, E_i will be based on (3').

O_i^e and E_i can be conceived as two dissimilar kinds of judgments regarding the allotment of income to specific individuals. To emphasize that these judgments pertain to microlevel phenomena, they will be dubbed *microjudgments*. More specifically, O_i^e reflects the amount of income that a judge deems just for individual i, and E_i reflects the direction and degree of deviation between the income that is actually received by i and the amount of income adjudged just for this individual.

Analogous to the relationship between just incomes and microcharacteristics such as achievements and needs, it is possible to relate actual incomes with those microcharacteristics:

$$O_i^a = (O_{tot}^a/I_{tot}^a)I_i^a, \tag{4}$$

$$I_i^a = \sum_{i=1}^{m} \alpha_k^a K_{ki}. \tag{5}$$

The preceding equations describe a theoretical relationship between micro-principles, microcharacteristics, and microjudgments. More specifically, these equations constitute a model to explain justice judgments regarding individual incomes of n persons who are defined in terms of m microcharacteristics.

Let us now take into consideration the case in which people are asked to adjudge just incomes to two income recipients, who are defined by one and only one microcharacteristic. Individual 1 is defined by $K_{11} = 1$ and $K_{21} = 0$, and individual 2 is defined by $K_{12} = 0$ and $K_{22} = 1$. From (2) it follows then that $I_1^e = \alpha_1^e$ and $I_2^e = \alpha_2^e$. The just amount of income for i then equals $I_i^e/(I_1^e+I_2^e)O_{tot}^e$, implying that i's equitable income share equals $\alpha_i^e/(\alpha_1^e+\alpha_2^e) = \beta_i^e$. Since the β_i^es are rescaled α_i^es, they can be considered to constitute a *standardized microprinciple*. A standardized microprinciple can be used to establish which amounts of income are just for recipients characterized by certain microcharacteristics, since the incomes deemed just are given by $O_i^e = \beta_i^e O_{tot}^e$. From (5) it follows that $I_1^a = \alpha_1^a$ and $I_2^a = \alpha_2^a$. Consequently, i's actual income share equals $\alpha_1^a/(\alpha_1^a+\alpha_2^a) = \beta_i^a$. Since $O_i^e/O_{tot}^e = \beta_i^e$ and $O_i^a/O_{tot}^a = \beta_i^a$, Equation (3') effectively amounts to $E_i = \ln(\beta_i^a/\beta_i^e)$.

Consider a society in which each individual either possesses characteristic 1 *or* 2. Let set 1 be the collection of individuals i with $K_{1i} = 1$ and $K_{2i} = 0$ and let set 2 be the collection of individuals with $K_{1i} = 0$ and $K_{2i} = 1$.[5] Assume, for convenience, that both sets comprise half of the population. In that case, the equitable income share of set 1 is given by $\beta_1^e = I_1^e/(I_1^e+I_2^e)$, and the actual income share of set 1 is given by $\beta_1^a = I_1^a/(I_1^a+I_2^a)$. If the actual income share of set 1 is smaller than the equitable income share, i.e., $\beta_1^a < \beta_1^e$, the individuals in this set are underrewarded. The Jasso type of microjudgment regarding the income share of the individuals in this set is given by $E_1 = \ln(\beta_1^a/\beta_1^e)$. Similar expressions apply to (the individuals in) set 2.

The preceding discussion presented an explanation for microjudgments, i.e., judgments regarding the incomes of individual income recipients. We will now turn our attention to macrojudgments, i.e., judgments regarding the income distribution as a whole. For that purpose we reconsider the two sets of individuals who have been introduced in the preceding paragraph. Assume that the individuals in the set 1 have a lower input than the individuals in set 2, i.e., $\beta_1^e < \beta_2^e$. Since the equitable share of set 1 is smaller than the equitable share of set 2, the individuals in set 1 would receive a lower income than the individuals in set 2 if all individuals receive an equitable reward. That is to say, as long as the individuals in set 1 are not overrewarded, set 1 represents the individuals on lower income. Consider the case where the individuals in set 1 are underrewarded, i.e., $\beta_1^a < \beta_1^e$. By implication, the individuals in set 2 are then overrewarded, i.e., $\beta_2^a > \beta_2^e$. The lower β_1^a relative to β_1^e, and the higher β_2^a relative to β_2^e, the more the individuals on lower income are underrewarded and the more the individuals on higher income are overrewarded, i.e., the more the differences in income will be judged "too large."[6] At least this would be the case if there is a consistent relation between microjudgments, i.e., E_1 and E_2, and macrojudgments. When we assume that the latter judgment, which we will call J from now on, is a linear additive function of E_1 and E_2, then:

$$J = \gamma_1 E_1 + \gamma_2 E_2. \tag{6}$$

If the judgment "too large" is represented by a low value of J, then $\gamma_1 > 0$ and $\gamma_2 < 0$. It is important to note that Equation (6) incorporates the aimed-for micromacro link, since it expresses how macrojudgments are (expected to be) influenced by microjudgments.

2.2   Frames, Ideology, and Self-Interest

In the preceding section we have emphasized the psychological regularities that are assumed to underlie the evaluation of income distributions. In this section, however, we will pay attention to more variable aspects involved in the evaluation process. Building on previous research and theory construction (cf. Arts and van Wijck 1991; Arts and van der Veen 1992; Törnblom 1992; Wegener and Steinmann, Chapter 7 of this volume) we take for granted that this process tends to be influenced by contextual factors. Before those factors can exercise any influence they are first filtered by frames of reference. Those frames affect people's definitions of the situation at hand and prestructure their choices and judgments. This prestructuring is perhaps better known in the literature as the framing or cognitive representation of a situation. There are *grosso modo* two distinct modes of framing justice principles and judgments. These principles and judgments can be shaped by the social context in the past and by the way in which pertinent information is framed by the researcher(s) (cf. Markovsky 1988:222). In this paper only the former possibility, i.e., situational framing, will be treated.[7] Such a frame is a general image of the situation. It is mainly a product of situations in the past and the prevailing cultural perspective, and partly of the norms, habits, and personal characteristics of those concerned.

In equity theory the potential role of frames of reference has been largely neglected. Berger, Zelditch, Anderson, and Cohen (1972:122) have criticized equity theory by arguing that issues of distributive justice only arise in the presence of stable frames of reference. According to Berger, Fisek, Norman, and Wagner (1985:222) referential structures describe distribution principles that are thought to be true as a matter of social fact and can serve as generalized standards whereby individuals eventually develop expectations for rewards in specific situations. Berger et al. (1972:139) advance the hypothesis that as a consequence of beliefs about what is typically the case, expectations come to be formed about what one can legitimately claim ought to be the case. A similar hypothesis can be found in framing theory: "Any stable state of affairs tends to become accepted eventually, at least in the sense that alternatives to it no longer readily come to mind" (Kahneman, Knetsch, and Thaler 1986:730–31). This idea is consistent with Homans's observation that "the rule of distributive justice is a statement of what ought to be, and what people say ought to be is determined in the long run and with some lag by what they find in fact to be the case" (1974:249–50).

What implications does the preceding discussion have for the explanation of possible differences in choices of justice principles between East and West? It is implied that the choice of justice principles will be influenced by the existing frames of reference in the East and the West. Consequently, if these frames are different, this difference will be reflected in the choice of justice principles. Lindenberg (1992) has formulated the hypothesis that due to different political and economic experiences, the frames of reference in East and West vary considerably. These frames might be called, respectively, a *state frame* and a *market frame*. He hypothesized that the state frame is inter alia characterized by less inequality than the market frame. By Homans's hypothesis, a state frame would then involve a more egalitarian attitude than a market frame.[8]

Because societal conditions in contemporary Eastern Europe are subject to considerable changes, the traditional frame of reference is eroding. Traditions, however, do not change overnight. Changes invariable take generations to develop. The state frame will thus continue to influence, although to a lesser degree, the choice of justice principles and the justice evaluation of income distribution. However, in the West, where social change has been much less radical in the last decade, the market frame has hardly been affected by erosion recently. The opposite seems to be true.

The implication of state and market frames for the evaluation of income distributions can be readily stated in terms of the two-set variant of our model. If a state frame is characterized by less inequality than a market frame, then the implication is that β_2^a should be lower in the East than in the West. Homans's hypothesis suggests that the same holds for β_2^e, i.e., a state frame involves a more egalitarian attitude than a market frame.

It is, however, immediately apparent that the choice of a standardized microprinciple will not be completely determined by contextual factors such as "the distribution principle that is thought to be true as a matter of social fact," i.e., $\beta_2^e \neq \beta_2^a$, or more generally $\alpha^e \neq \alpha^a$. This conclusion can be readily demonstrated by considering the case where a given sum O_{tot} is being distributed. If the distribution rule that ought to be applied coincides with the distribution rule that is actually thought to be applied, i.e., $\alpha^e = \alpha^a$, then it follows that all individuals are considered to receive an equitable reward, i.e., $E_i = 0 \ \forall i$, and the income differences are considered to be perfectly just, i.e., $J = 0$. Since this is highly unlikely to be an adequate representation of reality, supplementary determinants of the choice of principles of justice will have to be considered.

In investigating the choice of a standardized microprinciple, one must recognize that the choice of β_i^e is unlikely to be only influenced by β_i^a. In fact, the sociological literature furnishes a number of additional factors that would influence this choice. Supplementary determinants can be found, as mentioned before, in the individual's characteristics. We first assume that the choice of a standardized microprinciple will be influenced by an individual's ideological convictions. Research findings indicate that individuals who place themselves on the left (right) tend to prefer relatively low (high) inequality. Consequently, one would expect that individuals on the left (right) of the political spectrum tend to choose a standardized microprinciple that implies relatively low (high) inequality. Though the choice of a standardized microprinciple is most likely to be influenced by an individual's political beliefs, it is important to recognize that an individual's political ideology is merely a rough indicator of his/her normative conceptions. A number of more specific normative factors might influence the choice of a standardized microprinciple. Individuals who attach relatively high weight to need characteristics as characteristics that entitle people to income apportionment are most likely to choose a standardized microprinciple that implies relatively small inequality, whereas those who attach relatively high weight to achievements will most likely choose a standardized microprinciple that implies relatively great inequality. Furthermore, individuals who are, in the broadest sense, egalitarian minded might be expected to choose a standardized microprinciple that implies a relatively small degree of inequality. Finally, individuals might self-servingly adhere to norms that offer a legitimization for their personal gain (see Wegener and Liebig, Chapter 11 in this volume). More specifically, the higher an individual's position in the income hierarchy, the higher the inequality implied by his/her preferred standardized microprinciple.[9]

Assuming that the choice of a standardized microprinciple of justice is linearly related to these determinants, we arrive at the following equation pertaining to the two set case:

$$\beta_i^e = \xi_b\beta_i^a + \xi_p P + \xi_n N + \xi_c C + \xi_m M + \xi_y Y, \tag{7}$$

where β_i^e and β_i^a have been defined previously. The variable P represents the political orientation of the judging individual, N and C represent the weight he or she attaches to needs and contributions, M represents egalitarian mindedness, and Y represents his or her position in the income hierarchy. It goes without saying that the expected sign of the ξs depends on the operationalization of the respective variables.

In the preceding discussion, we highlighted the relation between β_i^e and β_i^a, i.e., a state frame (market frame) leads to the choice of a standardized microprinciple that implies relatively small (great) differences in income. Such a frame, however, will not completely determine the choice of a standardized microprinciple. We take it for granted that actual choices are not only a product of the circumstances, but also determined by the convictions and interests of those who choose.

Just as the choice of a "standardized microprinciple" can be expected to be influenced by more variables than merely "the distribution principle that is thought to be true as a matter of social fact" (β^a), it can be expected that the judgments regarding differences of income (J) will not only be influenced by judgments regarding individual incomes (E_i). In passing judgments regarding income differences, people will not only be guided by their microlevel opinions. Most notably, these judgments tend to be influenced by macroprinciples of justice, i.e., standards that are used in judging the income distributions as a whole, rather than the incomes apportioned to individual income units (see Arts et al. 1991). In fact, such a principle reflects an individual's egalitarian mindedness. Furthermore, one can expect an individual's self-interest and ideology to be echoed in the judgments on income differences he or she formulates. It can be expected, for example, that people on higher incomes are less inclined to deem income differences too large. After all, if a wealthy person thinks that the income differences are too large, he/she is implicitly questioning his/her income position. Assuming that judgments regarding income differences are linearly related to these determinants, we must add three variables to Equation (6):

$$J = \gamma_1 E_1 + \gamma_2 E_2 + \gamma_m M + \gamma_p P + \gamma_y Y. \tag{8}$$

The relation between judgments regarding income differences J and microjudgments E_1 and E_2 was already incorporated in Equation (6). Now, the variables M, P, and Y have been added. These variables reflect respectively the egalitarian mindedness, the political ideology, and position in the income hierarchy of the judge.

3. DATA SET AND OPERATIONALIZATION

3.1 Data Set

We tested the hypotheses using the data set from the international survey fielded in 1991 by the ISJP group. The population consisted of a representative sample (all countries $N \geq 1000$ except Japan, $N = 777$) of the adult population aged 18 years and above (Russia 16+, Japan 20+) of each of the countries participating in the project (Bulgaria, Czechoslovakia, Estonia, East and West Germany, Great Britain, Hungary, Japan, the Netherlands, Poland, Russia, Slovenia, United States). The observational method involved was a combination of questionnaires handed out to the respondents and face-to-face standardized interviews (in the United States interviews were conducted by telephone; in the

Netherlands they were self-administered via computer; see the Appendix to this volume for details).

3.2 Operationalization of the Variables

The theoretical variables incorporated in Equations (7) and (8) need to be operationalized for the empirical analysis. The dependent variable in Equation (7) is the standardized microprinciple β_i^e. In the questionnaire, people were asked what income would be just for two types of income units. The variables IEARNDIR and IEARNFAC indicate what income would be considered just for a chairman or managing director of a large cooperation and an unskilled worker, respectively. On the premise that these types are representative for the top and bottom half of the income distribution, the standardized microprinciple pertaining to these types of income units can be computed as

$$\beta_{fac}^e = \text{IEARNFAC}/(\text{IEARNFAC}+\text{IEARNDIR}),$$
$$\beta_{dir}^e = \text{IEARNDIR}/(\text{IEARNFAC}+\text{IEARNDIR}).$$

The distribution principles that are thought to be true as a matter of social fact, i.e., the β_i^as, can be similarly operationalized. In the questionnaire people were asked to estimate the income of those who held the previously mentioned positions. The variables EARNDIR and EARNFAC describe the respondents' perceptions of the amount of income that these types of income units actually earn. The β_i^as can be computed accordingly, i.e.,

$$\beta_{fac}^a = \text{EARNFAC}/(\text{EARNFAC}+\text{EARNDIR}),$$
$$\beta_{dir}^a = \text{EARNDIR}/(\text{EARNFAC}+\text{EARNDIR}).$$

A number of questions in the questionnaire asked the respondents to assess the role that certain microcharacteristics ought to play in determining the level of incomes. Owing to economical and theoretical considerations (the distinction between contribution and need characteristics), we only incorporated the weight attached to one contribution characteristic and the weight attached to one need characteristic in our empirical model. The variable PAYEDUC, indicating the importance attached to education, is used as operationalization of the weight attached to contributions, i.e., the variable C from Equation (7). The higher the value of PAYEDUC, the less influence education should have in determining the level of income. The variable PAYSIZE, indicating the importance attached to the size of the family an employee supports, is used as operationalization of the weight attached to need, i.e., the variable N from Equation (7). The higher the value of PAYSIZE, the less influence family size should have in determining the level of income.

As an operationalization of "egalitarian mindedness," i.e., of the variable M, we made use of the attitude toward the statement that "the fairest way of distributing wealth and income would be to give everyone equal shares." The value of the variable EQSHARE is inversely related to the strength of the respondent's agreement with the statement.

The variable P, representing the political ideology of the respondent, has been operationalized by using the answers to the question to indicate one's position on a left-right scale. The higher POLVIEW, the more the respondent places him-/ herself to the right of the political scale.

The variable Y, representing the respondent's position in the income hierarchy in his or her country, is operationalized on the basis of household incomes. The variable RELINC is defined as an individual's household income divided by the average household income in his/her country. Note that household incomes are specified in national currencies. By dividing household incomes by the average household income in a country, one obtains an indicator of relative income positions that is independent of the nation's currency, thus enabling international comparisons.

For the operationalization of judgments on income differences, i.e., the variable J, we used the answers to the question of what the respondents think about the differences between incomes in their country. The lower DIFFINC, the more the income differences are considered to be too large.

Finally, we computed the variables E_1 and E_2, indicating the degree to which the individuals in sets 1 and 2 are considered to be under- or overrewarded, using Equation (3′) and the operationalization of the fair and actual shares of both aforementioned sets. For the sake of convenience, the theoretical variables, their operationalization, and their meaning are summarized in Table 6.1.

3.3 Operationalization of the Hypotheses

Equation (7) incorporates six hypotheses regarding influences on the choice of standardized microprinciples. Effectively, these hypotheses can be expressed as

Table 6.1. Variables and Operationalization

Theoretical variable	Operationalization	Higher value indicates
β_2^e	β_{dir}^e	Higher equitable share of top set
β_2^a	β_{dir}^a	Higher perceived share of top set
P	POLVIEW	More to the right of the political spectrum
N	PAYSIZE	Less importance attached to need
C	PAYEDUC	Less importance attached to contributions
M	EQSHARE	Less egalitarian
J	DIFFINC	Judgment tends toward "too small"
E_1	E_{fac}	Bottom set tends to be overrewarded
E_2	E_{dir}	Top set tends to be overrewarded
Y	RELINC	Higher income position

Table 6.2. Hypotheses for Standardized Microprinciples

H1:	$\xi_b > 0$.	The higher β_{dir}^a, the higher β_{dir}^e
H2:	$\xi_c < 0$.	The less important education, the lower β_{dir}^e
H3:	$\xi_n > 0$.	The less important family-size, the higher β_{dir}^e
H4:	$\xi_m > 0$.	The less egalitarian, the higher β_{dir}^e
H5:	$\xi_p > 0$.	The more to the right politically, the higher β_{dir}^e
H6:	$\xi_y > 0$.	The higher one's income position, the higher β_{dir}^e

expectations of the signs of the coefficients in the equation. In analyzing a two-set case, one only needs to consider the expectation of one of the sets since the expectations regarding the other set are implied by $\beta_1^e + \beta_2^e = 1$. Since the expected signs depend on the operationalization of the variables in the equation, now that these variables have been operationalized, we can record these expectations. On reflection, the expectations regarding β_{dir}^e are as stated in Table 6.2.

Equation (8) incorporates five hypotheses regarding influences on the judgments of income differences. They are concisely as stated in Table 6.3.

It is important to note that Equation (8) is obtained by adding three variables to Equation (6). Consequently, it is implicitly assumed that judgments regarding income differences are based on the evaluation of the incomes received by two sets of income units only. This clearly constitutes a heroic assumption. It goes without saying that a larger number of sets may be relevant. Since only two sets are included in the dataset, we are obliged to use the two-set variant.[10] As a result, one would not anticipate that Equation (8) yields a particularly powerful explanation of judgments regarding income differences.

4. ANALYSIS

In Section 2.2 the expectation was formulated that β_{dir}^a will be smaller in the East than in the West.[11] Empirically, for the West an average value of 0.8698 and a standard error of 0.0011 are obtained. For the East these data are 0.8347

Table 6.3. Hypotheses Regarding Macro-judgments

H7:	$\gamma_1 > 0$.	The higher *EARNFAC*, the higher E_1, the higher J
H8:	$\gamma_2 < 0$.	The higher *EARNDIR*, the higher E_2, the lower J
H9:	$\gamma_m > 0$.	The less egalitarian, the higher J
H10:	$\gamma_p > 0$.	The more to the right politically, the higher J
H11:	$\gamma_y > 0$.	The higher one's income position, the higher J

and 0.0012. These findings are consistent with the expectation formulated above. Homans's hypothesis suggests that the same holds for β^e_{dir}. For β^e_{dir} we obtained an average value of 0.7875 and a standard error of 0.0015 for the West; these data are 0.7130 and 0.0014 for the East. Consequently, the average value of β^e_{dir} appears to be significantly lower in the East than in the West.

In order to test the hypotheses incorporated in Equations (7) and (8), we estimated both equations using regression analysis. In Equation (7) the choice of a standardized microprinciple has been related to a number of variables that are expected to influence that choice. We are, however, not only interested in the question of whether these variables significantly influence this choice, but also in the question of whether this influence is identical in the East and in the West. Therefore, separate equations have been estimated for the East and the West. While a state frame is expected to be salient in Eastern countries like Bulgaria, Czechoslovakia, East Germany, Estonia, Hungary, Poland, Russia, and Slovenia, a market frame is expected to be salient in Western countries like Great Britain, Japan, the Netherlands, West Germany, and the United States. The results of estimating the equations for the standardized microprinciples, β^e_{dir}, can be found in Table 6.4.[12] This table depicts unstandardized regression coefficients and standard errors.

From these results the following conclusions can be drawn. The results for the East indicate that all coefficients are significantly different from zero. The coefficient of the variable POLVIEW, however, has the wrong sign. The coefficients of

Table 6.4. Estimations for Standardized Microprinciples

	East	West
β^a_{dir}	0.5077**	0.8181**
	0.0148	0.0127
PAYEDUC	−0.0104**	−0.0082**
	0.0018	0.0014
PAYSIZE	0.0134**	0.0056**
	0.0013	0.0012
EQSHARE	0.0150**	0.0131**
	0.0011	0.0001
POLVIEW	−0.0014*	0.0066**
	0.0007	0.0007
RELINC	0.0022**	0.0066**
	0.0006	0.0013
CONSTANT	0.2288**	−0.0113**
	0.0140	0.0120
N	5416	5047
R^2	0.24	0.51

$^*p < 0.05.$ $^{**}p < 0.01.$

the remaining variables have the expected signs. Consequently, hypotheses 1, 2, 3, 4, and 6 cannot be rejected for the East. The results for the West indicate that all coefficients have the expected sign and are significantly different from zero. Consequently, hypotheses 1–6 cannot be rejected for the West.[13]

A comparison of the results that have been found for the East and the West show that the estimated models are not identical. First of all, the variable POLVIEW obtains a different coefficient. Furthermore, there appears to be a stronger relation between β_{dir}^e and β_{dir}^a in the West than in the East. This is a very interesting result since it supports a previously formulated idea whereby the normative effect of an applied distribution rule tends to be larger in a stable environment than in a rapidly changing environment.[14,15]

In Equation (8) judgments regarding differences of income are related to a number of variables that are expected to influence these judgments. The estimation results pertaining to the East and the West can be found in Table 6.5.

Except for EQSHARE in the East, all coefficients are significantly different from zero and have the expected signs. Consequently, hypotheses 7–10 cannot be rejected for the West. For the East, only hypothesis 9 is rejected. It is to be noted, however, that the explained variance is rather low. Several phenomena might account for this finding. As explained in Section 3.3, Equation (8) assumes that judgments regarding income differences are based on the evaluation of the incomes received by two sets of income units only. A larger number of categories may be relevant. Furthermore, judging individuals might attach dissimilar weights to E_{fac} and E_{dir} or they might have dissimilar "styles of expression" (cf. Jasso 1993).

Table 6.5. Estimations for Macrojudgments

	EAST	WEST
E_{fac}	0.2467**	0.2322**
	0.0253	0.0208
E_{dir}	−0.5628**	−0.7577**
	0.1045	0.0987
EQSHARE	0.0170	0.0753**
	0.0111	0.0069
POLVIEW	0.0270**	0.0620**
	0.0076	0.0069
RELINC	0.0184**	0.0371**
	0.0063	0.0146
CONSTANT	1.8927**	1.5197**
	0.0625	0.0536
N	5314	4977
R^2	0.06	0.12

$^*p < .05$ $^{**}p < .01$.

5. CONCLUSION

This paper is an attempt to gain an insight into the choice of justice principles that are used as standards in judging the apportionment of incomes and into the formation of judgments regarding the distribution of income. We focused on the question of whether these principles and judgments are formed in a similar way in the East and in the West. A theoretical model of justice evaluation was constructed to answer this question. At the core of this model lies the premise that certain psychological regularities always and everywhere underlie the evaluation of the distribution of income, whereas the exact formulations of the principles and judgments of justice depend on contextual factors, which are not always and everywhere the same, and on individual specific characteristics. The theoretical basis of the model originates from equity theory as well as framing theory.

The data used to test the hypotheses of the model stem from the International Social Justice Project. Since we addressed the question of whether these principles and judgments are formed in a similar way in the East and in the West, we estimated separate models for the East and the West. It turns out that the models for the East and the West are not identical. Most interestingly, there appears to be a stronger relation in the West than in the East between the chosen principle of justice, i.e., the distribution rule that ought to be applied and the distribution principle that is thought to be applied. This finding is perfectly consistent with Homans's observation that "the rule of distributive justice is a statement of what ought to be, and what people say ought to be is determined in the long run and with some lag by what they find in fact to be the case" (1974:250). An important result is that the constructed model can successfully explain the choice of justice principles and the formation of justice judgments indeed, albeit only to a certain degree. The reason for this can be sought both in the unrefined measurement of some of the theoretical variables and in a too parsimonious model.

Appendix 6.A1. Estimation Results for Standardized Microprinciples

	W. Germany	Japan	Nether-lands	U.K.	U.S.	Bulgaria	Czech.	Estonia	E. Germany	Hungary	Poland	Russia	Slovenia
β^a_{dir}	0.7889**	1.0140**	0.6645**	0.8684**	0.8218**	0.2567**	0.4882**	0.2211**	0.8107**	0.2996**	0.4590**	0.3953**	0.4637**
	0.0288	0.0529	0.0239	0.0340	0.0254	0.0433	0.0448	0.0636	0.0337	0.0546	0.0308	0.0545	0.0582
PAYEDUC	-0.0095**	-0.0059	-0.0147**	-0.0113**	-0.0029	-0.0108*	-0.0176**	-0.0318**	-0.0031	-0.0034	-0.0203**	-0.0092	-0.0159**
	0.0026	0.0051	0.0028	0.0034	0.0035	0.0047	0.0042	0.0010	0.0039	0.0056	0.0035	0.0066	0.0050
PAYSIZE	0.0095**	0.0090	0.0108**	0.0103**	0.0030	0.0115**	0.0118**	0.0130*	0.0048	0.0002	0.0130**	-0.0030	0.0112**
	0.0022	0.0058	0.0023	0.0031	0.0025	0.0037	0.0032	0.0064	0.0030	0.0041	0.0025	0.0051	0.0037
EQSHARE	0.0132**	0.0033	0.0149**	0.0136**	0.0168**	0.0122**	0.0224**	0.0061	0.0152**	0.0162**	0.0179**	0.0145**	0.0099**
	0.0018	0.0036	0.0016	0.0026	0.0022	0.0029	0.0024	0.0063	0.0024	0.0031	0.0022	0.0040	0.0024
POLVIEW	0.0082**	-0.0019	0.0057**	0.0083**	0.0045**	-0.0028	0.0017	-0.0017	0.0015	0.0000	0.0030*	-0.0068*	0.0004
	0.0014	0.0027	0.0011	0.0016	0.0013	0.0017	0.0016	0.0036	0.0018	0.0024	0.0014	0.0031	0.0020
RELINC	0.0061	0.0091	0.0240**	0.0038	0.0035	0.0168**	0.0012*	0.0058	0.0147**	0.0311**	0.0106**	0.0239**	0.0262**
	0.0032	0.0061	0.0047	0.0033	0.0021	0.0079	0.0006	0.0032	0.0069	0.0069	0.0031	0.0083	0.0061
CONSTANT	0.0045	-0.0791	0.0875**	-0.0798**	-0.0155	0.3843**	0.2370**	0.4909**	-0.0163	0.3883**	0.2213**	0.3849**	0.2753**
	0.0282	0.0524	0.0228	0.0309	0.0227	0.0381	0.0392	0.0649	0.0328	0.0511	0.0283	0.0509	0.0559
N	1198	315	1567	843	1124	479	905	426	712	553	1198	441	702
R^2	0.46	0.56	0.44	0.52	0.58	0.15	0.25	0.06	0.52	0.14	0.27	0.16	0.17

$*p < .05.$ $**p < .01.$

Appendix 6.A2. Estimation Results for Macrojudgments

	W. Germany	Japan	Nether-lands	U.K.	U.S.	Bulgaria	Czech.	Estonia	E. Germany	Hungary	Poland	Russia	Slovenia
E_{fac}	0.0918**	0.2253**	0.4777**	0.4274**	0.3400**	0.1322	0.8396**	0.0558	-0.1203	0.4439**	0.4940**	0.1644	0.1236**
	0.0260	0.0058	0.0662	0.0588	0.0560	0.0966	0.1232	0.0822	0.0630	0.1174	0.1132	0.1693	0.0263
E_{dir}	-0.4516*	-0.3339	-0.8750**	-0.1615	-0.5396*	-0.1891	-0.0220	-0.2437	-0.2199	-0.1383	-0.0563	0.0783	-0.7011**
	0.1590	0.4491	0.2402	0.2729	0.0263	0.2273	0.4035	0.2028	0.4075	0.3563	0.3906	0.4405	0.2280
EQSHARE	0.0662**	0.0340	0.1461**	0.0242	-0.0112	0.0247	0.0743**	0.0808**	0.0404	-0.0307	0.0159	-0.0612	0.0000
	0.0173	0.0395	0.0168	0.0262	0.0224	0.0199	0.0281	0.0407	0.0332	0.0253	0.0319	0.0375	0.0179
POLVIEW	0.0874**	0.0118	0.0706**	0.0658**	0.0317*	0.0034	0.0263	0.0039	0.0441	0.0304	0.0200	-0.0681*	0.0183
	0.0131	0.0301	0.0120	0.0174	0.0143	0.0113	0.0180	0.0232	0.0246	0.0206	0.0201	0.0299	0.0157
RELINC	0.1353**	0.2406**	0.2611**	-0.0069	-0.0134	0.0007	0.0120	0.0238	-0.0913	0.1017	0.1205	-0.1383	0.1887**
	0.0303	0.0684	0.0476	0.0344	0.0227	0.0544	0.0066	0.0207	0.0958	0.0592	0.0438	0.0787	0.0471
CONSTANT	1.1608**	1.5883**	1.0969*	0.1697**	2.2261**	1.2536**	2.0377**	0.1481	2.2275**	1.7030**	2.0576**	2.7692**	1.3988**
	0.0988	0.2227	0.1000	0.1324	0.1238	0.1874	0.1515	0.2176	0.2122	0.1701	0.1873	0.2239	0.1230
N	1201	313	1507	842	1114	483	881	415	695	555	1132	438	715
R^2	0.12	0.08	0.27	0.14	0.08	0.08	0.18	0.03	0.02	0.10	0.06	0.03	0.12

*$p < .05$.   **$p < .01$.

NOTES

1. We gratefully acknowledge helpful comments by Jim Kluegel and Bernd Wegener.
2. This model builds on ideas previously formulated in Arts et al. (1991); Arts, Hermkens, and van Wijck (1992) and van Wijck (1993, 1994).
3. The principles of equity, equality, and need are special cases of a general microprinciple, since they can be obtained by imposing certain restrictions on the vector α^e.
4. In a recent paper, Jasso (1990) presented a proof that, for the case of cardinally measurable goods, the logarithmic form is the unique solution to a system of partial differential equations representing three relatively mild conditions on the comparison function.
5. It is important to note that the individuals in a set have nothing in common except that they possess a certain characteristic. Such a set of individuals does not, or does not necessarily, constitute a social class.
6. By thus relating judgments about income differences to judgments regarding individual incomes, one recognizes that different judges may not only use dissimilar microprinciples, but they may also have dissimilar perceptions of individual incomes. This constitutes an extension to the model presented in Arts et al. (1991), since the latter model only recognizes the first mechanism.
7. The question of how the choice of justice principles and the passing of justice judgments is influenced by informational framing is dealt with in Arts et al. (1991).
8. Although the communist ideology in Eastern Europe was a very egalitarian one, one can doubt whether the income distribution in the countries of Eastern Europe really was much less unequal than in the West, especially if and when the privileges and the income in kind of the *nomenklatura* are accounted for (cf. Morrison 1984:131–33).
9. One caveat is in order: Circumstances determine how much leeway there is for pursuing self-interest and the attainment of ideological values. In the former communist countries of Eastern Europe, where totalitarian, monocultural ideologies and command political and economic systems operated, the leeway was restricted. In contrast, the democratic, pluralist ideologies and the political and economic market system of the West allowed more elbow room. Consequently, one could expect more variety in choices and judgments in the West than in the East. The current erosion of the traditional state frame in the now "post"-communist countries of the East, however, has led to anomie for some (see Wegener and Liebig, Chapter 11 of this volume). And in an anomic environment opportunism runs riot. Ideas of justice are considered obsolete or are guilefully used to maximize personal gains and minimize personal losses.
10. These sets have not been chosen haphazardly. We assume that they function as "anchors" in the process of judging the distribution. Such end-points are more meaningful reference points than intermediate categories (cf. Wegener 1987:7).
11. This expectation was based on the idea that in Eastern countries a state frame is the salient one, and in the Western countries a market frame is dominant. Furthermore, it was expected that a state frame would be more egalitarian than a market one. The answers to a number of questions regarding the role of the state do, indeed, suggest that a more extensive role of the state is thought to be more appropriate in the East than in the West.

12. Since we are especially interested in differences between East and West, our discussion is confined to the results of the East and the West. The country-specific results are presented in the Appendix to this chapter.

13. In order to check whether these results are sensitive to the operationalization of the variables, we tried a number of alternative operationalizations. First of all, as an alternative operationalization of C, the weight attached to contributions, we used the weights attached to efforts and responsibilities rather than education. In the second place, we tried out an operationalization of Y, an individual's income position, on the basis of household income divided by the number of people living in the household. Furthermore, we tried out the income the respondent receives from his job or business rather than household income. Finally, as an alternative operationalization we looked at the subjective standing of the respondents. None of these alternative operationalizations led to any modification of the conclusions. In the third place, we attempted to operationalize P by looking at party sympathy and party identification. This proved to be fruitless, since it resulted in a loss of two-thirds of our observations.

14. There is further evidence that the situation in the Eastern countries tends to be more anomic than in Western countries. The respondents have been asked whether they agree with the statement "The way things are these days, it is hard to know what is just anymore." In the East a considerably larger part of the populations agrees with this statement than in the West. Furthermore, a higher explained variance for the West than for the East suggests a smaller individual specific variation in the choice of a standardized microprinciple in the West and indicates the existence of a higher degree of consensus in the West.

15. Because the traditional notions of left and right have become diffuse categories in contemporary Eastern Europe, the variable POLVIEW is of questionable quality. Therefore, we also have estimated the equations for the explanation of β_{dir}^e and J for the East and the West without the variable POLVIEW. This yielded results that were virtually identical to the ones presented in Tables 6.2 and 6.3. Other variables yielded the interesting finding that respondents in the Eastern countries are remarkably nonideological in their orientations (Mason, Chapter 3 in this volume).

7

Justice Psychophysics in the Real World: Comparing Income Justice and Income Satisfaction in East and West Germany

Bernd Wegener and Susanne Steinmann

INTERDISCIPLINARY SOCIAL JUSTICE RESEARCH

There are many ways one can do justice research. Indeed, different academic disciplines have developed, which taken together constitute the *justice studies*. Unfortunately, however, there is little traffic across disciplinary borders within these studies (Miller 1992) and, more important, there is a complete lack of understanding of how one area of justice research can be of relevance to another. To begin communication between the different fields of justice research, one would have to start with a taxonomy of what social justice research is and which different disciplines exist within the justice studies. As a second step then, the relations of how results from one discipline can influence another must be studied. Based on a suggestion for a taxonomy of justice research, this paper attempts to make vivid the idea that there is much to be gained if interdisciplinary exchange would become the rule, not the exception in this area of research.

The case we address in this paper in particular is the *psychophysics of distributive justice*. This social justice discipline focuses on the causal relationship between individual justice judgments and the objective features of the distributed goods. While considerable progress has been made in determining how object characteristics influence individual justice responses in experimental situations (see Törnblom 1992 for the most recent review), little is known about the generalizability of these findings to the "real world." What we propose here is that applying the psychophysical justice laws—what Guillermina Jasso (1980) has called the *distributive-justice force*—outside the laboratory calls for considering the likely effects of circumstances the psychological laboratory tends to neglect, but that have long been studied in other domains of justice research. What we ask in this chapter then is whether the established psychophysical formulas are valid under all circumstances, and whether, in trying to answer this question, we can profit from the results of other types of social justice research.

Testing for the validity of "justice psychophysics in the real world" we use the perceived justice, or injustice for that matter, of incomes in now unified Germany. Individuals in East and West Germany receive incomes that differ depending on whether they live in the East or in the West. Are the amounts people obtain on both sides of the former border considered to be just? How can the justice judgments people make be explained? Appropriate answers can only be found, we argue, by looking also at approaches to social justice research other than that of psychophysics.

We begin by addressing the issue of the many different approaches taken in social justice research and offer a way to classify them.

APPROACHES TO SOCIAL JUSTICE

The most basic distinction is the Kantian one between the normative and the descriptive, between ought and is. How *should* goods be distributed in order to be just, and what distributions *are actually* perceived as being just? It is true that recent debates among philosophers of justice, dealing with John Rawls's revisions of *A Theory of Justice* (1971), have brought to bear that the normative and the descriptive approaches to justice cannot really be separated because normative decisions about justice policies are in the final analysis political, not metaphysical (Rorty 1991; Rawls 1993). This is why empirical descriptions of what people actually think about justice is one of the constituent factors for deriving what justice ought to be (Miller 1992; Wegener 1994; Swift, Marshall, Burgoyne, and Roth, Chapter 2 in this volume). But separating empirical analyses from normative justice deliberations is still important because the former must stay free from all normative constraints if these analyses should reveal what is empirically the fact.

Normative theories are usually philosophical in nature, reflecting on what individuals should do in order to be just or what principles or laws should be applied when justice is at stake. Thus, for instance, Kant's *Metaphysik der Sitten* (1797) is certainly a book in the normative realm. It tells people what they should do, but deals with justice only indirectly, by specifying laws that are morally good and by presuming that acting according to these laws is just. Justice is thus a very formal concept in Kant's understanding, but he definitely uses it in a normative sense. Rawls (1971), of course, is a genuine proponent of normative justice theory making prescriptive deductions on how we should distribute goods, and especially how institutions and certain "representative individuals" should act in order to make for an ethically justified society. Institutions must observe, in Rawls's view, a single justice principle, "fairness," when distributing valued goods. "Justice as fairness" implies that every individual should have an equal right to basic liberties and that all social values are to be distributed equally unless an unequal distribution is to everyone's advantage (Rawls 1971:62). Other contemporary philosophers see reasons to replace the criterion of "justice as fairness" by different criteria, e.g., "justice as entitlement" (Nozick 1974), "justice as equality" (Nielson 1979), and "justice as impartiality" (Barry 1989a). On the other hand, economic models of distributive justice are also normative when they define social welfare functions, that is, who in a society should get what. Most often the normative premises economists make are implicit to their models (Schokkaert 1992).

Other types of normative theories do not primarily consider what an individual or institution should do but rather ask how a society should look if it is to have stability and duration. Usually the answer is that such a society must be a just society. Most of Durkheim's theorizing is based on this very idea, but it is also implicit to American functionalism and to the functionalist theory of social stratification (Davis and Moore 1945). In his later writings, for instance, Parsons has explicitly addressed the justice issue as a prerequisite for a socially ordered society (Parsons 1970); so has Weber, but in contrast to Parsons he sees conflicting spheres of society characterized by different standards of justice—a conclusion to be drawn also by Michael Walzer (1983) much later (Müller 1994). Of course, Karl Marx deals with the very essence of justice when he identifies particular stages in human history by their typical production relations, unmasking these relations as exploitative (Buchanan 1982; Dahrendorf 1971).

So there are two very different approaches to *normative* justice theories: Those directed toward the individual, being prescriptive as to what he or she should do or get; and those directed toward the social order of society. This distinction can well be said to be reminiscent of Parsons's action-order distinction (1951), expressing an individual-related orientation of action vs. an order-related orientation.

Descriptive justice theories also come in two forms. These theories deal with actual distribution behavior and with beliefs and perceptions of such behavior. But these beliefs and perceptions can either be directed toward actual amounts that are being distributed, or toward the rules, practices, and principles by which distributions are made. Justice psychophysics (Stevens 1975; Wegener 1982) addresses the former by asking primarily two kinds of questions: What constitutes a *just reward* for an individual? and What determines an individual's *justice evaluation* when his or her actual reward deviates from the just reward? Both types of questions deal with judgments individuals make with regard to the distribution of goods they or other individuals receive. Descriptive justice research can, however, also study the beliefs and perceptions someone has regarding the general distribution rules, practices, and principles of a society (i.e., Lane 1986). These types of judgments take, for instance, the form "all members of society should receive identical shares" or "those who contribute to the well-being of society should receive according to their contribution." Both statements express ideological convictions or partisan beliefs. While psychophysical justice judgments address the justice of individual-related shares, judgments of the second type address principles that are believed to work in a society or that should be applied in order to make for a justly ordered society. Individuals in different social positions may, of course, have different views about what the prerequisites of a justly ordered society are. Thus, similar to normative justice theories, with descriptive justice research, we deal either with an individual-related approach and an order-related approach.

Table 7.1 represents an overall schema for describing justice research in its different disciplines. What should become apparent from this schema is that justice studies can be pursued along very different tracks depending on whether they are normative or descriptive and whether they are focused on the individual or on society. Clearly there are limits to the interdisciplinarity of justice research (Scherer 1992) because the different orientations do not reconcile easily. However, what should in particular be evident from Table 7.1 is that normative philosophical and sociological reasoning (A and B) may well have the force to determine socially what justice beliefs people actually hold (D) and what kinds of allotments they consider to be just or unjust (C). Thus, while it is important to know what people think about justice (descriptively), in order to validate the normative justice discourse it is no less important to consider how the normative statements may influence peoples' actual perceptions of justice and of just distributions. Furthermore, the ideological justice beliefs people actually hold (as in D) will certainly be influential in shaping their views about the justness of the rewards they themselves or other individuals receive (C). Thus, reconstructing individual-related justice judgments empirically calls for going beyond considering only perceptual or psychophysical regularities as such, but also requires putting the likely influence of normative and ideological justice beliefs on micro-justice judgments on the research agenda. We would argue, therefore, that for the measurement of psychophysical phenomena to which research of C is aimed, A,

Table 7.1. Disciplinary Domains of Justice Research

	Individual-related	*Order-related*
Normative	A. Practical Philosophy and Normative Economic Model Building	B. Justice Implications of Social Theory
Descriptive	C. Justice Psychophysics and the Study of Individual Distribution Behavior	D. Study of Distributive-Justice Ideologies and Inequality Perceptions

B, and D form possible contextual domains, whose influences on such phenomena have yet to be properly charted.

Addressing the question of how judgments on *earnings* are determined by different contexts, we use unified Germany as an example. We look specifically at the differences between former East and West Germany and at the possible *ideological* and *factual* conditions affiliated with the transformation experiences in both parts of the country. Will the established laws of justice psychophysics also hold in this context? Various theories concerned with microjustice serve as the theoretical framework of this study. However, we will look only at the *formal structures* òf these theories in order to determine what place contextual factors can have in the formulations of these theories.

THE "DISTRIBUTIVE-JUSTICE FORCE"

The study of individual-related justice judgments has long reached the level of a formalized discipline, the work by Berger et al. (1972) being of seminal importance in this respect. As a formalized discipline, individual-related justice research aims for deductive-nomological explanations of justice responses (Hempel and Oppenheim 1948). Basic to this idea is the assumption that we make justice judgments in a regular and predetermined way, so that generalizations with regard to these judgments can be formulated in terms of functional relationships. According to Jasso (1989:354) three types of relationships constitute what she terms the *distributive-justice force*. The respective three central questions are:

1. What are the determining factors in a society for the distribution of rewards individuals receive?
2. What do individuals and collectives think is a just reward?
3. What is the magnitude of the perceived injustice associated with given departures from rewards that are just?[1]

Each of these questions addresses a different phenomenon and accordingly the questions point to different functional relationships that need to be specified. With the first question, we are looking for the set of independent variables $\mathbf{X} = x_1, \ldots, x_n$ and the related set of parameters $\mathbf{A} = a_1, \ldots, a_n$ for predicting the *reward* variable R according to a *reward function* (RF) f:

$$R = f(\mathbf{X}; \mathbf{A}). \qquad (1)$$

Considering only the metric or cardinal case, one frequent application of Equation (1) are earnings equations [also termed income determination functions in economic contexts and human capital research in particular (Mincer 1974;

Becker 1964)]. Here linear relations with regard to the logarithmic values of R (earnings) are usually proposed such that

$$\ln R = a_1 x_1 + a_2 x_2 + \cdots + a_n x_n. \tag{2}$$

When posing the second question above, not simply reward but specifically the reward that is considered to be just, the *just reward (JR)*, is the explanandum. For JR, $\mathbf{X} = x_1, \ldots, x_k$ is the set of possible predictors assuming that more than one factor may be responsible for the determination of JR. h being the *just-reward function (JRF)*, we have

$$JR = h(x_1, \ldots, x_k), \tag{3}$$

and more specifically,

$$JR = h(\mathbf{X}; \mathbf{B}), \tag{4}$$

if $\mathbf{B} = b_1, \ldots, b_k$ is the set of relevant parameters for estimating h. In empirical application the just-reward function is most conveniently specified as a power function (Jasso 1978), this choice being in accord with Stevensian psychophysics (Stevens 1975):

$$JR = b_1 X^{b_2}, \tag{5}$$

or equivalently,

$$\ln JR = \ln b_1 + b_2 \ln X. \tag{6}$$

But other forms of the just-reward function have also been proposed and tested [see Jasso (1980:360) for an overview].[2]

The third type of questions deals with how satisfied or dissatisfied a person is if he or she is not receiving the amounts considered to be just (see Chapter 5 in this volume). How is justice *evaluated* if it deviates from perfect justice? Following the early works of Jasso and Rossi (1977) and Jasso (1978), the theory of distributive-justice force answers this question with the *justice evaluation function (JEF)* g, which involves a comparison between the *actual reward* and the *just reward*. A *justice evaluation* then is

$$JE = g(\text{actual reward, just reward})$$

or

$$JE = g(R, JR). \tag{7}$$

Based on the Berger et al. (1972) referential-comparison theory, Jasso (1978) first proposed specifying g as the logarithm of the ratio of the actual reward to the just reward:

$$JE = \ln(R/JR). \tag{8}$$

This enables us to represent JE in the full real-number continuum, with zero representing the point of perfect justice, negative numbers representing the degrees of unjust underreward, and positive numbers representing the degrees of unjust overreward. In addition, this choice of the justice evaluation function is able to express the common human experience that unjust underreward is felt more keenly than comparable unjust overreward. It has become customary to speak of $\ln(R/JR)$ as the *Jasso ratio J*, so that Equation (8) is also written as

$$JE = J. \tag{9}$$

With Equations (1) to (9), a sketch of the formal structure of justice psychophysics—termed the distributive-justice force by Jasso—is given.

FRAMES, CORES, AND EXPANDED CORES
OF JUSTICE PSYCHOPHYSICS

The reported statements characterizing the distributive-justice force do not, however, all reach the same level of concreteness. Because this is so, we will say that while part of the statements represent only the *frame* for the psychophysics of justice, the remaining statements represent the justice psychophysics' *core*. As is easily seen, Equations (1), (4), and (7) leave the form of the respective reward, the just reward, as well as the justice evaluation functions unspecified. Based on definitions with which we will deal immediately, they provide only a frame for the theory. In contrast, in Equations (2), (5), and (8) specific empirical functions are postulated, which is why these equations form the core for the psychophysical theory of justice.

With this terminology we draw on Joseph Sneed's (1971) *The Logical Structure of Mathematical Physics* and on the *nonstatement view of theories* that he put forth in that book. According to this view, empirical theories are set-theoretical entities, not systems of predicate statements. The *empirical claim of a theory* (Sneed 1971:42) is then conceived as a formal structure S expressed by the set or sets of models M by which S may be satisfied. It is fundamental to the empirical claim of a theory, from the nonstatement perspective, that the elements of M are characterized by all being *extensions* of possible and possible partial models. Consider the sentence of the form

$$(\exists x)(x \text{ is an } E_{PP} \wedge x \text{ is an } S), \tag{10}$$

where PP is a possible partial model for S and E_{PP} expressing "an extension of PP."

Intuitively, Equation (10) says that there is some extension of PP that is a model for S. If we regard PP as a description of the observed facts about a situation,[3] then Equation (10) says that this description of the observed facts can be "filled out" in some way to produce a model for S. That is, one can find theoretical functions, values, and, if necessary, supplementary laws that, when combined with PP, yield a model for S. With this idea of theories being formal structures satisfied by models such that $M \subseteq S$, and of models being extensions of incomplete models, it is possible to define theories with different levels of empirical content, being either frames, cores or expanded cores for theories (Stegmüller 1973; Wegener 1982).

Based on this logic, a *frame F* for a theory consists not only of the set of models M that actually satisfy S, but also of the sets of possible partial models PP and possible models P. Leaving aside the comprehensive formal definitions given by Sneed (1971:Chapter VII), possible partial models are built from descriptions of observable facts plus nontheoretical (empirical) functions, whereas possible models also include theoretical functions.[4] In order to produce a *core H* for a theory, the frame needs to be extended by specific *constraints C* that hold if the possible models are being applied to particular empirical settings. The constraints guarantee that the possible models P yield identical theoretical functions in these different applications.[5] However, characteristics of different intended applications are likely to call for different laws within one and the same theory. Considering this will yield an *expanded core E* for a theory consisting of the core H and sets of laws L.[6] Accordingly, an *applied core for a theory* can be written as $T_E = \langle E, I \rangle$, I representing the area of intended applications. T_E may also be called an *expanded theory* (Sneed 1971:178).[7]

One of the challenging problem the nonstatement view has found a solution for, is the *incommensurability problem* that is given if one follows Kuhn's (1970) description of scientific revolutions. Scientific revolutions embrace shifts of paradigms implying that theories before and after a revolution cannot be compared— they are incommensurable. From the nonstatement perspective, the dynamics of theories (Sneed 1971:Chapter VIII), however, can be preserved in spite of scientific revolutions. If theories are conceived as set-theoretical extensions of other theories, a "progressive" development of theories (Lakatós 1970) is possible as long as the superseding theories can be reduced to the frames or cores of earlier theories. But also when scientific revolutions are not of relevance, incommensurability may become a problem because the frame and core for a theory need to be expanded in different ways in order to be useful for diverse areas of intended applications. Applying the distributive-justice force to the real world would be a likely example. We therefore suggest making use of the nonstatement view of theories in this area of research.

Since a *frame* for a theory is one in which no special constraints are made with regard to particular intended applications, it is easy to see that Equations (1), (4), and (7) of the distributive-justice force together form the frame F for that theory. Specifying the functional forms, as in Equations (2), (5), and (8) then yields the theory's core H with regard to R, JR, and JE. It is also easy to see, however, that the core of the distributive-justice force needs to be extended as well. In order to make the theory applicable to concrete intended areas of application and to ensure that the respective reward, just-reward, and justice evaluation functions have validity in the different areas of these applications, special laws and special constraints must be added to the core. Going beyond the basic frame and core structure of the distributive-justice force, the question must be raised of how to extend this structure in order to make it fit to the real world.

The basis for such an extension is given with Berger et al.'s (1972) status-value theory and the idea of a referential structure that this theory implies. A referential structure, according to Berger et al. (1972:133), consists of four components: individuals, their characteristics, their goal objects, and the status values of characteristics and goal objects. Any applied core for a theory of justice psychophysics must therefore take into consideration not only variations in time and space conditions, but also sociostructural as well as psychodynamic specifics of the individuals to which the core should apply. The constraints that need to be specified must also be directed toward the kinds of rewards that are being distributed and evaluated for their justice. Jasso in her exhaustive review article of 1980 mentions these constraints, which constitute different contexts for the distributive-justice force (Jasso 1980:361), but she does not seem to realize that only a core for a theory expanded by these constraints will produce an applied core $T_E = \langle E, I \rangle$ that is of use in the real world. What is of particular importance is how *distributive-justice ideologies* and *normative justice beliefs* (situated in Sections A, B, and D of Table 7.1, respectively) affect the regularities of psychophysical justice judgments.

If Equations (2), (5), and (8) make up the nonexpanded core for the distributive-justice force theory with regard to *R*, *JR*, and *JE*, and if we let $\mathbf{Z} = z_1, \ldots, z_i$ be the set of special constraints by which to expand the core, the following *Reward, Just-Reward,* and *Justice Evaluation Models* result:

$$\ln R = a_1 x_1 + a_2 x_2 + \cdots + a_n x_n + c_1 z_1 + c_2 z_2 + \cdots + c_i z_i, \quad (11)$$

$$\ln JR = \ln b_1 + b_2 \ln X + d_1 z_1 + d_2 z_2 + \cdots + d_i z_i, \quad (12)$$

$$JE = \ln(R/JR) + e_1 z_1 + e_2 z_2 + \cdots + e_i z_i. \quad (13)$$

Thereby, $\mathbf{C} = c_1, \ldots, c_i, \mathbf{D} = d_1, \ldots, d_i,$ and $\mathbf{E} = e_1, \ldots, e_i$ represent sets of parameters for the sets of special constraints for each respective model. It may well be possible, however, that in Equation (11), $\mathbf{X}$ and $\mathbf{Z}$ form one overlapping set of variables since the Reward Model has its most common application in earnings equations; the relevant independent variables in that context are well established, making unlikely the necessity of extensions.

As Jasso asserts, the justice evaluation function is valid for all areas of social life. This would mean that the justice evaluation function should serve as a useful instrument to predict *satisfaction with material well-being* as well. Using this as a theoretical cornerstone, we discuss in the following a possible extension of the distributive-justice force to include satisfaction with material well-being and the special constraints associated with that particular application. Formally, this extension follows Equation (13).

JUSTICE EVALUATIONS AND SATISFACTION
WITH MATERIAL WELL-BEING

Satisfaction with economic or material well-being may be understood as an expression of agreement with the existing structures of resource distribution in a society. The *objective* criteria for distribution include the amount of available material resources (e.g., net earnings). The *subjective* factors consist of referential standards of comparison, meaning certain social norms and expectations with regard to particular distributions and distributive mechanisms. They are an expression of the expected or just level of well-being. Based on this reasoning, Alwin (1987) formulates a model for dealing with satisfaction with material well-being that is easily recognized as deriving from Jasso's justice evaluation formula of Equation (8) (see also Shepelak and Alwin 1986; Alwin, Khakhulina, Hermkens, Antoncic, and Arts 1992). If the material well-being of a person deviates from the expected and perceived justice level, then these deviations would have an independent effect on material well-being. Since, according to Jasso, positive deviations (overreward) do not have the same meaning as negative deviations (underreward), it can be expected that underreward has a stronger effect than overreward on the relevant measure of well-being. Alwin derives from this three hypotheses: First, that satisfaction with the level of objective rewards is a monotonically increasing function of the level of objective rewards; second, that satisfaction with the level of objective rewards is a monotonically decreasing function of the negative deviations of expected and actual level of rewards; and third that the effects of negative deviations from expected and actual reward (underreward) are substantially greater than the effects of comparable positive deviations (overreward). To test for these hypotheses, it is necessary to specify the effects of over- and underreward separately, as in the following regression equation (Shepelak and Alwin 1986):

$$y = a + b_1x_1 + b_2x_2 + b_3x_3 + b_4x_4 + u, \qquad (14)$$

where y is the level of satisfaction, x_1 represents earnings in units of $100, x_2 is the absolute value of the Jasso ratio $\ln(R/JR)$, x_3 the direction of Jasso's ratio with 1 for positive values and 0 for negative values, and x_4 the product of x_2 and x_3.

Evidently, the effects of underreward are measured by the parameters a and b_2, of overreward by the parameters a, b_2, b_3, and b_4. However, the only causal link that exists is between the level of actual earnings and the level of satisfaction, thereby excluding the causal attribution of deviations, either positive or negative. This led Alwin et al. (1992) to modify the regression equation in the following way:

$$y = a + b_1x_1 + b_2x_2 + b_3x_3 + b_4x_4 + b_5x_5 + u, \qquad (15)$$

where now x_1 is the logarithm of household earnings, x_2 and x_3 are two dummy variables that measure the individuals' evaluation of household earning as being less than, exactly, or more than the amount that the individual perceives as being justly deserved, x_2 is 1 for underreward, x_3 is 1 for overreward, and x_4 and x_5 are two product variables: $x_4 = x_2\ln(needed$ household earnings) and $x_5 = x_3\ln$ (*needed* household earnings). According to Alwin, the variables x_4 and x_5 measure the amount of deviation. In this model the justice evaluation function according to Jasso is used in the form of Justice Evaluation = ln(Actual Reward) − ln(Just Reward), with Just Reward, however, estimated separately in the regression equation for over- and underrewarded. In Alwin's formulation, what we have then is first a reconstruction of the *comparison process* itself captured by Jasso's ratio; and second what may conveniently be summarized as the *microjustice force,* consisting first of the overreward/underreward distinction, second of the needs component, and third of a referential comparison standard involving whether earnings are less than, exactly, or more than the amount that the individual perceives as being justly deserved.

This model, however, has the disadvantage of disregarding social-structural variables as well as the influence of macrojustice principles. In addition, in view of applying the model to a country that was until recently divided into two separate parts each of which is now struggling with particular transformation problems, *regional* effects also need to be considered. Do East-West differences within Germany affect the satisfaction with material well-being? Models like Jasso's and Alwin's assume that individuals have certain perceptions about just distributions that are not, or at least not significantly affected by sociostructural criteria. There can be no doubt, however, that particularly societies that are presently forced to adapt to processes of profound transformation provide insight into the questionability of such an assumption.

In societies under transition, individuals should find it more difficult to formulate their notion of a just claim. In the transformation of socialist into capitalist systems this difficulty is related to the requisite processes of redefining distribution rules. Within these societies, there is a growing tendency for individuals to support new distributive mechanisms, namely those that operate in accordance with principles of effort, achievement, and economic liberalism. At the same time, however, it cannot be expected that these individuals dissociate themselves altogether from the "old" dominant socialist values of *egalitarianism.* While in capitalist societies, the predominance of achievement-based distributive mechanisms continues to find widespread acceptance, in societies under transformation it can be expected to find the *simultaneous* acceptance of inegalitarian as well as egalitarian modes of distribution (Kluegel and Matějů, Chapter 4 in this volume).

In addition, there is evidence that the variation in justice beliefs within a country is also determined by structural differences such as those associated with the social positions individuals have, their level of education, sex, or specific types of employment relations (Wegener and Liebig, Chapters 10 and 11 in this volume). For the purpose of some studies, regional differences, of course, will also play a role.

Considering these different kinds of *special constraints*, in Sneed's terminology, besides Jasso's ratio the following elements of an *expanded* core for the distributive-justice force theory are thus of relevance:

- The microjustice force: under-/overreward, need, referential comparison
- The macrojustice force: e.g., inegalitarianism vs. egalitarianism
- Sociostructural constraints: sex, age, education, size of firms, etc.
- Regional differences: e.g., East-West comparison

In the following we will try to determine the effects of these constraints on the distributive-justice force empirically, that is, we will apply the expanded Reward, Just-Reward, and Justice Evaluation Models following Equations (11) through (13), comparing the populations in East and West Germany. For the Justice Evaluation Model, we will use satisfaction with material well-being as an instance of the justice evaluations *JE*.

DATA AND RESEARCH METHODS

We make use of data from the German part of the International Social Justice Project (ISJP) in which separate samples were drawn for East and West Germany. There were 1837 interviews completed in the east and 1019 in the west (Kleebaur and Wegener 1991; Appendix to this volume). Our model consists of the family of three models—the Reward Model, the Just-Reward Model, and the Justice Evaluation Model. These three models are being estimated simultaneously using a structural equation approach. Separate models for East and West Germany are estimated and then compared statistically for significant differences using Bentler's (1989) EQS version of the Lagrangian multiplier test.[8]

The first model has, as its dependent variable, the respondents' net income in logarithmic form—this is the Reward Model given in Equation (11) or, more simply, Equation (2). It can be expected that a large part of the variation in objective income is explained by structural variables. Among these variables are respondent's sex, level of education, age, firm size, and employment type contrasting employment in the private and the public sector. Table 7.2 describes these variables in detail.

In the second model, the logarithmic income is used as an independent variable for predicting the logarithm of the just income for *JR* according to Equation (12), the expanded Just-Reward Model. In addition, the effects of the individual variables (sex, education, age, firm size, employment type), which were also included in the first model, are estimated, thereby allowing us to control for the

Table 7.2. Description of Variables

Actual income	*R*'s income
Just income	Income *R* feels he or she deserved
Satisfaction with income	"Please indicate how satisfied or dissatisfied you are with your income." (1, completely dissatisfied; 7, completely satisfied)
Satisfaction with standard of living	"Please indicate how satisfied or dissatisfied you are with your standard of living." (1, completely dissatisfied; 7, completely satisfied)
Sex	1, men
Education	Level 1a: Less than general formal education; Level 1b: general formal education; level 1c: general formal education and basic vocational training; level 2a: medium vocational training; level 2b: medium formal education; level 3a: secondary formal education; level 3b: lower tertiary training; level 3c: higher tertiary training
Age	Years
Firm size	1, small firms (up to 100 employees); 0, more than 100
Type of organization	1, public sector; 2, private sector
Underreward	1, job income is "much less" or "somewhat less" than deserved
Overreward	1, job income is "much more" or "somewhat more" than deserved
Need	If the difference between *R*'s needed and *R*'s actual household income is greater than zero, 1; otherwise 0
Referential comparison (below average)	1, income is "somewhat below" or "far below" the average compared to "people in similar jobs"
Referential comparison (above average)	1, income is "somewhat above" or "far above" the average compared to "people in similar jobs"
Inegalitarianism	"It is all right if businessmen make good profits because everyone benefits in the end." (1, strongly disagree; 5, strongly agree)
Egalitarianism	"The state has the duty to care for the welfare of its citizens and has to finance protection against personal risks out of tax revenues." (1, strongly disagree; 5, strongly agree)

direct and indirect effects on the just income. These variables represent objective or existential criteria. Researchers conducting studies on the justice of earnings in Western industrialized countries (Dornstein 1991; Shepelak and Alwin 1986; Wegener 1991; Norden 1985) agree that the perceived level of just earnings is strongly affected by the level of actual earnings. This is very much in accord with Homans's (1974) dictum that "the ought is determined in the long run by the is." Thus, it is the existential or "real" criteria that determine the definition of just earnings. The underlying norm for that is prescribed by market mechanisms and is widely accepted in capitalist societies (Alwin, Chapter 5 in this volume; Wegener 1992c). Just earnings must, however, be regarded as a function of various factors. Not only existential measures, but nonexistential or utopian standards as well (Jasso and Rossi 1977) affect the perception and evaluation of just earnings. As Alwin (Chapter 5 in this volume) predicts, nonexistential variables should be of more importance in societies undergoing transformation from socialist to capitalist societies. It is also imaginable, however, that structural differentiations play an increasingly more important role in such societies.

The evaluation of one's own personal income, as being either just or unjust, is not independent of the financial resources that are available to one's household. When reflecting upon one's personal income, individuals have a perception of having either more or less income at their disposal than what they actually need. Thus, it is important for questions pertaining to household income to reflect this *needs* factor. Also, the two variables for felt *overreward* and *underreward* are included in the model. These variables allow us to account for the different types of injustice, as postulated by Jasso (1978, 1980). Finally, also describing an element of the microjustice force, a *referential comparison* of individuals is considered. The referential comparison we include consists of two dummy variables expressing whether respondents believe that their income was below or above the average for people in similar jobs.

The macroprinciple justice force includes the two basic macrolevel distribution principles of economic *inegalitarianism* and *egalitarianism*. Both represent principles that have been frequently analyzed (Wegener 1992c; Wegener and Liebig, Chapter 12 in this volume; Kluegel and Matějů, Chapter 9 in this volume; Deutsch 1975, 1985; Della Fave 1986b; Ritzman and Tomaskovic-Devey 1992). The operationalization of respondents' attitudes toward economic inegalitarianism uses a variable with a 5-point response scale to the statement: "It is all right if businessmen make good profits because everyone benefits in the end." Egalitarianism is measured by the item "The state has the duty to care for the welfare of its citizens and has to finance protection against personal risks out of tax revenues."

The third model, finally, is the Justice Evaluation Model. Its dependent latent construct, satisfaction with material well-being, is composed of two measures of satisfaction: the first with earnings and the second with one's standard of living (see Table 7.2). According to Equations (8) and (13), Jasso's ratio is used to predict this construct. The ratio, however, is entered into the model as the difference of two separate linear terms: $\ln(\text{Reward}) - \ln(\text{Just Reward})$. The Reward term—the actual income—coincides with the dependent variable of the first model and the Just Reward—the just income—coincides with the dependent variable of the second model, thus permitting us to control for direct and indirect effects on satisfaction. In addition to this, the third model contains the respective independent variables from the Just-Reward Model. This means that the third model considers not only the effects of the comparison process captured by Jasso's ratio, but also elements of the micro- and macrojustice forces as well as sociostructural variables. In addition to this, the models are estimated for both regions of Germany separately.

RESULTS

The Reward Model

Table 7.3 presents the estimates of a structural equation model in which the reward (as income), the just reward (as just income), and the justice evaluation (as satisfaction with material well-being) are three dependent variables and latent constructs. As independent variables, Jasso's comparison ratio, elements of the microjustice and the macrojustice forces, as well as sociostructural variables appear. Table 7.3 presents *one* model but it incorporates the three models that are of interest to us, the Reward Model, the expanded Just-Reward Model, and the expanded Justice Evaluation Model, which are being estimated simultaneously. Separate parameter estimates for East and West Germany are reported. In addition, the levels of statistical significance for differences between the East and the West using the group comparison option within the structural equation approach are indexed (either by *a*, *b*, or *c* for different levels). Goodness-of-fit indices refer to the East and the West models separately.

We begin by looking at the Reward Model presented in the two leftmost columns of Table 7.3. The determining factors for the respondents' income for East Germany, and partly for West Germany, correspond with the results also found in other studies (Bellmann 1992; Szydlik 1992; Schwarze 1991a, 1991b). Men have significantly higher wages than women (also Frick, Krause, and Schwarze 1991; Schupp and Wagner 1991; Bellmann 1992; Szydlik 1992). This correlation holds true for both East and West Germany.[9] In spite of these similarities, the statistical group comparison of the two structural equation models reveals differences within the two regions of Germany: The earnings differential between men and women is much larger in West Germany than in East Germany, but also in East Germany earnings differentials are significant. This comes as somewhat of a surprise, in light of the ideological and political commitment of official socialist policy to sexual equality. In reality, such policies have systematically failed to extend to women the socialist notion of egalitarianism, thereby explaining the evidenced, statistically significant differences in remuneration (Winkler 1990a, 1990b; Stephan and Wiedemann 1990). At this point, it is difficult to assess whether these differences are attributable to the past policies of the former Socialist Party in East Germany or to the present process of adaptation to West German remuneration mechanisms brought about by the unification of the economic systems and currencies.

The relationship between education and income is consistent with expectations based on human-capital theory. Significant effects are evident for both East and West Germany. What is of more importance is the job-related knowledge that individuals are able to acquire during their working lives—captured by age as a

Table 7.3. Results of Structural Equation Models for East and West Germany (Standardized Coefficients, *t*-Value in Parentheses)

| | Measurement model | | | | | |
| | Reward model Income | | Just reward model Just income | | Justice evaluation model Material satisfaction | |
	West-G.	East-G.	West-G.	East-G.	West-G.	East-G.
Job income	1.000	1.000				
Deserved job income			1.000	1.000		
Satisfaction with income					.936	.818
Satisfaction with standard of living					.674	.520
	Structural model					
	West-G.	East-G.	West-G.	East-G.	West-G.	East-G.
Sociostructural Variables:						
Sex (1 = men)	.479***	.387***	−.012	.096**	−.131**	−.136**
	(12.868)[a]	(8.946)	(−.872)[b]	(2.859)	(−2.616)	(−2.388)
Education	.319***	.364***	.016	.209***	.103*	.055
	(8.379)	(8.394)	(1.269)[a]	(6.278)	(2.123)	(.924)
Age	.984***	.927**	.089	−.053	.068	.156**
	(3.900)	(3.072)	(1.124)	(−.244)	(1.506)	(2.993)
Age²	−.795**	−.895**	−.044	.135		
	(−3.099)	(−2.949)	(−.562)	(.616)		
Firm size (1 = small firms)	−.076*	−.038	.009	−.013	.071	−.081
	(−2.088)	(−.887)	(.773)	(−.391)	(1.667)	(−1.562)
Type of organization (1 = public sector)	−.043	.096*	−.019	.140***	−.056	−.028
	(−1.129)[a]	(2.168)	(−1.606)[a]	(4.369)	(−1.215)	(−.518)

Comparison Process:				
Income	.957*** (67.843)[a]	.511*** (14.754)	.602** (3.343)[c]	.237*** (3.572)
Just income			−.472** (−2.635)[c]	−.181* (−2.175)
Microjustice Force:				
Underreward	.235*** (18.838)[a]	.412*** (12.897)	−.258*** (−4.065)	−.267*** (−4.171)
Overreward	−.008 (−.607)[a]	.111*** (3.657)	−.011 (−.244)	−.010 (−.192)
Need	.054*** (4.719)[c]	.052* (1.982)	−.164** (−3.679)	−.281*** (−5.411)
Referential Comparison				
(below average)	.031** (2.617)	.023 (.732)	−.038 (−.791)	−.053 (−1.021)
(above average)	.003 (.228)	.028 (.918)	.123** (2.774)	.181*** (3.687)
Macrojustice Force:				
Inegalitarianism	.001 (.046)	−.063* (−2.105)	.131** (3.077)	.109* (2.162)
Egalitarianism	.011 (.981)	.049 (1.626)	−.108** (−2.512)	.007 (.143)
R^2	.946	.647	.393	.391

	West-G.	East-G.
R^2	.407	.291
n	454	412
Chi-square	37.562	68.337
df	22	22
GFI	.991	.982
Bentler's Comparative Fit Index	.990	.953

*** $p_t < .001$. ** $p_t < .01$. * $p_t < .05$; group comparison with Lagrangian multiplier test: [a] $p < .001$. [b] $p < .01$. [c] $p < .05$.

variable in our modeling. However, the significant effect of age on net earnings is evident only in West Germany. Much of the firm-specific and job-related knowledge that East Germans have gained from previous employment experiences is not applicable to the needs of the West German labor market. The more sophisticated level of high technology in West Germany is a frequently cited cause of this value depreciation of their work experience (Bellmann 1992; Schwarze 1991a, 1991b).

Individuals employed in small firms in West Germany earn less than those employed in large firms. In East Germany, employment in the public sector has a positive effect on net earnings; firm size on the other hand does not. Thus, reliable predictors for net earnings in West Germany are those usually found to be of relevance in Western industrial societies. Deviations from this pattern are still evident in East Germany. The main difference between East and West Germany that the group comparison reveals lies, first, in the stronger effect of the respondent's sex on income in West Germany and, second, in the differential effect of employment type (private vs. public sector). Civil servants have a greater likelihood of earning more in East Germany than in West Germany.

The Just-Reward Model

In the Just-Reward Model in Table 7.3, the effects on individuals' notions of just earnings in logarithmic form are determined. This model includes as an independent variable the net income, also in logarithmic form, thereby allowing us to control for the direct and indirect effects of the variables sex, education, age, firm size, and type of organization. Direct income effects are visible in both East and West Germany. Because individuals employed in small West German firms are faced with lower actual earnings, they view higher earnings as just. On the other hand, individuals employed outside the public sector (in the private sector or as self-employed individuals) demand higher just earnings, although their factual income level is higher than that of the civil servants. In East Germany, the effect is reversed. Civil servants have higher earnings and regard an even higher level of earnings as just. This suggests that East Germans make comparisons with similarly employed West Germans and explains the positive effects for male and highly educated employees as well. Individuals take their own qualities and attributes into consideration, as well as their position of employment to make comparisons with West German employees who are similar to them in this respect. This inevitably leads to the viewpoint that an adequate income would have to be at a higher level. It also means that in East Germany it would be a mistake to ignore the effect of sociostructural variables. They are even stronger predictors of individual sentiments toward just earnings in East Germany than they are in West Germany.

In both populations it is true, however, that a large part of the explained variation for just earnings is attributed to actual earnings. This finding is consistent with results found in other studies and underscores the validity of Homan's statement, cited above, that the ought is determined in the long run by the is. This effect is stronger, however, for West Germany than for East Germany, as the statistical parameter comparison between both groups reveals. This is also most likely the result of the higher earnings level in West Germany, which serves as a reference point for individuals in their perceptions of a just income.

In addition to these sociostructural variables, the Just-Reward Model also includes variables that measure the microjustice force according to the expanded core of Equation (12). The saliency of these measures is apparent. Individuals who feel underrewarded demand a higher just income. This causal link may be found in both East and West Germany. Moreover, even East Germans who state that they are overrewarded, that is, who receive more than they feel that they are justly entitled to, demand that their wages be higher in order to be considered just. A shift in the unit of comparison is a likely explanation of this phenomenon. East Germans who make evaluations about the adequacy of their earnings in terms of overrewardedness look to other East Germans for a point of reference. When making justice judgments about their actual earnings, however, East Germans tend to look beyond their neighbors's fence, and use the earnings of West Germans as a basis of comparison (Adler 1991a). A similar argument applies to referential comparisons in which respondents see themselves as "below average." In the West this comparison raises the just income significantly, but this is not so in East Germany. Obviously, because of the fact that until recently East German income differences were rather small, present comparisons with job-holders in similar jobs are not of relevance for their perception of a just income. However, in terms of their general sense of over- or underrewardedness, East Germans compare themselves with West German income earners.

However, the main effect of underreward is much stronger than that of overreward in both East and West Germany. This result confirms Jasso's expectation that underreward is felt more keenly than overreward. It is also consistent with the result that individuals who state that they need higher household incomes incorporate this needs component into their just income demands. In this sense, we find, especially for West Germany, a high level of significance of the need variable. It can be argued that this is so because, in West Germany, household income coincides more often with individuals' net income, since the labor force participation of wives is not as common in West Germany as it is in East Germany.

Finally, including also the beliefs in macrojustice principles in the model reveals that East Germans who have strong inegalitarian justice beliefs have lower just income demands. It should be noted that this also tends to be true for East Germans with an high egalitarian conviction (t-value $= -1.626$). We take this as evidence that in East Germany the transformation process has not yet brought about a consistent structure of justice beliefs. In West Germany both kinds of justice beliefs do not affect just-reward claims at all.

Comparing the estimates of the sociostructural variables across both parts of Germany statistically shows that, whereas in West Germany, women view higher earnings as just, in East Germany it is the men who harbor similar sentiments. The level of education has a greater influence on the perception of just earnings in the East than in the West. This is also the case for individuals who are public sector employees. Thus, men, those who are higher educated, and the civil servants in East Germany feel that they are unjustly rewarded at this stage of the transformation.

The Justice Evaluation Model

Using the same independent variables as in the Just-Reward Model, we determine the effects of these variables on the satisfaction of material well-being. By including the just-reward variable as an independent variable, that is, just income in logarithmic form, we are able to expand the Justice Evaluation Model, as outlined in Equation (13).

The degree of satisfaction with material well-being is determined to a large extent by the perceived level of income sufficiency. This can be inferred from the strong effects both actual and just incomes have, the sign of just income being negative, as the application of Jasso's ratio would require. It also agrees with the core model for justice evaluations that feelings of underreward exercise a much stronger effect on satisfaction scores than feelings of overreward. Equivalently, respondents who say that their household income is less than what they would need are less satisfied. Those who perceive their individual income as above average, in comparison to similar jobholders, are significantly more satisfied than those with below average income. With regard to these variables then, the Justice Evaluation Model, applied to satisfaction with material well-being, is in full agreement with the predictions. This is true for East and for West Germany, though, as the group comparison reveals, the influence of Jasso's ratio is statistically somewhat stronger in the West than in the East (see also Chapter 5 in this volume).

Out of the two macrojustice distribution principles, the indicator for economic inegalitarianism has a positive effect on satisfaction with material well-being in both populations. Individuals who support this principle internalize its values and apply them to their own lives. They believe that this principle works and that their own success is closely linked to the realization of it. Thus these individuals also claim to be more satisfied with their material living conditions. In contrast, the egalitarian justice belief reduces satisfaction, this being so, however, only in West Germany.

One interesting feature of how the macrojustice principles affect satisfaction differently in East and West Germany can be drawn from Table 7.4. We include this table in order to demonstrate the differential explanatory power of the groups of variables added to Jasso's original formulation. Restricted to the Justice Eval-

Table 7.4. Hierarchical Justice Evaluation Models, Excluding Sociostructural Variables (Standardized Coefficients, t-Values in Parenthesis)

Structural model	Material satisfaction		Material satisfaction		Material satisfaction		Material satisfaction	
	West-G.	East-G.	West-G.	East-G.	West-G.	East-G.	West-G.	East-G.
Comparison process (Jasso ratio)								
Income	1.238***	.498***	.697***	.333***	.526**	.209**	.475**	.202**
	(10.939)	(7.117)	(4.257)	(4.543)	(3.018)	(2.906)	(2.863)	(2.813)
Just income	−1.112***	−.445***	−.562***	−.219**	−.411**	−.173*	−.376**	−.158*
	(−9.809)	(−6.374)	(−3.401)	(−2.686)	(−2.644)	(−2.170)	(−2.597)	(−2.085)
Microjustice force								
Underreward			−.293***	−.342***	−.306***	−.284***	−.297***	−.293***
			(−4.999)	(−5.199)	(−4.993)	(−4.327)	(−4.725)	(−4.484)
Overreward			−.006	−.062	−.011	−.014	−.001	−.010
			(−.134)	(−1.109)	(−.253)	(−.247)	(−.107)	(−.182)
Need					−.167***	−.284***	−.171***	−.279***
					(−3.788)	(−5.308)	(−3.793)	(−5.257)
Referential comparison								
(below average)					−.008	−.065	−.026	−.060
					(−.169)	(−1.228)	(−.545)	(−1.126)
(above average)					.115**	.197***	.137**	.187***
					(2.624)	(3.705)	(3.064)	(3.579)
Macrojustice force								
Inegalitarianism							.123**	.101*
							(2.837)	(2.129)
Egalitarianism							−.135**	.014
							(−3.140)	(.271)
R^2	.198	.166	.247	.235	.305	.357	.366	.369
n	454	412	454	412	454	412	454	412
GFI	.989	.969	.989	.979	.990	.981	.991	.982
Bentler's Fit Index	.979	.933	.978	.942	.988	.946	.990	.953

*p < .05.   **p < .01.   ***p < .001.

uation Model only, Table 7.4 presents hierarchical model estimates, beginning with the inclusion of only the Jasso ratio (in linear form, of course), then successively adding the variables of the microjustice force (overreward/underreward, household needs, referential comparison) in the next models and, finally, including also the macrojustice force in terms of the two inegalitarianism and egalitarianism items. What is most noteworthy for the present context is that, in West Germany, adding the macrojustice beliefs raises R^2 from .305 to .366; in East Germany the respective increase is much smaller. We conclude from this that the micro-/macrojustice consistency is much stronger in West compared to East Germany.

In addition to these effects, respondents' sex is an important determining factor. In general, women indicate that they are more satisfied than men. Particularly in East Germany, this comes as a surprise, since women have been forced into the category of the "losers" in the transformation process. Women are faced with fewer employment alternatives in their struggle to subsist under the new and devastating labor market conditions (Blaschke et al. 1992; Brinkmann et al. 1992). However, our sample includes only those women who were successful at retaining their jobs despite the turmoil of the reunification. Assuming that these women compare themselves to the East German female "losers," then their greater satisfaction becomes a matter of course.

In summarizing we find that the results of our study confirm the laws of justice psychophysics quite impressively, but that in application to the real world it is necessary to apply the distributive-justice force by considering extensions. As can be seen most clearly from Table 7.4, only the inclusion of special constraints that are related to both the microjustice and the macrojustice force and to sociostructural determinants will provide justice psychophysics with enough explanatory strength to be of predictive value. Restricting the Justice Evaluation Model to only the comparison process, to Jasso's ratio that is, we are able to explain just 19 percent of variation in West Germany and 17 percent in East Germany (Table 7.4), but considering the model expansions, these values approach the 40 percent mark.

DISCUSSION

The acceptance of prevailing mechanisms of distribution has taken a forefront position in the present difficult process of transformation in Germany. Noll sees a possible cause "in the collective conviction of a relative deprivation of the East German population" (1992b:9), not least resulting from "the separate tariff regulations that conflict with the generally recognized principle of equal pay for equal effort" (ibid.). Certain mechanisms of distribution have a direct effect on the income that individuals have at their disposal. This makes the distribution of earnings a measure of success or possibly failure when assessing the politics of unification. The promise of improvements in living standards to bring East Germany up to par with West German standards is slow to unfold, and for many East Germans, it is simply too slow. The acceptance and even legitimacy of factual distributive structures is open for debate. In fact, various crisis scenarios predict increased conflict and the intensification of resource competition. Their existence points to the urgency of the rapid correlation of East German wages with West German wages. Separate tariff policies and a dual system of remuneration are acceptable only on an exceptional basis. As soon as this situation turns into the norm, the acceptance disappears and conflict ensues. This potential for conflict can become a "threat to the legitimation of the political order and to the loyalty to the system" (ibid.).

Up against this background, in this chapter we have looked at the differential justice evaluations of personal earnings in East and West Germany, making this the cornerstone of this study. The Reward Model, the Just-Reward Model, and the Justice Evaluation Model served as the theoretical framework. According to Jasso's distributive-justice theory, and to its extended formulation by Shepelak and Alwin (1986) and Alwin et al. (1992), justice evaluations are a salient determinant of the subjective well-being of individuals. Its measurement serves as an important instrument that may be used to predict individuals' satisfaction with their material well-being.

Our study offers a confirmation of the psychophysical model in many respects, although it also showed that the impact of sociostructural factors deserves equal consideration. The level of one's own income is of primary importance in determining evaluations of the just level of earnings. Nevertheless, subjective attitudes toward over- and underreward took on a different meaning. One difference between East and West Germany was evident in the stronger effect of actual earnings in West Germany. Another was the positive effect that feeling over-rewarded elicited in East Germany. We interpret this to mean that, whereas the East German population bases its justice evaluations of earnings on the corresponding reference group in the West, it bases its evaluation of the appropriate earnings on reference groups in the East. For justice evaluations in East Germany, structural variables, like education, employment type, and sex are of additional importance.

Terms estimated from the Justice Evaluation Model are good predictors of the level of satisfaction with material living conditions. Apart from the households' general financial situation, the most important determinants of subjective well-being include both objective factors, meaning primarily disposal of material resources, and subjective factors, like justice sentiments on the level of micro- as well as macrojustice principles. Although East and West Germany differ in their satisfaction with material well-being, the causal attribution explaining these differences is, for both regions of Germany, relatively similar.[10] The transformation process appears to be less a matter of "growing together," than of East Germany assimilating to West German ways of thinking and behaving.

We also emphasize that especially the justice sentiments existing during the time of the former East Germany continue to have a strong effect on individuals' subjective well-being. This is reflective of the uneasy alliance existing within East Germany: between East Germans' willingness to accept and to legitimize new distribution mechanisms on the one hand and their awareness of the effect of such mechanisms on individual outcomes, especially in the form of earnings, on the other. It is futile to speculate over the future intensity of resource competition in Germany. However, the present situation is critical enough to allow us to reasonably conjecture the imperativeness of working toward the rapid reduction of the differential standards of living in East and West Germany.

The contribution social justice research can offer in this context is that it can direct attention to the psychophysical regularities with which individuals perceive and evaluate justice. Applying this knowledge to justice responses in the real world, however, calls for expanding the core of justice psychophysics and for incorporating social, political, and attitudinal effects on our justice judgments. As this example demonstrates, social justice research cannot be applied to areas of political and practical importance without also taking into account approaches that go beyond reconstructing the individual-related justice judgments empirically, but it also requires us to study the likely influence of normative and ideological justice beliefs on microjustice judgments. While it may be important for justice researchers to work in relative isolation in their different special domains in order to pursue the growth of knowledge within these specialities, we argue that the interest the public will take in this knowledge demands that we begin to open up to the possibilities of the interdisciplinarity of justice studies.

NOTES

1. Jasso (1980) mentions an additional set of questions: What are the behavioral and social consequences of perceived injustice? In our view, however, this goes beyond the mere distributive-justice force since it involves the more general problem of how attitudes determine behavior (see Swift et al. in this volume).

2. Linear: Alves and Rossi (1978), Alves (1982); square root: Jasso and Rossi (1977); exponential: Jasso (1978).

3. *PP may* refer to observables since x may name or describe some entity that is composed in part of concrete physical objects. But *PP* may also refer to completely abstract entities.

4. A frame for a theory is then defined as $F = \langle P, PP, r, M \rangle$; $M \subseteq P$ and $PP \subseteq P$, r representing a function mapping P into PP.

5. A core thus represents an extension of a particular frame for a theory consisting of the elements $\langle P, PP, r, M, C \rangle$. To the extent that the core H for a theory is directed toward a specific area of intended application I, that theory is defined as $T = \langle H, I \rangle$, if $I \subseteq PP$.

6. In order to be applicable to different sets of intended applications I, special constraints C_L with regard to those possible partial models for which the laws L are to

apply must be included in the expanded core along with a specific binary relation α, which assigns members of PP to laws in L. Omitting the apparatus of formal definitions for L, C_L and α, the expanded core for a theory may be expressed as $E = \langle P, PP, r, M, C, L, C_L, \alpha \rangle$.

7. With the nonstatement view of theories, a number of problems can be solved that have burdened the philosophy of science for a long time. One of these problems has been the *problem of theoretical terms*. Very simply, this problem consists in the fact that it is logically impossible to define what a theoretical term is independent from the theory of which that term is a part; therefore, it is impossible to define what a theoretical term is. Carnap's (1954) attempt to circumvent this impossibility by postulating two different kinds of languages, one theoretical and one empirical, did not prove successful. Only if predicates of theories are understood as set-theoretical extensions of other predicates of these theories can the circularity of defining theoretical terms be eliminated (Ramsey 1965).

8. We use maximum-likelihood parameter estimates for all models that follow.

9. Based on our samples, the mean monthly net income is 2984 D-Marks in West Germany, and 1288 in East Germany. East German women receive 1143, East German men 1417; in West Germany women receive 2292, men 3214.

10. The means for the item measuring satisfaction with one's *earnings* was higher in West Germany (4.49, coefficient of variation .328) than in East Germany (3.10, coefficient of variation .519). Similarly, the means for the item measuring satisfaction with the *standard of living* was higher in West Germany (5.23, coefficient of variation .246) than in East Germany (4.51, coefficient of variation .305).

III
IDEOLOGY AND JUSTICE

8

Accounting for the Rich and the Poor: Existential Justice in Comparative Perspective

James R. Kluegel, György Csepeli, Tamás Kolosi,
Antal Örkény, and Mária Neményi

The rich and the poor personify economic inequality. Whereas the concept of distributive justice applied to society as a whole is quite abstract, the rich and poor in a given society are quite real and quite visible. In addition, their visibility beyond that in daily life is promoted by their use as political symbols (Edelman 1971; Lewis 1978).

Put in terms of contemporary social science theories of justice (Alwin 1992a; Brickman et al. 1981), perceptions of the rich and the poor provide a vehicle for studying how the public evaluates existential macrojustice. Studying popular explanations for the rich and the poor gives us insight into the perceived legitimacy (justice) of the stratification order in fact (cf. Della Fave 1980, 1986a, 1986b). Except in the case where complete equality is held to be the standard of justice, the stratification order is working as it should if both the rich and the poor are seen as deserving their fates. On the other hand, should either or both be seen as predominantly undeserving, it may occasion demands for political action or in the extreme cause people to strongly doubt or reject the legitimacy of the prevailing normative justifications for inequality. Popular beliefs about who is responsible for poverty and wealth strongly affect a wide range of public attitudes toward inequality-related policy in the United States (Feagin 1975; Iyengar 1990; Kluegel and Smith 1986; Bobo and Kluegel 1993). Research reported in Chapter 4 of this book shows that these beliefs are consequential for support of government intervention to reduce inequalities in advanced capitalist countries more broadly.

The study of popular explanations of wealth and poverty to date has been pursued primarily in English-speaking countries, and mainly in the United States. Furthermore, little of this research is truly comparative, i.e., using the same sampling procedures and measures in all countries studied. This chapter presents research expanding the scope of our comparative understanding of popular explanations of wealth and poverty. Here we examine beliefs about wealth and poverty in twelve nations: Bulgaria, Czechoslovakia, Estonia, Germany (both the former East and West), Great Britain, Hungary, Japan, the Netherlands, Poland, Russia, Slovenia, and the United States.

THEORY

The central question addressed by research on popular explanations for wealth and poverty is, Do people explain poverty and wealth primarily in individualist or social terms, and why? Though the opposites are not logically precluded, to see poverty and wealth in individualist terms—to see it respectively as the product of negative or positive personal traits—is to see the stratification order as legitimate, hence fair. To see poverty and wealth as the product of social factors— as due to lack of opportunity or the failure of the economic system to provide jobs—implies that the existing order is seen in some measure as illegitimate, hence unfair. Explanations of wealth, however, are an exception in that wealth may be attributed to either positive traits such as hard work and ability, or negative traits such as dishonesty and corruption. Prior research (Kluegel and Smith 1986) has shown both types of explanations of wealth are prevalent in the United States.

In addition to comparative analysis of data, we also take a comparative approach to theory testing. Several scholars offer theories of the legitimation of inequality in industrial societies from which we may derive hypotheses about country-level and individual-level differences in popular explanations of poverty and wealth. As we will develop below, some of these theories give competing hypotheses. Theories also differ in focusing on extraindividual, or macrolevel, factors such as ideology and social structure versus focusing on individual or microlevel factors such as psychological motives and self-interest calculations. In our analyses we will compare the merits of hypotheses taken from major theoretical perspectives on legitimation that concern both macrolevel and microlevel determinants of popular explanations of poverty and wealth. We will also compare how theories developed for the case of stable Western, capitalist countries apply in the transition countries of Central and Eastern Europe.

Macrolevel Factors in Capitalist Countries

Dominant Ideology. An influential perspective on the macrolevel determination of stratification beliefs has been labeled the "dominant ideology thesis"—as summarized by Abercrombie, Hill, and Turner:

> The [dominant ideology] thesis argues that in all societies based on class divisions there is a dominant class which enjoys control of both the means of material production and the means of mental production. Through its control of ideological

production, the dominant class is able to supervise the construction of a set of coherent beliefs. These dominant beliefs of the dominant class are more powerful, dense and coherent than those of the subordinate classes. The dominant ideology penetrates . . . the consciousness of the working class, because the working class comes to see and to experience reality through the conceptual categories of the dominant class. (1980:1)

Of most relevance to our concerns is the place of individualistic explanations of poverty and wealth as part of the dominant ideology in capitalist societies. Several scholars (Anderson 1974; Feagin 1975; Offe 1976; Therborn 1980) have proposed that promulgating individualistic explanations of economic success and failure legitimates inequality under capitalism. From the dominant-ideology perspective we may derive two hypotheses about individualistic explanations of poverty and wealth in capitalist nations:

Hypothesis 1: *In capitalist societies, positive individualistic explanations of wealth and negative individualistic explanations of poverty are more prevalently held by the public than are social explanations.*

Hypothesis 2: *In capitalist societies, individualistic explanations of wealth and poverty prevail among all classes. In other words, economic groups (classes) in capitalist societies will differ little among themselves in the level of adherence to individualistic explanations and rejection of social explanations.*

The dominant-ideology thesis argues that not only will the overall level of adherence to an individualistic interpretation of the causes of poverty and wealth be high (Hypothesis 1), but it will be uniformly held by the more and less privileged. In other words, according to the dominant-ideology thesis, in capitalist societies individualistic interpretations are consensually held. It also is implicit in the dominant ideology thesis that acceptance of individualistic explanations in effect drives social explanations from the popular consciousness of inequality, i.e., an uncritical or wholesale acceptance of economic inequality as legitimate results. A key component of Hypotheses 1 and 2, then, is the proposed *rejection of social explanations* of poverty and wealth simultaneous with the *acceptance of individualistic* ones.

Critique of the Dominant-Ideology Thesis. Abercrombie, Hill, and Turner offer a broad-ranging critique of the dominant-ideology thesis, elaborated over a decade in three books (1980, 1986, 1990), that essentially makes two major assertions. First, their critique questions the extent to which beliefs justifying inequality espoused by the most privileged are in fact "dominant," i.e., it claims that much more disagreement among economic classes regarding justifying beliefs promulgated by the privileged exists than is proposed by the dominant-ideology thesis. In their view, the stability of the stratification order results more from "dull economic compulsion" than from indoctrination.

Second, they question the link between capitalism and individualism (Abercrombie et al. 1986). Pointing especially to the case of Japan, Abercrombie et al. (1986) argue that individualism does not necessarily develop as a consequence of advanced capitalism. They argue that more attention must be paid to history and culture as autonomous factors, shaping ideology independent of class interests.

Historical and cultural differences may lead to substantial differences among capitalist countries in the use of individualist versus structural attributions. The United States is unique among the countries in this study in its long period of frontier development and the individualism that this nurtured. As underscored by Rimlinger (1971), these countries also differ in historical political traditions. The United States, according to Rimlinger, shares with Great Britain the liberal tradition, stressing individual rights and responsibilities. Accordingly, we might expect to find similar levels of attribution to individualist causes of wealth and poverty in these two nations. However, Northern Europe historically has been characterized by what Rimlinger has called a "patriarchal tradition"—where the government has taken an active role in providing for basic wants and needs of individuals. This has served as the basis for welfare state developments in Northern Europe, and may discourage individualist attributions of poverty (in our case in West Germany and the Netherlands), at least to the extent that government actions are seen as responsible for producing inequality. The collectivist emphasis in Japanese history and culture (Abercrombie et al. 1986; Hofstede 1984) may produce a lower level of adherence to individualist explanations and a higher level of adherence to social explanations of poverty and wealth in Japan than found in the United States and Great Britain, which occupy the individualist end of the cultural spectrum.

Split Consciousness. What may be labeled the *split consciousness* perspective has its roots in the work of Gramsci (Sassoon 1987), but aspects of it have been elaborated by numerous other scholars (Cheal 1979; Halle 1984; Mann 1973; Nichols and Armstrong 1976; Parkin 19712; Sennett and Cobb 1973; Therborn 1980; Willis 1977). The split-consciousness perspective proposes that beliefs about social inequality are formed by two broad influences. First, they are the product of inculcation of dominant-ideology beliefs. Second, beliefs are the product of everyday, stratification-related experience. Beliefs of this second kind may be labeled "challenging beliefs" (Kluegel and Smith 1986). Split-consciousness theory represents a kind of compromise between the strong claim of total acceptance of elite-promulgated stratification ideology made in the dominant-ideology thesis, and the claim by Abercrombie et al. that the dominant ideology essentially has no influence.

Split-consciousness perspectives propose that dominant and potentially challenging beliefs may coexist without any necessary force toward change. They may be in Lane's (1962) terms "compartmentalized," or in the terms of Sennett and Cobb (1973) people may maintain "divided selves," i.e., some people may rarely if at all bring them together in their consciousness. The two types of beliefs may also be more actively accommodated by forming composite explanations that incorporate both dominant-ideology and challenging beliefs (Hochschild 1981; Kluegel and Smith 1986).

Above we identified negative individualist explanations of poverty and positive individualist explanations of wealth as *dominant-ideology* beliefs in capitalist societies. Social explanations of poverty and wealth, and negative individualist explanations of wealth may be seen as *challenging* beliefs in capitalist societies. Applying the split-consciousness perspective to beliefs about the causes of poverty and wealth yields the following hypotheses:

Hypothesis 3: *In capitalist societies, items measuring individualist and social explanations of poverty and wealth form independent factors, and the correlation between these factors is low.*

Hypothesis 4: *Economic groups (classes) in capitalist societies differ little among themselves in the level of adherence to negative individualistic explanations of poverty and positive individualist explanations of wealth. Much more substantial differences exist, however, among economic groups in adherence to social explanations of poverty and wealth, and in negative individualist explanations of wealth.*

Hypothesis 3 follows from the proposition that dominant-ideology and challenging beliefs coexist. Hypothesis 4 follows from the proposition in the split-consciousness perspective that challenging beliefs respond more to everyday, stratification-related experience than do dominant-ideology beliefs.

Macrolevel Factors in Postcommunist Countries

History. We find it useful to briefly consider the historical bases of explanations of poverty and wealth in central and eastern Europe, i.e., their roots in economic and political structures of the recent past. We lack both space and expertise to discuss the relevant historical features of the economic and political structures of each country in our study. We focus instead on the case most familiar to the authors, Hungary. The economic and political histories of the other Central and Eastern European countries in this study, of course, differ in important ways from that of Hungary, and from one another. Nevertheless, they also share enough broad similarities of economic and political history to allow reasonable generalization from the Hungarian case.

In the several decades prior to its absorption into the Soviet Union, Hungary shared an economic structure heavily based in agriculture. Industrialization took place in urban areas, but at a very slow pace that made migration from rural to urban areas impossible. Poverty was rampant in the countryside. A weak capitalist economy struggled to exist alongside the predominant semifeudal economy.

Politically, this period was characterized by monarchy and other forms of authoritarian rule. The ruling political, economic, and bureaucratic elites showed little sympathy toward issues of economic inequality, perpetuating a conservative ideology that encouraged a censorious view of the poor. Poverty was explained as the consequence of laziness, drunkenness, and lack of moral or religious virtue. Conservative ideology, however, offered little justification of wealth beyond notions of noble birth or inherited superiority.

It is unsurprising then that the rich were ready targets for socialist movements of the Great Depression era, as wealth could find no justification in merit or equity explanations. The socialist condemnation of wealth as due to exploitation of the workers (Ferge 1986) joined the strongly latent antimonarchy sentiment to produce strongly negative and hostile attitudes toward wealth and toward rich people. National Socialism also encouraged hostility toward the rich by propagating a widely perceived false correlation between being rich and being a Jew (Csepeli 1991).

Restoring social justice was the leading ideological motive in Eastern Europe after World War II, following the forced establishment of state socialism. Although the official Communist ideology stressed egalitarianism, the state-socialist system proved unable to deter development of economic inequalities. Because of its inconsistency with official ideology, discussion of structural sources of poverty was forbidden, and the existence of wealth was denied. The public, however, was aware of both poverty and wealth. A 1976 survey of Hungarians found that the explanations of poverty and wealth that prevailed in the period prior to communist takeover appeared to have continued popularity well into the era of domination by the Soviet Union (Kolosi, Papp, Pal, and Bara 1980:138–39). In this study, only a minority of respondents denied the existence of wealth. Wealth was for the most part seen as a "social dysfunction," and frequently attributed to bureaucratic power, corruption, and inheritance. This study showed also that more than half of the working class and nearly a third of university graduates denied the existence of poverty or explained it as the result of individual failings on the part of the poor themselves. Other research showed that individualistic explanations of poverty played a dominant role in prejudice against Gypsies in Hungary (Tauber 1986).

Contemporary Ideology.   Although the dominant-ideology thesis has focused on capitalist societies, one might well apply its logic and dynamics to generate hypotheses about adherence to individual or social explanations of poverty and wealth in other types of societies. Until recently, of course, the postcommunist countries in our study were subject to the ideological influence of the Soviet government. At issue is the question of how much the influence of the years of Soviet communism persists, if at all.

During the several years prior to our survey in 1991, the elite-promulgated ideology in these countries increasingly promoted notions of market justice. However, the virtues of market vs. socialist justice were matters of much debate among elites (cf. Yanowitch 1989). The number of years during which elites openly advocated market justice ideology differs among these countries, but in all cases it is small in comparison to the years of exposure to elite-promulgated justifications of socialist justice. One might well question the success of elite efforts to promote notions of market justice in the face of internal divisions and in light of the historical entrenchment of socialist justice notions. Indeed, there is evidence that the influence of one central tenet of the dominant stratification ideology under Soviet socialism continues: that egalitarian norms persist among the publics of the postcommunist countries (Mason and Sydorenko 1992; Csepeli and Örkény 1992a; Pakulski 1990; Connors 1991).

The dominant-ideology thesis leads one to expect that positive individualistic explanations of wealth prevail in capitalist societies. State socialist ideology, however, encouraged the view of wealth as the result of negative personal traits (Connors 1991). In Russia (Batygin 1989; Mason and Sydorenko 1992) and perhaps other postcommunist nations as well (Csepeli and Örkény 1992a) a widespread strain of hostility toward the well-to-do and elite privilege remains. The high valuation of equality may lead people to view wealth in general as illegitimate, and thereby the wealthy as possessing "personally illegitimate" traits as it were (Mason and Sydorenko 1992; Csepeli and Örkény 1992a). This gives the following additional hypothesis:

Hypothesis 5: *In postcommunist societies negative individualistic explanations of wealth prevail.*

Interestingly, if the influence of another important tenet of the Soviet-promulgated dominant ideology persists, then we would expect to find that the same kinds of beliefs about poverty hold in capitalist and postcommunist countries. In both capitalist and postcommunist countries, poverty should predominantly be seen as the product of negative individual factors. In official Soviet ideology state socialist societies are "classless" and equal opportunity is present (Ossowski 1963; Pakulski 1990). Since in the respective "official ideologies" of both capitalist and state socialist societies equality of opportunity exists, it follows that in both cases the perception of poverty as the product of individual failings is encouraged.

In all postcommunist countries, the recent history is one of declining standards of living and increasing poverty. On its face, this growing poverty seems to question individualist explanations and encourage social explanations of poverty. On the other hand, as noted above, individualist explanations are rooted in the political and economic structures of the recent past in Eastern Europe and were encouraged or at least not discouraged under Soviet rule. This suggests that split consciousness also may characterize postcommunist countries, and indeed may be more pronounced. That is, the dire economic problems faced in the transition may strongly dispose people toward social explanations of poverty that are added to historically and ideologically rooted individualistic explanations.

Microlevel Processes

Some scholars have called upon social psychology theory and research to explain the prevalence of individualistic explanations of poverty and wealth. Della Fave (1980, 1986a, 1986b) argues that self-evaluation and status attribution processes serve to lead people in capitalist societies to believe that the wealthy deserve their privileged position. He proposes, however, that at the same time other aspects of the self-evaluation process dispose people to doubt that the stratification order is just; in his words:

> just as concentrations of wealth and power are impressive and generate legitima-
> tion, according to self-evaluation theory people find the asymmetrical power and
> control relationships generated by such concentrations inherently alienating. Thus
> the disadvantaged may utter "good reasons" for stratification while resenting it all
> along. (1986: 493)

Della Fave's perspective, then, gives the same prediction of split-consciousness theory regarding individualist and social explanations, i.e., they may coexist in the same persons.

Della Fave focuses on explanations legitimating the wealth of the rich, though a like argument has been applied to the poor as well. That is, the very poverty of the poor is taken as evidence that they have personal character deficits that make or keep them poor (cf. Kluegel and Smith 1986). Beyond this, people may be motivated out of what Lerner (1980) has called the just world belief to see the poor as responsible for their own fates. Attribution theory, through what has been labeled the "fundamental attribution error," holds that human cognition is in effect biased against situational (i.e., social) explanations and toward dispositional (i.e., individual) explanations of human action. Social-psychological theory suggests that at least in prosperous capitalist societies we need not appeal to macrolevel factors to account for the prevalence of individualistic explanations. Because these theories take the motives and cognitive processes they propose to be part of human nature, they should hold in capitalist and postcommunist countries alike. Social-psychological theory seems then to join macrolevel theory in predicting that individualistic explanations of poverty prevail in capitalist and postcommunist countries. The two seem, however, to differ regarding individualistic explanations of wealth. Strict generalization from the assumed universality of motives and cognitive processes biasing people toward individual explanations of human action implies that these theories predict the prevalence of individualistic explanations of wealth in both capitalist and postcommunist countries.

In all of the above perspectives on macrolevel influences, it is implicitly or explicitly assumed that those who benefit the most from a system of inequality— i.e., have the greatest self-interest in the existing order—endorse beliefs that justify it. These three perspectives differ however in the degree to which self-interest shapes the beliefs held by those who benefit the least. For dominant-ideology theorists, self-interest is an important latent force, but it is suppressed in advanced capitalism by elite-directed ideological indoctrination. For split-consciousness theorists, it has effects in one arena, but it does not affect core dominant-ideology beliefs. For the critique of dominant ideology, it presumably is free to have a broad-ranging influence.

Self-interest considerations direct our attention to the objective and subjective (perceived) statuses held by individuals. Recent work also directs our attention to persons' perceptions of the status' held by others, i.e., the perceived status distribution in a society (Wegener 1987; Evans, Kelley, and Kolosi 1992). Based upon results of a comparative study of Australia and Hungary, Evans et al. conclude:

> Centered in their own social milieu, most people see themselves in a middling position. As a result, high status people exaggerate the size of the higher classes and minimize the size of the lower classes, so envisioning a relatively equalitarian society. Conversely, low status people exaggerate the size of the lower classes which leads them to envision an elitist society. Prosperous people see others as prosperous while the poor see others as poor. (1992: 477)

The perceived-status distribution in society in turn may be linked to explanations of poverty and wealth through the "covariation principle" of attribution theory (Fiske and Taylor 1991), i.e., that people make causal inferences on the basis of rudimentary perceived covariation between attributes. The perceived-status distribution may shape the degree to which people infer it is possible for individual or social factors to be a cause of an outcome. For example, in the limiting case, if everyone is perceived to be poor, then people may infer it is not possible for poverty to be caused by individual traits, because no covariation can exist between individual traits and poverty. The reverse logic may also apply in that people may infer that if a small number of people are poor then it is unlikely that their behavior is due to a factor with a broad-ranging influence, i.e., a social cause. This then gives the following hypothesis:

Hypothesis 6:   *The larger the perceived middle class the greater the adherence to individualist beliefs and the less the adherence to social beliefs about poverty and wealth.*

This process then may result in a tendency in societies in which there is a large middle class, or at the least in societies where conditions permit people to perceive that most people are in the middle class, for individualist explanations to prevail. On the other hand, in societies where poverty is widespread and perceived to be increasing, we may expect to find that social explanations are more widely held.

Prior Research

Consistent with Hypothesis 1, survey-based research (Huber and Form 1973; Feagin 1975; Nilson 1981; Kluegel and Smith 1986) and qualitative research (Binzen 1970; Hochschild 1981; Lewis 1978) have shown the prevalence in the United States of blaming the poor personally for their own poverty, i.e., of attributing poverty to a lack of effort, poor morals, etc. This research also has shown that individualist explanations of wealth are prevalent. Americans strongly endorse the notions that the rich are rich because of superior personal attributes—hard work, willingness to take risks, exceptional abilities, and so on.

In contrast, explanations for poverty that appeal to social factors are not as broadly endorsed by the American public (Feagin 1975; Kluegel and Smith 1986). Similarly, individualist explanations of wealth are somewhat more prevalent than social ones (Kluegel and Smith 1986).

This research also gives initial support to Hypotheses 3 and 4. The American public does not view social and individualist explanations as mutually exclusive— many people endorse both types. Consistent with Hypothesis 3, two factors are needed to account for the correlations among responses to items used to measure social and individualist explanations (Kluegel and Smith 1986). There is only a small correlation between these two factors. Consistent with Hypothesis 4, social explanations of poverty, and less so for wealth, are more strongly affected by social status, race and other sociodemographic characteristics than are individualist explanations. Put another way, there is more consensus among the American public about individualist than about social explanations.

Research conducted outside the United States suggests that Hypothesis 3 holds in certain other nations. Factor-analytic studies in Great Britain and Australia also have found that the same two dimensions—social and individualist factors— underlay items used to measure explanations of poverty and wealth (Feather 1974; Furnham 1982 1983; Furnham and Lewis 1986). However, there also are indications—consistent with the argument of Rimlinger (1971)—that people in Northern European countries endorse individualist causes of poverty less often than the citizens of the United States and Great Britain (Coughlin 1980). We know virtually nothing about how these findings hold outside Western Europe and the United States. It is to this question, among others, that we now turn.

THE INTERNATIONAL DISTRIBUTION OF POVERTY
AND WEALTH EXPLANATIONS

The measure of explanations of poverty and wealth employed is based closely on instruments used in several studies (Feagin 1975; Kluegel and Smith 1986).

Respondents were asked, "In your view, how often is each of the following factors a reason why there are [poor/rich] people in [country] today?" They were asked to indicate if they believed that each factor listed below was (1) Very often, (2) Often, (3) Sometimes, (4) Rarely or, (5) Never a reason why there are [poor/rich] people. We presented respondents with three individualist reasons (numbers 1 through 3), and three social reasons (numbers 4 through 6) as potential causes respectively of poverty and wealth.

Poverty Factors
1. Lack of ability or talent (PABILITY)
2. Lack of effort by the poor themselves (PEFFORT)
3. Loose morals and drunkenness (PMORALS)
4. Prejudice and discrimination against certain groups in (COUNTRY) (PDISCRIM)
5. Lack of equal opportunity (POPPOR)
6. Failure of the economic system (PECONS)

Wealth Factors
1. Ability or talent (WABILITY)
2. Hard work (WHDWORK)
3. Dishonesty (WDISHON)
4. Having the right connections (WKNOW)
5. More opportunities to begin with (WOPPOR)
6. The economic system allows them to take unfair advantage (WECONS)

Hypotheses 1 and 4 call our attention to the distribution of individualistic and social explanations of poverty and wealth among countries. Table 8.1 is an array of *dominance scores*—the difference between the percentage of respondents who indicate that a given factor is Very often or Often a reason why there are poor or rich people and the percentage who indicate that they believe a given factor is Rarely or Never a reason—by country. These scores provide a measure of the relative importance given to individual and social causes of poverty and wealth.

There are three notable patterns in the distribution of explanations of poverty. First, hypothesis 1 is supported only for Japan. Although on balance our Japanese respondents deny the importance of lack of ability as a cause of poverty, they very strongly endorse lack of effort and poor morals. They also shade toward denial of social causes of poverty, with negative dominance scores for the attribution of poverty to discrimination or the lack of equal opportunity. Although among the other capitalist countries attribution to individualist factors is affirmed somewhat more often than it is denied, we also see that endorsement of social causes of poverty slightly dominates over rejection of them. Second, postcommunist and capitalist countries share similar profiles for the attribution of poverty and wealth to ability and effort. However, on average the attribution of poverty to poor morals is much higher in postcommunist than in capitalist countries (except Japan). Third, though the denial of discrimination is much stronger than in

Table 8.1   Dominance Scores for Explanations of Poverty and Wealth by Country[a]

	Poverty Explanation Items					
Country	PABILITY	PEFFORT	PMORALS	PDISCRIM	POPPOR	PECONS
Bulgaria	−6.5	27.6	37.6	−33.0	69.7	49.2
Czechoslovakia	−1.1	6.5	53.7	−40.9	17.2	29.7
E. Germany	−17.5	−10.1	39.9	14.6	27.8	18.0
Estonia	−11.5	17.3	51.8	−39.1	27.6	85.2
Hungary	20.2	−3.4	66.4	−15.4	38.7	65.1
Poland	11.0	26.7	72.2	−53.6	32.5	67.7
Russia	−9.0	9.8	76.3	−3.2	25.6	89.8
Slovenia	−9.4	1.5	31.9	−34.3	46.0	67.9
W. Germany	0.2	9.5	20.7	10.8	17.5	−4.3
Great Britain	11.3	15.1	5.0	9.3	15.4	36.7
Japan	−21.7	53.3	51.4	−24.0	−17.0	6.3
Netherlands	8.8	17.7	5.7	4.2	9.0	2.0
U.S.	13.2	36.9	22.4	16.8	8.3	27.7

	Wealth Explanation Items					
	WABILITY	WDISHON	WHDWORK	WKNOW	WOPPOR	WECONS
Bulgaria	19.9	65.4	32.3	84.8	77.2	62.0
Czechoslovakia	34.4	65.6	0.4	70.6	36.7	45.7
E. Germany	59.8	2.2	36.0	65.2	59.6	5.2
Estonia	38.2	79.2	−23.9	80.1	56.2	85.3
Hungary	46.0	60.0	4.6	64.8	45.1	36.8
Poland	26.3	56.3	−3.1	71.0	46.7	47.6
Russia	22.2	78.7	−18.9	87.0	31.1	79.4
Slovenia	42.5	52.9	−2.5	59.9	56.4	53.0
W. Germany	55.9	5.4	38.4	71.9	62.4	−12.1
Great Britain	46.2	14.4	40.5	75.3	60.2	32.2
Japan	56.5	−7.6	28.2	36.4	41.4	44.6
Netherlands	69.0	6.6	54.2	71.4	66.7	15.1
U.S.	52.3	24.2	57.6	72.4	54.7	17.3

[a] Individualist explanations are given in the first three columns and social explanations are given in the last three. Dominance scores equal the percent giving "often" or "very often" responses minus the percent giving "rare" or "never" responses.

capitalist countries, the endorsement of lack of equal opportunity and the failure of the economic system as causes of poverty is much higher in postcommunist countries. *In sum, with the exception of Japan, the view of poverty in capitalist countries is a mixed one with relatively equal percentages affirming and denying individualist and social causes of poverty. The view in postcommunist countries, except for the denial of discrimination, strongly emphasizes social causes, but combines this with strongly "moralistic" individualist blame.*

The view of wealth among respondents in our postcommunist countries is more consistently negative. Although they see ability or talent as often the cause of wealth, respondents in our postcommunist countries tend to be equally divided or to deny that wealth has come from hard work on the part of the rich. In addition, dishonesty is given great importance as a perceived cause of wealth; it was virtually a consensually held opinion in 1991. This pattern of prevailing negative individualist attributions for wealth shown in Table 8.1 gives strong support for hypothesis 3. This negative individualist view is matched by strong dominance of the attribution of wealth to social causes, giving an overall picture of a very negative view of wealth in postcommunist countries.

The view of wealth among our "capitalist" respondents is more mixed, but on balance is a much more positive one. Relatively equal percentages see the rich as often dishonest as see them as rarely or never dishonest. However, the "dishonesty" evaluation of the rich in capitalist countries is markedly lower than that prevailing in postcommunist nations. The attribution to ability or talent and hard work is high in absolute terms, and relative to the level in postcommunist countries as well. The high level of endorsement of "connections" and greater inherited opportunity suggests a composite view of the rich that includes both a sense that the rich have advantages others do not, and that they also deserve wealth on the basis of positive individual qualities. Though the dominance of endorsement of connections and greater opportunity is roughly equal in both regions, attributions to the economic system are markedly higher among respondents from postcommunist countries.

FACTOR STRUCTURES

Hypothesis 3 calls our attention to the factor structure underlying items measuring poverty and wealth explanations. Table 8.2 gives the results of model-fitting to test the hypothesis that a common factor structure underlies popular explanations of poverty and wealth. The results in this table are for a 10-item subset, excluding PABILITY and PDISCRIM.

Space considerations preclude giving all the factor analysis results in this chapter. In summary though, preliminary results show that the items attributing poverty to lack of ability (PABILITY) and discrimination (PDISCRIM), respectively, behave erratically in factor analyses. It appears that in some countries lack of ability is seen as an individual flaw, while in others it is viewed as extraindividually determined.[1] The item attributing poverty to discrimination (PDISCRIM) also was dropped for conceptual reasons. As seen in Table 8.1, there is a seeming contradiction in several of the postcommunist countries, where

Table 8.2. Tests of Fit of Factor Models for Correlations among Social and Individual Explanations of Poverty and Wealth[a]

Models

Country	One-factor (df = 35) Chi-Square	AGFI	Two-factor-A (df = 34) Chi-Square	AGFI	Two-factor-B (df = 34) Chi-Square	AGFI	Three-factor-A (df = 32) Chi-Square	AGFI	Three-factor-B (df = 32) Chi-Square	AGFI	Four-factor (df = 29) Chi-Square	AGFI	Five-factor (df = 26) Chi-Square	AGFI	Five-factor-Final (df = 22) Chi-Square	AGFI
Bulgaria	1791.6	0.62	1459.3	0.65	1083.3	0.77	746.4	0.84	522.0	0.87	439.3	0.88	353.7	0.90	205.4	0.93
Czechoslovakia	693.1	0.82	868.8	0.78	673.2	0.82	536.2	0.85	334.1	0.90	260.0	0.91	227.2	0.92	128.0	0.95
East Germany	554.7	0.84	554.4	0.83	500.6	0.85	402.0	0.87	263.3	0.91	234.1	0.92	223.2	0.91	196.6	0.95
Estonia	658.8	0.81	604.3	0.81	649.7	0.80	540.0	0.83	467.0	0.85	403.8	0.85	385.0	0.84	149.4	0.93
Hungary	508.8	0.84	460.2	0.85	576.9	0.83	511.2	0.84	282.3	0.90	204.0	0.93	185.7	0.92	77.1	0.96
Poland	771.4	0.85	746.1	0.85	721.8	0.85	797.7	0.86	401.0	0.92	344.7	0.92	297.4	0.93	195.9	0.94
Russia	1110.3	0.79	1355.6	0.73	1048.6	0.83	907.8	0.84	566.3	0.90	542.8	0.89	461.3	0.90	274.5	0.93
Slovenia	548.8	0.87	503.3	0.88	515.6	0.88	403.2	0.90	282.1	0.93	205.6	0.94	177.5	0.95	108.6	0.96
Great Britain	934.8	0.78	773.6	0.81	772.1	0.82	598.8	0.85	474.4	0.88	301.9	0.91	268.3	0.92	163.2	0.94
West Germany	1453.6	0.78	1334.5	0.79	1272.9	0.80	954.1	0.84	747.4	0.87	592.1	0.89	494.2	0.89	199.5	0.95
Japan	511.3	0.81	375.6	0.84	495.4	0.80	476.5	0.80	317.2	0.87	124.7	0.94	103.5	0.95	77.8	0.95
Netherlands	1761.6	0.71	1487.3	0.75	1748.1	0.73	1482.5	0.76	886.6	0.83	531.2	0.89	477.5	0.89	244.0	0.94
U.S.	1157.6	0.76	1413.6	0.67	956.5	0.80	786.0	0.82	625.3	0.86	432.8	0.89	293.2	0.92	195.3	0.93

[a] AGFI, adjusted goodness of fit index (Joreskog and Sorbom 1988). See text for descriptions of models tested. df, degrees of freedom.

a large percentage of respondents deny the importance of discrimination, but at the same time see lack of equal opportunity as an important cause of poverty. We speculate that this discrepancy may stem from a link between discrimination and the denial of equal opportunity to ethnic minorities. Ethnic homogeneity may play a role in producing the high rate of denial of discrimination as a factor in certain postcommunist countries. In countries with small ethnic minority populations, or where they lack visibility, it is quite possible that someone could perceive a denial of equal opportunity on class or status grounds, but see discrimination against ethnic minorities as rarely or never a cause of poverty. In light of the ambiguous meaning of the discrimination item, and because the item concerning the lack of equal opportunity provides a more general assessment of perceived social barriers to opportunity, we chose to employ it (POPPOR) alone.

We used maximum likelihood confirmatory factor analysis (Jöreskog and Sörbom 1989) to test separately in each country several hypotheses about the factor structures underlying explanations for poverty and wealth. We present the results of these hypothesis tests in Table 8.2. The first two columns give the results for testing the hypothesis that people think of poverty and wealth in a unitary fashion, viewing them along a single continuum from due exclusively to individualist causes to due to social causes. Values in the one-factor column test the strongest version of the "unitary" view, that people think of poverty and wealth along the same continuum. Values in the two-factor–A column test a weaker version, that people view the causes of poverty along one dimension and that they view the causes of wealth along a second, independent dimension. As seen in Table 8.2, the unitary-thinking hypotheses do not fare well. The chi-square values and adjusted goodness of fit indices show a very poor fit to the correlations in all countries.

Consequently, we developed and tested additional models incorporating different conceptual considerations. We sought in this process to find the fewest number of factors that provide the best fit to the correlations in each country. The two-factor–B column contains values from a model assuming that the correlations can be reproduced by two factors, one for items indicating social causes of wealth and poverty, and the second for individual causes. There is little to no improvement of fit over the two-factor–A model, and it also fits poorly. We next specified models with two factors for individualistic explanations of poverty and individualistic explanations of wealth. The models differ in whether the item attributing wealth to dishonesty (WDISHON) is considered to load on the individualist (two-factor–A) or the social explanation factor (two-factor b). Though conceptually WDISHON would seem best considered as an individualist explanation, fit diagnostic values from the two factor b model suggest that a better fit is achieved if it is grouped with the social explanation items. The values under the three factor–A and three-factor–B models show first that there is a significant improvement in fit in adding a third factor, and second that considering the attribution of wealth to dishonesty as a "social" explanation also results in a significantly better model. Though the fit of the three-factor–A model is for most countries significantly better than the two-factor models, a markedly better fit is achieved for the three-factor–B model. The adjusted goodness of fit index for this model in each country is near .9, a minimum value for judging the fit of a model to be adequate (Byrne 1989; Jöreskog and Sörbom 1988).[2]

We continued to seek a better fit by first estimating a four-factor model, specifying social poverty, social wealth, individualist poverty, and individualist wealth factors (WDISHON is assumed to load on the social wealth factor). The fit improved with this specification, and it continued to improve with a five-factor specification where the attribution of wealth to dishonesty is considered to be a single-item indicator of a separate factor. WDISHON is specified as the sole indicator of a negative individualist wealth factor. WABILITY and WHDWORK are specified as indicators of a positive individualist wealth factor. This five-factor specification follows from our earlier distinction made between positive and negative individualist explanations for wealth. The five-factor–FINAL model adds four terms for correlated errors to the five-factor model.[3]

Table 8.3 gives the loadings of items on four of the five factors (WDISHON is the only item specified to load on the fifth factor, and it is fixed at 1.0). There is a remarkable similarity among countries in the respective item loadings. Opportunity (WOPPOR) loads weakly on the Wealth Social factor in all countries, but all other items have moderate to high loadings in each country.

Table 8.4 gives the factor correlations, and provides evidence concerning hypothesis 3. We see here that this hypothesis is strongly confirmed as it involves explanations of poverty. In nine of the thirteen countries the correlation between the Poverty-Individual and Poverty-Social factors essentially is zero, and it is weak to moderate (with a high value of −.4) in the other four. Roughly the same pattern is found for the correlations between Poverty-Individual and Wealth-Social, and between Poverty-Social and Wealth-Individual Negative. Though the correlations between the Poverty-Social and Wealth-Individual Negative factors are consistently in the moderate range, we have seen that WDISHON behaves like an indicator of Social Wealth in all countries—thus we may see these as correlations between two social explanation factors. (Note also in this regard the weak correlations between the Poverty-Individual and Wealth-Individual Negative factors, and the moderate to high correlations between the Wealth-Social and Wealth-Individual Negative factors.) It is quite clear that respondents in all thirteen countries do not see individualist explanations of poverty as mutually exclusive of (or alternative to) social explanations of poverty or wealth. Correlations between the Wealth Individual Positive and Wealth Social factors are low to moderate on average, but within the range that gives general support to hypothesis 4.

Correlations between the two individual explanation factors are of consistently moderate value, and are quite high on average between the two social explanation factors. In all countries people are more consistent within types of explana-

Table 8.3. Factor Loadings from the Best-Fitting Model (Five-Factor-Final Model in Table 2)

Country	Poverty Individual		Poverty Social		Wealth Individual		Wealth Social		
	PMORALS	PEFFORT	POPPOR	PECONS	WABILITY	WHDWORK	WKNOW	WOPPOR	WECONS
Bulgaria	.67	.78	.68	.49	.64	.71	.62	.27	.41
Czechoslovakia	.59	.54	.43	.78	.59	.61	.47	.24	.79
East Germany	.63	.52	.58	.50	.69	.52	.45	.30	.65
Estonia	.59	.54	.63	.58	.60	.38	.43	.25	.80
Hungary	.72	.40	.63	.56	.75	.42	.71	.42	.56
Poland	.56	.57	.61	.52	.46	.68	.68	.30	.57
Russia	.48	.64	.29	.58	.56	.62	.59	.08	.41
Slovenia	.63	.46	.60	.60	.51	.51	.62	.30	.74
Great Britain	.56	.65	.55	.73	.69	.68	.37	.39	.98
West Germany	.56	.72	.70	.62	.70	.57	.36	.21	.62
Japan	.87	.64	.55	.95	.59	.66	.55	.54	.61
Netherlands	.61	.65	.69	.69	.61	.85	.43	.28	.78
U.S.	.72	.60	.52	.81	.51	.71	.47	.38	.65

Table 8.4. Correlations between Factors from the Best Fitting Model (Five-Factor-Final Model in Table 2)[a]

	PI,WIP	PI,PS	PI,WS	PI,WIN	PS,WS	PS,WIP	PS,WIN	WS,WIN	WIP,WIN	WIP,WS
Bulgaria	0.47	-0.05	0.20	0.10	0.84	-0.11	0.33	0.63	-0.27	-0.17
Czechoslovakia	0.39	-0.10	0.19	0.22	0.59	-0.16	0.33	0.54	-0.31	-0.35
East Germany	0.42	-0.11	0.16	0.16	0.83	-0.33	0.46	0.53	-0.18	-0.21
Estonia	0.56	-0.24	-0.03	0.11	0.45	-0.34	0.39	0.62	-0.33	-0.46
Hungary	0.30	-0.08	0.08	0.18	0.61	-0.20	0.40	0.57	0.06	-0.09
Poland	0.36	0.09	0.25	0.30	0.63	-0.22	0.44	0.66	-0.19	-0.15
Russia	0.55	-0.04	0.00	0.13	0.83	-0.36	0.39	0.76	-0.29	-0.32
Slovenia	0.41	0.17	0.29	0.29	0.70	-0.10	0.49	0.77	-0.33	-0.34
Great Britain	0.33	-0.41	-0.12	0.19	0.56	-0.12	0.23	0.36	-0.14	-0.36
West Germany	0.39	-0.17	0.04	0.19	0.75	0.04	0.28	0.68	-0.20	-0.36
Japan	0.56	0.03	0.40	0.15	0.30	0.40	0.35	0.53	0.08	0.35
Netherlands	0.37	-0.39	0.01	0.09	0.65	0.01	0.48	0.80	-0.32	-0.32
U.S.A.	0.26	-0.15	0.07	0.29	0.56	0.07	0.33	0.51	-0.24	-0.09

[a] PI, poverty-individual; PS, poverty-social; WIP, wealth-individual positive; WIN, wealth-individual negative; WS, wealth-social.

tion (individual or social) than between them. Indeed, the correlations between the POVERTY-SOCIAL and WEALTH-SOCIAL factors are such that we may conclude that most people consistently apply social explanations to poverty and wealth.

Taken together the results in Tables 8.2–8.4 argue that in all important respects we are measuring the same underlying constructs in all countries. Put another way, people in all thirteen of our countries view our items as indicative of the same interpretations of the causes of poverty and wealth. Importantly, this enables us to validly compare the determinants of explanations of poverty and wealth among our thirteen countries.

DETERMINANTS

To test hypotheses 4 and 6, we regressed four indices for explanations of poverty and wealth on measures of objective and "subjective" social and economic status. These indices follow from the factor analysis results above. POVERTY INDIVIDUAL equals the average of PMORALS and PEFFORT. POVERTY SOCIAL equals the average of POPPOR and PECONS. WEALTH INDIVIDUAL averages WABILITY and WHRDWORK. WEALTH NEGATIVE is the average of WKNOW, WECONS, and WDISHON. In forming WEALTH NEGATIVE we dropped WOPPOR because of its weak loadings on the Wealth-Social factor (Table 8.3), and because three of the four correlated errors needed to achieve a good fit involve this item; in general this is a poor item. We add WDISHON to the mix because our results show that it is highly correlated with the Wealth-Social factor, and for many of our countries a five-factor solution has only a marginally better fit over a four-factor solution with WDISHON loading on a factor with WKNOW and WECONS.

Social and Economic Status Measures. Age is measured in years, and we include an *Age-squared* term in the regression equations to allow for possible nonlinear patterns in the relationship of age to explanations of poverty and wealth. *Gender* is a 0, 1 variable, with 1 assigned to males. *Education* is measured in CASMIN levels, i.e., in seven categories from less than primary education to higher tertiary (König et al. 1988; see Appendix). We include three variables to tap the effects of job-based stratification-related experience. *Time unemployed* gives the amount of time in months that a respondent has spent unemployed. We measure job authority by an item asking for the total number of employees one supervises (*Number supervised*). The third of these is a 0, 1 variable, with 1 assigned to respondents reporting that they are *Self-employed*.

Perceived Status. Income need is based on the respondent's assessment of whether her or his family income is "much less than that needed," "somewhat less than that needed," "about what is needed," "somewhat more than needed," or "much more than needed"—on a scale from 1 to 5, with 5 indicating "much more than needed." This measure allows us to assess the effects of income in subjectively comparable terms. Perceived *Social standing* is measured on a ten-category scale with 1 low and 10 high. We include a measure of self-reported political ideology to determine if explanations of poverty and wealth are tied to broader political perspectives. *Liberalism* is measured on a ten-point scale, with 10 indicating perceiving oneself on the left of the political spectrum and 1 on the right (reverse coded from the response format in the questionnaire).

We also employed two measures of the perceived societal distribution of income. The first measure is based on two questions asking respondents to respectively indicate their estimate of the percentage of poor and of rich. *Middle percent* is formed by subtracting the sum of the perceived percentage of poor and rich from one hundred. The second measure is constructed from two items to give the perceived trend in inequality. Respondents were asked to indicate whether they thought the percentage of poor and rich, respectively, in their country would decrease, stay the same, or increase. We assigned a score of -1 to respondents choosing "decrease," 0 to those choosing "same," and $+1$ to those choosing "increase." The scores for the two items were summed to create *Trend in middle percent*, giving a measure varying from -2 to $+2$, with the high score indicating a strong perception that the middle class is getting smaller (the rich and poor percentages are both increasing) and the low score indicating a strong perception that the middle class is increasing (the rich and the poor percentages are both decreasing). The higher the value of Middle percent the *larger* is the perceived relative size of the middle class in a country. The higher the value of Trend in Middle Percent the *smaller* the middle class is perceived to become in the future.[4]

Table 8.5 gives means for perceived personal status, the perceived societal distribution of poverty and wealth, and self-rated liberalism by country. Reflecting the economic austerity prevailing in these countries at the time of the survey, the mean for Income need is markedly lower in postcommunist than in our capitalist nations. Although Social Standing is assessed relative to the distribution in a specific country, postcommunist respondents in general see themselves as having below-average status, and (with the exception of Japan) on average respondents from capitalist nations see themselves as occupying an above-average status. Wegener (1987) has spoken of a tendency for persons to overestimate their relative standing in the societal status hierarchy and has argued that there is consequently a bias toward what he labeled the "illusion of distributive justice." It appears that this holds for Western capitalist countries, except Japan; but among the postcommunist states the bias seems to be in the other direction. That is, among respondents in these nations, there may exist an illusion of distributive *injustice*.

Respondents in the postcommunist countries clearly perceive poverty as wide-

Table 8.5.   Country Means for Status Perceptions, Perceived Poverty and Wealth Distributions, and Self-Rated Liberalism-Conservatism[a]

	Social standing	Income need	Poor percent	Rich percent	Trend in middle percent	Liberalism
Bulgaria	3.92	1.53	43.27	19.69	1.46	5.93
Estonia	4.82	1.54	44.92	19.01	1.05	4.95
Russia	4.03	1.39	53.49	18.40	1.44	6.28
Czechosolvakia	4.64	2.05	22.89	21.36	1.17	5.13
East Germany	4.81	2.60	18.04	14.53	1.07	6.07
Hungary	4.24	1.87	49.84	19.53	1.21	5.77
Poland	4.51	1.63	36.67	23.28	1.23	5.15
Slovenia	4.28	2.00	39.14	24.15	0.85	6.05
Great Britain	5.29	2.44	23.59	21.68	0.78	5.42
West Germany	5.77	2.94	15.02	25.19	0.76	5.59
Netherlands	6.26	3.07	11.77	26.29	0.87	5.64
U.S.A.	5.81	2.46	26.55	20.66	0.82	5.42
Japan	4.32	2.54	11.77	20.59	0.49	5.14
Eta	0.43	0.56	0.59	0.18	0.29	0.19

[a] A high value of Social standing indicates higher perceived status. A high value of Income need indicates that one has more than one needs. A high value of Trend in middle percent indicates a perception that the middle class will get smaller in the future. A high value of Liberalism indicates stronger self-rated political liberalism

spread. Indeed, in the three Eastern European countries (Bulgaria, Estonia, and Russia) the mean percentage of poor is seen to be higher than the mean size of the middle class. The perception of poverty in Central Europe is quite varied, ranging from roughly one-fifth of the population on average in Czechoslovakia and East Germany, to nearly 50 percent in Hungary. Though the perceived percentage in poverty varies substantially among countries, the perceived percentage of rich varies little: from about one-fifth to one-quarter of the population is seen as rich. The perception of wealth then seems to be largely based on relative status, while the calculus of poverty is based more on considerations of absolute need.

On average, respondents in all of our nations see the middle class as shrinking in the future, i.e., see the percentages of rich and poor as increasing. Again, there are sizable differences between respondents from postcommunist and capitalist nations. There is an order of pessimism that flows generally from East to West, with Eastern Europeans being most pessimistic about the future of the middle class, followed by Central Europeans, and Western capitalist respondents— though respondents from our eastern capitalist state, Japan, are the most optimistic of all countries on average.

To the degree that these aspects of perceived personal and societal status influence explanations of poverty and wealth, we may potentially account for the differences observed in Table 8.1. To examine the nature and strength of this potential influence we conducted the regressions reported in Tables 6 and 7.

We conducted these regressions for four groupings of countries: (1) Eastern Europe combines respondents from Bulgaria, Estonia, and Russia, (2) Central Europe combines respondents from Czechoslovakia, East Germany, Hungary, Poland, and Slovenia, (3) the Western Capitalist grouping combines West Germany, Great Britain, the Netherlands, and the United States, and (4) Japan. The groupings are based on two considerations. First, they are grouped on conceptual grounds, to reflect common levels of experience and types of market economies. Eastern European countries share a lack of historical experience with a market economy prior to the ascendancy of communist rule and little contemporary experience with it before the fall of Soviet hegemony. Central European countries share both at least rudimentary experience before Soviet domination, and varying amounts, but at least some recent development of markets in the last several years before the collapse of Soviet rule. Our Western capitalist countries, of course, have highly developed market economies rooted in Western European cultures. Questions about the relative impact of culture and capitalism lead us to treat Japan as a separate grouping unto itself (cf. Abercrombie et al. 1986). We restrict analyses here to people currently in the labor force, to provide the most appropriate sample for testing the effects of job characteristics (Time unemployed, Number supervised, and Self-employed).[5] Second, they are grouped on empirical grounds, placing together countries that share similar profiles of perceived personal status and the perceived societal status distribution (Table 8.5). We also note that the regression equations of Tables 8.5 and 8.6 have been estimated individually within each of the thirteen countries. Though there are small variations within each of the four groupings, the regression coefficients from the individual country equations on the whole differ very little from those estimated within the pertinent country group. Categorical variables for the countries within each of three groupings (not, of course, for Japan) are included in the regressions to assess country differences net of the effects of individual-level variables.

Table 8.6 gives regression results for intermediate variables in the assumed causal ordering. We assume that the perceived status distribution and self-rated liberalism are in part products of objective and subjective personal status, and the predominant direction of causation is from these intermediate variables in turn to explanations. As seen in Table 8.6, the perceived size of the middle class is clearly shaped by personal status, and the influence is much the same in all four country groupings. Consistent with the view advanced by Evans et al. (1992), there is a marked tendency for people with high status to see a larger middle class, and for people with low status to see a smaller one. There also is a consistent gender difference across groupings, such that women see a smaller middle class on average than do men. In contrast, status

Table 8.6. Regression Results (Unstandardized Coefficients) for Perceived Percentage in the Middle Class, Perceived Trend in the Middle Class, and Liberalism on Sociodemographic Variables (Respondents Currently in the Labor Force)[a]

	Eastern countries			Central countries			W. capitalist countries			Japan		
	Middle %	Middle Trend	Liberalism	Middle %	Middle Trend	Liberalism	Middle %	Middle Trend	Liberalism	Middle %	Middle Trend	Liberalism
Age					0.04	0.04	0.82	0.03				
Age squared (× 100)					-0.03	-0.04	-0.83	-0.03				
Gender (1 = male)	4.19			6.27			12.37		-0.20	6.83		
Education	0.90			3.34	0.07	0.08	4.42		0.11	5.25		
Income need	6.30			4.67			2.63	-0.05		3.34		
Social standing	1.82	-0.04		1.07	-0.03	-0.11	-0.31		-0.15		-0.09	-0.14
Time unemployed					-0.01				0.01			
Number supervised			-0.05						-0.01			
Self-employed					-0.20	-0.31		-0.12	-0.21			-0.63
Estonia	-9.43	-0.37	-0.75									
Russia			0.52									
Czechoslovakia				10.88	-0.23	0.95						
East Germany				19.36	-0.11	0.51						
Hungary				-11.45	-0.34	0.79						
Slovenia				-3.19								
West Germany									0.32			
Netherlands							-2.51	0.13	0.34			
U.S.							-4.90					
R^2	0.10	0.05	0.07	0.29	0.04	0.08	0.18	0.01	0.04	0.13	0.05	0.11

[a] Only coefficients significant at the .05 level are reported in this table. "Eastern" combines Bulgaria, Estonia, and Russia. Bulgaria is the reference (excluded) group for regressions. "Central" combines Czechoslovakia, East Germany, Hungary, Poland, and Slovenia. Poland is the reference (excluded) group for regressions. "W. Capitalist" combines Great Britain, West Germany, the Netherlands, and the U.S. Great Britain is the reference (excluded) group for regressions.

Table 8.7. Coefficients (Unstandardized) from Regressions of Poverty and Wealth Explanations Factors on Sociodemographic Variables, Perceived Size and Trend of the Middle Class, and Liberalism. Separately by Four Country Groupings (Respondents in the Labor Force)[a]

	Poverty-individual				Poverty-social				Wealth-individual				Wealth-negative			
	Eastern	Central	W. Capital	Japan	Eastern	Central	W. Capital	Japan	Eastern	Central	W. Capital	Japan	Eastern	Central	W. Capital	Japan
Age	-0.139								-0.024							
Age squared (× 100)			-0.016	-0.034											-0.049	-0.077
Gender (1 = male)	-0.043	-0.030	0.021	0.038											-0.019	-0.121
Education			-0.104			0.026	-0.125	-0.207		-0.022					-0.085	
Income need	-0.103					-0.088	-0.086	-0.146	0.091	0.047	0.036		-0.074	-0.064		
Social standing	-0.046	0.025	0.027			-0.041			0.028	0.051	0.033		-0.033	-0.028		
Time unemployed																
Number supervised						0.010										
Self-employed	0.462	0.115	0.077						0.313	0.138	0.083					0.204
Middle percent (× 10)	0.030	0.016	-0.014		-0.049	-0.065	-0.046	-0.072	0.071	0.024	-0.062		-0.023	-0.037	-0.028	
Middle % trend		-0.031				0.070	0.154	0.101					0.047	0.061	0.121	
Liberalism		-0.023	-0.074			0.042	0.099	0.098		-0.048	-0.049		-0.023	0.018	0.053	
Estonia		—	—	—	-0.223	—	—	—	-0.395	—	—	—		—	—	—
Russia		—	—	—	-0.398	—	—	—	-0.291	—	—	—		—	—	—
Czechoslovakia	—	-0.240	—	—	—	-0.205	—	—	—	0.339	—	—	—	0.159	—	—
East Germany	—	-0.567	—	—	—	-0.154	—	—	—	0.197	—	—	—	-0.378	—	—
Hungary	—	-0.275	—	—	—		—	—	—	0.104	—	—	—	-0.141	—	—
Slovenia	—	-0.543	—	—	—	0.113	—	—	—		—	—	—		—	—
Netherlands	—	—	0.109	—	—	—	-0.246	—	—	—	0.093	—	—	—	-0.070	—
West Germany	—	—	0.097	—	—	—	-0.214	—	—	—	-0.119	—	—	—	-0.199	—
U.S.	—	—	0.394	—	—	—	-0.145	—	—	—	0.154	—	—	—		—
R²	0.02	0.08	0.08	0.03	0.10	0.14	0.14	0.14	0.05	0.05	0.05	0.02	0.05	0.12	0.13	0.07
R without countries	0.14	0.14	0.26		0.25	0.35	0.36		0.17	0.20	0.17		0.22	0.26	0.33	

[a] Only coefficients significant at the .05 level are reported in this table. "Eastern" combines Bulgaria, Estonia, and Russia. Bulgaria is the reference (excluded) group for regressions. "Central" combines Czechoslovakia, East Germany, Hungary, Poland, and Slovenia. Poland is the reference (excluded) group for regressions. "W. capitalist" combines Great Britain, West Germany, the Netherlands, and the U.S. Great Britain is the reference (excluded) group for regressions. "R without countries" equals the multiple correlation of sociodemographic variables, perceived size and trend of the middle class, and liberalism with factors for explanations of poverty and wealth.

weakly affects the perceived trend in the size of the middle class and self-rated liberalism.

Table 8.7 arrays the direct effects of objective and subjective status on explanations of poverty and wealth. These results support hypothesis 4, and give partial support to hypothesis 6. Consistent with hypothesis 4, we find that individualist explanations are more weakly affected by individual differences in personal status and perceived societal status. This is shown in two ways. First, the individual regression coefficients for the effects of personal status and perceived societal status are more consistently statistically significant, and on the whole are larger for POVERTY SOCIAL and WEALTH NEGATIVE than for POVERTY INDIVIDUAL and WEALTH INDIVIDUAL. Second, it is shown in the values of the R without countries row of Table 8.7. These values are from regressions that include all independent variables in Table 8.7 except the categorical variables for country, and so estimate the combined correlation of sociodemographic factors, the perceived societal status distribution, and liberalism with explanations of wealth and poverty. As can be seen in this row, the combined influence of individual-level variables is substantially stronger on social than on individual explanations.

Focusing on individual variables, we see that on the whole Age, Education, and Gender have weak or statistically insignificant direct effects on explanations of poverty and wealth. However, we should keep in mind that both Gender and Education have indirect effects through the perceived size of the middle class. Thus the total effects of Gender and Education are such that women and those with lower education levels on average see social explanations of poverty and wealth as more important than do men and the more highly educated. Replicating a finding in U.S. data (Kluegel and Smith 1986), there is a tendency for education to have "self-canceling" effects. The total effect of education on Poverty-individual (except in Japan) is such that lesser educated tend to have a higher level of individualistic attribution, and as we have seen the total effect of education on Poverty-social is such that the same group also has a higher level of social attribution. Aside from a small tendency for the self-employed to give more individualistic explanations of poverty and wealth, explanations essentially are uninfluenced by job characteristics. This again is consistent with a negative body of evidence concerning such effects in the United States (Schlozman and Verba 1979; Kluegel and Smith 1986; Kluegel 1988).

Hypothesis 6 is supported only as it applies to social explanations of poverty and wealth. Both the perceived Middle percent, and the perceived Trend in middle percent have statistically significant and consistent effects on Poverty-social and Wealth-negative. However these variables have quite weak or statistically insignificant effects on Poverty-individual and Wealth-individual.

Table 8.8 gives the final analysis results, bringing our attention back to macro-level differences. Here we ask how much of the country differences in emphasis given to individual and social explanations can be accounted for by perceived

Table 8.8. Regression Results (Unstandardized Coefficients) for Poverty and Wealth Explantion Factors on Perceived Status and Country (Respondents from All Countries Combined)[a]

	Poverty individual		Poverty social		Wealth individual		Wealth negative	
	I	II	I	II	I	II	I	II
Income need		0.023*		-0.083*		0.051*		-0.079*
Social standing		0.015*		-0.030*		0.030*		-0.027*
Middle percent (× 10)	-0.001			-0.051*		0.017*		-0.034*
Middle percent		-0.017*		0.110*		-0.022*		0.096*
U.S.	0.318*	0.313*	-0.076*	-0.092*	0.131*	0.126*	0.013	0.005
Netherlands	0.047	0.022	-0.246*	-0.158*	0.097*	0.035	-0.128*	-0.053
Japan	0.715*	0.727*	-0.402*	-0.345*	0.022	0.028*	-0.186*	-0.153*
Great Britain	—	—	—	—	—	—	—	—
West Germany	0.061	0.045	-0.264*	-0.204*	-0.028	-0.067	-0.259*	-0.205*
Bulgaria	0.382*	0.435*	0.846*	0.533*	-0.236*	-0.095*	0.643	0.394*
Estonia	0.331*	0.364*	0.596*	0.341*	-0.553*	-0.444*	0.715	0.521
Russia	0.484*	0.537*	0.518*	0.153*	-0.610*	-0.454*	0.674	0.392*
Czechoslovakia	0.326*	0.354*	0.012	-0.107*	-0.381*	-0.324*	0.364	0.260*
E. Germany	0.057	0.069*	-0.046	-0.033	-0.030	-0.028	-0.223	-0.227*
Hungary	0.332*	0.370*	0.410*	0.125*	-0.306*	-0.186*	0.233	0.021
Poland	0.587*	0.626*	0.363*	0.108*	-0.468*	-0.357*	0.306	0.105*
Slovenia	0.050	0.078*	0.470*	0.268*	-0.392*	-0.298*	0.244	0.096*
Constant	3.127	3.006	3.338	3.960	3.648	3.280	3.558	4.028
R^2	.06	.06	0.16	0.21	0.08	0.09	0.19	0.23

* $p < .05$.

[a] Column I gives coefficients for regressions on country variables only. Column II gives coefficients for regressions on country variables and perceived status variables.
Great Britain is the reference (excluded) group for the country variables in all regressions.

personal and societal status. In other words, to what extent do we need to appeal to ideological, cultural or historical macrolevel factors to account for the country level differences described earlier in this paper? Because other factors have little impact and because the effects of perceived status are generally the same in all the country groupings, we can validly approach this question by performing two sets of regressions. The first set of regressions, given in column I of coefficients for each explanation factor in Table 8.8, contains categorical variables for country alone. The second set, in the column II includes country variables, and perceived personal status and the perceived societal status distribution. To the degree that the coefficients in column II are smaller than those in column I, we may conclude that country differences in average levels of social and individual explanations of poverty and wealth are explained by country differences in perceived personal status and perceived societal status.

Two major findings are shown in this table: (a) significant country-level mean differences in all four of the explanation factors remain controlling for status perceptions, but (b) much more of the country-level differences in social explanations are accounted for by status perceptions than in individual explanations—especially so for individualist poverty, where none of the country differences can be accounted for in this manner. In answer to the above questions, these findings argue that to explain country differences in individual and social explanations of poverty and wealth one must appeal to macrolevel factors in some measure. However, one must appeal to such factors much more for individual explanations than for social explanations.

CONCLUSIONS

Our results are substantially consistent with the split-consciousness perspective on the legitimation of the stratification order. We found evidence for split consciousness in explanations of poverty and wealth in both capitalist countries for which split-consciousness theory was developed, and postcommunist countries for which it was not. In all countries, people do not see individual explanations and social explanations as mutually exclusive alternatives, especially for explanations of poverty. In all countries, the popular view of poverty and wealth is very much bicausal.

In all countries, social explanations are more open to influence by stratification-related factors than are individual explanations. In all countries then, it seems that in response to one's position in the stratification order, social explanations in effect are added on top of a base of individual explanations. This appears to be so even in postcommunist countries, where the marked economic troubles of the transition period might well be expected to challenge individual explanations of poverty. Yet, as we have seen, persons who perceive little poverty and persons who perceive rampant poverty differ little or not at all in adherence to individual explanations of poverty and wealth.

Were we to focus on explanations for wealth only, we would conclude that ideology is the primary determinant of individualist attribution. East Germany is the only exception to an otherwise wide gap in popular views of the rich, with a positive view in capitalist countries and a strongly negative view in postcommunist countries. Individualist explanations for poverty, however, do not admit to such a straightforward accounting. We find no parallel capitalist-postcommunist gap in individual explanations of poverty. Indeed, differences among capitalist countries and among postcommunist countries in the average level of individualist attribution for poverty are as large as the difference between countries in the respective two groupings.

It is beyond our scope in this paper to attempt to account for country differences in individualist explanations of poverty. We can only speculate about why attribution to individual causes of poverty is higher in the United States and still higher yet in Japan then in the other capitalist countries; or why individual explanations of poverty are more popular among Poles and much less popular among East Germans and Slovenians than among respondents from our other postcommunist nations. Answers to these questions await research that brings to bear historical and other macrolevel data.

Our results have implications for the legitimation of economic inequality in capitalist and postcommunist countries. On the capitalist side, the split-consciousness pattern supports Mann's (1973) assertion that the stability of the stratification order results more from self-canceling beliefs among the working class than from uncritical belief in its legitimacy. The effect of status variables on social explanations coupled with the lack of such effects on individual explanations implies that the bicausal view of the causes of poverty and wealth is strongest among lower status persons, i.e., among the working classes. The presence of a bicausal view of poverty and wealth has implications for the politics of welfare state redistribution. It presents a fertile ground for framing effects (Iyengar 1990) as political actors compete to make salient either the social explanations of poverty and wealth in support of redistribution or the individual explanations to motivate opposition to the welfare state.

On the postcommunist side, we consider the implications of our results for the transition to a market economy. Some argue that the hostility toward wealth prevalent in the transition period has hindered the growth of entrepreneurship and risk-taking important to the development of market economies (Csepeli and Örkény 1992a). A critical question concerns the staying power of beliefs about the causes of poverty and wealth. Have these beliefs—as Feagin (1975) has argued is the case for individual explanations of poverty in the United States—taken on a life of their own, exerting an influence on politics that is now independent of the economic and cultural conditions that originally produced them?

Della Fave's self-evaluation perspective on the legitimation of wealth in this regard has an interesting implication for the acceptance of inequalities generated by market economies among people in postcommunist countries. It suggests that such legitimacy in effect must be "bootstrapped." As he argued, exposure to successful capitalism is a strong force legitimating wealth. One of the problems faced by postcommunist countries in the transition is changing the reference groups for explanations of wealth from the authoritarian and political figures of the recent past to "modern" capitalist entrepreneurs. Former East Germany, in effect, boot-strapped exposure to successful capitalism in the merger with former West Germany, and through the media and family relations in the years prior to the merger. Such exposure may account for the markedly more positive view of the rich that prevails in East Germany than in the other postcommunist countries. Given the historical and ideological roots of antirich sentiment in other postcommunist countries, and the fact that they cannot simply annex successful capitalism as happened in East Germany, they are likely to experience a more difficult road in boot-strapping the legitimacy of inequality.

NOTES

1. In several countries PABILITY loads highly on a "luck" factor measured by two items that attribute poverty to bad luck and wealth to good luck. In other cases it simply loads poorly on all factors.

2. In assessing how well models fit in our tests, keep in mind that goodness of fit measures are sensitive to sample size, especially sample sizes of 1000 or more cases—which we have for all but one of our countries. We estimated numerous additional models to those reported in Table 8.2, adding more correlated errors and allowing items to load on more than one factor. In all cases these additional parameters have trivial values, and the values for factor loadings and correlations differ from very little to not at all from those reported in Tables 8.3 and 8.4.

3. Averaged across countries, these correlations are WOPPOR with POPPOR .11, WOPPOR with WHDWORK .06, WOPPOR with WKNOW .19, and WECONS with PECONS .12.

4. Respondents in former East and West Germany were asked about the distribution and trend in poverty and wealth for both East and West Germany. The analyses in this paper employ respondents' perceptions concerning their own regions: perceptions of poverty and wealth in East Germany among East Germans and in West Germany among West Germans.

5. We have run all the regressions reported in this paper in the full sample of respondents as well. In these equations we exclude the measures of job characteristics. The results for the effects of the other variables are in all important respects the same.

9

Egalitarian vs. Inegalitarian Principles of Distributive Justice

James R. Kluegel and Petr Matějů

Studying the social distribution of beliefs and norms about economic inequality speaks to theories of the legitimation and "delegitimation" processes (cf. Ritzman and Tomaskovic-Devey 1992). The social distribution of beliefs and norms about the justice of economic equality and inequality is an important characteristic of the political landscape of any society. To the degree that major social and economic groups in a country differ among themselves in adherence to egalitarian vs. inegalitarian norms and beliefs, the potential for group conflict, of course, is heightened.

Intriguingly, several scholars have argued that not only are there divisions among groups, but that essentially many persons are internally divided as well. That is, both qualitative and quantitative evidence suggests that many individuals simultaneously affirm both egalitarian and inegalitarian beliefs about economic justice (Halle 1984; Hochschild 1981; Huber and Form 1973; Hyman and Brough 1975; Kluegel and Smith 1986; Lane 1962; Mann 1970; Nichols and Armstrong 1976; Sennett and Cobb 1973; Willis 1977). The presence of such duality in popular thinking about economic justice has important political implications. It implies that in societies where it is particularly strong there exists a large "swing vote" regarding policy concerning economic inequality. Depending upon who succeeds in political battles over how policy is framed, citizens may be persuaded to support or oppose policy that promotes greater economic equality or inequality (cf. Iyengar 1990). The existence of this duality then gives at least a strong potential for volatility in the politics of distribution and redistribution.

In this chapter we compare norms about societal-level economic justice held by the citizens of the thirteen nations participating in the International Social Justice Project (ISJP). We first compare the general level of legitimacy of distributive systems in these nations, and explore the internal structure of legitimacy. In a second step we use the principal dimensions of legitimacy to group individual countries into clusters representing distributive systems that differ in extent and kind of perceived legitimacy. Third, we develop a measurement model for egalitarian and inegalitarian orientations, and test its cross-system generality. Fourth, we develop and test a nonrecursive structural model of the determinants of egalitarian and inegalitarian orientations, of how they are shaped by social attributes or "life chances" in different distributive systems. Results of these latter two analyses are used to test hypotheses taken from recent theoretical perspectives on the legitimation of economic inequality.

THEORETICAL BACKGROUND

Theories proposing an egalitarian-inegalitarian duality have employed microlevel and macrolevel frameworks.[1]

Microlevel Theory. Della Fave (1980, 1986a, 1986b) offers a perspective on the duality of how people evaluate economic justice, stressing what he calls legitimation norms and counternorms. He differentiates between equity norms that legitimate inequality and equality counternorms. Della Fave focuses on self-evaluation processes, proposing that certain processes serve to reinforce equity norms, but that others lead to equality counternorms; thus "[t]he result is that legitimating norms and counternorms exist in a state of continual tension." (1986a:480). In his terms

[W]e humans are very impressed by our own or others' ability to control the environment, physical and social, successfully. Those in the upper reaches of the stratification system—that is, those with the most primary resources (wealth, institutional power, status)—are, thus the most impressive. (Della Fave 1986:478)

Through the process of status attribution, argues Della Fave, the well-to-do in capitalist societies come to be seen as deserving their status, and this buttresses support for equity (i.e inegalitarian) norms and beliefs. Della Fave proposes that the power of the state and force of day-to-day dealings with the economy are such that equity norms are widespread and self-reinforcing; hence they are unlikely to be affected by one's position in the stratification order. He argues, however, that at the same time people find asymmetrical power and control relationships alienating, and come to resent the stratification order.

Macrolevel Theory. Another influential explanation of the egalitarian-inegalitarian duality is provided by what may be called the "split-consciousness" perspective held by many students of subjective social inequality (Cheal 1979; Halle 1984; Hochschild 1981; Huber and Form 1973; Kluegel and Smith 1986; Lane 1962; Parkin 1971; Mann 1970, 1973; Sennett and Cobb 1973). Though it cannot be said that there is a single or unified theory of split consciousness regarding norms and beliefs about economic justice, split-consciousness advocates share common propositions from which empirically testable hypotheses may be derived. All proponents of this perspective begin with the proposition that in every society there is an ideology that serves to justify the privileged status of economic elites. Likewise, split-consciousness perspectives share the premise that elites have the upper hand in putting this interpretation of how the economic order works before the general public, principally through ideological hegemony. Privileged elites act to have this justifying set of beliefs or "dominant ideology" promulgated to the public through the schools, the church, the arts, popular media, and other institutions over which they exert a strong influence. Because the dominant ideology is put before the public often and in many different ways, over time it takes on the force of the "accepted explanation of things."

Split-consciousness perspectives also share the proposition that a second category or level of beliefs exists that are in some respect inconsistent with the dominant ideology. In one way or another these beliefs seem to question or challenge the fairness of the economic order as portrayed by the dominant ideology. Whereas dominant-ideology beliefs often are explicitly taught by various agents of socialization, challenging beliefs and norms derive more informally, from everyday experience. According to split-consciousness theory, challenging beliefs and norms largely derive from the struggle to make do with limited resources, from feelings of blocked opportunity due to race or gender, experience at the workplace, or simple economic self-interest.

A key proposition of split-consciousness views is that dominant and potentially challenging norms and beliefs may coexist without any necessary force toward change. They may simply occupy separate places in a person's consciousness; in Lane's (1962) terms "compartmentalized" or in the terms of Sennett and Cobb (1973) working-class individuals may maintain "divided selves." Because these two types of norms or beliefs stem from different sources, some people may rarely if at all bring them together in their consciousness, thus never activating a potential challenge.

Hypotheses

Capitalist Countries. From the shared propositions of split-consciousness theories and Della Fave's self-evaluation perspective, two central hypotheses about economic justice beliefs in capitalist countries may be derived.

Hypothesis 1: *In capitalist societies, the structure of beliefs and norms about economic justice is at least bidimensional. Specifically, if split-consciousness perspectives have merit, then: (a) we would expect to be able to identify at least two factors underlying a set of items concerning justifications of inequality, i.e., inegalitarianism, and of egalitarian beliefs and norms, respectively; (b) these two*

*factors will show principally a competing relationship (represented by a signifi-
cant negative correlation), but not mutual exclusiveness.*

Hypothesis 2: *Reflecting the influence of common socialization, in capitalist
societies support for inequality is weakly affected by stratification-related experience. However, support for equality is more strongly shaped by such experience.
In operational terms, this hypothesis implies that, on the one hand, groups
defined by socioeconomic status, class, or other stratification-related criteria will
differ little or not at all in their level of support for economic inequality. On the
other hand, the same groups should differ significantly in their average level of
support for equality—with challenging beliefs more strongly held by the less
privileged.*

Postcommunist Countries. Do these perspectives apply also to postcommunist countries? Do we expect to find the same duality and differences in the
effects of class and status as hypothesized for capitalist countries?

Questions may be raised about the applicability of both the split-consciousness
and the self-evaluation perspectives to postcommunist countries during the transition period in which this study was conducted. For the split-consciousness
perspective, one may question whether or not a dominant ideology existed at the
time of the study. Had this study been done several years earlier, one would
certainly argue for the dominance of egalitarian ideology. In the recent history of
each country, however, justifications of economic inequality in Western capitalist
terms have been promoted by political elites, so it is arguable that equity is now
the dominant justification for inequality. On the other hand, it is only within the
past few years that market justice has been emphasized by elites, in contrast to
the several decades of socialist justice as dominant ideology.

A central aspect of Della Fave's self-evaluation perspective is the existence of
successful capitalism, *successful* here meaning that there exists a visible, powerful economic elite who display an apparent ability to control the economic
environment. A related argument is made by Lane, who asserts that in order for
the market to be considered fair, "there must be perceived openness if not
equality of opportunity, and the market must be considered responsive to
effort—to hard work" (1986:386). Although some of the postcommunist countries have had more experience with capitalist markets than others, at the time of
our survey none can be said to have had experience with successful capitalism.
Quite to the contrary, of course, the economies of these countries were badly
foundering and economic austerity prevailed in all of them. This combination of
competing ideologies and poor economic conditions implies that the duality in
beliefs and norms about equality and inequality will exist as well and may be
even be more pronounced in postcommunist than capitalist countries. The newness of equity and market justice ideas and the lack of experience with capitalism
may mean that fewer people in postcommunist than in capitalist societies see
these ideas as inconsistent with egalitarian beliefs and norms.

Although we thus expect hypothesis 1 above to hold in both capitalist and postcommunist countries, we may specify this hypothesis for postcommunist countries:

Hypothesis 1b: *In postcommunist countries, in light of the transition between two different systems of legitimation and the profound transformation of the stratification system, changing the life chances of social groups and strata, the two economic justice orientations (i.e., egalitarian and inegalitarian) are not as often seen to be opposed as in capitalist countries. Consequently, we predict that the (negative) correlation between egalitarian and inegalitarian norms (ideologies) of distributive justice in postcommunist countries will be smaller than in capitalist countries. In other words, split-consciousness theory may find stronger support in analyses of data from postcommunist countries than from capitalist countries.*

We also expect hypothesis 2 to hold in postcommunist countries, but for a different reason than in capitalist countries. In capitalist countries, inegalitarian norms are widely held both because of common socialization and the experience of successful capitalism, but in postcommunist societies only the former is present. In postcommunist countries equity norms are now held out by elites as necessary for making the transition from failed socialist to market economies; so we may expect uniform and, in many cases perhaps, superficial acceptance of inegalitarianism. However, though people in these countries have experience on which to base a rejection of egalitarianism, most have little to no experience on which to evaluate equity beliefs. It is much clearer to most people, then, who potentially may gain and lose under egalitarian norms. Formalizing this, then, we have:

Hypothesis 2b: *In postcommunist countries the ideology of inequality is a widely supported "new ideology," and consequently is little affected by stratification-related experience. However, those who belong to higher social strata (people with the highest educational credentials, professionals, new entrepreneurs, and like others) whose life chances gradually increase as egalitarian ideology and policy is being dismantled will more strongly oppose egalitarianism. Thus in postcommunist countries it is not support for inegalitarianism, but disagreement with egalitarian ideology that is strongly affected by stratification-related experience.*

Prior Research

A recent study by Ritzman and Tomaskovic-Devey (1992) directly tests hypothesis 2 and finds clear support for it in data from the United States; showing that having more favorable life chances (more favorable position in the stratification system) weakly affects support for equity, but leads to strong rejection of equality norms. Although they do not test hypothesis 1 directly, they do provide evidence that speaks to its merits. In particular, they show a moderately sized negative correlation between indices of egalitarian and equity norms, as expected under hypothesis 1.

In Chapter 10 of this book, Wegener and Liebig employ historical and cultural argumentation to define primary and secondary distributive ideologies in different social systems (United States, West Germany, East Germany). They analyze the differential effects of social background on the two ideologies, reaching conclusions that, in our view, are consistent with Ritzman and Tomaskovic-Devey's findings. They find that in the United States "functionalism" (rooted in the equity principle) is a widely held distributive ideology across all class positions. Also significant for our study is their finding that East German data do not provide conclusive evidence as to which is the primary and which the secondary ideology. They conclude that East Germany, a society in transition, does not exhibit the specific patterns of normative and rational justice ideologies typical of either a welfare or a meritocratic society. We now turn to the question of whether there is evidence for our hypotheses in other capitalist societies and indeed in postcommunist societies as well.

MEASURES

In our analyses we use three sets of variables: (a) variables describing the legitimacy of a current distributive system, (b) variables capturing respondents' views of principles of a just distribution of income and wealth, and (c) socio-demographic variables.

For the classification of nations into clusters (as described subsequently) on the bases of the prevailing level and kind of the perceived legitimacy of the distributive system, a set of four variables was used:

- EQOPPOR: In [country], people have equal opportunities to get ahead.
- GETNEED: In [country], people get what they need.
- REWEFFR: In [country], people get rewarded for their effort.
- REWSKLL: In [country], people get rewarded for their intelligence and skill.

The original response scale for these variables (1, strongly agree, to 5, strongly disagree) has been reversed for our analyses.

We use these four items because they correspond to the generally recognized dimensions on which the fairness of distributive systems are evaluated.

EQOPPOR, of course, concerns the ability of a society to provide equality of opportunity. GETNEED concerns the ability of a society to provide for the basic welfare of all citizens, or "need." REWEFFER and REWSKLL concern the meritocratic functioning of a stratification order.[2]

Popular sentiment toward distributive justice principles is measured by a set of six items. The first three concern equality norms, and the second three items concern inequality norms:

- EQSHR: The fairest way of distributing wealth and income would be to give everyone equal shares.
- WNEED: The most important thing is that people get what they need, even if this means allocating money from those who have earned more than they need.
- PAYFAM: How much influence should each of these factors have in determining the level of pay for an employee? [The size of the family the employee supports.]
- KEARN: People are entitled to keep what they have earned—even if this means some people will be wealthier than others.
- WORKH: People who work hard deserve to earn more than those who do not.
- PASSW: People are entitled to pass on their wealth to their children.

The original response scale for EQSHR, WNEED, WORKH, KEARN, and PASSW (1, strongly agree, to 5, strongly disagree) and the original scale for the variable PAYFAM (1, a great deal, to 4, none) also have been reversed for analysis.

Several other possible indicators of egalitarian or inegalitarian sentiment are present in the ISJP common survey. We limit our attention to these six variables for two reasons. First, these items tap only basic or general egalitarian or inegalitarian orientations, and are not confounded with evaluations of concrete measures that may be taken to achieve "just inequality" (e.g., pay for education, responsibility, difficult conditions) or "just equality."[3] Second, these items concern egalitarian and inegalitarian norms that scholars have identified as central to judgments of fairness in industrial societies. The three egalitarian items (EQSHR, WNEED, PAYFAM) measure adherence to three major, different principles of distribution: (1) the principle of equality of outcomes (EQSHR), (2) an abstract or general need principle (WNEED), and (3) a specific need principle, based on family as a distributive unit (PAYFAM) (Deutsch 1975). The three inegalitarian items (WORKH, KEARN, PASSW) measure adherence to the equity principle (WORKH) and to two slightly different expressions of the principle of entitlement (KEARN, PASSW), which is a key aspect of notions of inegalitarian or "market" justice (Rawls 1971; DiQuattro 1986). Accordingly, these are norms that are encouraged by privileged elites or, as Della Fave (1986b) suggests, come to be adopted by the force of day-to-day dealings with the economy.

There are nine "exogenous" variables in the structural model. AGE is in years, and GENDER is coded 1, male, and 0, female. Some of them require explanation. RSEI is a standard international socioeconomic index of occupational status (Ganzeboom, De Graaf, and Treiman 1992) for respondent's present job. FSEI is the same index for father's occupation when respondent was about sixteen years old. COLLEGE is a categorical variable with a value of one for respondents who reported having a tertiary education diploma. HIPROF is also a categorical variable distinguishing higher professionals or managers from other occupations. Another categorical variable, SELFEMPL, distinguishes self-employed or entrepreneurs from employees. We employ a measure of personal INCOME from a respondent's job. To allow comparability, INCOME was recoded from the original monetary units of each country to income deciles (defined within each country). RIGHTOR is respondent's self-identified position on a left-right political continuum (with 1 representing extreme left and 10 representing extreme right).

With the exception of political identification, these variables concern what have been called "life chances," factors that shape the opportunity for people to share in the valued goods made available by a society (Dahrendorf 1979; cf. Ritzman and Tomaskovic-Devey 1992). In our context, each of these variables is of interest because they potentially relate to the perceived prospects for benefiting from different distributive justice principles. We include political identification to examine the political-ideological shaping of preference for egalitarian or inegalitarian principles. Prior research suggests that in the United States the political determination of egalitarianism and inegalitarianism follows a split-consciousness pattern, such that there are much larger differences between liberals and conservatives in adherence to egalitarian than in adherence to inegalitarian principles (Kluegel and Smith 1986).

STRATIFICATION SYSTEM LEGITIMACY

On the one hand, the large number of countries and respondents in our study is a strong point, permitting us to test hypotheses in a broad comparative context, ranging from the West to the East. On the other hand, we undoubtedly face large heterogeneity and variation not only among Western countries, but also within the postcommunist block. The task for every comparative analyst is to solve the problem of relevant criteria for the classification of units that will be compared. If we take into account all relevant economic, social, political, and cultural criteria, each country in our study is a unique social system, which creates specific conditions for the crystallization of distributive ideologies. However, to specify and test for the potential effects of all relevant country-specific conditions on the formation of beliefs about distributive justice is a task not only beyond our level of knowledge, but makes the task of comparing results formidable. To address this problem we start by classifying countries into meaningful clusters, based on the similarity of countries in the level and structure of the perceived legitimacy of the distributive system. As discussed above, the theory we call on to derive hypotheses for capitalist countries assumes "successful" capitalism; it assumes that the economic system is functioning well enough to at least permit people to believe that the stratification order is fair. The level of legitimacy of the distributive system, in fact, then is a limiting condition of this theory, and tests of hypotheses should take it into account.

We assume that a "belief" about a phenomenon serves as a basis both for inferring other information and for action (Kluegel and Smith 1981)—in line with an assumption of much social-psychological theory that how people interpret the situation is more important than its objective parameters. Although for our study how people in a given country perceive the distributive system is more important than how it really works, there is no reason to assume that there is a large discrepancy between belief and reality.

Figure 9.1 displays means and confidence intervals of an index of legitimacy of distributive systems in individual countries.[4] Although the index is a simple descriptive measure, the information in Figure 9.1 is quite telling. First, all Western countries are located above symbolic "zero legitimacy" (which, of course, has no substantive interpretation), while all postcommunist countries (again except hybrid East Germany) fall below this line. The division line between West and East is the most evident result, but we should not overlook the variation within the two blocs. West Germany and Japan show a very high level of system legitimacy, followed by the United States and the Netherlands. Britain is located quite near the East-West division line, at the same level as East Germany. Similar variation exists among postcommunist countries. The highest legitimacy of distributive system was found in Slovenia; Hungary, Czechoslovakia, and Poland are located in the middle of the area occupied by postcommunist countries, while Russia, Estonia, and Bulgaria are located at the bottom.

We next applied discriminant function analysis to assess the discriminant capacity of single indicators of system legitimacy (EQOPPOR, GETNEED, REWEFFR, REWSKLL) and to standardize scales of variables for correspondence analysis. At the country level, the four extracted discriminant functions correspond to the four original variables.

The matrix of group centroids of individual discriminant functions was entered into a correspondence analysis, which revealed three relatively strong factors and resulted in the location of individual countries within a three-dimensional space of system legitimacy.[5] Figure 9.2, in which results of the correspondence analysis are displayed, supports the assumption that legitimacy of a distributive system is not one-dimensional phenomenon, and that the East-West division line is not the only one we should take into consideration.

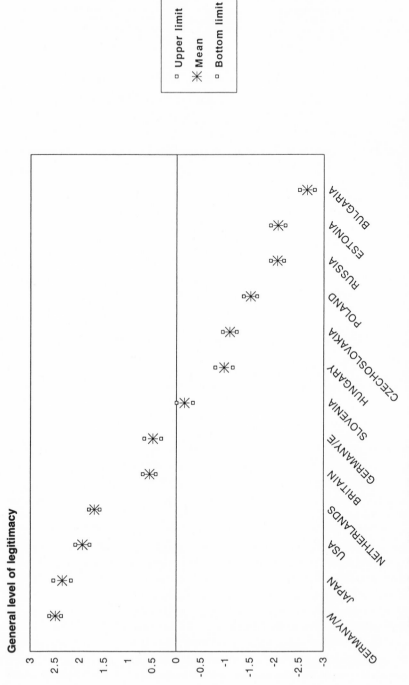

Figure 9.1. Legitimacy of distributive system. Means and 95% confidence intervals for the variable LEGITIMACY.

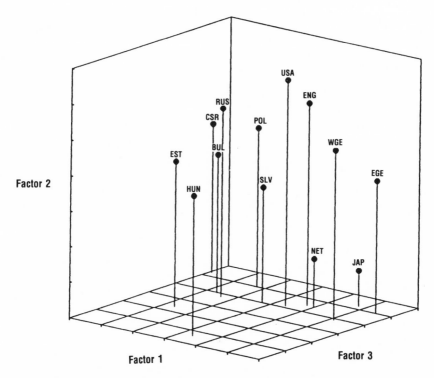

Figure 9.2. Countries in the three-dimensional space of system legitimacy. Results from correspondence analysis (LINDA).

In general, all postcommunist countries (except East Germany) occupy one part of the "cube" (though there is significant variation among them) and all Western countries are located on the other side. However, there are two segments in the western part of the cube: the upper segment (the United States, Britain, and West Germany), and the bottom one (Netherlands and Japan). These two segments are separated by a vertical axis (factor 2) representing the tendency to believe that the distributive system of a given country is "welfare oriented" ("People get what they need").[6] The results of correspondence analysis permit us to define three major clusters of countries: Western capitalist (W-CAP): United States, West Germany, Britain; Welfare capitalist (WLF-CAP): Netherlands and Japan; and East (postcommunist): Bulgaria, Czechoslovakia, Estonia, East Germany, Hungary, Poland, Russia, and Slovenia. A subsequent discriminant analysis with the three clusters as a grouping variable shows that there are two general dimensions of legitimacy: meritocratic orientation (first discriminant function with 83 percent of explained variance) and welfare orientation (second discriminant function with 17 percent of explained variance). Figure 9.3 displays the

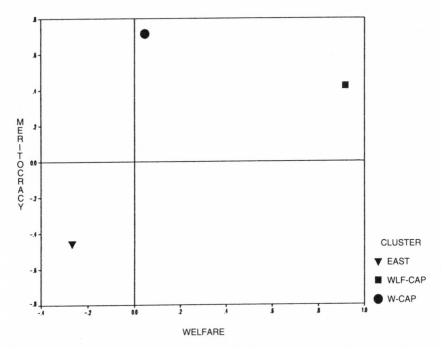

Figure 9.3. Clusters of countries in the two-dimensional space of system legitimacy. Results from discriminant analysis (group centroids).

location of the three clusters in the two-dimensional space of legitimacy. In our view, this figure strongly supports the conclusion that the legitimacy of a distributive system is at least a two-dimensional phenomenon, and that countries in our analysis can be effectively clustered in three distinct systems of legitimacy: high legitimacy due to a strong meritocratic orientation (cluster 1—W-CAP), high legitimacy due to both meritocratic and welfare orientation of the distributive system (cluster 2—WLF-CAP), and low level of legitimacy due to the failure of the distributive system to follow either of the two major principles (cluster 3— EAST). Classification results show that the two functions quite successfully locate respondents from thirteen countries back in the initial clusters (61 percent of cases are correctly classified, but if the West is treated as one cluster, then 74 percent of cases are correctly classified in their initial clusters).

MODELS OF DISTRIBUTIVE JUSTICE PRINCIPLES

Three correlation matrices between six endogenous variables capturing beliefs about distributive justice (EQSHR, WNEED, PAYFAM, WORKH, KEARN,

PASSW) and nine exogenous (descriptive) variables (sex, age, socioeconomic status, etc.) were computed, one for each cluster. Because the meaning of our occupationally based variables is clearest for those currently economically active, we restrict our sample to respondents currently in the labor force. We also restrict our sample to those with complete data on all variables (i.e., use listwise deletion). Because information needed to code occupations in Russia and Estonia to the same categories as in the other countries is not available, we excluded respondents from these two countries (Bulgaria, Czechoslovakia, East Germany, Hungary, Poland, and Slovenia remain in our East grouping).[7]

Models representing our major hypotheses are displayed in Figures 9.4 and 9.5. Figure 9.4 presents the model for a confirmatory factor analysis of beliefs about distributive justice. It serves for testing hypotheses 1 and 1b. Figure 9.5 is a model designed to test hypotheses 2 and 2B concerning the effects of social background characteristics on egalitarianism and inegalitarianism. All models were estimated by LISREL VII (Jöreskog and Sörbom 1988). Instead of visual comparisons among models estimated separately in each individual cluster, we chose multisample analysis, in which one model is tested simultaneously on a number of covariance (correlation) matrices representing different populations (e.g., countries) or groups within one population. This permits us to test both the general fit of the model and the similarity or dissimilarity of its parameters among groups. As will be shown later, multisample analysis—among other things—permits us to fix the measurement models for the two distributive justice ideologies (EQUALITY and INEQUALITY) for all three clusters. This decision, which of course cannot be made unless there is sufficient statistical evidence that such equality constraints posed on parameters hold, makes the estimation of causal links between exogenous variables and variables representing competing distributive ideologies far more simple and straightforward than if performed on unconstrained measurement models.

In accordance with hypothesis 1, we predict the existence of two latent variables, one representing egalitarian orientation (EQUALITY), the other one representing preference for inegalitarian norms (INEQUALITY). We also predict a significant negative correlation between the two latent variables. In addition, hypothesis 1b predicts that the correlation between the two latent variables is significantly weaker in postcommunist countries. We in fact did not explicitly predict a difference between the two Western clusters, but we conjecture that—if there is any difference—there will be a significantly lower correlation in systems with a more welfare-based legitimacy than in systems with a more meritocratic-based legitimacy.

Because our models contain two different types of variables (both continuous and ordinal) we produced correlation matrices for individual clusters combining three types of correlation coefficients (a) polychoric correlations (between two ordinal variables), (b) polyserial correlations (between one ordinal and one continuous variable), and (c) product moment correlations (between two continuous variables).[8] The correlation matrices employed in our LISREL modeling are displayed in the Appendix to this chapter.

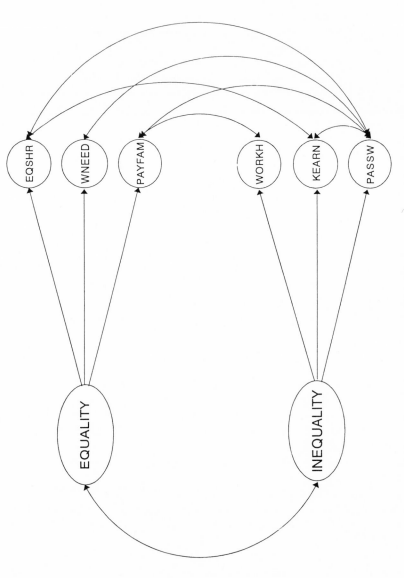

Figure 9.4. Measurement model for EQUALITY and INEQUALITY.

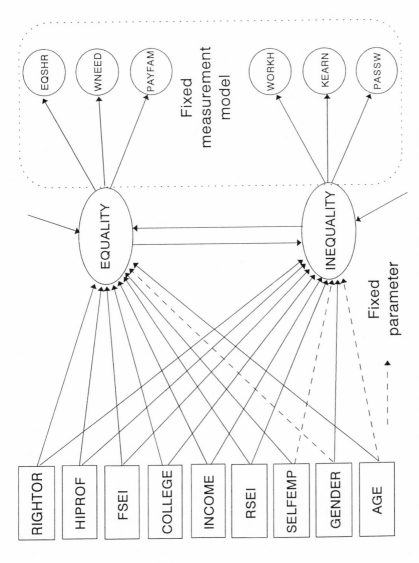

Figure 9.5. Structural model for EQUALITY and INEQUALITY.

Parameters of the model displayed in Figure 9.4 and corresponding fit statistics estimated for the three samples (for each cluster) are displayed in Table 9.1. Three results are relevant. First, to achieve an acceptable fit we must assume the existence of two latent variables representing two competing distributive norms (EQUALITY and INEQUALITY).[9] Second, there is cross-system similarity of the definition of these latent variables, i.e., there are no significant differences

Table 9.1. Parameters of a Measurement Model for EQUALITY and INEQUALITY— Results of a Multisample Analysis across Three Types of Countries

(a) Factor loadings (LAMBDA)—invariant parameters

	EQUALITY	EQUITY
EQSHR	.690[a]	.000
WNEED	.303***	.000
PAYFAM	.403***	.000
WORKH	.000	.587***
KEARN	.000	.749***
PASSW	.000	.578[a]

(b) Correlations between factors (PSI)

	W-CAP	WLF-CAP	EAST
EQUALITY-EQUITY	−.551***	−.450***	−.161***

(c) Correlations between errors of measurement (THETA EPS)

	W-CAP	WLF-CAP	EAST
EQSHR-KEARN	−.089***	−.057	
WNEED-WORKH	.087**	.068*	.115***
WNEED-PASSW	−.171***	.048	−.128**
PAYFAM-WORKH	—	.190***	.081
PAYFAM-PASSW	—	—	.118***
KEARN-PASSW	—	—	−.169***
EQSHR-PASSW	—	—	−.127

(d) Statistics of model fit (for the multisample analysis)

N of cases	1796 + 794 + 2882
df	19
Chi square	57.97
df	3.05
p	.001
GFI (goodness-of-fit index)	.999
RMR (root mean square residual)	.013

*.05 > p > .01.   **.01 > p > .001.   ***.001 > p.
[a] Fixed parameter.

among corresponding factor loadings from the three clusters. Third, we find that there are system-specific, but in each case negative correlations between the two latent variables. To perform a direct test of cross-system differences in correlations between the two latent variables we set the model in Figure 9.4 as the baseline and fitted other models: (a) one with the assumption that all three correlations are equal ($k$df $= 2$, $k\chi^2 = 62$, $kp = .000$); and (b) three with equality constraints put on these correlations between pairs of clusters.[10] The result is that all three correlations cannot be considered equal ($kp = .000$), but we may accept the hypothesis that the correlations between latent traits are equal in the two capitalist clusters ($kp = .204$). It follows that we must reject the hypothesis that the correlations between latent traits are equal in the capitalist clusters and the postcommunist cluster. In sum, we have strong evidence favoring both hypotheses 1 and 1B.

That the other parameters of the measurement model do not show significant cross-system variation may be taken to indicate cross-national similarity in the popular definitions of the two distributive ideologies.[11] This result has both theoretical significance and practical consequences. It has the practical consequence of simplifying construction of a structural model for the multisample comparative analysis of the impact of social background variables on the two general justice norms. Because of the cross-system similarity in how the latent variables EQUALITY and INEQUALITY are defined, we fix the measurement model for further analyses.[12]

The model in Figure 9.5 contains three sets of exogenous variables, as described above: six indicators of socioeconomic status (RSEI, FSEI, HIPROF, SELFEMP, COLLEGE, and INCOME), one indicator of general political orientation (RIGHTOR), and two instrumental demographic variables (AGE and GENDER). To estimate the overall effect of the exogenous variables on the latent traits for the two competing justice norms, we start with a recursive version of the model in Figure 9.4, in which we do not estimate causal relationships between EQUALITY and INEQUALITY, but do estimate the correlation between the disturbances for these two latent variables. Table 9.2 gives the results of this analysis. Even without detailed inspection of the individual effects of exogenous variables, it is clear that the EQUALITY counternorm indeed is more strongly linked to one's position in the system of social stratification than the INEQUALITY norm [see coefficients of determination in panel (a) of Table 9.2]. Nevertheless, there are quite interesting differences among the three clusters. First, the strongest effect of position in the system of social stratification on endorsement of EQUALITY is found in postcommunist countries ($R^2 = .377$ for EAST, .360 for W-CAP, and .217 for WLF-CAP). Second, in countries that are perceived as strongly welfare-oriented this link turns out to be the weakest. Third, the most universal support for inequality is shown in postcommunist countries ($R^2 = .030$ for EAST, .119 for W-CAP, and .106 for WLF-CAP). And fourth, the relative differences among clusters in the value of the correlation

Table 9.2. Parameters of a Recursive Structural Model for EQUALITY and INEQUALI-
TY: EQUALITY and INEQUALITY Correlated—Results of a Multisample Analysis with a Fixed Measurement Model

(a) Direct effects (GAMMA)—standardized coefficients

Dependent variable

	W-CAP		WLF-CAP		EAST	
	EQUALITY	*INEQUAL*	*EQUALITY*	*INEQUAL*	*EQUALITY*	*INEQUAL*
RIGHTOR	−.250***	.235***	−.220***	.173***	−.070***	.040*
HIPROF	−.256***	.089*	−.117*	.059	−.158***	−.002
FSEI	−.062*	.144***	−.124***	.073*	−.128***	−.013
COLLEGE	−.102***	−.209***	−.078	−.229***	−.419***	.117***
INCOME	−.121***	.089**	−.130*	.049	−.128***	.065**
RSEI	−.022	.012	−.091	.041	.070**	−.088**
SELFEMPL	−.250***	.099***	.013	.100**	−.160***	.026
GENDER	.084**	−.002	.073	−.002	.089***	−.039
AGE	−.043*	.037	.172***	.007	−.014	.088***
$R2$	.360	.119	.217	.106	.377	.030

(b) Correlations between EQUALITY and INEQUALITY (PSI)

	W-CAP	WLF-CAP	EAST
r	−.421***	−.378***	−.110***

(c) Statistics of model fit (for the multisample analysis)

N of cases	1796 + 794 + 2882
df	0
Chi square	0
df	
p	0.000
GFI (goodness-of-fit-index)	1.000
RMR (root mean square residual)	0.000

*.05 > p > .01.   **.01 > p > .001.   ***.001 > p.

between the two norms remain unchanged (−.110 for East, −.421 for W-CAP
and −0.378 for WLF-CAP).

Individual parameters for the effects of the exogenous variables vary substantially in value across the systems. First, holders of a college or university diploma
both reject egalitarian norms and endorse inegalitarian norms much more strongly in the postcommunist cluster than in the capitalist countries. Indeed, people
with a tertiary education in the West are somewhat more likely than those with
less education to reject inegalitarian norms. Second, new entrepreneurs in our

East countries show a tendency to reject egalitarian norms equal to their counterparts in Western capitalist countries and greater than that found in the Welfare capitalist countries. Finally, left-right political orientation predicts both egalitarian and inegalitarian inclinations in the West (including Japan) much better than in the East.

Although the modified (recursive) model discussed above speaks clearly in favor of hypothesis 2, we may proceed still further to examine the causal relationship between inequality and equality inclinations and their power to challenge each other in different systems. For this purpose the nonrecursive model shown in Figure 9.5 was estimated, with the results given in Table 9.3. To

Table 9.3. Parameters of a Nonrecursive Structural Model for EQUALITY and INEQUALITY–in a Simultaneous Causal Relationship—Results of Multisample Analysis with Fixed Measurement Model

(a) Direct effects (gamma, beta)—standardized coefficients

Dependent variable

	W-CAP		WLF-CAP		EAST	
	EQUALITY	*INEQUAL*	*EQUALITY*	*INEQUAL*	*EQUALITY*	*INEQUAL*
RIGHTOR	−.206***	.126***	−.138***	.189***	−.080***	.084
HIPROF	−.235***	−.018	−.100**	.068	−.155***	−.032
FSEI	−.031	.116***	−.087**	.083	−.129***	−.040
COLLEGE	−.142***	−.255***	−.181***	−.222***	−.421***	.029
INCOME	−.157***	.037	−.135***	.057	−.130***	.037
RSEI	.043	−.013	−.059	.048	.071**	−.074
SELFEMPL	−.243***	.000[a]	.059***	.097*	−.168***	.000[a]
GENDER	.000[a]	−.059	.000[a]	−.089	.089	−.019
AGE	−.029	.016	.178***	.000[a]	.000[a]	.090***
EQUALITY	.000	−.433***	.000	.078	.000	−.209
INEQUALITY	−.204**	.000	−.476***	.000	.023	.000
R^2	.492	.365	.373	.042	.371	.049

(b) Statistics of model fit (for the multisample analysis)

N of cases	1796 + 794 + 2882
df	3
Chi square	16.58
df	6
p	0.000
GFI (goodness of fit index)	1.000
RMR (root mean square residual)	0.002

*.05 > p > .01.   **.01 > p > .001.   ***.001 > p.

[a] Fixed parameter.

identify this nonrecursive model, we fixed the effects of certain exogenous variables at zero. Two major criteria were used in deciding which parameters would be fixed in our model: the size of the parameter if set free for estimation in the recursive variant of the model (Table 9.2) and the modification index if the parameter were fixed in the nonrecursive model. Parameters were fixed at zero for variables that had a nonsignificant partial effect in Table 9.2, and that produced a nonsubstantial modification index in the nonrecursive model estimation.

Again, the model was estimated simultaneously in the three groups (clusters). This model (Table 9.3) permits cross-system variation in all the effects of exogenous variables on the endogenous variables, in the disturbances of the latent variables, and in the reciprocal causal (simultaneous) effects between the two latent variables.

Before interpreting parameters of the nonrecursive model, its overall fit should be evaluated. As shown in Table 9.3, the likelihood ratio for the model tested simultaneously on all three subsamples is 16.6 with 3 degrees of freedom (p = .001). Even though this conventional statistic for the evaluation of the goodness of fit is highly sensitive to sample size, which in our case is very high (5468 for all respondents combined), our model has a very good fit. If the sample size is larger than 1000 cases, models for which the ratio of chi square divided by its degrees of freedom is less than 2 are statistically acceptable (Carmines and McIver 1981; Wheaton, Muthen, Alwin, and Summers 1977; Byrne 1989). As shown in Table 9.3, our model exceeds this line (chi square/df = 6), but other criteria also show an excellent fit. The GFI index (Jöreskog and Sörbom 1988), which indicates quite satisfactory fit if it approaches a value of .9, is 1.000 for our model. Also the RMR (root mean square residual) index is highly satisfactory: our model has a value of .002, whereas the suggested upper limit for acceptable models is .05. Using all the above criteria, we may conclude that the model displayed in Figure 9.5 (applied simultaneously on three subpopulations with fixed measurement model for the two latent variables) is a statistically acceptable causal representation of the correlations among the variables in each cluster.

The parameters of the model lend high credence to hypotheses 2 and 2b. First, as already demonstrated by the results from the recursive version of this model (Table 9.2), in all three clusters of countries inequality norms behave like a dominant ideology, as predicted by the theory. Its determination by respondent's socioeconomic position is weaker than that of the equality counternorm. Second, while the inequality norm receives quite similar support from different social groups and classes, the equality counternorm shows a statistically significant tendency to attract adherence from the lower socioeconomic strata and classes (less-educated individuals, lower-income categories, etc.). Nevertheless, there are interesting cross-system differences, to which we will return later.

The third important result concerns the relationship between the two ideologies. Both the stand-alone measurement model and the modified version of the structural model reveal a principally competitive relationship between equality and inequality inclinations embodied in significant negative correlations (less sharp in the East than in the West). The final model goes beyond this, to address the question of causal links between them.

Taking first the Western world, we find that indeed the two different systems differ not only in the level and kind of legitimacy, but also in the relationship between justice ideologies. In the Western capitalist cluster, the parameters of the nonrecursive model show support for the thesis that egalitarian and inegalitarian tendencies are, as Della Fave proposes in "continual tension," i.e., they stand in a relationship of mutual challenge to each other. An egalitarian orientation is clearly in opposition to a dominant and strong inegalitarian (meritocratic) ideology, and therefore it represents a serious challenge to inequality norms ($-.396$). Nevertheless, inequality norms show a significant capacity to prevent a "swing" to egalitarian ideology ($-.187$). In the other capitalist cluster (WLF-CAP) the parameters suggest quite a different interplay of the two ideologies. Egalitarian norms apparently do not represent a strong challenge to inequality norms—they in fact show limited compatibility ($.078$)—but inequality norms seem to play a strong role as a challenging ideology ($-.476$).

Our results confirm hypothesis 2b for the postcommunist countries, that inequality principles serve as a kind of "new ideology" that everybody at least superficially endorses ($R^2 = .049$). Consistent with our hypothesis, individuals in the East who belong to higher social strata—especially those with higher education—reject egalitarian ideology as strongly or more strongly than similar people in capitalist countries. In postcommunist countries rejection of equality norms is strongest among those whose life chances were most restricted by the egalitarian policy of the previous regime, i.e., the highly educated and the new entrepreneurs.

CONCLUSIONS

In this chapter we addressed two general hypotheses derived from micro- and macrolevel theoretical perspectives on adherence to egalitarian and inegalitarian norms (ideologies) concerning the distribution of income and wealth in industrial societies. Both hypotheses were modified to apply to postcommunist countries, where profound changes in both the dominant distributive ideology and in the stratification system itself are taking place.

Tests of these hypotheses were conducted with data from thirteen countries participating in the International Social Justice Project. To establish contrasting conditions for testing these hypotheses, the thirteen countries were classified in three clusters according to the level and kind of legitimacy of their distributive systems: Western capitalist countries with a high level of legitimacy based on the strong meritocratic orientation of their distributive system, capitalist countries with a high level of legitimacy stemming from a strong welfare orientation, and postcommunist countries with a very low general level of legitimacy due to their failure to meet either of these two criteria of distribution.

We first tested a measurement model for egalitarian and inegalitarian norms. The model and its parameters provided strong evidence in favor of split-consciousness theory. Two separate latent variables were delimited by confirmatory factor analysis. One represented egalitarian norms (EQUALITY) and the other inegalitarian norms (INEQUALITY). Although we found no significant cross-system variation in the definition of the two ideologies, we did find significant cross-system variation in the correlation between the two ideologies. A negative correlation at a medium level exists in Western countries, but the correlation is much weaker in postcommunist countries.

The conclusions from the first part of the chapter are straightforward. In capitalist societies, the structure of beliefs about economic justice is bidimensional. The split-consciousness perspective has merit in that we have shown the existence of two factors underlying a set of items concerning justifications of inequality and of egalitarian beliefs and norms, respectively. As expected, these two factors show a primarily competing relationship (represented by a significant negative correlation), but not mutual exclusiveness.

The markedly weaker correlation between egalitarian and inegalitarian norms (ideologies) of distributive justice in the postcommunist bloc suggests that the two ideologies are not yet as well crystallized in these countries as they are in Western capitalist world, where the "battle" between them has been fought much longer. Though very likely for different reasons, split-consciousness theory finds even stronger support in data from postcommunist countries than from Western countries.

In the second part of the chapter, hypotheses were tested that addressed the theory of dominant inequality distributive norms and challenging equality counternorms. The results we obtained from testing both recursive and nonrecursive models supported this theory. Both in the West and in the East, inequality beliefs form a dominant distributive ideology. In accordance with the theory, the effect of one's position in the system of social stratification on the adherence to inequality principles is much weaker than its effect on inclination to egalitarian principles. However, there are significant differences even within the Western world. It seems that the dominant (inequality) ideology is exposed to a much stronger challenge from egalitarian norms in systems that are perceived as primarily meritocratic than in welfare-oriented systems. On the other hand, in welfare-oriented systems, there is a much stronger tendency of inequality principles to challenge existing egalitarian orientations. Thus we may conclude that in more classically liberal capitalist systems, egalitarian counternorms represent an ongoing and quite strong challenge to the dominant ideology, while in more welfare-oriented systems it is inequality ideology that stands in a challenging position, regardless of its near universal adherence (as measured by the lack of effect of social stratification variables). In more meritocratic distributive systems, lower social strata more strongly embrace egalitarian ideology and higher social strata more strongly reject egalitarian norms than they do in more welfare-oriented systems.

In postcommunist countries, our results confirm the hypothesis that inequality norms serve as a kind of "new ideology" that everyone feels compelled to endorse, regardless of lacking experience with which to judge it—in contrast to the prevailing negative experience with which to judge egalitarian ideology. Inegalitarian principles receive special support from holders of a college or university diploma, whose income and life chances were the most limited by the egalitarian ideology of the communist regime. Also, it is no surprise to see that those with higher education and those who are in the new entrepreneurial class, those whose life chances suffered the most under the previous egalitarian regimes, most strongly reject egalitarian ideology—even more strongly than similar people in the West.

The results of this chapter argue that duality in thinking about principles of economic justice is a universal feature of capitalist economic societies, and of the postcommunist region as well. We have also seen the universality of a pattern such that those who occupy less privileged positions in the stratification order—i.e., those with more limited life chances—are substantially more likely to express egalitarian sentiment than are the more privileged, but that these two groups differ little in their endorsement of inegalitarian norms. This suggests that in all these countries the working classes form a swing vote group in the politics of distribution and redistribution.

APPENDIX: MEANS AND STANDARD DEVIATIONS (STD), AND
CORRELATION MATRICES

Table 9.A1.   Means and Standard Deviations

	W-CAP		WLF-CAP		EAST	
	Mean	*S.D.*	*Mean*	*S.D.*	*Mean*	*S.D.*
EQSHR	2.121	1.234	2.514	1.362	2.114	1.354
WNEED	3.254	1.361	2.960	1.267	3.306	1.389
PAYFAM	2.073	.981	2.185	.929	2.370	1.056
WORKH	4.556	.705	4.344	.782	4.628	.743
KEARN	4.340	.838	4.033	.964	4.214	1.041
PASSW	4.513	.787	4.457	.814	4.685	.735
RIGHTOR	5.513	1.779	5.482	1.673	5.372	1.934
HIPROF	.345	.475	.300	.458	.228	.419
FSEI	43.835	15.783	42.311	15.758	37.413	15.471
COLLEGE	.289	.453	.288	.453	.228	.420
INCOME	5.459	2.908	5.651	2.853	5.498	2.830
RSEI	49.113	15.106	47.742	15.290	45.083	16.005
SELFEMP	.138	.345	.205	.404	.097	.296
SEX	1.454	.498	1.348	.477	1.453	.498
AGE	38.490	11.712	41.026	10.493	38.625	10.634

Table 9.A2.   Correlation Matrix for Measurement Model: W-CAP

	EQSHR	*WNEED*	*PAYFAM*	*WORKH*	*KEEP*	*PASSW*
EQSHR	1.000					
WNEED	.141	1.000				
PAYFAM	.256	.036	1.000			
WORKH	−.234	−.011	−.109	1.000		
KEEP	−.399	−.133	−.154	.461	1.000	
PASSW	−.178	−.256	−.110	.354	.436	1.000

Table 9.A3.   Correlation Matrix for Measurement Model: WLF-CAP

	EQSHR	*WNEED*	*PAYFAM*	*WORKH*	*KEEP*	*PASSW*
EQSHR	1.000					
WNEED	.237	1.000				
PAYFAM	.295	.101	1.000			
WORKH	−.118	−.034	.040	1.000		
KEEP	−.260	−.158	−.226	.433	1.000	
PASSW	−.124	−.052	−.201	.393	.497	1.000

Table 9.A4.   Correlation Matrix for Measurement Model: EAST

	EQSHR	*WNEED*	*PAYFAM*	*WORKH*	*KEEP*	*PASSW*
EQSHR	1.000					
WNEED	.243	1.000				
PAYFAM	.301	.131	1.000			
WORKH	−.068	.094	.022	1.000		
KEEP	−.157	−.013	−.091	.416	1.000	
PASSW	−.193	−.155	.071	.315	.227	1.000

Table 9.A5. Correlation Matrix for Structural Model: W-CAP

	EQUAL	EQUIT	RIGHT	HIPRF	FSEI	COLL	INC	RSEI	SELF	GEND	AGE
EQUALITY	1.000										
EQUITY	-.554	1.000									
RIGHTOR	-.285	.261	1.000								
HIPROF	-.378	.041	.003	1.000							
FSEI	-.217	.115	-.027	.304	1.000						
COLLEGE	-.349	-.055	-.062	.668	.383	1.000					
INCOME	-.369	.107	.053	.464	.175	.385	1.000				
RSEI	-.307	.030	-.041	.720	.347	.627	.351	1.000			
SELFEMP	-.310	.127	.088	-.059	.131	.117	.086	.106	1.000		
GENDER	.231	-.086	-.102	-.034	.003	-.035	-.530	.079	-.171	1.000	
AGE	-.173	.096	.102	.089	-.057	.022	.165	.093	.244	-.042	1.000

Table 9.A6. Correlation Matrix for Structural Model: WLF-CAP

	EQUAL	EQUIT	RIGHT	HIPRF	FSEI	COLL	INC	RSEI	SELF	GEND	AGE
EQUALITY	1.000										
EQUITY	-.416	1.000									
RIGHTOR	-.169	.236	1.000								
HIPROF	-.289	-.010	-.115	1.000							
FSEI	-.204	-.001	-.026	.190	1.000						
COLLEGE	-.239	-.168	-.188	.542	.328	1.000					
INCOME	-.267	.075	.038	.408	.031	.339	1.000				
RSEI	-.295	-.035	-.082	.767	.250	.591	.339	1.000			
SELFEMP	.051	.138	.246	-.102	-.119	-.066	-.140	-.141	1.000		
GENDER	.182	-.131	-.058	-.268	.110	-.056	-.748	-.042	-.044	1.000	
AGE	.133	.076	.159	-.025	-.092	-.031	.156	-.052	.296	-.102	1.000

Table 9.A7. Correlation Matrix for Structural Model: EAST

	EQUAL	EQUIT	RIGHT	HIPRF	FSEI	COLL	INC	RSEI	SELF	GEND	AGE
EQUALITY	1.000										
EQUITY	-.175	1.000									
RIGHTOR	-.077	.041	1.000								
HIPROF	-.449	.039	-.085	1.000							
FSEI	-.283	-.006	.023	.285	1.000						
COLLEGE	-.531	.071	-.046	.798	.322	1.000					
INCOME	-.383	.103	.029	.409	.129	.369	1.000				
RSEI	-.374	.003	-.030	.808	.303	.729	.294	1.000			
SELFEMP	-.055	.051	.101	-.328	-.099	-.233	.053	-.283	1.000		
GENDER	.114	-.082	-.065	.164	.083	.102	-.338	.189	-.272	1.000	
AGE	-.083	.105	-.041	.170	-.078	.142	.093	.100	.084	-.060	1.000

NOTES

1. Because the same micro- and macrolevel theoretical frameworks are used in this chapter and in Chapter 8 of this book, the respective theory sections in each paper contain some redundancy. Rather than inconvenience the reader by referring to material in the previous chapter, we decided to tolerate redundancy, making each chapter stand alone, obviating the need to reread parts of another chapter.

2. Legitimacy is often defined in terms of the correspondence between the real and the ideal, i.e., between "what is" and "what should be." These items only concern the "what is" dimension of evaluations of the economic distributive system. We did not ask directly parallel questions about "what should be." However, we believe it is reasonable to assume that abstract or general values of equality of opportunity, provision of need, and the reward of effort and skill are endorsed by substantial majorities in all countries. Accordingly, an index formed from questions about the real only likely correlates highly with a hypothetical one formed using difference scores for the real minus the ideal. In addition, analyses of questions about how important certain factors are and should be in determining pay—in particular about "individual effort" and "responsibility held"—give parallel results. (Details of these analyses are available from the authors.) See also the discussion of legitimacy presented in Chapter 5 in this volume.

3. Nevertheless, our measure of inegalitarian orientation is substantially correlated with a measure constructed from items that have been used in other research to measure "equity" norms (Ritzman and Tomakovic-Devey 1992) or popular "functionalism" (Kluegel and Smith 1986; see also Chapter 10 in this volume). Using LISREL we estimated the correlation between a factor underlying our inequality measures (WORKH, KEARN, PASSW) and a factor underlying three items commonly used to measure commitment to equity or popular functionalism (an item concerning general societal benefit to good profits, the need for inequality to motivate hard work, and the need to have inequality to encourage people to take on responsibility) in each of the three groupings of countries. These three correlations are, respectively, W-CAP = .43, WLF-CAP = .61, and EAST = .44.

4. The index was computed as a sum of Z-scores of the variables EQOPPOR, GETNEED, REWEFFR, REWSKILL. We chose this index for two reasons: first it standardizes national scales, and second it is more sensitive to those items with generally higher variation.

5. Details of the discriminant function and correspondence analyses are available from the authors.

6. Recall that the scale of this factor is coded such that a higher value indicates lower agreement with the statement, "People get what they need."

7. For each country, the number of cases analyzed is Great Britain, 516; Bulgaria, 507; Czechoslovakia, 553; East Germany, 429; West Germany, 541; Hungary, 319; Japan, 462; the Netherlands, 462; Poland, 614; Slovenia, 460; and the United States, 739.

8. These correlations were computed by PRELIS, a preprocessor for LISREL.

9. We also directly tested the hypothesis that the correlations among the indicators of equality and equity could be represented by a single factor, in other words, the hypothesis that thinking about principles of justice is unitary or that equality and inequality are viewed as mutually exclusive principles. The single-factor model has the following fit statistics: chi square, 514; df, 37; AGF, .911; RMR, .106. In absolute terms, the single-

factor model is a poor fit. In relative terms, a two-factor model (without the corre-lated errors of Table 9.1) has a markedly better fit: chi square, 286; df, 32; AGF, .960; RMR, .067.

10.   The value $k$df is the change in the number of degrees of freedom due to imposed equality constraints; $k\chi^2$ is the corresponding change in the chi-square statistic; kp is the level of statistical significance of the change in $k\chi^2$.

11.   As shown in panel (b) of Table 9.1, there are statistically significant correlations between errors of measurement.

12.   The correlation matrices used in structural modeling (in the Appendix) were obtained by first estimating structural and measurement model parameters for a recursive model (including a correlation between disturbances for EQUALITY and INEQUALITY). Covariance matrices for ETAs and KSIs were then extracted to enter further analyses.

10

Dominant Ideologies and the Variation of Distributive Justice Norms: A Comparison of East and West Germany, and the United States[1]

Bernd Wegener and Stefan Liebig

In comparative social justice research, one of the unresolved research topics is whether views on distributive justice vary with the social structure and the political organization of a society. For instance, based on survey results, Haller (1989) compared nine nations and concluded that there is such a variation. According to his reasoning, in societies that are strongly class based and welfare oriented, the majority tends to demand a strong redistributing state for minimizing social inequality. In societies, on the other hand, with more open mobility chances and weakly developed welfare rules, most people feel that the unequal distribution of goods that results from economic exchange is deserved and that there is no need for the state to redistribute. In terms of justice norms, what we have then is the norm of egalitarian statism versus a justice norm favoring self-interest and an individualistic reward system (see Chapter 6 of this volume). According to Haller, egalitarian statism is tied to welfare-directed class societies, whereas individualism is preferred in competitive, meritocratic societies. This view, however, has been contradicted by arguments put forth recently by Lane (1986). Though addressing primarily justice beliefs in the United States, Lane is convinced that in all advanced industrial societies self-interest and individualistic ideology has widely spread, implying the rejection of egalitarian statism. Lane reports empirical data of comparative social justice studies that evidence, across different types of countries, a general preference for the market distributions of goods. In advanced societies, distributions that are due to market processes are more likely to be accepted as just than distributions that are the product of state allocations because, as Lane argues, the "sense of controlling one's own destiny in the market, but not in politics, leads to more of a sense of political injustice than of market injustice" (1986:385). This idea would be in line with Parsons's (1970) conclusion that in modern societies the principle of freedom is valued higher than the principle of equality. But Lane's results dispute the assumption that justice ideologies depend on structural characteristics of a society.

How can the contradiction between these two positions be resolved? As we will show in this chapter, the contradiction results because, in each of the two views, either a *normative* or a *rational* argumentation is used (see also Chapters 11 and 12 of this volume). Only the normative side is considered by Haller (1989) and by all those who wish to defend that different societies have different dominant justice norms. Proponents of this view base their argument on particular "culture values" (Weber 1972b:34) that have developed over history and shaped the distributional institutions of a society such that the institutions correspond with the culture values. Thus, one would argue, for instance, that the evolution of meritocratic societies is based on the values of a Calvinist religious doctrine that demands of the individual to strive for inner-worldly success as a religious duty. In contrast, welfare societies may well have their roots in Lutheran religious doctrines in which acceptance of the state authority and patrimonial tenets play a major role (Troeltsch 1961). Thus, in both types of societies, different preferences for justice rules have evolved because both originate from different "normative cultures" (Parsons 1970). On the other hand, arguing for identical justice preferences in different societies, as Lane (1986) does, disregards the normative and cultural background of a society's development. Instead, when discussing the difference between market justice and political justice, Lane points to the likely psychological reactions people experience when confronted with either a market distribution system or a distribution system organized by the state. Lane's conclusion is that a market system offers greater advantages to the individual, and it is therefore rational to prefer a market system over a system in which the state allocates the goods. Since individuals in all societies tend to be rational, Lane seems to say, their preferences will be with the market system, regardless of the different normative cultures that may exist in these societies.

However, from an action theory point of view, normative and rational considerations are both needed if we want to explain why people have preferences for certain justice rules. Therefore, to make predictions as to which justice norms are cherished by members of different societies, we must consider the culture values characterizing a society, but we must also consider the rational interests individuals in different social positions of a society have. Both factors jointly determine the justice response of an individual. For instance, in a dominantly meritocratic society the majority, if not all of its members, endorse the individualistic justice norm because, as could be argued, it is the normative culture of "heroic individualism" that has given that society its particular structure. But meritocratic societies typically disadvantage certain groups of the population—in particular the not so well to do and those who do not achieve. It is in the rational interest of these groups, then, to favor egalitarianism and to call upon the state to distribute to them what they were unable to obtain by their own achievement. Conversely, in a welfare society, the normatively accepted justice principle will very likely be egalitarianism. But those who are particularly well off tend to be disadvantaged by that principle, since redistribution measures aim at taking from the affluent. The affluent, therefore, will favor the individualistic distribution rule in spite of the normatively accepted ideology of egalitarian statism prevalent in welfare societies. What we see, then, is that there is a certain interaction between the normative and the rational contingencies of justice beliefs in a society. Only by considering both, will it be possible to come to grips with the problem of whether members of different societies prefer either the same or different distributional justice rules and whether, in one and the same society, all of its members agree as to which rules are just.

In this chapter, we demonstrate that, in comparative social justice research, both the normative and the rational reasoning are necessary. As an example, we will contrast Germany and the United States. Germany can be viewed as an illustration of a class-based and welfare-oriented society, and the United States as an illustration of a meritocratic society. Of course, this distinction is ideal-typical, since institutionalized meritocratic rules will be found in Germany as well as in the United States and, conversely, in both societies, varying degrees of welfare regulations are existent. It is generally acknowledged, however, that historically these two societies form the extremes when placing societies on a continuum between class-based welfare societies and meritocracy (Rokkan 1974; Alber 1982; Flora and Heidenheimer 1987; Haller 1989; Esping-Andersen 1990).

PATTERNS OF NORMATIVE AND RATIONAL
JUSTICE IDEOLOGIES

One way of dealing with the contradiction between Haller's and Lane's views is to call into question the assumption, implicit in both, that there are such things as *dominant ideologies*. The dominant-ideology thesis (Abercrombie et al. 1980) assumes that a particular society has a consistent ideology for evaluating distributions of goods that is shared by virtually all members of that society. As is also assumed, this ideology serves the interests of the ruling class (Poulantzas 1974). The ruling class is thus viewed as an indoctrination agency being successful in forcing the subordinate classes to believe that the ways in which goods are distributed are normatively correct. For theoretical and historical reasons, however, the existence of dominant ideologies is unlikely. As Abercrombie and Turner (1978; Abercrombie et al. 1990) have argued, even in Marx's theory, the ideology of the ruling class is opposed by the class interests of the subordinate class, inasmuch as this class has moved from a class in itself to a class "for itself." Therefore, the ideology of the ruling class is not *the* dominant ideology. Historically, moreover, ruling-class ideologies were usually not available to the subordinate classes because these ideologies were either intellectually too demanding or simply irrelevant for the everyday lives of the subordinated. The purpose of the ruling ideologies was rather to secure the coherence and legitimation of the ruling class itself. For reaching that goal, no other classes were necessary to participate in these ideologies.

Social justice research has produced an additional argument against the assumption of dominant ideologies. Justice ideologies are rarely encompassing and consistent bodies of beliefs. As Kluegel (1989; Kluegel and Smith 1986; see also Chapter 9 of this volume) and others have pointed out, individuals often endorse more than one, and even contradictory ideologies. Kluegel's split-consciousness theory, for instance, assumes that, in the United States, a majority is in favor of material social inequality created by economic exchange, but that, at the same time, a substantial proportion of the population also prefer to have the state take measures to reduce social inequality (also Lane 1962; Sennett and Cobb 1973; Hochschild 1981). This challenging belief, as Kluegel calls it, is clearly inconsistent with the underlying acceptance of social inequality, but people seem to be able to hold both views. So it will be difficult to decide which of these views can be stamped the "dominant" ideology.

In order to free ourselves from the ambiguities tied to the concept of a dominant ideology, it will be useful to distinguish *primary* justice ideologies from *secondary* ideologies (Wegener and Liebig 1991; Wegener 1992c). We define primary ideologies as ideologies that are held by the majority of a society, ideal-typically by all of its members, whereas secondary ideologies are maintained by only particular groups in a society—possibly simultaneously with primary ideologies. The advantage is that the concept of justice ideologies is thus freed from the association with a ruling class that forces the dominated into believing existing distributions to be just. Instead, primary and secondary ideologies are distinguished only in quantitative terms: primary ideologies characterize a whole society, secondary ideologies characterize subgroups within that society.

However, the assumption that primary justice ideologies are held by the total population of a society implies that some mechanism is at work creating an encompassing consensus. This mechanism provides the basis for a society's legitimization. As such, it will be rooted in the cultural history of a society, exerting a normative influence on the beliefs most or even all people have about how goods should be distributed. Therefore, the nature of these beliefs must be reconstructed by going back to the cultural values that have developed in a society's history. In contrast, for secondary ideologies, being relevant only to specific groups in a society, we must look for other forces shaping these ideologies. One approach is to try to assess the rational motives members of subgroups in a society have, motives that can be held responsible for particular secondary justice ideologies to emerge. Thus, apart from the difference in number—

primary ideologies being endorsed by all, secondary ideologies only by certain individuals in a society—the two types of ideologies can be distinguished by focusing on the *normative* descent in the case of primary, and on *rational* motives in the case of secondary ideologies. This scheme would allow that, in one and the same society, individuals as members of particular subgroups may simultaneously uphold secondary ideologies, not necessarily consistent with the primary justice ideology, though everyone is normatively compelled to endorse society's primary justice ideology (see also Chapter 11 of this volume).

RELIGIOUS ROOTS OF CULTURE VALUES IN GERMANY AND THE UNITED STATES

When we ask which ideologies we can expect in class-based welfare societies and in meritocratic societies, it will not be sufficient to argue, as Haller (1989) does, that in class-based societies social inequality is particularly visible and strong, such that the cry for a powerful and equalizing state will ensue—resulting in egalitarian statism as the general justice ideology. Conversely, in meritocratic societies, Haller argues, willingness to achieve is given priority—yielding an individualistic ideology. This line of argument cannot explain why in both cases there is the astonishing congruency between the ideologies and the respective functioning of both types of societies. Why do Germans, for instance, when faced with social inequality, react with a preference for equality (calling upon the state to provide that equality), and why do Americans, also faced with social inequality, react with a preference for inequality (permitting the state to interfere as little as possible). For an answer, we must try to discover the culture values that form the roots of both kinds of justice ideologies. As is generally held, these values can be found in the two different variants of Protestantism: in Luther's and Calvin's Protestant religious doctrines. Following Weber (1972a, 1979), Troeltsch (1961), and others (Bendix 1970; Kalberg 1987; Marshall 1982), we will briefly sketch out how the two Protestant doctrines may have produced two different justice ideologies in these two countries.

In the preindustrialization epoch, both variants of Protestantism have differently shaped the *public sphere*, i.e., the occupational, the economic, and the political realm. In the *occupational realm*, the Lutheran doctrine adopted the feudal notion of craftsmanship and added to it the idea of a vocation or "calling." The disciplined and diligent performance of tasks became a religious duty—a duty, however, that was restricted to the fulfillment of work (Weber 1972b, 1979; Mühlen 1986; Volf 1987). For salvation, faith was a more important prerequisite than this inner-worldly sense of duty. In contrast, for the Puritanic tradition based on Calvinism in North America, diligent work habits were not simply a matter of religious duty but the single means of acquiring a sense of inner certainty of being among the eternally saved. Thus, in the United States, worldly success constituted a sign of God's favor and even of membership among the predestined few.

In the *economic realm*, the Calvinist tradition dictated to the member of the church or religious group to establish his reputation as an honest merchant who could be relied upon to give truthful advice and set a fair price. Only rational actions on the basis of these principles demonstrated loyalty to God. Therefore, trust in the reliance on "unknown others" as potential economic partners expanded beyond its original locus, the community of friends and church members, to the sphere of economic transactions (Wolfe 1989). Although the Protestantism of Luther cultivated the craftsmanship ideal and understood methodical labor as a religious duty, it failed to dissolve the traditional economic dualism inherent in medieval Catholicism. Economic transactions were still viewed as governed primarily by suspicion, dishonesty, and greedy calculation (Weber 1979:337–38). In Germany, therefore, the basic distrust in the economic domain constituted an important factor leading to an enormous proliferation of laws and a strengthening of the state.

As a third component that shaped the public sphere, the *relationship of the individual to the state* was conceptualized differently in both religious doctrines. In Lutheranism this relationship was authoritarian. Not only were the sovereigns deeply involved in the advancement of the German reformation, the alliance of throne and altar also played a major role in institutionalizing Lutheran Protestantism (Moeller 1988). This alliance, however, was an obstacle to overcoming the ideology of feudal hierarchies and the authoritarian mentality tied to that ideology (Schwarz 1978). According to Luther, the rulers and their subjects were, in the political realm, in a different position before God (Luther 1900, 1908a, 1908b). Whereas subjects were obliged as a matter of religious duty to be obedient to the state, the rulers were responsible before God to further the material and spiritual well-being of their subordinates, that is, they were representatives of a patrimonial state. In contrast, Calvinism was based on the covenant ideal (Calvin 1984), which required that all individuals, subjects and rulers alike, acted according to God's commandments, observing the ideals of truthfulness and fair play in particular. This gave subjects not only the right to criticize the acts of rulers, but also the obligation to overthrow tyrants who deviated from these commandments (Moeller 1987, 1988; Hill 1964).

LUTHERANISM, CALVINISM, AND PIETISM

With the advent of industrialization and the expansion of the public sphere in the nineteenth century, the configuration of the religious values in America proved not only particularly appropriate for the new mode of production and exchange, but these values could also be generalized to all realms of life, public or private (Kalberg 1987). This is what Parsons (1971) labeled *value generalization* as one of the exigencies of modernization. In the United States, this generalization was effected by extending the values of the public sphere into the private sphere. Being thus ideologically unified, "heroic individualism" and antistatism became, using the terminology suggested here, the *primary* ideology in America. In Germany, the Lutheran heritage was unable to provide a legitimizing ideology of an equally encompassing nature. Instead, what we observe here, is a deep gulf between the public and the private spheres (Kalberg 1987) reflecting Luther's doctrine of the two kingdoms. The notion of labor as being only methodical craftsmanship, and the failure to establish a trust relationship in economic transactions, left the expanding public sphere devoid of a value base in Germany. Given the necessity for a regulation of commercial relationships, this vacuum at the level of values was filled by state power and the development of an extensive legal apparatus far more comprehensive than in the United States. In addition, the private sphere in Germany was governed by values that were, by their very nature, opposed to the demands of modern economic transactions. The ideal of *gemeinschaft,* the ethics of neighborhood, and status equality in the family and among intimate friends was strengthened by Lutheranism and continued to prevail in the private sector (Kalberg 1987). Thus, in diametrical opposition to the American situation, German public sphere values had no foundation in private socialization practices. In fact, there was a distinct cleavage between the private and the public sphere. In obvious contradiction to Parsons's claim, value generalization was not a phenomenon to be observed in industrializing Germany.

We must, however, not end our analysis at this point. It is likely that Germany has undergone a process of value generalization of its own, but unlike the earlier value generalization in the United States, this value generalization is characterized by the penetration of the private values, favoring social equality, into the public sphere, i.e., by blending statism with egalitarianism (Mosse 1964; Dahrendorf 1965:144–75; Herf 1984). According to some authors (Wacker 1922; Hinrichs 1941; Deppermann 1961), this shift was well prepared by the particular German *Pietistic* tradition within Lutheranism that came into existence as early as the eighteenth century. One of the chief promoters of Pietism had been August Hermann Francke (1663–1727) of Halle. His variant of Pietism had a strong paternalistic and welfare component. Against Weber's somewhat simplistic dichotomy of Calvinism vs. Lutheranism in his *Protestant Ethics*, it must be recognized that Hallensian Pietism in Germany introduced the notion of *gemeinwohl*, or welfare, to the occupational and economic as well as to the political realm. Contrasting Luther's understanding of work as being a religious duty to be fulfilled with passion and craftsmanship, but contrasting the Calvinist idea of "salvation through worldly success" as well, Pietism valued work first of all as a means for fostering the public welfare and providing help for those in need. In fact, Francke's exemplary charitable institutions, like asylums and orphanages in

Halle (*Franckesche Stiftungen*) became a model for the unfolding Prussian state, its compulsory school system and welfare institutions. Pietism was also most likely influential in building the unique German social insurance system in the 1880s under Bismarck (Flora and Heidenheimer 1987). While Pietism in Germany, then, continued to value the authority of the state, it modified Luther's religious state doctrine in that patrimony had as its first goal the welfare of all. As one early commentator remarked, being uneasy with Weber's equating anglo-saxon Puritanism with German Pietism: "In Britain (*viz.* the United States) with Puritanism capitalism begins, in Germany socialism" (Hinrichs 1941:561). The pietistic version of Lutheranism is thus an important current characterizing public sphere values of the Protestant population in Germany since the eighteenth century. It was in particular part of the ethos of the higher Prussian state servants and the nobility that the state was to be responsible for the well-being of the impoverished. The concurrence of this moral view with major elements of the *gemeinschaft* belief in the private sphere can well said to have advanced the process of modern value generalization in both spheres. From this would follow that egalitarian statism has become the primary ideology in Germany.

To the extent that this is in fact what happened, we must go on and ask who has profited from this unification of value spheres and who has lost. In Germany, clearly, those affected most were the members of the *service class*, i.e., that group of individuals who are in top occupational positions in either the industrial or state bureaucratic hierarchies (Geiger [1932] 1972; Ringer 1969; Renner 1953; Dahrendorf 1965). Service class members could not expect to gain from egalitarian doctrines. This is why—following Dahrendorf's (1965) analysis—the German service class must be held responsible for the distinctive antimodernism in Germany and for the long-lasting separation of the public and the private spheres. Members of the service class were guided by a particular "German ideology" (Dahrendorf) of which the most important ingredients were the illusionary beliefs in social equality, *gemeinschaft* values, and the idealization of "culture" as opposed to "civilization" (Tönnies [1935] 1979). To the extent that egalitarian principles became blended with the idea of a welfare state, however, privileges of the service class were eroded (Ringer 1969). Thus, it can be assumed that these professionals, managers, and high state employees will, in addition to the primary ideology of egalitarian statism, seek a basis for legitimizing their own interests. Opposed to egalitarian statism, this would be the ideology of the minimal state and the endorsement of individualistic ideals. Therefore, by this historical reasoning, in contemporary Germany egalitarian statism is assumed to be the primary ideology everyone is willing to accept, but the German service class differs from the rest by upholding the self-interested individualistic ideology in addition. The latter is, therefore, Germany's *secondary* justice ideology.

Based on a parallel argument there is also a secondary ideology in the United States. Assuming that individualism is the primary ideology in America, we must also ask who is benefiting from this ideology and who is disadvantaged. As we can conjecture, those will feel disadvantaged by the "minimal state" who would gain by an "equalizing state," i.e., the minimal-state ideology is not to the advantage of the not so well to do. In the United States, therefore, the not so well to do—the non–service class members—are likely to support an opposing ideology. Egalitarian statism, in other words, is likely to be the *secondary* ideology in the United States, upheld by those who are not members of the service class. The non–service class members in America are expected to support this ideology *in addition to* the primary individualistic ideology being endorsed by everyone.

What has been said can be summarized as in Table 10.1. Empirically, do we find, as primary justice ideology, egalitarian statism in Germany and self-interested individualism in the United States? With primary ideology we mean that an ideology is maintained by the total population of a society and that it is rooted in the cultural history of that society. In contrast to primary ideologies which exert, due to their cultural descendence, a normative pressure on all members of a society, secondary ideologies originate from rational considerations of particular classes. Second, we ask whether there are secondary ideologies in both countries such that, in Germany, members of the service class endorse individualism besides egalitarian statism; and that, in the United States, all members outside the service class approve of egalitarian statism though they share with everyone else the preference for individualism?

EAST GERMANY

Speaking of Germany in the 1990s, however, must not leave unconsidered that Germany is two societies in one. Both were only very recently united, East Germany—what has been the German Democratic Republic—integrating with the West only gradually. Therefore, the predictions we make for Germany as a society, may not apply to East Germany. Both parts of Germany should be

Table 10.1. Distribution of Primary and Secondary Justice Ideologies in Germany and the United States

	GERMANY	*USA*
Primary ideology	Egalitarian statism (total population)	Self-interested individualism (total population)
Secondary ideology	Self-interested individualism (service class)	Egalitarian statism (non–service class)

treated separately therefore. It is safe to assume, however, that East Germany is, like the West, firmly rooted in the German welfare and authoritarian state tradition. This is what East Germans have, in its most extreme form, been experiencing for the last sixty years. In addition, the East German population is of predominantly Lutheran origin, thereby making the acceptance of a strong state something one would expect to find. But the wrenching transformation East Germany is undergoing presently has led many to believe that the East German society today is in a severer state of anomie (Habich, Landua, Seifert, and Spellerberg 1991; Habich, Häder, Krause, and Piller 1991; Fuchs, Klingemann, and Schöbel 1991; Wegener and Liebig, Chapter 11 in this volume). An immediate reflection of this would be the presence of particularly inconsistent justice beliefs. Also, we cannot expect the distribution of justice norms to be very structured in East Germany. Having been shielded from meritocratic economics for so long, the population will now support individualistic principles with great enthusiasm. But, at the same time, well aware of the blessings the socialist distribution system did provide, egalitarian principles and statism would be the values East Germans are still likely to cherish. Members of the service class in the East, having lost virtually over night the privileges they had in the old system, are particularly likely to hold on to these values (Wegener and Liebig, Chapter 11 in this volume). Therefore, we do not expect the East German service class to be an exceptionally strong proponent of Germany's secondary justice ideology (self-interested individualism). We rather expect that, in East Germany, members of all classes will favor individualism, but that more or less all will also favor egalitarian statism—regardless of the obvious inconsistencies this combination of beliefs implies (see Chapter 3 of this volume).

To the extent that there are ideological differences in the East German population at all, these will most likely be due to *age* differences. While we may conjecture that age is in general a factor determining justice beliefs strongly since persons of different age have experienced different socialization environments, in Eastern Germany it is particularly important at what time period an individual was socialized. Assuming that life experiences in our formative years are of special importance for which values and action orientations we will treasure over the life span (Mannheim 1928; Inglehart 1977), one must consider the fact that the East German history was marked by decisive political and economical discontinuities. A look at the educational and occupational opportunities reveals marked differences between the different age groups (Huinink and Mayer 1993) directly related to the economical strategies and policy shifts implemented by the regime (Ludz 1968; Glaeßner 1977). Thus, for instance, those born before 1930 were molded in the fifties by genuinely socialist values. The forced transformation of the East German social structure after World War II allowed this generation to experience rapid upward social mobility, presumably resulting in a strong attachment to the system they helped to rebuild. Moreover, the mass exodus of the educated middle class to the West, before the Berlin wall was put up, most likely strengthened the sense of identification with the regime and its socialist ideology among those left behind. In contrast, for those born after the war and for the very young, identification with the ideals of socialism gradually became questionable. They were early in their lives confronted with the lure of Western material goods and the freedom they were deprived of. This most likely weakened the appeal of the egalitarian convictions held by their parents and the acceptance of a strong state. Instead, they looked to affluence, wealth, and individualism as a source of legitimation. Contrasting sharply, therefore, with the generational value change in Western democracies that has brought younger people to identify with egalitarian, antistate, and antiachievement values, we expect in East Germany that older persons identify with egalitarian statism.

RESEARCH METHODS

We use data from the International Social Justice Project (ISJP) comparing only the data for the United States and Germany. There are 1414 completed interviews available for the United States, 2856 for Germany. In Germany, however, separate samples for East and West Germany were drawn, resulting in 1019 cases in the East and 1837 in the West (Kleebaur and Wegener 1991; Appendix of this volume).

From the questionnaire, the following items were selected to represent the two justice ideologies under study. This selection was the result of a detailed exploratory factor analysis involving many more items. The following six map the two theoretical concepts best:

Egalitarian statism: (1) "The government should guarantee everyone a minimum standard of living." (2) "The government should provide a job for everyone who wants one." (3) "The most important thing is that people get what they need, even if this means allocating money from those who have earned more than they need." (5-point response scales were provided.)

Self-interested individualism: "Please tell me how much influence each of these factors should have in determining the level of pay for an employee on the job: (4) The employee's individual effort, (5) the responsibility held by the employee on the job" (4-point response scales were provided for both items). (6) "People are entitled to pass on their wealth to their children" (5-point response scale).

As the main independent variable, service class membership is used (Kurz 1989; Herz 1990). Service class is determined by applying, to the respondents' present occupations, the *International Standard Classification of Occupations* in its 1968 version (International Labour Office 1968). ISCO's major groups 0, 1, and 2 are selected excluding, however, all technical and nonprofessional occupations[2] as well as all respondents who report to have no supervisory responsibility in their job. "General managers" (unit groups 300, 400, 500, and 600) are added.

With this classification, we define as service class a relatively small group of high-ranking managers in private enterprises, and executive public servants. This definition is much more restrictive than that used, for instance, by Goldthorpe (1987). For the United States, we find that there are somewhat less than 17 percent of service class members, according to our classification. In Germany there are 9 percent.

Beginning our analyses, we will look at the differences in mean factor scores of egalitarian statism and individualism between East and West Germany and the United States and also between service class members and nonmembers. Following that we use structural equation models in which the two ideology factors are treated as endogenous latent variables. For each country, we fit identical models—for reasons discussed above, East Germany will be treated as a separate population so that three data sets are compared. Results are evaluated by looking at goodness-of-fit indices and the significance levels of the structural parameters. Here, the most important question is whether service class membership has the predicted reciprocal effect in both Germanies compared to the United States.

Other independent, structural variables are respondents' age, the highest level of education they received, and their sex. In the course of our analyses we also use two attitudinal variables: First, respondents' preferences for a low level of income differences in their society as proxy for the preferred level of social inequality; this was measured by determining the quotient of the amount the respondent thought to be appropriate ("just and fair") to earn for an "unskilled manual worker" and a "chairman or managing director of a large corporation." The second item reads: "Would you say your (household) income is much less than you need, somewhat less than you need, about what you need, somewhat more than you need, or much more than you need?" These two items are used as control variables since it can be assumed that both affect the respondents' preferences for either of the two justice ideologies. Someone preferring large income differences will most likely not be in favor of the egalitarian distribution principle and will advocate individualism instead. Conversely, to the extent that someone feels deprived in terms of having not a high enough income to satisfy his or her needs, it can be predicted that that person would strive towards the state implementing redistribution measures, distrusting individualistic maneuvers to better his situation. We begin by using first the structural variables as controls adding the attitudinal variables next. Again, the important question is whether the predicted effects of service class membership "survive" even when age, sex, education level, and the attitudinal variables are considered.

RESULTS

Table 10.2 compares mean values of factor scores in West and East Germany and the United States. The factor scores result from a confirmatory factor

Table 10.2. Mean Factor Scores of Egalitarian Statism and Self-Interested Individualism by Country and Class: April/May 1991[a]

| | Primary ideology | | |
| | Egalitarian statism | | Self-interested individualism |
	W. Germany	E. Germany	
Country mean	2.36	7.09	5.26
	(7.64)	(5.13)	(8.28)
Service class	2.42	6.81	5.79
	(7.72)	(6.45)	(6.80)
Non–service class	2.35	7.12	5.14
	(7.64)	(4.98)	(8.56)
t-value for difference	.097	.344	.903
	Secondary ideology		
	Self-interested individualism		Egalitarian statism, U.S.
	W. Germany	E. Germany	
Country mean	−3.65	−3.44	−6.48
	(9.43)	(9.56)	(10.16)
Service class	−1.62	−0.78	−8.88
	(9.10)	(7.88)	(10.08)
Non–service class	−4.01	−3.37	−5.97
	(9.44)	(9.68)	(10.11)
t-value for difference	**2.539***	**2.183***	**3.351*****

[a] Factor scores are multiplied by 10;
standard deviations in parentheses. $N = 2311$.
*$p \leq .05$.   **$p \leq .01$.   ***$p \leq .001$.

analysis of the six justice items we chose to measure egalitarian statism and self-interested individualism in the three populations. In Table 10.3, separate confirmatory analyses for West Germany, East Germany, and the United States are reported. As can be seen from the measurement models in the upper panel of Table 10.3, egalitarian statism and individualism are both well captured using the six items; the factor structure is basically the same for both Germanies and the United States. Based on this result, the factor score means of Table 10.2 have been derived from a single confirmatory analysis that is by treating all three populations as one sample.[3] The comparison of the country means in Table 10.2 reveals that egalitarian statism is highest in East Germany and lowest in the United States, West Germany being placed in a position in between but closer to East Germany. For individualism the United States comes out highest, both Germanies showing much lower values. So clearly—as would be predicted by proponents of the dominant-ideology thesis—the United States, being a mer-

Table 10.3. Estimates of a Structural Equation Model (Nonstandardized Coefficients) for Determining Egalitarian Statism and Self-Interested Individualism in West Germany, East Germany, and United States of America: April/May 1991[a]

	Egalitarian statism			Self-interested individualism		
	West Germany	East Germany	United States of America	West Germany	East Germany	United States of America
Measurement model						
State should guarantee standard of living	1.000	1.000	1.000			
State should guarantee that people have jobs	1.625*** (4.804)	1.068* (2.428)	.932*** (9.394)			
People should get what they need, if necessary by redistribution	1.012*** (5.900)	.482* (2.429)	.326*** (5.405)			
Job income should be determined by achievement				1.000	1.000	1.000
Job income should be determined by responsibility				.909*** (9.041)	.564*** (3.816)	1.232*** (3.262)
People are entitled to keep what they have earned				.873*** (9.050)	.242** (2.989)	.275* (2.329)

Structural model

Service class (= 1)	.023	−.018	−.062*	.079*	.047	.007
	(1.032)	(−.585)	(−2.211)	(2.481)	(1.160)	(.292)
Control variables						
Sex (female =1)	.044*	.037	.124***	−.056	−.026	.073**
	(2.101)	(1.207)	(4.484)	(−1.916)	(−.650)	(2.731)
Age	−.024	.069*	−.130***	.065*	−.089*	−.029
	(−1.202)	(2.025)	(−4.629)	(2.216)	(−2.226)	(−1.236)
Education	.006	−.032	−.119***	−.006	.175***	.079**
	(.297)	(−1.017)	(−4.199)	(−.181)	(4.260)	(2.838)
Goodness of fit						
Chi square	85.256	75.161	57.484			
df	25	25	25			
N	785	591	935			
GFI	.979	.975	.988			
RMR	.043	.053	.034			
R^2	.019	.039	.123	.040	.072	.058

*$p \leq .05$.   **$p \leq .01$.   ***$p \leq .001$.

[a] *t*-statistics in parentheses.

itocratic society, is more individualistic; Germany, having a strong welfare state tradition, is more egalitarian.

But if we distinguish between class membership in the three populations, also in Table 10.2, we see that the differences in mean values of individualism between service class and non–service class members are statistically significant in West and East Germany, but not in the United States. What this tells us is that individualism in both Germanies is the secondary justice ideology since members of the service class endorse that ideology more strongly than individuals not belonging to that class, whereas in the United States individualism is an ideology shared by all, regardless of class. Thus, according to our definition, individualism qualifies as a primary ideology in the United States. This being what we expect, we also see that for egalitarian statism the picture is the perfect mirror image. In the United States, the service class favors egalitarian statism more than the non–service class, proving that ideology to be a secondary ideology in the United States; whereas in both Germanies egalitarian statism is a primary justice ideology cherished by all, independent of class.

Next we show that service class membership has the described effects also when controlling for the basic covariates age, sex, and education level. In the lower panel of Table 10.3 the results of a structural equation model are given in which class membership as well as age, sex, and education are included as exogenous observed variables, egalitarian statism and self-interested individualism being latent constructs.

In terms of significant regression coefficients[4] we see here that, in both Germanies, being a member of the service class does not affect the belief in egalitarian statism as a distribution norm; service class members and nonmembers alike endorse that norm. Thus, even controlling for age, sex, and education, this is what we expect, since egalitarian statism has the role of a primary ideology in Germany. In the United States, however, those who are not members of the service class support egalitarian statism. This behavior is, as we argue, rational since redistribution measures tend to benefit the disadvantaged; that is, non–service class members react rationally in the face of an opposing primary ideology (individualism) in the United States. Hence, controlling for age, sex, and education, egalitarian statism proves to be secondary in the United States and primary in the two Germanies with regard to class membership.

The situation is turned around with respect to the individualistic ideology. In the United States, more or less all support that ideology, regardless of class. In Germany, however, when controlling for the other variables, it is West Germany that most clearly presents the predicted picture, in that service class members favor individualism more than non–service class members. Clearly, self-interested individualism is, in West Germany, a secondary ideology. In East Germany, however, the population behaves differently. Here, those not in the service class prefer individualism to the same extent as those in the service class. In contrast to what we find when comparing factor score means within the East

German population (as in Table 10.2), controlling for other structural variables does not yield a significant difference of service class members and nonmembers. Instead, the structural model demonstrates that in East Germany age is more important than class in explaining justice beliefs. In sharp contrast to West Germany and the United States, older Eastern Germans support egalitarian statism and resent individualism. Obviously, older citizens of East Germany identified with the socialist regime early in their lives and find it difficult now to turn their backs on these beliefs (Wegener and Liebig, Chapter 11 of this volume). In addition, the significant influence of education level on individualism speaks to the fact that those with high education in East Germany seem to be able to free themselves from their former socialist, egalitarian convictions more easily. Indeed, if we look at the interaction of age and education (not shown in Table 10.3) it becomes clear that even older respondents with a high level of education in Eastern Germany now favor self-interested individualism.

While service class is the most important independent variable in the present context, in Table 10.4 we also look at the attitudinal realm, examining whether class differences continue to be effective when controlling for justice-related attitudes. If respondents feel that their household income is insufficient for satisfying their *needs*, they tend to support egalitarian statism; this is evident for the United States at least, but the relatively high, though statistically insignificant coefficients for West and East Germany should be observed as well.

Preferring large *income differences*, on the other hand, leads to not preferring egalitarian statism in the United States. Here, the preference for large income differences makes people support individualism, as the rather high but insignificant *t*-value seems to suggest. In West Germany, however, we find that those not wishing to see large income differences in their country do *not* support individualism. While this may well be a reflection of Germany's welfare tradition, opposed to American meritocracy, it is noteworthy that in the United States the well educated diverge from the general population. As can be seen from the effects of the interaction terms with education, in the United States the better educated, who hold large income differences to be desirable, prefer egalitarian statism. This is consistent with Kluegel's (1989) result that higher-educated Americans tend to promote what he calls "challenging beliefs." In fact, not only in the United States but in West Germany as well, the better-educated "challenge" whatever is the primary ideology in their respective countries—self-interested individualism in the United States, egalitarian statism in West Germany. In the latter case, however, the respective interaction coefficient with $t = 1.382$ stays below the statistical significant level.

In East Germany, it should be observed that preferring large income differences results in also preferring egalitarianism; only the better educated seem to be resistant to this obvious cognitive inconsistency, as the negative interaction effect with education in Table 10.4 suggests. In addition, East Germany does not exhibit the typical class-related pattern of primary and secondary ideologies

Table 10.4. Estimates of a Structural Equation Model (Nonstandardized Coefficients) for Determining Egalitarian Statism and Self-Interested Individualism in West Germany, East Germany, and United States of America, without Measurement Model (see Table 10.3): April/May 1991[a]

	Egalitarian statism			Self-interested individualism		
	West Germany	East Germany	United States of America	West Germany	East Germany	United States of America
Structural model						
Service class (= 1)	.053	−.014	−.060**	.085**	.043	.005
	(1.493)	(−.493)	(−2.599)	(2.732)	(1.067)	(.226)
Control variables						
Sex (female = 1)	.064*	.028	.073**	−.059*	−.017	.071**
	(1.963)	(1.017)	(3.157)	(−2.060)	(−.435)	(2.794)
Age	−.037	.057*	−.069**	.069*	−.079*	.030
	(−1.137)	(1.977)	(−2.996)	(2.419)	(−1.995)	(1.395)
Education	.032	−.042	−.139***	−.020	.138*	.078*
	(.877)	(−.927)	(−4.559)	(−.621)	(2.126)	(2.495)

Attitudes					
Household income is less than needed	.049 (1.474)	.045 (1.144)	.084*** (3.533)	−.018 (−.615)	−.045 (−1.144)	.004 (.172)
Preferring large income differences	−.039 (−.314)	1.220* (2.078)	−.441*** (−3.362)	−.295** (−2.670)	−.473 (−.588)	.184 (1.487)
Preferring large income differences × education	−.117 (−.927)	−1.242* (−2.106)	.368*** (2.727)	.152 (1.382)	.514 (.636)	−.157 (−1.240)
Goodness of fit:						
Chi square	99.621	87.515	93.389			
df	36	36	36			
N	785	591	935			
GFI	.981	.978	.985			
RMR	.036	.040	.036			
R^2	.078	.072	.192	.103	.082	.064

*$p \leq .05$.   **$p \leq .01$.   ***$p \leq .001$.

[a] t-statistics in parentheses.

found in both West Germany and the United States. From this it can be concluded that East Germany's distribution of justice beliefs is presently without much structure. This does not mean that the East German population is unaware of the distinction between egalitarian statism and individualism, but that no decision can be made presently as to what the primary and what the secondary ideology in that part of Germany is. In East Germany, most people seem to have a preference for egalitarian statism *as well as* for self-interested individualism. Only their age and, regarding the preference for individualism, their education seem to distinguish Eastern Germans in terms of what distributive justice beliefs they have. But East Germany, being a society in transition, does not yet exhibit the specific pattern of normative and rational justice ideologies typical of either a welfare or a meritocratic society.

CONCLUSION

In a recent review, Arts and van der Veen (1992) distinguish between the Durkheimian approach to social justice and the exchange perspective. Durkheim presupposes that a society is characterized by certain moral ideas and norms grounded in specific features of solidarity having emerged in the society. While societies may well differ in accordance with the social conditions and the type of solidarity reached, within any one society the moral ideas are cherished by all of its members alike and thus constitute the normative culture of a society on which legitimation is based (Müller 1992). The exchange approach to social justice, in contrast, reflects on the individual and on his or her motivation in social interaction. Human beings are motivated by the gains they can expect in exchange relations, but moral considerations do play a role. According to Homans (1974) and proponents of equity theory, the limitless thirst for ever greater profits is counterbalanced by a general feeling that returns should be proportional to costs and investments. The exchange reasoning proposes a "model of man" (Skidmore 1984) that conceives human beings as rational as well as moral, if only according to Aristotle's proportionality rule.

The argument we put forth in this chapter represents the attempt to merge Durkheim's with the exchange perspective. While it is well evidenced that different societies have typical dominant justice ideologies as their primary ideologies, there are also justice beliefs within a society that challenge these primary convictions. The secondary justice beliefs are maintained by members of particular groups in a society, usually by those groups who would be disadvantaged if the primary ideologies were enforced throughout. In spite of the normatively established primary distribution rules in a society, therefore, it is rational for the members of these groups to call the primary justice rules into question and to support alternative rules from which they can hope to benefit. To the extent that egalitarian statism is rooted in the pietistic Lutheran tradition in Germany, and that, in the United States, self-interested individualism has its foundation in the Calvinistic religious doctrine, both respective ideologies have become the dominant ideologies in these countries. But, as could be demonstrated here, service class members in West Germany and non–service class members in the United States maintain secondary justice beliefs that are directed against what the respective religious traditions promote as norms in both countries, because it is rational for them to do so. In societies where other cleavages besides class boundaries are pronounced, as is true of East Germany in its present transition phase, it is interesting to see that the structure of primary and secondary justice ideologies is less clear. Here one could argue that the transitory period will not have ended before justice beliefs have gained structure.

What results then is not that societies simply differ in their normative traditions and dominant ideologies, but that different *patterns* of primary and secondary justice norms have emerged in different types of societies. This raises the question of how legitimation is possible under these various conditions. How much justice norms consensus is necessary for a society to form a "normative order" (Parsons 1937)? This question has been central to the long debate between proponents of consensus and conflict theories. One of the lessons to be learned from that debate is that it is not so much consensus of norms that keeps a society in balance but the *lack* of consensus in the areas where the deprived translate these norms into concrete demands (Mann 1970:436). The relationships between the macrolevel justice norms discussed in this paper and the microlevel claims people make for improving their personal well-being in everyday life is something social justice research must focus attention on.

NOTES

1. An earlier version of this paper was presented by Stefan Liebig at the Eighty-Seventh Annual Meeting of the American Sociological Association, Pittsburgh, August 20–24, 1992.

2. On the unit groups level, we exclude 022–029 (engineers, technologists), 031–039 (assistants, technicians), 043 (ship engineers), 071–079 (medical assistants), 084 (programmers), 133–139 (primary school teachers, kindergarten teachers, etc.), 161–163, 171–190 (artists, musicians), 193–196 (social workers).

3. The goodness-of-fit index (Jöreskog and Sörbom 1985) for this analysis is .995; chi square = 63.503 with 8 degrees of freedom.

4. Since we analyze the relationship between justice ideologies and occupational classes, the samples we study include only respondents who report ever having had a job. Controlling for selectivity bias, however, by applying the usual two-step instrumental variable procedure (Berk and Ray 1982) does not result in noticeable changes of the estimated coefficients.

IV

SOCIAL STRUCTURE AND
JUSTICE BELIEFS

11

Hierarchical and Social Closure Conceptions of Distributive Social Justice: A Comparison of East and West Germany[1]

Bernd Wegener and Stefan Liebig

The reunification of Germany is tied to many unmet demands for a better distribution of resources between East and West. In view of the high unemployment rate of almost 40 percent in some parts of the former German Democratic Republic (GDR), in many cases the situation amounts to actual disaster and individual tragedy. As Judith Shklar argues in her *Faces of Injustice* (1992), individuals in a modern democratic state who experience disaster often redefine their misfortune as injustice. It is therefore pertinent to know with which principles Germans living on both sides of the former border, come to view their misfortune as injustice or, on a more general level, which norms of distribution they accept as morally good.

In dealing with a society that was divided for forty years, it seems plausible to assume that the different political and economic "systems" have produced different standards of social justice. The distinct ideological features of the East and the West may well have induced differences in the socialization of values. On the other hand, if there are such differences, it is also possible that they were generated by differing material conditions and dissimilarities in the respective social structures. These two possibilities raise the problem of uncovering the determinants of justice beliefs. On the abstract level there are two causal explanations in this context (Archer 1988): It is either assumed that the structural characteristics of a society determine justice perceptions (for which Marxism would be a prime example) or that the consensus over norms that exists in a society generates that society's perception of justice (as would be argued by proponents of functionalism). The task of the sociology of culture has been to integrate both points of view (Archer 1988; Thompson 1990). From an empirical standpoint, however, it is unavoidable to keep both views separate and to proceed

263

step by step. Thus, the important question is first, What kind of justice reactions to specific structural conditions are to be expected? Whether there are also justice beliefs in a society that are rooted in norms typical of that society, in cultural traditions, or in religious doctrines is a question of a separate causal concern.

Two problems arise by separating the two perspectives. The first is related to the structural characteristics of a society. Which structural conditions are relevant for the development of attitudes and values? Anthropologist Mary Douglas attempted to answer this question (Douglas 1982). She proposes that the specific mode of *social control* operating within societies is responsible for the acceptance and bearing of the society's "cosmologies," with justice beliefs being an important ingredient of these cosmologies. This perspective gives rise to the hypothesis that the regions of former East and West Germany, which until recently cultivated different forms of social control, should also display different justice norms. The second problem is of a methodological nature. What is the best way to separate the effects of social structure from those of cultural consensus? The separation of the two types of effects can be best realized through comparative measures, that is, through comparing at least two societies with each other and using a two-step procedure (Przeworski and Teune 1970). The first step requires determining what effects structural determinants have on the perceptions of individuals living in a specific society. If there is variation that remains unexplained, that is, that cannot be attributed to structural factors, then, second, this variation may be ascribed to the influence of "culture."

Based on this theoretical and methodological background, we examine any differences between Eastern and Western Germany in justice beliefs and try to determine whether the causal factors that are responsible for diverging beliefs are more "cultural" or more "structural." To test for which influence is more dominant, we use data stemming from the International Social Justice Project (ISJP). In order to apply the two-step procedure outlined above to this data, we must first decide on a theory that outlines how *structural* conditions affect value orientations and beliefs. Such a theory can be formulated on varying levels of abstraction. It is possible first to reduce the determinants to effects that are general enough to apply to all social situations. The results would then correspond to an abstract causal model without any specific empirical effects. Subsequent to this, it is possible to introduce specific structural constraints that may affect justice perceptions. In particular, these structural constraints can be tied to concrete historical settings, e.g., Germany's forty-year-long separation. Only a concrete model such as this may be empirically tested. We adopt the anthropological ideas expounded by Mary Douglas (1982; Douglas and Wildavsky 1982) as an introduction for an abstract model, which we then attempt to steadily concretize. The following is a short presentation of her ideas.

ANTHROPOLOGICAL FOUNDATIONS OF JUSTICE

In her article *Cultural Bias*, Douglas (1982) assumes that the convictions and values that individuals have are reactions to the social conditions in which they live. Prevailing convictions and values help individuals to justify their actions in relation to their social environment. These convictions and values represent "implicit cosmologies" (Douglas 1982:190) or our *ways of life* as Thompson, Ellis, and Wildavsky (1990:3) put it. Douglas sets very high standards, positing that there are only four social environments and hence also only four cosmologies. Her approach may leave a vaguely familiar Parsonian aftertaste but is, in fact, actually directed against Parsons (Thompson et al. 1990:179–88). While Parsons's AGIL model (1951) is based on dichotomies (instrumental vs. consummatory orientation of action and internal vs. external order relations), Douglas proposes a *dimensional* schema. The social conditions in which we live vary— using Mary Douglas's own terminology—in gradations of *grid* and *group*. *Grid* represents the "dimension of individuation." *Group*, on the other hand, represents "social incorporation" (Douglas 1982:190). This means that the social environments in which all individuals operate have two characteristics: First, all social environments have, to some extent, external constraints. They typically stem from hierarchical structures and the regulations associated with such social constructions (*grid*). The stricter and more extensive these constraints are, the less individuals may dictate their own actions. Second, all social environments are characterized by the extent to which individuals are part of demarcated social entities (*group*). The more closely individuals are incorporated into such social entities, the more likely their decisions will be affected by group norms. The social environment can vary in both respects independently from one another: It contains either strong or weak hierarchical constraints and involves individuals in either strong or weak social closure. In this sense, grid and group appear in orthogonal gradations.

The group dimension describes the extent to which individual lives are influenced by group membership. Individuals tied to others through close living arrangements, shared employment or leisure activities, the use of mutual resources, or similar "social honor" rank high on the group dimension. As the sharpness of the group borders, the monopolization and exclusivity of entry increase, the stronger the group dimension becomes. On the other hand, the grid aspect describes a type of framework of regulations similar to that used by Durkheim to describe anomic suicide (Durkheim 1983:273–318). In highly regulated social contexts it is the institutionalized ordering of social positions that define and restrict the individual's interaction therein. The positional ordering of individuals within a social hierarchy casts the die for interaction such that those in higher positions cannot compete or associate freely with those in lower positions or vice versa. The weaker the grid aspect becomes, however, the more possibilities open up to the individual, for control over his or her own situation through activities of negotiation and compromise with others. Thus, both the grid and group dimensions represent modes of social control. But in one case group norms and decisions subjugate the individual (group), in the other case regulations that stem from a hierarchy of social positions act as a force of subjugation (grid). By considering only the extreme forms of both dimensions we are able to construct a taxonomy of four typical social constellations (Table 11.1; Douglas 1982; Thompson et al. 1990): On the one hand there can be conditions of strong social closure and group ties, in which the closed social formations may either operate within the framework of a distinct hierarchical structure (strong group/ high grid) or a weak or absent hierarchical differentiation (strong group/low grid). In the first case, constraints produced by the positional ordering of the social environment are strong, in the second case weak. On the other hand, the social system may be permeable, consisting of relatively weak group ties. Here too, the social structure may be either distinctly hierarchical (weak group/high grid) or only weakly differentiated by rank (weak group/low grid). According to Douglas, these four social conditions are associated with four types of cosmologies: *ascriptivism, egalitarianism, individualism,* and *fatalism.*[2] These cosmologies must be understood as reactions to the social circumstances in which individuals live.

Ascriptivism

In the situation of both strong group ties and strong hierarchical structures within a society, individuals find it only natural to live in closed groups and to be subjugated to the norms of this group. They are used to the rigid rules dictated by their "place" in that society. Thompson et al. (1990:9) describe the male Hindu member of a high social caste as being the prototype thereof, deriving his rights and duties from his social position and living in strict separation from other social groups. His social and hierarchical position is given to him *ascriptively*. This describes the grid under which the individual lives. At the same time the individual is fully aware that s/he shares his or her fate only with the members of his or her own group, leading to exclusion of the nonmembers (Weber 1972b:23; Parkin 1979).

Table 11.1.   The Grid-Group Paradigm

	Weak group	*Strong group*
High grid	Fatalism	Ascriptivism
Low grid	Economic liberalism	Egalitarianism

Egalitarianism

An egalitarian cosmology consists of individuals who also have strong group ties but, contrary to ascriptivists, do not feel the dictates of hierarchically dictated restrictions. Group borders are weakly differentiated and have a tendency to be open. Strong group/low grid means that individuals are likely to give in to the pressures of group solidarity. Incumbents of positions of any level are usually denied any type of special rights. An extreme example of this cosmology would be a member of a commune or a cult (Thompson et al. 1990:9), where all material and symbolically created inequalities have been abolished. Here the process of conflict resolution would have to be closely watched to avoid the exercise of power.

Individualism

Individualism results from a situation in which not only the hierarchically determined constraints are weak, but with them also group pressure and solidarity, thereby allowing the individual a type of freedom of movement independent from such restrictions. The self-made entrepreneur represents the prototype of this cosmology, since his or her success lies in the conviction that the only thing that counts is individual achievement (Thompson et al. 1990:7). This form of individualism is allowed to develop in a society in which the individual operates relatively free from the pressures of both group ties and social hierarchy.

Fatalism

Individuals exposed to tenacious restrictions stemming from his or her position within a social hierarchy without having the support of group solidarity (high grid/weak group) will in time come to fatalistically comply to the inevitable and to acquiesce in what fate decrees. The nonunionized textile worker of nineteenth-century England is an example of this type of social condition. S/he was forced to accept the dictates of the social environment and was, as an isolated individual, at its mercy. With time, the fatalistically oriented individual comes to learn that s/he is always the loser in the end and that all attempts made to change the situation are virtually useless (Runciman 1966).

RESPONSIBILITY AND DISTRIBUTIVE SOCIAL JUSTICE

These four social types and their unique social structural antecedents make up the panorama of ideological biases and *ways of life*.[3] The ideological contents may be applied to any imaginable sphere of life. They determine which preferences take form in the various spheres, which in turn are determinants of individual action. Nevertheless it is important to remember that individuals are seldom conscious of their preferences, which explains the frequent inconsistency and the lack of strategic rationality in their preferences. To make preferences visible requires drawing upon existing ends-means situations and the related ways of life. In this way, if individuals could consciously react to their individual grid-group positions. For example, an egalitarist could be made aware of his or her preference for a specific political measure simply by posing the question whether or not it would increase or decrease inequality. Far more frequent, however, is the situation in which our preferences arise as an unintentional consequence of attempts to organize our lives in a specific way and to associate with other individuals (Thompson et al. 1990:57). Those living in rigid, socially closed groups, for example, in which membership is relatively free from external constraint (low grid/strong group) will inevitably regard outsiders quite negatively and even with hostility, whereas one's own group members are held in high esteem. Such preferences are not the result of some conscious plan for a desired way of life, but rather the unintentional result of factual social relationships. These shared convictions and expectations permeate all spheres of life, yet their origins remain well hidden from view.

Preferences that deal with questions such as who is assigned responsibility and who gets what are particularly salient for the way in which people live together. Together they build the basis of the way distributive social justice is perceived in a society by offering acceptable answers to the questions Who should distribute resources? and How should the resulting distributional outcomes appear? Because the answers to these questions have direct implications for the way in which people live together, there will be varying answers within a single society. Ascriptivists, for example, have a vested interest in keeping the responsibility for prevailing social inequalities impersonal. They maintain that the factual distribution of privileges and goods is natural and self-evident and that inequality is ascriptively determined and good. Egalitarists, on the other hand, appeal to authority. They hold the state ultimately responsible for the unjust distribution of wealth. Hence, a redistribution of societal resources that aims to fulfill the egalitarian wish for maximum equality should, in their view, also be the responsibility of the state. Individualists relate their own failures to personal incapabilities: only achievers are rewarded with success. They hold a system of free competition to be fair because it bestows the individual with responsibility. This is in direct contrast to the fatalistic viewpoint, which blames the system for one's unfortunate situation. In this outlook, individuals have an ominous sense of being at the mercy of a system that denies justice to the individual.

The above description gives rise to the assumption that the four grid-group types also differ in their preferences for distributional social justice. Each defines the responsibility for the allocation of resources differently and strives toward different distributional outcomes. While in ascriptivism the responsibility remains relatively hidden (Thompson et al. 1990:59), in egalitarianism it is given to central authorities. In individualism, it is the individual who takes responsibility. The fatalist holds destiny to be responsible. As far as the hoped for outcome of resource distribution goes, there are also important distinctions: The ascriptivist hopes to maintain the existing conditions of inequality, the egalitarist hopes to overturn them. Individualists view differential rewards as just as long as those who work hard receive more than those who do not. Essentially, this of course is what the doctrine of economic liberalism entails. Fatalists react with resignation: of course, they would prefer the reduction of social inequality, but the prevailing circumstances are unfortunately unalterable.

The differences in the attribution of responsibility and in preferences for distributional outcomes offer an important basis for the operationalization of Douglas's social-justice-related cosmologies, which play a role in the empirical part of this paper.[4] Of great importance to the empirical application of this paradigm is that specific structural conditions give rise to typical ideological reactions. Hence, making predictions about ideologies first requires being able to recognize the concrete social structural conditions. The following attempts to show how the abstract model may be increasingly influenced by circumstances in Eastern and Western Germany.

GRID AND GROUP IN EAST AND WEST GERMANY

Many authors provide evidence that the extent of subjectively felt social inequalities was, on the average, less distinct in the former GDR than in West Germany (Korte 1990; Adler 1991a, 1991b; Schupp and Wagner 1991; Noll 1992a; Szydlik 1992). Of course, there were enormous factual differences based on power, influence, and income (Pollack 1990; Mayer 1992a, 1992b) firmly cemented through the acquisition of organizational assets (Wright 1985) as well as loyalty (Adler 1991b). However, the fact that income leveling is an integral part of the socialist ideology of *gemeinschaft* caused many Germans living in the former GDR to overlook hierarchy-produced obstacles. In this sense, the former GDR population could be described as having lived under low-grid conditions. West Germany, on the other hand, is a highly stratified society with pronounced hierarchical restrictions (high grid). By the same token, it would seem plausible to assume that the former East Germans shared feelings of solidarity, making strong use of available social networks. This would mean that the group factor was of more importance in East than in West Germany. This idea is supported by the saliency of social ties as a valued resource in the GDR, as well as the many East German support networks that successfully operated outside the iron grip of the totalitarian organization (Pollack 1990; Adler 1991b; Huinink and Mayer

1993; Mayer 1992a; Thomas 1991). Individuals living in West Germany, on the other hand, are often described as existing under conditions of isolation and "individualization," this being characteristics of competitive societies.

This application of the Douglasian paradigm is however very schematic. It implies the demarcation of the two German societies according to a particular combination of grid and group—East Germany being supposedly an exemplar of low grid/strong group, West Germany of high grid/weak group. In reality, however, the differences are never so absolute as to lead to complete reciprocal exclusion. The relevant question at this point is how the actual empirical reality in Germany and the socially relevant characteristics of individuals affect their justice perceptions. Thus, other variables besides territory should come into play. We proceed on the assumption that class membership, social mobility, age, and sex are all factors that work in this way to influence the assignment of individuals to one of the four types of ideology.

By considering these structural characteristics and their influence on the formation of justice perceptions, our viewpoint challenges the idea that for every society there is but one typical dominant ideology. This stance is also implied by Douglas, however. She posits that the position of any type of society in the two-dimensional space defined by grid and group determines its dominant ideology. In this sense, Douglas finds herself in a curious alliance with both Marx and Parsons, both of whom hold the belief that there exists a uniform system of norms for every society. Marx describes this situation by claiming that in every epoch the ideas of the ruling class are turned into the dominant ideas of the total society (Marx [1845/46] 1968). This concept makes up the popularly held *dominant-ideology thesis* (Poulantzas 1974), one that has, however, also been disputed (Abercrombie, Hill and Turner 1980). Marx himself undermines the idea of a top-to-bottom diffusion of a dominant ideology on a theoretical level by positing that, in capitalism, members of the class-conscious working class will come to develop ideas quite different from those of the ruling class. Furthermore, the dominant-ideology thesis has been proven to be historically incorrect (Abercrombie et al. 1980; see Chapter 10 of this volume). A kind of "contamination of the masses" through the ideology of the ruling class (Poulantzas 1974) stands contrary to the fact that the content of such ideologies was frequently incomprehensible to the masses and often lacked relevance to their day-to-day existence. Moreover, empirical social justice research has been especially fruitful in showing that justice perceptions within societies are in themselves heterogeneous and even contradictory. One and the same circle of individuals may support two contradicting ideologies (*split consciousness*; Kluegel and Smith 1986; Kluegel 1989). Under these conditions it is difficult to describe societies as having a single dominant ideology.[5] In view of the task of separating "structural" from "cultural" determinants of justice ideologies within Germany, we are therefore left with the question, To what extent do class membership, social mobility, age, and sex affect the formation of justice perceptions in both parts of Germany?

Class Membership

Class membership may affect the individual mentalities. This idea has, in fact, been employed for demarcating different classes (Geiger [1932] 1972). The approach is particularly appropriate in the case of classes that attain a distinguished demographical identity and a high degree of unity. According to Goldthorpe (1987) this is especially characteristic of the *service class*, a categorization stemming from the writings of Renner (1953) and Dahrendorf (1965, 1969; Wegener and Liebig, Chapter 10 of this volume). The service class consists of individuals in top positions in state bureaucratic institutions or private organizations, having for the most part a tertiary education, who in some form share in the "exercise of power" (Dahrendorf 1965:106) and who are able to set their own working conditions in a relatively autonomous fashion. Dahrendorf (1965) reminds us that this class along with its "German ideology" was responsible for the antimodernism and for the prolonged segmentation of the private and public spheres in Germany. This not only led to a delayed generalization of values (Parsons) within these spheres (Kalberg 1987), but also to ambivalent values: On the one hand, members of this social class rejected social inequality, since it conflicted ideologically with their ideals of *gemeinschaft* upheld in the private sphere; on the other hand, they were well aware that under the cloak of this image they were free to secure their own interests (Dahrendorf 1965:17–242; Mosse 1964; Stern 1961; Herf 1984; Eley 1986). The classification of members of the service class within the framework of the grid-group paradigm is then based on their self-image, characterized by both a conscious awareness of their own hierarchical and privileged position and a deep-seated feeling of belonging to a privileged group. High grid and strong group thus describe their social condition. This would mean that ascriptivism should be the preferred ideology of members of the service class. An ascriptive understanding of justice allows individuals to champion the safeguarding of one's own interests and to advocate the preservation of prevailing inequalities at the same time (Wegener 1992a, 1992c; Wegener and Liebig, Chapter 10 of this volume).

What relevance does this have for the comparison between Eastern and Western Germany? Is it safe to assume that ascriptivism guides the conduct of service class members in general? This would imply that, ideologically, belonging to a privileged class in the former GDR had no impact on the individual, especially in terms of the individual internalization of socialist values. This is highly unlikely, since we know that class position in the former GDR was tied to conformity and loyalty to the party. Furthermore, the popular state-sponsored advanced training programs—the key to career opportunities—were tied to a lifetime of conformity and the assimilation of socialist values (Glaeßner 1977; Weidig 1988; Meier 1990; Adler 1991b). It is to be expected from the successful former East German professionals that their identification with the GDR regime and its ideology was not merely superficial or feigned, perhaps brought about by "force" or "discipline" (Mayer 1992a). Instead their identification was real and deep-seated, a product of an intensive and long-standing socialization. In contrast to the West German service class members, therefore, who perceive ascriptivism as the means to safeguarding their own interests, the East German service class members may very likely still cling to the egalitarian ideology and will reject the privilege-securing justice ideology of ascriptivism.

Social Mobility

In addition to class membership, experiences that individuals make in the course of their careers play an important role in the development of their justice perceptions. Of primary importance in this respect is social mobility. Other studies have shown (Boudon 1986; Wegener 1991) that the upward and downward movement associated with social mobility and the personal experiences individuals have with social mobility help shape individual justice judgments. Those on the way up the career ladder are more likely to support justice principles being in line with the doctrine of economic liberalism. Contrary to those on the way down and the nonmovers, they are skeptical of any egalitarian measures and its corollary, state intervention. These findings then stand in accordance with Mary Douglas's theory, since individuals who were successful in attaining a higher occupational position have managed to struggle for that freedom of action typical of the low-grid/weak-group environment, economic liberalism being the corresponding justice ideology. In addition to that, the psychology of motivation offers a variety of possible explanations (Atkinson 1964; Weiner 1976), arguing either with learning theory (Bandura 1979) or attribution theory (Heider 1958) or the development of either internal or external control expectations (Rotter 1966; Phares 1976). The multiple-principle approach to justice research (Deutsch 1975, 1985) describes how in competitive contexts, for example, in the work setting, the achievement principle, which describes a liberal justice perception, outweighs all others in making judgments about distributional outcomes (Sampson 1975; Schwinger 1980b; Lerner and Whitehead 1980; Hochschild 1981). Based on this approach, we may predict that upwardly mobile individuals are more likely to have a preference for economic liberalism, since occupational work represents a sphere of deep-seated importance to them. This psychological mechanism, finding empirical support in the above-mentioned areas of research, seems so strong that the influence of all other factors appear as secondary. This means that in both the eastern and western populations of Germany it should hold true that upwardly mobile individuals should tend toward an economically liberal oriented justice ideology.

Age

The idea that age determines justice perceptions is founded on the thesis of the determining force of socialization. Life experiences in our formative years are the most important (Inglehart 1977), since they result in the emergence of values and orientations of action that prove to be remarkably stable throughout the entire life span (Alwin, Cohen, and Newcomb 1991). Mannheim's (1928) definition of generation is founded on the legitimacy of this concept. His approach is especially important for the reconstruction of the long-term values held by the GDR population branded by the political and economical discontinuities characterizing its history. A look at the educational and occupational opportunities reveals marked differences between the different cohorts (Huinink and Mayer 1993; Trappe 1992) directly related to the economical strategies and policy shifts experienced by this country (Ludz 1968; Glaeßner 1977). Bürklin (1992) links the political-historical conditions of the GDR to the emergence of distinct "generations" of East Germans: the "Weimar generation" experienced its political socialization before 1933; the "transitory generation" was reared in the era of the Third Reich; the "Ulbricht" and the "Honecker" generations describe the two postwar generations. His results show age-specific differences in the acceptance of economic social inequalities, that is, of conditions that are basically irreconcilable with socialist ideals, in Eastern Germany today. Those belonging to the Honecker generation found it easier to accept such conditions than the older members of society, particularly those of the transitory generation. Mayer (1992a) describes a "reconstruction generation" and an "intermediate generation" and contrasts them with the present-day thirty-five- and forty-year-olds. The reconstruction generation of the former GDR (the 1920 to 1930 age groups) was molded in the fifties by genuinely socialist values. The forced transformation of the East German social structure after World War II allowed this generation to experience rapid upward social mobility (Korte 1990; Geißler 1991). This resulted in a strong attachment to a system they helped to rebuild and whose reconstruction cost them a great deal of self-sacrifice. Moreover, the mass exodus of the educated middle class to the West most likely strengthened the sense of identification with the regime and its socialist ideology among those left behind, in an attempt to uphold their self-consistency. Those born after this time frame were forced to come to terms with the existing circumstances with the means available to them. Applying Pizzorno's (1991) classification of theories of social order,[6] Mayer posits that for the intermediate generation, disciplinary measures take the place of internalized beliefs and values as the central mode of achieving social order. In the day care center, at school, in collectively organized vacations, or in the military, discipline was publicly displayed and clearly evident for all to see. In direct contrast to this, the private sphere was consumer-oriented, thus leading to a nichelike existence for many in the GDR society (Gaus 1983). "The good life had to take place in the GDR" (Mayer 1992a:14), even if this meant having to don the mask of feigned conformity once outside the private sphere. For those born after the war and for the very young, however, discipline has lost its attraction as a source of legitimation. For them, even the sense of identification with the ideals of socialism has become questionable. They not only experienced the double standards of conformity and silent fortune-seeking embodied by their parents, but were also confronted with the lure of Western material goods. Together, these experiences worked to weaken the appeal of formerly held sources of legitimation. Instead, the Honecker generation looked to affluence and wealth as a source of legitimation, thereby closing their eyes to its affiliation with social inequality and disproportionate privileging.

In this light, it is highly probable that the egalitarian socialist ideals belong to the long-term values of the older people within East Germany—in Douglasian terms they perceive their social environment as characterized by low grid/strong group. The younger are more likely to reject egalitarian values. These tendencies stand in direct opposition to those operating in Western Germany. There, the younger generation identifies more with egalitarian and antihierarchical values, thereby validating the Inglehartian thesis of a shift toward postmaterialism.

Sex

The former East German concept of the ideal normal life biography as one constituted by unintermittent, full-time employment outside the home applies not only to men, but to women as well. Enders (1986) describes how this idea existed side by side with the East German definition of productive labor, which idealized domestic activities and seemed to hold them in higher esteem than marketplace activities. This ambiguousness left women saddled with the responsibility of working out the details of making activities in both spheres compatible with one another. And as life course studies reveal (Trappe 1992), women living in the former GDR did not find the double burden abnormal. It is therefore likely that the socialization of Eastern German women have caused them to be oriented more toward individual achievement and less affected by sentiments of fatalism than their Western German sisters.[7] This tendency should be especially evident among those East German women who are presently employed.

From the above reflections concerning the likely influences of service class membership, job mobility, age, and sex, Table 11.2 selects the four most appar-

Table 11.2. Hypothetical Distribution of Grid-Group Types in East and West Germany[a]

	Weak group	Strong group
High grid	Fatalism	Ascriptivism
	Women West: high	Service class West: high
	Women East: low	Service class East: low
Low grid	Economic liberalism	Egalitarianism
	Upward mover West: high	Old age group West: low
	Upward mover East: high	Old age group East: high

[a] See text for more detailed hypotheses.

ent hypotheses and places them within the grid-group schema. Rather than expecting that East and West Germany represent undivided examples of grid-group combinations and their associated cosmologies, there will very likely be differences in justice beliefs in East and West depending on the basic structural characteristics of individuals.

DATA, VARIABLES, AND RESEARCH METHODS

We use data from the German part of the ISJP (see Appendix to this volume). The surveys resulted in 1839 cases in Western and 1017 cases in Eastern Germany (Kleebaur and Wegener 1991; Appendix to this volume). Table 11.3 pre-

Table 11.3.   Description of Variables

Dependent variables	
Economic liberalism	There is an incentive for individual effort only if differences in income are large enough (5-point scale).
	It is all right if businessmen make good profits because everyone benefits in the end (5-point scale).
Egalitarianism	The government should place an upper limit on the amount of money any one person can make (5-point scale).
	The state should own the electric power plants (5-point scale).
	The state has the duty to care for the welfare of its citizens and has to finance the protection against personal risks out of tax revenues (5-point scale).
Ascriptivism	[Criteria for queuing for hospital treatment]
	The patient who can afford to pay most is treated first (4-point scale).
	Ratio of the just monthly income for a "chairman or managing director of a large corporation" and an "unskilled worker, such as a factory line worker."
Fatalism	[How often is each of the following factors a reason why there are poor people in Germany today?]
	Prejudice and discrimination against certain groups in Germany (5-point scale).
	Lack of equal opportunity (5-point scale).
	Failure of the economic system (5-point scale).
Independent variables	
Region	West, 0; East, 1
Structural variables:	
Service class	Members of the service class, 1; others, 0
Job mobility	Upward move at last job shift, 1; others, 0 (see text)
Age	Respondents' age in years
Sex	Male, 0; female, 1

sents the description of variables serving as a basis of the operationalization of the four justice types used for this study. The selected ten items out of a large number of possible variables together make up the four constructs used to study the two German populations. This is a sufficient number of variables to capture reliably the structure representing the prevailing justice ideologies. The results are presented in the upper part of Table 11.4 and are the estimation result of a confirmatory factor analysis for the joint populations of both Germanies.[8] Separate analyses lead to identical measurement models, meaning that the structure of justice perceptions is relatively similar in both parts of Germany.

We continue our analysis by utilizing confirmatory structural equation models to analyze the relationship between justice ideologies in Eastern and Western Germany and the structural variables class,[9] mobility,[10] age, and sex. All models

Table 11.4. Justice Beliefs in East and West Germany; Standardized Coefficients of a Structural Equation Model: April/May 1991

	Economic liberalism	Egalitarianism	Ascriptivism	Fatalism
Differences in income: incentive for individual effort	.383			
Differences in income: everyone benefits	.722			
State should place an upper limit on income		.465		
State-owned power plants		.700		
State has to care for the welfare of its citizens		.376		
Richness as a privilege (hospital treatment)			.266	
Preferred extent of social inequality			.878	
Poverty due to discrimination				.490
No equal opportunity				.593
Poverty due to the economic system				.526
Region[a] (East = 1)	−.200** (−3.300)	.664*** (11.611)	−.239** (−2.902)	.196*** (4.010)
R^2	.040	.440	.057	.038
Goodness of fit[b] GFI = .988 CFI = .970	Chi square = 68.589 df = 31 RMR = .215		N = 1057	

*$p_t \leq .05.$ **$p_t \leq .01.$ ***$p_t \leq .001.$

[a] t-value in parentheses

[b] GFI: goodness-of-fit index (Jöreskog and Sörbom 1985), CFI: Bentler's comparative fit index (Bentler 1989), RMR: root mean square residual (Jöreskog and Sörbom 1985).

employ the same measurement model for determining the endogenous justice constructs (presented in Table 11.4). As described earlier, the aim of this study is to discover if the differences in justice ideologies may be explained merely through structural effects or if, in addition, there is an East-West effect. In simple terms this means asking, Does living and having been raised in one or the other part of Germany make any difference at all in terms of justice perceptions? If, after controlling for structural variables there is still an East-West effect, then we may assume that cultural differences do indeed produce differences between the two Germanies.

RESULTS

As mentioned earlier, both parts of Germany exhibit a common factorial structure of justice beliefs (Table 11.4). This does not mean that there are no differences between the East and the West. The bottom part of Table 11.4 presents the estimated parameters of a structural equation model using the four justice factors as endogenous, latent constructs and the East-West dummy variables as exogenous variable. In Table 11.5 four additional control variables have

Table 11.5. Justice Beliefs in East and West Germany and Structural Variables; Standardized Coefficients of a Structural Equation Model: April/May 1991[a]

	Economic liberalism	Egalitarianism	Ascriptivism	Fatalism
Region	$-.196^{***}$	$.651^{***}$	$-.207^{**}$	$.160^{***}$
(East = 1)	(-3.790)	(11.762)	(-3.081)	(3.648)
Structural variables				
Service class (= 1)	$-.095^{*}$	$-.029$	$.094^{*}$	$.034$
	(-2.072)	$(-.825)$	(2.183)	$(.820)$
Job mobility	$.123^{**}$	$-.046$	$.009$	$.020$
(upward move = 1)	(2.626)	(-1.314)	$(.250)$	$(.490)$
Age	$.152^{**}$	$-.023$	$.052$	$-.148^{***}$
	(3.124)	$(-.664)$	(1.408)	(-3.414)
Sex	$-.132^{**}$	$.102^{**}$	$-.159^{**}$	$.174^{***}$
(female = 1)	(-2.777)	(2.837)	(-2.827)	(3.899)
R^2	$.112$	$.457$	$.098$	$.094$
Goodness of fit:	GFI = .986	Chi square = 112.147 df = 55		$N = 1057$
	CFI = .962	RMR = .165		

[a] See notes to Table 11.4.

been included: membership to the service class, an upward move in position, age, and sex. The two tables reveal that with regard to justice perceptions which part of Germany one comes from is statistically significant. Eastern Germans have a stronger preference for egalitarianism and distributional fatalism than Western Germans and tend to reject economic liberalism and ascriptivism. Controlling for the four structural variables (as in Table 11.5) does not result in a change in the direction or in the strength of the results: Both parts of Germany display a homogeneous structure with regard to justice perceptions, but the intensity of the individual perceptions do vary.

At the same time, the effects of the control variables reveal structural differences in the preferences for justice ideologies. As expected, ascriptivism appeals more to members of the service class in reasoning about the distribution of resources. Similarly, and in accordance with the ideal of *gemeinschaft*, they tend to reject economic liberalism as a justice ideology. It appears that the described relationship between mobility experiences and justice ideology is confirmed by our results as well. Those who experienced an increase in position at their most recent job shift are inclined to favor economic liberalism as a justice ideology, thereby indirectly voicing their support for individual achievement as a just principle for the distribution of resources. Age is a statistically significant factor only with regard to the justice ideologies economic liberalism and fatalism. Older respondents tend to favor liberalism and reject fatalism. Their rejection of fatalism reveals the older respondents' stronger attachment to norms, as compared to younger respondents. Sex appears to have the strongest determining effect on justice ideologies. All four justice ideologies are clearly influenced by the respondent's sex. In particular by favoring egalitarianism, women express their disagreement with modes of distribution based on achievement or social origins.

The conclusion of our analysis of justice perceptions at this point that the results serve as evidence for basic structural similarities between Eastern and Western Germany would be premature, however. The supposition, in particular, that class, age, and sex of respondents should elicit different effects, depending upon which part of Germany the respondent is from based on the idea of the differential developments of the two Germanies, remains yet to be tested. In order to account for these differences, it is necessary to test for interaction effects, that is, for the interaction between these variables and the region of Germany one is from. Only if the overall East-West effect stays constant in spite of having introduced the interaction terms will we be able to conclude that "culture" matters.

As Table 11.6 reveals, the East-West effect is all but stable. The addition of region-specific structural measures as independent interaction variables results in the disappearance of the formerly significant variable "region," i.e., the East-West distinction.[11] Instead, the differences in intensity of the justice perceptions are reducible to their individual structural effects acting within both Germanies. This is especially true for the ideologies egalitarianism and ascriptivism. Where-

Table 11.6. Justice Beliefs in East and West Germany and Structural Variables and Interactions; Standardized Coefficients of a Structural Equation Model: April/May 1991[a]

	Economic liberalism	Egalitarianism	Ascriptivism	Fatalism
Region	−.042	.049	−.075	.019
(East = 1)	(−.253)	(.363)	(−.566)	(.120)
Structural variables with interactions				
Service class (= 1)	−.041	−.023	**.163****	.006
	(−.760)	(−.516)	**(2.655)**	(.117)
Service class × region	−.095	−.030	**−.122***	.063
	(−1.617)	(−.634)	**(−2.173)**	(1.160)
Job mobility	**.179****	−.075	.008	.063
(upward move = 1)	**(2.878)**	(−1.616)	(.188)	(1.178)
Job mobility × region	−.088	.068	−.002	−.072
	(−1.416)	(1.353)	(−.044)	(−1.242)
Age	**.145***	**−.098***	**.099***	**−.163****
	(2.481)	**(−2.178)**	**(1.960)**	**(−3.027)**
Age × region	−.001	**.618*****	−.218	.057
	(−.005)	**(4.431)**	(−1.534)	(.369)
Sex	**−.185****	**.098***	**−.174****	**.241*****
(female = 1)	**(−2.882)**	**(2.032)**	**(−2.638)**	**(4.023)**
Sex × region	.125	.004	.047	−.131
	(1.665)	(.066)	(.795)	(−1.863)
R^2	.124	.487	.112	.104
Goodness of fit:	GFI = .987	Chi square = 128.953 df = 79		N = 1057
	CFI = .993	RMR = .164		

[a] See note to Table 11.4.

as in Western Germany older respondents reject egalitarianism, older respondents in the East continue to feel attached to egalitarian, socialist ideals and express preference for an egalitarian justice ideology. Of particular interest here is that the strong effect region appeared to have, explaining by itself 44 percent of the variation in the egalitarian factor (Table 11.4), practically disappears. Hence, a large part of the variation in egalitarianism does not exist between Eastern and Western Germany, but between different age groups within the two Germanies.

A look at the ascriptivistic justice ideology and its significance to class membership reveals a similar picture. In Western Germany it is the member of the service class who rationally prefers distribution rules that safeguard his or her privileges. The same class in Eastern Germany does not support this type of distribution to the same degree. This result reflects the persistence of socialist beliefs within the service class in East Germany.

As to the other individual characteristics apart from class membership, most noteworthy is here that in East Germany, older respondents are clearly more egalitarian than those in West Germany. At the same time, in both parts of the country, the economically liberal justice belief increases with age, while the strength with which fatalism is endorsed is lessening as people get older. Of interest, however, is that women in East Germany tend to be less fatalistic than their West German sisters, showing a higher degree of preference for economic liberalism at the same time. While both effects are visible, as was predicted, in numbers both effects fall short of being statistically significant. Finally, respondents in both parts of Germany do not differ in that those who have experienced upward occupational mobility in their most recent job shift are spurred into more strongly favoring economic liberalism as a justice ideology.

In sum, controlling for region-specific structural effects revealed that originating from either part of the two Germanies, in and of itself, does not affect individual preferences for justice ideologies significantly. Instead the region-specific *structural* effects are responsible for the variation between the two parts of Germany. Hence, the differences between the Germanies are of a structural, and not a cultural nature. However, the two Germanies do differ from one another in the way in which the structural effects work to influence justice ideologies.

DISCUSSION

Based on Mary Douglas's anthropological model, we may identify four types of justice ideologies in Eastern and Western Germany. The different intensities with which these four justice ideologies appear in Eastern and Western Germany cannot be explained by cultural differences existing between the two Germanies. Instead we must attribute the different preferences for justice ideologies in East and West Germany to the different structural conditions under which an individual exists and that make up his or her social environment. However, while this is the major conclusion we draw from our results, in the following we discuss in particular four problems that must not be left unconsidered.

First, the conclusiveness of our results may be somewhat narrowed through the sample of study. Since we analyzed the relationship between justice ideologies and class as well as occupational mobility, we were forced to limit our sample to include only those who had ever had a job and who had experienced at least one job shift. Thus our sample was systematically selected. The proper analysis of this sample calls for controlling for selectivity bias, and if necessary, for correcting it. Table 11.7 shows the results of a structural equation model using the inclusion probability as an instrumental variable (Berk 1983; Berk and Ray 1982).[12] The addition of this variable did not result in any changes, neither for

Table 11.7. Justice Beliefs in East and West Germany Controlling for Selectivity Bias; Standardized Coefficients of a Structural Equation Model: April/May 1991[a]

	Economic liberalism	Egalitarianism	Ascriptivism	Fatalism
Region	−.042	.144	−.016	−.028
(East = 1)	(−.250)	(1.040)	(−.116)	(−.327)
Structural variables with interactions				
Service class (= 1)	−.043	−.028	**.131***	.002
	(−.759)	(−.597)	**(2.317)**	(.045)
Service class × region	−.984	−.033	**−.120***	.065
	(−1.602)	(−.700)	**(−2.171)**	(1.199)
Job mobility	**.178****	−.074	.010	.061
(upward move = 1)	**(2.862)**	(−1.601)	(.220)	(1.140)
Job mobility × region	−.088	.064	−.003	−.068
	(−1.408)	(1.289)	(−.071)	(−1.181)
Age	**.145***	**−.094***	.098	**−.165****
	(2.486)	**(−2.098)**	(1.952)	**(−3.063)**
Age × region	−.003	**.594***	−.200	.071
	(−.017)	**(2.283)**	(−1.430)	(.458)
Sex	**−.185****	**.105***	**−.180****	**.241*****
(female = 1)	**(−2.882)**	**(2.186)**	**(−2.709)**	**(4.026)**
Sex × region	.126	.002	.050	−.132
	(1.673)	(.032)	(.844)	(−1.880)
Inclusion probability	.005	**−.162*****	**.098***	.007
	(.108)	**(−3.877)**	**(2.076)**	(.149)
R^2	.124	.509	.121	.104

Goodness of fit	GFI = .986	Chi square = 147.386 df = 85		N = 1057
	CFI = .991	RMR = .172		

[a] See notes to Table 11.4.

the coefficients for country, class, age, or sex, nor for the corresponding interaction effects. We are therefore relatively safe in assuming, that our results do not suffer from selectivity bias. The significant effects of the inclusion probabilities themselves simply mean that we overestimated the mean values of egalitarianism and underestimated those of ascriptivism. Employed respondents (with at least one job shift) tend to prefer the justice ideology of ascriptivism more than the unemployed, while the unemployed prefer egalitarianism more strongly. But the stable regression coefficients reveal that the observed differences in justice perceptions in Eastern and Western Germany are structurally produced regardless of employment status.

The second problem concerns the proposed linearity of age with the justice beliefs and the separation of age and cohort effects. Does the succession of "generations" really amount to a steadily increasing rejection of egalitarianism in the East and to its increasing acceptance in the West? And do comparable relationships hold with regard to the other justice beliefs? We tested for that by replacing the age variable and its respective interaction term with age group dummy variables that corresponded roughly with Bürklin's (1992) transitory, Ulbricht, and Honecker generations. The results exhibited the same reciprocal pattern of coefficients for Eastern and Western Germany that we find when using age as a continuous variable, but they led to a decrease of the respective R^2. So we can assume that age is linearly related to the justice beliefs we study. Using age instead of age groups is warranted in particular because the nonlongitudinal character of the data prohibits us from saying anything about what part of the variation in justice beliefs is age and what is cohort produced.

The third problem we address deals with the specification of our models. Is it safe to assume that being a member of a specific class and having experienced an upward mobility move *causes* certain justice beliefs? Could it not be that the justice beliefs have primacy and are responsible, at least in part, for someone reaching a high status position and for being upwardly mobile, e.g., by shaping his or her motivation for attainment? Although we do not think that this is a very probable path of influence since status attainment and mobility moves are known to be affected only very little by psychological attributes (Sewell, Haller, and Ohlendorf 1970; Wilson and Portes 1975; Alexander, Eckland, and Griffin 1975; Kerckhoff 1989), we have estimated alternative models. In these models we replaced service class membership and upward mobility by prestige of respondent's father and respondent's education, respectively, considering the fact that father's prestige predicts class position to a substantial degree and that high education increases the probability of shifting jobs (Sørensen and Tuma 1981; Carroll and Mayer 1986). While, in these models, the coefficients for father's prestige and education usually do not reach the level of statistical significance (the negative influence of father's prestige on egalitarianism being a noteworthy exception), the important part is here that by including these instrumental variables, the East-West effect disappears just as when using the variables for class and mobility themselves. So evidence seems to prove that our models are not wrongly specified.

Finally, we wish to point out that the strict distinction we make in this paper between "structure" and "culture" is at best an exaggeration. What we find is that variations in justice beliefs can be explained by variations of class, mobility, age, and sex, and that coming from East or West Germany is negligible vis-à-vis that finding. However, as we have argued in several different instances, class, mobility, age, and sex are attributes that may well be seen as reflecting different *socialization histories*, which are partly the product of *cultural* circumstances. Thus, the correct statement is not that "culture" does not matter, but that in East and West Germany the cultural forces have elicited different justice preferences depending on individuals' class, mobility experiences, age, and sex.

NOTES

1. An earlier version of this paper was presented by Bernd Wegener at the Fourth International Conference on Social Justice in Trier, Germany, July 1–3, 1993.

2. Douglas proposes a fifth cosmology, namely *hermeticism*, reserved for those individuals living outside of any social order and who have, in this way, attained absolute autonomy (Douglas 1982:231–38). The hermetical life-style, however, disqualifies itself from being defined as a kind of social type in the same manner as the other four types have been defined. Houghton (1991) suggests adding another dimension to the grid-group dichotomy: power. This addition makes for eight types of social environments, only five of which Houghton views as having distinct cosmologies (see also Thompson 1982). Thompson et al. (1990) also utilize the labels egalitarianism, individualism, and fatalism and replace ascriptivism simply with *hierarchy*.

3. The classification is exhaustive, fulfilling an important condition of scientific concept formation (Hempel 1965:137–54): The classification of all four types along the same dimensions results in categories that are logically distinct from one another. This is why the combination of hierarchy and social closure is also a possible basis for classifying the most important theories of social inequality (Wegener 1992b).

4. Other attempts to operationalize the four social types were undertaken by Gross and Rayner (1985), Hampton (1982), and Houghton (1991).

5. These same conditions have caused the Parsonian viewpoint (and the even more extreme standpoint of Davis 1948) of a uniform normative consensus to come under fire. While conflict theorists have always rejected the idea of normative consensus due to its implications to their theoretical construct (Dahrendorf 1974; Lockwood 1964), other theorists have come forward with criticisms of this idea, arguing that it represents an inadmissible application of "presuppositional" arguments to empirical conditions (Smelser 1985; Holton and Turner 1986; Alexander 1987).

6. According to Pizzorno (1991:233) there are four possible modalities to legitimate and secure social order, thereby resulting in four types of societies: those which are upheld by physical force (*Leviathan*), and those which are upheld by its members' use of inner control, that is, through disciplinary measures. Social order can also be upheld through incentives, which may be of a material nature, operating through the marketplace, or of a moral nature, working through the satisfaction of having firm principles (*value integration*).

7. This expectation is countered by the finding that a general tendency exists among women to support egalitarian and reject strict achievement-based principles of resource distribution (Davidson, Steinmann, and Wegener, Chapter 12 in this volume). Whether this is a reflection of a different, gender-specific morality (Gilligan 1982) and its influence on justice judgments is left undecided for our purposes. The empirical confirmation of the theses we propose would provide evidence of a structural determinacy of moral principles and its specifically "feminine" outcome.

8. Maximum-likelihood estimates were used for all structural equation models presented in this study (PROC CALIS of SAS).

9. The operationalization of the service class is based on the works of Kurz (1989) and Herz (1990), who tailored Goldthorpe's *Class Scheme* to suit the unique German situation (Goldthorpe 1987). The service class includes those employed as scientists, skilled laborers, and similar personnel or in managerial and executive positions within the

civil service or public administration. In addition to this, we included the occupations in the main categories of 0, 1, and 2 of the *International Standard Classification of Occupations* (International Labour Office 1968) into the classification as well (for exceptions to this, see Kurz 1989). This method allows us to exclude university graduates working in purely technical fields.

10.   Here, we calculated the bivariate regression of occupational prestige (Wegener 1988) after job shift on occupational prestige before the job shift. Individuals with positive residuals are considered upwardly mobile and those with negative residuals count as being downwardly mobile. In this way, the direction of mobility is determined independently from the "normal" upward mobility characteristic for any labor market system.

11.   The GFI and CFI coefficients' values of .987 and .993 point to the relatively good fit of the model (Table 11.6). This model offers with $\rho = .479$ the highest level of improvement in fit in relation to the original model. The model without interaction effects (Table 11.5) achieved a much lower level of improvement: $\rho = .143$ (Bollen 1989).

12.   We used logistic regression to estimate the probability of being included in the sample. The dependent variable hereto was a dummy variable, for which all respondents from the reduced sample were assigned 1; those excluded were assigned 0. Independent variables were education, prestige of father, region, and marital status, resulting in close to 60 percent of the respondents being correctly classified.

12

The Caring But Unjust Women? A Comparative Study of Gender Differences in Perceptions of Social Justice in Four Countries[1]

Pamela Davidson, Susanne Steinmann, and Bernd Wegener

Psychoanalytical and cognitive-developmental psychologists have long studied the formation and growth of individual moral perceptions. In linking these to gender differences in justice perceptions, such researchers make the claim that women's tendency to feel empathy and charity thwart their ability to reflect upon abstract principles of fairness. Women's capacity for abstract moral reasoning is described as being less developed or even nonexistent, overridden by women's contextuality, emotionality, and inconsistency. Freud ([1925] 1964:257) maintained that women "show less sense of justice than men" and attributed this to women's stunted ego development. After studying children's games, Piaget concluded that "the legal sense is far less developed in little girls than in boys" (1965:77). Kohlberg (Kohlberg and Kramer 1969; Kohlberg 1981, 1984) argued that women's lack of opportunities to engage in experiences that widen the moral perspective results in women's "stunted" sense of justice. Gilligan (1982, 1991) attempts to counter the gender bias inherent in such interpretations. She contends that women's moral development is qualitatively comparable to men's. In the same breath, however, she argues that women's moral perceptions are "different" from men's since women base their moral decisions on other, more "feminine" criteria. This, of course, puts Gilligan's feminist-psychoanalytic approach neatly in line with the very theories that she seeks to criticize. Gilligan argues that women cannot have justice perceptions, but that we should also come to recognize the merit in women's compassion, empathy, and moral "goodness." For Carol Gilligan, because women "care," they cannot be just in their moral decisions, but since both caring and justice are necessary in this world, why should this bother anyone (see also Flanagan and Jackson 1987)?

We argue that such an approach is not only overly simplistic, but is in many cases misleading for attempting to explain gender-specific variations in justice norm preferences. Both Gilligan's "difference feminism" (Pollitt 1992) and Kohlberg's unidirectional liberalism turn a blind eye away from the effects of differential economic and social positions in society. Highly hypothetical moral dilemmas, usually used in Gilligan's and Kohlberg's empirical research, tell us very little about how individuals would reason in real-life situations in which real interests are at stake. Hypothetical moral dilemmas ignore differing economic and social positions as well as differing levels of power that spark the rational considerations that work to shape perceptions of social justice. Such forces should be most apparent when looking at real-life situations requiring justice reasoning. An aroused sense of injustice is often the source of an alternative justice perception. Sexual inequality is the single most important issue affecting the interests of women. It is for this reason that we predict that women who are sensitive to the issue of sexual inequality may come to view justice differently then men. This in no way discounts the important role that the normative culture of a society plays. Beliefs and myths surrounding the normative culture may block the development of a sense of injustice and thereby the rational preference for specific justice principles. Justice ideologies represent one materialization of the "normative culture." A comparative study of different countries is for this reason especially relevant, since in different societies there are different justice ideologies in operation (see Wegener and Liebig, Chapter 10 of this volume).

Our comparative analysis includes the countries Russia, Poland, Western Germany, and the United States. The section that follows outlines the most important theoretical ideas found in the works of Lawrence Kohlberg and Carol Gilligan in their separate attempts to explain gender-related differences in justice perceptions. We then go on to look at approaches taken in the field of social justice research to explain gender-related variations in perceptions of social justice. By comparing these with the approaches taken by Kohlberg and Gilligan, we show how dissenting conclusions drawn from the various fields derive from the use of different measurement strategies. Whereas Kohlberg and Gilligan take a *hypothetical moral dilemma approach*, research in the field of social justice research favors a *real-life approach* to distributive justice situations. We then apply both approaches to our comparative study of justice perceptions of individuals in situations requiring a "just" allocation of scarce resources in order to test for their effectiveness in explaining gender differences.

MORAL DEVELOPMENT AND JUSTICE:
THE KOHLBERG-GILLIGAN DEBATE

Building on Piaget's cognitive developmental theory of moral psychology, Kohlberg employs a three-tiered model of six "universal" stages of moral development as the cornerstone of his empirical research (1973, 1981, 1982; Kohlberg and Kramer 1969). Not the content of moral beliefs, but rather the invariant sequence through which all individuals move at varying speeds and end points of development marks the universal structure underlying moral development that Kohlberg describes. Much of Kohlberg's research concentrates on making the level of moral maturity empirically tangible. This is done by evaluating the verbal justifications of respondents for moral action in hypothetical situations. In moving toward the highest stage, individuals rise above conventional beliefs, majority opinion, and concerns over the consequences of actions on specific persons. This is requisite for the development of abstract justice perceptions: Individuals learn to base moral behavior and judgments on abstract and universal standards that are guided by one moral principle, the *golden rule*. Closely following the Rawlsian view of justice as reversibility, Kohlberg argues that the most rational and just principles are those that we would still find fair, even if we ourselves were disadvantaged by their application. Only by viewing moral dilemmas from an abstract vantage point, paralleling Rawls's (1971) "original position under the veil of ignorance," are individuals able to act as any rational moral agent in a similar situation.

Despite his claimed universality, Kohlberg's own empirical results show that certain groups of individuals and certain cultures score consistently lower (Kohlberg and Kramer 1969). Among the groups are women who appear to be arrested at the conventional level of moral development.[2] Kohlberg (1973) interprets the interpersonal, conciliatory approach of these groups of individuals as evidence for their weakly developed justice reasoning abilities. He explains the empirical results pointing to women's "moral deficiency" as being the result of society's defined gender roles; he argues that isolation in the domestic sphere prevents women from engaging in the public sphere's *Socratic dialogue* found exclusively in educational or employment activities or in other experiences of participation, responsibility, and role-taking in society's institutions. These activities allow individuals to detach themselves from ego-centered or consensus-based judgments and to take on an impartial vantage point from which to evaluate the fairness of individual or social practices (Kohlberg, Levine, and Hewer 1983). Hence, Kohlberg predicted that controlling for gender differences in education and employment activities would cause differences between women's and men's moral reasoning to vanish (Kohlberg 1984:347).

Gilligan's work can be described as the attempt to discount Kohlberg's tenant of male moral superiority, by redefining women's "goodness" in a way that allows women to reach the postconventional stage of moral development. Gilligan writes: "Yet herein lies a paradox, for the very traits that traditionally have defined the 'goodness' of women, their care for and sensitivity to the needs of others, are those that mark them as deficient in moral development" (1982:18). Gilligan attributes women's evidenced lack of justice-oriented behavior, that is, their deviation from the Kohlbergian definition of moral maturity, to the presence of an alternative morality: a female "voice" based on an "ethic of care." Unlike Kohlberg, who localizes the domestic sphere and women's isolation therein as the point of divergence in moral development, Gilligan describes how women miss the chance to develop justice perception in early childhood due to the fusion with their mothers. Closely oriented toward Chodorow's (1974) psychoanalytic approach to the study of gender identity, Gilligan argues that processes of attachment to and separation from the mother have a determining effect on the direction of moral development. She writes, "Given that for both sexes the primary caregiver in the first three years of life is typically female, the interpersonal dynamics of gender identity formation are different for boys than for girls" (1982:7). She goes on to describe how boys' separation from their mothers is compensated for by firmer ego boundaries and emphatic individuation that germinate rational thinking processes necessary for a principled moral perspective. Girls' intense identification with their mothers produces a "basis for 'empathy' built into their primary definition of self" (Gilligan 1982:8) and a sense of connectedness that impedes the development of similar reasoning abilities in women. Thus, whereas in Kohlberg's interactionist-developmental perspective, moral perspectives are alterable through experiences in secondary institutions of society, in Gilligan's "feminist"-psychoanalytical perspective, the course that moral perceptions take is fixed early in life and unalterable in early adulthood.

The results of Gilligan's statistically somewhat questionable research (see Broughton 1983; Nails 1991; Faludi 1991; Pollitt 1992) lead her to conclude that women's moral understanding lies outside the moral domain covered by Kohlberg's "universal" model of development. Gilligan argues that women have a different moral understanding since women's moral development has its own distinct developmental stages. Closely following Kohlberg's three stages of moral development, Gilligan describes three alternative ways for women to include self and others when making moral decisions and defines them as varying levels of moral maturity that are universal for women. Women who reach the highest level attain an extended view of equality, one that goes beyond concentrating only on the needs of others, to include caring for and feeling responsible toward oneself (Gilligan 1982:147). Gilligan asserts that women's lower scores along the Kohlbergian scale are evidence for the duality of human nature. She argues that Kohlberg's approach concentrates on the "ethics of rights" and is, as such, gender-biased since women typically do not seek an objectively fair or just resolution to moral dilemmas. Instead, women's moral reasoning is firmly rooted in an "ethics of responsibility." This leads women to contextual and narrative thinking, as opposed to men's formal and abstract mode of thinking.[3] Since contextual judgments exclude reasoning by principles of justice, Gilligan agrees with Kohlberg that only very few women base their moral decisions and actions on principles of justice (Gilligan 1982:30).

HYPOTHETICAL AND REAL-LIFE APPROACHES TO JUSTICE

Although in many ways similar (see Broughton 1983), Kohlberg's and Gilligan's research on justice perceptions make different claims that have far-reaching implications for understanding gender-related variations in justice reasoning. Divergences that arise between their studies as well as between various other studies on justice perceptions have two sources. Not only are researchers divided over the *origins* of justice perceptions, but the *approaches* that they take to measure justice perceptions differ as well. The explanations for variations in justice perceptions and the conclusions drawn from such studies depend upon how the social researcher combines these two factors. In discussing the origins of justice perceptions, some social justice researchers have argued that justice perceptions are deeply entwined with normative considerations that are borne out of socialization experiences. Despite consensus within this framework of thought over the influence of normative factors, researchers are divided over the concept of a singular, "universal" concept of justice and the concept of multiple justice perceptions. Contending researchers argue that rational self-interest is the determining factor in shaping justice perceptions. Research on gender-related differences in justice perceptions is not exempt from such discourse.

In the following, we compare three research strategies whose different combination of the two factors makes up the chief line of discernment. We then go on to present our own strategical variant. As will be discussed below, measurement approaches alternate between hypothetical and real-life approaches, but also may fall somewhere in between the two. Similarly, social justice researchers may attribute the origins of justice perceptions to either *normative* or *rational* factors. More common, however, is to take the safer middle-of-the-road approach by recognizing the importance of both. It also is of importance to note that the belief in a singular, "universal" concept of social justice generally stems from the combination of a hypothetical research approach coupled with an orthodox view of normative influences. All other combinations usually recognize the presence of multiple justice perceptions.

Kohlberg and Gilligan reflect upon only the *normative* origins of justice perceptions. Normative influences activated during early psychosexual development (Gilligan) or during later socialization experiences within different spheres of society (Kohlberg) either guide or hinder the formation of justice perceptions. Kohlberg argues that role-taking enlightens individuals by making them generalize their perception of justice to the point of universality and to choose justice norms that are in the interest of all. To discover the level of universal moral reasoning in individuals and across societies, Kohlberg uses as the basis of his empirical research hypothetical moral dilemmas. Gilligan also reduces her research to the verbal behavior of individuals in response to hypothetical dilemmas. However, as Pollitt (1992) asks in her article criticizing Gilligan's "difference feminism," do expressed sentiments toward the moral dilemma of whether or not a poor man should steal drugs to save a dying wife really reveal how individuals reason in real-life situations or do they reveal what respondents think makes them sound good? A woman may feel that it is normatively expected of her to express compassion, thereby making her appear to be less "just" in Kohlberg's and Gilligan's eyes. If this is true, then gender differences uncovered in hypothetical approaches may not measure justice perceptions at all, but rather gender-related, differential definitions of being "good."

In contrast, research conducted within the *social-psychological justice framework* avoids using hypothetical moral dilemmas to measure justice perceptions. In these studies, patterns in preferences for distribution rules are obtained from either vignettes or group interactions in laboratory settings. Thus, such research also refrains from taking a true real-life approach. Real-life situations are artificially created, making long-term self-interest a variable that remains uncontrolled for. Social-psychological social justice researchers favor the view that there are several distinct norms of justice. The causal factors underlying preferences for distribution rules are thought to have both normative and rational roots. This idea is found within social exchange theories (Homans 1974; Blau 1964; Deutsch 1975; Leventhal 1976; Reis 1984; Leventhal, Koruza, and Frye 1980) as well as in allocation studies (Leventhal et al. 1980). Proponents of this approach argue that rational self-interest converges with the collective good of society, through mutual advantage (Barry 1989b), a mutually agreeable exchange (Reis 1986), or individual insight into social cooperations's ability to foster individual well-being or reward maximization (Deutsch 1975; Walster, Walster, and Berscheid 1978). Despite the usual adherence to a mixed approach, when explaining gender-related differences in justice perceptions, these researchers resort to the familiar normative explanations. Experiments in these settings reveal that whereas women are more likely to prefer resource distribution behavior based on equality, men tend to view resource distribution behavior based on meritorious equity as fair (Leventhal and Lane 1970; Leventhal and Anderson 1970; Benton 1971; Wahba 1972; Major and Adams 1983; Kahn, O'Leary, Krulewitz, and Lamm 1980; Sampson 1975). Researchers explain this through gender-specific interpersonal values (Deaux 1976; Kahn et al. 1980) evident in women's acute interest in interpersonal harmony and solidarity (Leventhal 1976; Sampson 1975; Deutsch 1975; Bierhoff, Buck, and Klein 1986) due to gender-specific differences in goals (Deutsch 1975; Sampson 1975), women's perception of others as persons instead of interchangeable occupants of positions (Lerner 1975), or to differential socialization, such that "women's behaviors are maximally tailored to the world of love, men's to the world of work" (Kidder, Fagan, and Cohn 1981:246; also Bernard 1981; but see Major and Adams 1983). Research limited to dyadic relations in laboratory settings leaves unanswered the familiar question of how individuals perceive just allocations in their own lives, as members of particular groups or social systems. Since allocations in laboratory settings have no effect on individuals' own economic and social position, researchers are free to concentrate solely on socialization as the determinant of gender-related differences in justice perceptions. Similar to the hypothetical approach, the effect of socialization that these studies capture may simply be gendered definitions of acting "good." Playing the role requires only minimal effort since, like going to church on Sundays, the moral situation is only temporary.

Comparative social justice research overcomes this problem by taking a *real-life approach.* Taking a macrolevel viewpoint of social justice, comparative social justice researchers attempt to measure the extent to which the social structure and the political organization of societies affect individuals' views on distributive justice (Wegener 1992a; Haller 1989; Lane 1986). Researchers within this framework argue that the normative forces acting to shape justice perceptions within a society may be countered by the *rational* considerations that individuals engage upon as a result of their position within society. Within the framework of inequality, every individual is affected differently by the application of the principles of distribution associated with that society's justice ideology. Proponents of this approach remain divided over whether societies have homogeneous preference distributions dictated by the society's particular normative and cultural background (e.g., Haller 1989) or by a conception of the rationally more adequate mode of distribution (e.g., Lane 1986), or whether societies may be described as exhibiting multiple justice perceptions in the shape of dominant or primary justice perceptions and secondary justice perceptions (Abercrombie and Turner 1978; Hochschild 1981; Abercrombie et al. 1990; Wegener and Liebig 1991, and Chapter 10 of this volume). Despite their disagreement over normative consensus within societies, the empirical results stemming from comparative research unite these social justice researchers in their skepticism over the concept of one universal concept of social justice. In this light, the basic problem inherent in Kohlberg's and Gilligan's own research appears solvable. Benhabib (1992) points out that the invisible, fictitiously defined *generalized other*, whose impartial standpoint Kohlberg uses to ascertain the just solution to moral dilemmas, is most likely a white, Anglo male professional (see also Haan 1978; Karniol and Miller 1981). The dictates of universal rationality, although claiming to apply to all individuals in all societies alike, would seem only to be reflected upon by some individuals living in certain societies. A comparative social justice researcher, on the other hand, would argue that this "universal" definition of justice is simply a primary justice perception of certain societies, thereby leaving open the possibility of other justice perceptions of a primary or secondary nature (Wegener and Liebig, Chapter 10 of this volume).

In our approach, we argue that justice perceptions are the product of both normative and rational forces. These sources are not only to be regarded separately, but it is important to realize that they are often contradictory.[4] Distribution norm preferences are closely linked to normative processes mandated by the "cultural values" characterizing a society. The "normative culture" of a society that Parsons (1970) describes that gives rise to such values is also deeply entwined with the "patriarchal culture" (Connell 1992) and its definitions of men's and women's proper ways of thinking and acting. Patriarchal society prescribes women an others-oriented, nurturant role.[5] Although normatively prescribed, values associated with this role may be inconsistent with the "primary justice ideology" (Wegener 1992c; Wegener and Liebig, Chapter 10 of this volume) of the society in which women live. Women may then feel two types of normative constraints: those stemming from the society's cultural background in which women live, and those related to the values of "patriarchal culture" specific to the society in which they live.

Taken together, we predict that both types of normative constraints will result in country-specific differences in female justice perceptions. Nevertheless, normative explanations alone disregard the implications of differential privileges stemming from alternative distributive justice norms on the legitimacy of these norms. It is for this reason that our approach tests for the influence of both forces. Döbert and Nunner-Winkler's (1986) criticism of Gilligan's segregation of morality along gender lines is also formulated in these terms. Döbert and Nunner-Winkler argue that differential perceptions of justice arise whenever individuals are personally affected by the application of specific justice principles. This means that if an individual's interests are affected or even endangered by the application of a specific moral principle, it would cause the individual to reflect upon the justice of that principle and to look for "justifiable alternatives." One implication would be that it is not gender role socialization that mandates different interpretations of justice, but rather the perceived bearing that the application of distribution norms has on getting ahead in life as members of one of the two sexes.

Real-life distributive justice situations are best suited to control for the effect of rational self-interest on the emergence of differential justice perceptions. Behind the "veil of ignorance" (Rawls 1971), the status of being a "winner" or "loser" in the allocation of societal resources may be of unwarranted concern. Restricting research to *hypothetical* moral dilemmas, then, neatly works to conceal the effect of such a status. In situations in which resources are allocated, it is unavoidable that the interests of some individuals will be better met than those of others.

What affect does this have on perceptions of social justice? Within the context of real societies, women are disadvantaged both in the work force and in the home. We predict that this will cause some women to identify with egalitarian justice norms, not because such norms are more compassionate, but because their interests directly depend upon a redistributing state. If women are unaware of the structural inequalities related to gender then they will most likely base their distributive judgments on normative considerations. Awareness is often affected by cultural values. If the normative culture succeeds in camouflaging gender-based inequalities, then this could lead to women's justice perceptions being more determined by normative values than by rational considerations. In this light, the relevance of a comparative study of gender differences in justice perceptions becomes particularly evident. A comparative approach is ideally suited to uncover the factors that determine whether women's beliefs in justice norms are predominantly products of normative or rational considerations.

METHODS AND HYPOTHESES

We make use of data from the International Social Justice Project (ISJP) restricting our comparative analysis to four countries: two former socialist (Russia and Poland) and two Western capitalist countries (West Germany and the United States). We chose these four countries because of their appropriateness for a dichotomized comparison between East and West. By taking into account the differences within each of the market systems, we are able to imagine a continuum between Russia and the United States as extreme poles, and Poland and West Germany as weaker variations of these two types of social structure. The surveys resulted in 1839 cases in West Germany, followed by Russia with 1783 cases, Poland with 1542 cases, and the United States with 1414 cases (see Alwin et al. 1993 and the Appendix to this volume).

Table 12.1 gives a description of the operationalization of the variables used in this study. For justice perceptions associated with hypothetical moral decisions, the results of confirmatory factor analyses support a two-factor model. These factors serve as dependent variables in the first part of this study. One deals with a situation in an hospital where a decision must be made regarding who should receive an operation first; the other calls for a decision as to which employee of a firm should get the chance to rent one of the firm's apartments. As Table 12.2 reveals, *need* and *desert* are the two common criteria by which both decisions may be guided.

In the second part of the study, we utilize justice perceptions involving real-life distributive situations as dependent variables. These variables are the result of a three-factor model that is based on nine items, three of these items expressing in turn *egalitarian, economic inegalitarian*, and *fatalistic* justice beliefs (Table 12.3). Both confirmatory analyses use the pooled samples of all four countries, but separate latent variable models for the individual countries revealed almost identical factor structures.[6]

Our empirical analysis is based on the idea that women's justice perceptions are shaped by the conflict between two forces: the force of prescribed societal norms rooted in the society's cultural history, in which "normative cultures" (Parsons 1970) may give rise to moral convictions that conflict with those of the "patriarchal culture" (Connell 1992), and the force of rational motives, whose

Table 12.1. Description of Variables

Dependent variables	
Justice factors for hypothetical moral dilemmas	*Situation in hospital:* Three patients are admitted to a hospital at the same time, all suffering from a form of heart disease requiring surgery. However, the limited resources of the hospital allow only one heart operation each month. All three cases are equally urgent. The patient who is treated first will have better chance of survival. What would be your view of the following decisions?
	Apartment situation: A small firm has an apartment to rent. Three of its employees want the apartment. A selection has to be made. What would be your view of the following decisions?
Need	The employee with the lowest income gets the apartment. The employee supporting the largest family gets the apartment.
	Four-point scale: 1, very unjust; 4, very just
Desert	The decision about which patient goes first is made by judging the usefulness of each patient for society at large.
	The decision about who gets the apartment is made by judging the usefulness of each employee to the firm.
	Four-point scale: 1, very unjust; 4, very just
Justice factors for real-life distributive justice situations	
Fatalism	How often is *prejudice and discrimination against certain groups* a reason for poverty today?
	How often is *the failure of the economic system* a reason for poverty today?
	How often is the *lack of equal opportunity* a reason for poverty today?
	Five-point scale: 1, never; 5, very often
Economic inegalitarianism	It is all right if businessmen make good profits because *everyone benefits* in the end.
	People would not want to take *additional responsibility* at work unless they were paid extra for it.
	There is an *incentive for individual effort* only if differences in income are large enough.
	Five-point scale: 1, strongly disagree; 5, strongly agree
Egalitarianism	The government should provide *a job for everyone* who wants one.
	The government should place *an upper limit on the amount of money* any one person can make.
	The government should guarantee everyone *a minimum standard of living*.
	Five-point scale: 1, strongly disagree; 5, strongly agree

(*continued*)

Table 12.1. Continued

Independent Variables

Region	Dummy coded: 1, Eastern European countries (Poland and Russia); 0, Western countries (western Germany and the United States)
Sex	Dummy coded: women, 1; men, 0
Lower education	Dummy coded: 1, 1 and 2 of the CASMIN EDUCATION variable; 0, other
Intermediate education	Dummy coded: 1, 3 and 4 of the CASMIN EDUCATION variable; 0, other
Marital status	Dummy coded: 1, married, divorced, or widowed persons, living together partners; 0. other
Size of household 1 (2–3 persons)	Dummy coded: 1, two or three persons, living in the household; 0, other
Size of household 2 (more than 3 persons)	Dummy coded: 1, more than three persons living in the household; 0, other.
Age	Age in years
Employment	Dummy coded: 1, working full- or part-time; 0, other
Gender injustice variables	
Personal experience with gender injustice	How often have you personally experienced injustice because of your sex?
	Five-point scale: 1, never; 5, very often
Gender as determinant of success	Please tell me how important you think one's sex is for success in our society today?
	Four-point scale: 1, not at all important; 4, very important

Table 12.2. Results of Aggregate Confirmatory Factor Analysis for Determining Hypothetical Justice Perceptions in the Eastern European (Russia and Poland) and Western (Germany and the United States) Countries

	Latent-factor model	
	Need	*Desert*
Apartment: the employee with the lowest income	.518 (5.110)	
Apartment: the employee supporting the largest family	1.000	
Hospital: the usefulness of patient for society		.747 (16.306)
Apartment: the usefulness of employee to the firm		1.000
Goodness-of-fit index (GFI)	.993	
CFI Bentler's (1989) Comparative Fit Index (CFI)	.987	
Root mean square residual (RMR)	.151	
n	5111	

Table 12.3.   Results of Aggregate Confirmatory Factor Analysis for Determining Real-Life Justice Perceptions in Russia, Poland, West Germany, and the United States

	Latent factor model		
	Fatalism	*Economic inegalitarianism*	*Egalitarianism*
Poverty due to discrimination	.328		
	(20.649)		
Poverty due to the economic system	.301		
	(19.102)		
No equal opportunity	1.000		
Differences in income: everyone		.204	
benefits		(12.411)	
Differences in income: responsibility		.191	
		(13.797)	
Differences in income: incentive for		1.000	
individual effort			
Government should provide a job			.393
for everyone			(15.178)
Government should place an upper			.274
limit on income			(13.447)
Government should guarantee			1.000
minimum standard of living			
Goodness of fit index (GFI)	.992		
GFI adjusted for degrees of freedom (AGFI)	.980		
Bentler's (1989) comparative fit index (CFI)	.959		
Root mean square residual (RMR)	.034		
n	4954		

pursuit may be either blocked or prompted by the former. We argue that rational motives can only come into play if the distributive situation is taken out of its abstract context and is understood by the individual to place his/her interests at stake. In this, our analysis of gender-specific differences in perceptions of social justice is a two-part analysis: the first part deals with hypothetical moral dilemmas, the second with real-life distributive justice situations. Between-country differences of reactions to hypothetical moral dilemmas would reflect purely normative differences since one's own interests are not at stake; differences of reactions to real-life justice situations would reflect differences in the rational interests women have since negatively affected interests dislodge justice perceptions from their normative context.

Hypothetical Moral Dilemmas

The dependent variables we use for the first part are the justice factors for hypothetical moral dilemmas, need and desert (Table 12.2). In the operationalizations we use within the "hospital" and "firms" settings, preferences for either of the distribution norms describe support for unequal outcomes, either on the basis of individual needs or on individual usefulness to a collective or to society at large. In this, they roughly correspond to Gilligan's distinction between a female "ethics of care" and a male "ethics of rights." In granting large and low-income families more privileges, individuals express their preference for a distribution of scarce resources based on need. A preference for modes of distribution that grant "useful" individuals more privileges entails the idea of bringing about "the greatest good for the greatest number," since the social system at large stands to benefit from the survival of the "useful" patient, just as the firm is likely to benefit most if the most useful employee is securely sheltered. Both Gilligan and Kohlberg would classify only the latter preference as "just," making the liberal influence on their framework of thought immediately apparent.

For the two hypothetical dilemmas no other information is provided other than that there are variations in income level, family size, and usefulness to the firm or society. We argue that preferences will be determined by normative forces. We predict that intrasocietal differences between the sexes in just solutions to hypothetical moral dilemmas will be determined by socialization into "patriarchal culture." Intersocietal differences between members of the same sex are shaped by the dominant ideologies of the different economic systems in the East and West whereby gender-related normative prescriptions may or may not come into conflict with the mandates of the society's cultural values. A society's definition of proper gender roles clearly influences gendered individuals' framework of thought. Living up to this definition may result in the incorporation of moral convictions that contradict the cultural values of that same society.

Such contradictions are easily visible in capitalist societies. There, the patriarchal values associated with femininity and domesticity such as helplessness, self-sacrifice, vicarious achievement, the avoidance of aggressiveness, decisiveness, competitiveness, and independence are the antithesis of core values held in capitalist societies. In contrast to this, conventional definitions of femininity appear to be more in line with the socialist ideals of egalitarianism (Wolchik 1985; Deutsch 1985). As an important aspect of the ideology of egalitarianism, official socialist policy sought to reduce sexual inequality. Although the values of egalitarianism may appear to be more "feminine," a strong "patriarchal culture" in socialist societies produced highly inegalitarian tendencies between the sexes (Braun, Scott, and Alwin 1992). Similar to the West, the result is a contradiction between "patriarchal values" and the "cultural values" of socialism. The former state-bureaucratic countries have been only marginally successful in dispersing deep-seated gender role ideologies. This is especially true in Poland, which evidences a particularly strong religious culture under the stronghold of the Catholic Church.[7] On the other hand, labor shortages in the East have brought about an extensive integration of women into the labor market, thereby necessitating the supplementation of traditional values with new values. At least outside the domestic sphere this has led to a lessening of the conflict between the two normative spheres. The greater acceptance of nonfamilial roles for women in the East is linked to attitudinal changes, such that women living in the former East bloc countries may have become more open for more economically inegalitarian and therefore less "feminine" values than women living in Western societies (Wegener and Liebig, Chapter 11 of this volume). Thus, normative influences related to the normative culture of patriarchal society help shape gender-specific approaches to justice such that women may come to prefer justice norms that are more in line with their gender role as nurturer and caretaker. These influences may be transposed by the general cultural values and situative necessities of that society, which could lead to a lessening of conventional gender-related values.

To test for country-specific effects, we created the dummy variable for region by combining the four countries of analysis into the categories East and West. The reconstructed dummy variable is dichotomized with the two former socialist countries, Russia and Poland, forming one category and the two Western nations, Western Germany and the United States, forming the reference category. We felt justified in taking this step in this part of the analysis, because separate analyses of the four nations revealed striking similarities between the two Western nations and between the two former socialist nations. Thus, by consolidating the four countries into one variable, no information was lost.[8] Besides the East-West dichotomy, sex is of course the most important independent variable in our models. To capture the effect of gender role responsibilities we control for marital status and household size. Level of education, employment status, and age are used in order to account for Kohlberg's prediction that differences between women's and men's moral reasoning should vanish by controlling for these variables.

Real-Life Distributive-Justice Situations

In taking a real-life approach, we look at gender-specific differences in justice perceptions concerning the distribution of societal resources. In the tradition of comparative macrolevel social justice research, we include three norms of distribution that describe different standards of social justice. The content of the three justice factors used in this part of our analysis (Table 12.3) is oriented toward the Douglasian grid-group approach (Douglas 1982). This approach was utilized by Wegener and Liebig (Chapter 11 of this volume) to make predictions about justice perceptions based on the social environments in which individuals operate. Such predictions take into account the degree of hierarchical restrictions and social closure within a society as well as within groups within a society. *Economic inegalitarianism* describes the preference for unequal distributions based on effort and achievement. Social stratification is accepted as morally good, since it offers an avenue for ascent. *Egalitarianism* describes preferences for a more equal distribution of resources guided by the state. Not one particular criterion for redistribution (e.g., need) lies at the core of this principle, but rather the sentiments supporting a state-guided redistribution of societal resources and benefits that grants some groups more rights and resources in order to achieve greater equality between certain groups. *Fatalism* expresses disillusion with the system and a sense that the system is essentially unjust. Individuals whose perception of justice is guided by distributional fatalism blame the system for inequality.

Using these justice ideologies, we wish to test for the possibility that within the same society, women who perceive justice differently then men, do so out of *rational* considerations, that is in reaction to their conscious awareness of their own discriminated position within society. This should not be understood to mean a rebuke of the determining effect of the cultural values of a society. They often guide the course of direction that rational justice perceptions follow. The values and practices associated with the "meritocratic-competitive society" (Haller 1989) of the United States permeate American consciousness. These include, in addition to the doctrine of meritocratic individualism and equal opportunity (Hochschild 1981; Lane 1986), faith in an unregulated competitive market and distrust of government intervention (see Chapters 9 and 10 of this volume). In contrast to this, German history is firmly rooted in a welfare and authoritarian state tradition (Dahrendorf 1965). Germany as a "stratified class society" (Haller 1989) represents an interesting alternative model of capitalism that incorporates a welfare component. Germany's welfare capitalism and stratified class structure lead Wegener (1992c) to conclude that individuals in Germany are less inclined to support meritocratic principles, which reward individuals according to achievement, than individuals living in the United States. Instead of distrusting state involvement, the German public actively supports the state-guided egalitarian allocation processes. These differing historical developments are responsible for the operation of different primary distribution rules within the two capitalist societies, making Germany, with its preference for statist, egalitarian norms lean closer to state-socialist countries than the United States with its widespread preference for equitarian distribution norms (Wegener and Liebig, Chapter 10 of this volume).

Women who subscribe to the minimal-state ideology of the United States believe that they, like everyone else, have the ability to get ahead if they only work hard enough. Many of those who come up empty-handed feel personally responsible for their disadvantaged position (Lane 1986), attributing their failures to individual differences in input such as education, occupational choice (Jasso and Rossi 1977), intelligence, initiative, or other personality traits (Kluegel and Smith 1986). Many other female "losers" may feel that they were passed over in the system's reward allocation. This need not cause women to lose faith in market principles since alternatives to it do not fit within the framework of the minimal-state ideology. Despite their disillusion, American women tend to keep their distance from government interventionism. German women's experience with welfare capitalism on the other hand opens up more options for women who feel their disadvantaged position is the result of their gender membership. The welfare component of the German capitalist variant "creates a political climate in which government action on behalf of the disadvantaged (in this case women) becomes seen as legitimate in the popular mind" (Robinson and Davis 1990:34).

The socialist organization of society rests on state interventionism and egalitarian principles. Despite the overturn of communist rule and the enthusiasm affiliated with the new economic course taken by postcommunist states in the direction of market economy, individuals continue to support the deeply entrenched values of egalitarianism associated with their socialist past in addition to their new passion for the free market (Mason, Nelson, and Szklarski 1991; Chapter 3 of this volume). Postsocialist countries have achieved consensus in their support for creating a market economy, but this consensus is based on the idea that the transformation should be brought about by administrative action taken by the state (Tidmarsh 1993). Anxiety about the uncertain future of economic reform in terms of their own personal well-being, i.e., the growing fear of unemployment, has resulted in individuals' continued support of a distribution system based on need and their skepticism toward a system based on merit. In Poland, where popular movements overthrew Communist rule, the new private sector points to the country's active interest in adopting a capitalist culture. This interest existed before Poland's break with communism, making Poland lean closer to Western capitalist societies than Russia. The Russian public is more cautious, especially after six futile years of *perestroika* that brought about little or no economic progress, and is weary with and even disenchanted by the reformation process.

Women living in former socialist societies have profited from their welfare policies in many ways that Western women have not. Women are provided with day care and a variety of pregnancy-related benefits and job security protection. Through higher rates of labor force participation and continuous employment involvement, women living in communist societies were also likely to be covered by a retirement plan. These measures are prized examples of the socialist commitment to the emancipation of women as a part of its political program. Behind this facade, the reality of socialist women's lives was different. Women's status in communist societies was that of a labor reserve, with their mobilization contingent upon the economic planning and decision-making at the center (Wolchik 1985; Siemienska 1985). Despite laws that made the status of women equal to that of men, women were forced to carry the unequal double burden of outside employment and domestic responsibilities. Similar to women's movement into the work force in the West, in the East women's "intrusion" was closely controlled, leading to the segregation of women into specific sectors. Women were concentrated in "feminized" occupations, poorly remunerated, low in status, and had few opportunities for mobility. Furthermore, women were excluded from political life (Wolchik and Meyer 1985). "Feminism" was not a topic of discussion for Russian and Polish women (Rosenbaum 1991; Watson 1992). Women responded positively, when called upon to identify with their multidimensional roles as mother, comrade, worker, and wife, although they were offered no assistance in uniting the different roles (Rosenbaum 1991). Women's mobilization into the work force was less effective in Poland than in Russia. Living in a "society turned inward" (Mason et al. 1991:221), Polish women were expected to conform to traditional patriarchal values on gender roles. With such support at home, Polish men were then free to pursue an orientation of individualism and opportunism. The decline in popular approval of socialism and the growing legitimacy of the Church made this contradiction to socialist ideology possible (Jancar 1985).

In taking a real-life approach, we wish to uncover which of the two influences is the more dominant in shaping justice perceptions. Accordingly, we divide this second part of our analysis into two steps. In the first step, we look at the effect of normative influences and include the same independent variables that were also used in the first part of the analysis. In the second step, which measures the effect of rational considerations, we include two variables that capture an element of women's past experience with the distribution of societal resources on their own lives. The variables, *personal experience with gender injustice* and *gender as a determinant of success* (see Table 12.1), describe two variations of the same theme, namely, that the application of dominant justice ideologies within the society in which women live produces inequalities that have a negative impact on the interests of women as a group, including those of status attainment. These inequalities may not appear justifiable within the framework of the prevailing ideology. In this case, these ideologies would no longer appear legitimate, thereby leading to a type of questioning of the justice of their application and to the search for other, more just norms of distribution. Cross-cultural variations or commonalities in justice perceptions of women should then be affected by the different strategies enacted by the countries to equally include women in the allocation of societal resources and women's awareness of the effectiveness of these strategies to relieve sexual inequality.

To sum these ideas up, we argue in concrete terms that there are two determinants of justice perceptions. First, the *normative* order of society shapes women's justice perceptions in both hypothetical and real-life distributive situations and it has two sources. Those which are related to the normative order of patriarchal culture help to shape gender-specific approaches to justice such that women should prefer justice norms that are more in line with their gender role as nurturer and caretaker. In attempting to resolve hypothetical moral dilemmas, women should therefore prefer a *needs*-oriented distribution of resources. Faced with societal-level distributive situations, women whose justice perceptions are guided by normative forces should prefer *egalitarianism*. These forces could also lead women to support *fatalism*, since the culture of patriarchy supports women's helplessness. These influences may be transposed by the general "cultural values" (i.e., the values associated with the economically inegalitarian doctrine of capitalism) and by nontraditional gender role ideologies generated out of the situative necessities of a society (e.g., labor shortages). We predict that this would lead to a lessening of conventional gender-related values.

In addition, we control for the possibility that women's justice perceptions incorporate an element of rational self-interest. The stepwise inclusion of variables measuring an awareness of sexual discrimination should result in the disappearance of gender-related differences in preference for egalitarianism. This disappearance would provide evidence that differences in justice norm preferences are in actuality attributable to women's desire to have state-guided egalitarian measures eliminate sexual discrimination and inequality. Despite the implication of helplessness, we argue that women's support for distributional fatalism may also be the outgrowth of rational forces. Women's perception of distributional injustice that would normally be channelled into the expected rational-justice perception may be diluted by cultural values that oppose state-guided allocative mechanisms. We predict that, within the confines of a minimal-state ideology, American women are normatively restricted from calling upon the state for a redistribution of resources. Their awareness of gender-based hierarchical constraints is thus prevented from transforming into their hopeful support of egalitarianism. Thus, we expect to see that American women's awareness of their disadvantaged position will be channelled into their frustration and gender-related differences in fatalistic perceptions of social justice. If women's fatalism is in response to perceived sexual discrimination, then gender-related differences in fatalistic perceptions of justice should disappear after controlling for the items measuring gender injustice. Since the political climate of Germany, on the other hand, allows women to support interventionist activities of the state to reduce inequality, we predict that German women's awareness of gender injustice will explain gender differences in support for egalitarian justice norms. We predict the same effect for Polish and Russian women. On the other hand, the socialist ideology of egalitarianism and the associated doctrine of equality between the sexes has most likely worked to obliterate Eastern women's perception of gender injustice. Table 12.4 presents a summary of these hypotheses.

RESULTS

Hypothetical Moral Dilemmas

In Table 12.5, we report the estimated parameters of an aggregated structural equation model using the two justice factors, need and desert, as endogenous, latent constructs (whose measurement model is given in Table 12.2). As described above, instead of separate analyses for all four countries of study, a dummy variable, labeled Region (East vs. West) has been included in the

Table 12.4.   Outline of Hypotheses

	Forces determining justice perceptions	
Justice situations	*Normative forces*	*Rational forces*
Hypothetical moral dilemmas	Patriarchal culture determines women's support for *need* and rejection of *desert*. Cultural values of capitalism will weaken Western women's support for *need*. Extensive work experience and emergence of new "cultural values" associated with transformation will weaken Eastern women's rejection of *desert*.	
Real-life distributive justice situations	Patriarchal culture leads women to prefer *egalitarianism* and/or *fatalism*. Preferences for *egalitarianism* elicited by patriarchal culture are underscored by cultural values of socialism and welfare capitalism and countered by minimal-state ideology. Extensive work experience and emergence of new cultural values associated with transformation will weaken Eastern women's rejection of *economic inegalitarianism*.	Awareness of sexual discrimination or gender-based hierarchical constraints will elicit support for state-guided resource distribution if this is permitted by the dominant cultural values. Minimal-state ideology will channel women's awareness into *fatalism*. Cultural values of socialism curtailed process of becoming aware. Instead of awareness, fear of one's own uncertain future within postsocialist society is a more likely source of Eastern women's rational justice preferences.

model as an exogenous variable, with the two Western countries making up the reference category.

As predicted, the first three columns of Table 12.5 reveal that, after controlling for country-related differences, there are statistically significant differences between men and women with regard to using desert as a basis for distributing scarce resources. Women do not favor modes of distribution based on this justice norm. In fact, Region and Sex together explain 22 percent of variation in justice perceptions based on desert. Contrary to Kohlberg's predictions, however, controlling for differential educational and employment activities does not cause

Table 12.5. Hypothetical Justice Perceptions in Eastern European (Poland and Russia) and Western (Western Germany and the United States) Countries; Standardized Coefficients of Structural Equation Model[a]

	Need	*Desert*	*Need*	*Desert*
Region	.339***	.586***	.310***	.589***
(1 = East)	(13.399)	(22.096)	(10.548)	(16.452)
Sex	−.008	−.116***	−.041	−.113***
(1 = Female)	(−.510)	(−4.956)	(−1.844)	(−3.642)
Lower education	−.061*	−.154***	−.056*	−.154***
	(−2.263)	(−3.976)	(−2.003)	(−3.977)
Intermediate education	.018	−.067*	.024	−.067*
	(.904)	(−2.310)	(1.149)	(−2.313)
Marital status	.057**	−.105**	.059**	−.105**
	(2.659)	(−3.418)	(2.619)	(−3.411)
Household 1	.023	.121**	.025	.121**
(2–3 persons)	(.860)	(3.110)	(.881)	(3.101)
Household 2	.008	.157**	.009	.156***
(more than 3 persons)	(.251)	(3.560)	(.286)	(3.550)
Age	.001	.007***	.001	.007***
	(1.858)	(7.570)	(1.892)	(7.566)
Employment	−.002	.022	−.005	.022
(1 = full- or part-time)	(−.108)	(.854)	(−.278)	(.856)
Interaction sex × region			.076*	−.007
			(2.286)	(−.155)
R^2	.114	.268	.134	.272
Goodness-of-fit index (GFI)		.993		.995
Bentler's (1989) comparative fit index (CFI)		.987		.989
Root mean square residual (RMR)		.151		.140
n		5111		5111

[a] t-values in parentheses.

*$p_t \leq .05$.   **$p_t \leq .01$.   ***$p_t \leq .001$.

gender-related differences to dissipate. Gender role responsibilities represented by marital status and size of household have a significant effect on individuals' perception of desert as a fair basis for unequal distribution, but they also do not cause the gender effect to disappear. There do not, however, appear to be gender-related differences with regard to justice judgments based on need. In this, Gilligan's assumed female preference for "compassionate" solutions to moral dilemmas is only partially confirmed. The same holds true for our own assumptions of the effects of socialization into patriarchal culture.

It is interesting to note that region has a significant positive effect on both

distributive justice norms. Eastern Europeans experiencing the radical transformation of their society's economic and political structures have come to embrace
the more Western ideas of desert, without simultaneously retracting their loyalty
to the socialist ideology of "to each according to his/her need" (see also Kluegel
and Matějů, Chapter 9 in this volume; Wegener and Liebig, Chapter 11 in this
volume).

In the last two columns of Table 12.5, we controlled for the interaction effect
between region and sex. It is here that the predicted country-related differences
between men and women with regard to need being a valid criteria of resource
distribution becomes statistically significant. The significant positive effect gives
evidence to former East Bloc women's preference for a needs-based distribution
of scarce resources. Despite the process of transformation that their countries are
undergoing, women living in former socialist countries lean more toward the
traditional socialist ideals than the men in their societies do. At the same time, we
see a strengthening of the negative main effect of sex on the need-oriented justice
perception. Because this occurs simultaneously while controlling for the interaction effect, its strengthening is related to Western women's disagreement with
modes of distribution based on need. Western women have long been exposed to
the cultural values of capitalism. Exposure to these normative forces may have
worked to cancel out their potential support for a distribution of resources based
on need, one that socialization into patriarchal culture would tend to emphasize.
On the other hand, we predicted that Eastern women's extensive work experience
would lead to a strengthening of their support for modes of distributions based on
desert. This did not take place. Based on these results we may conclude that
whereas all women express disagreement with achievement-based modes of
distribution based on desert, only women living in former social states go as far
as supporting a needs-oriented mode of distribution.

These results seem to support normative explanations of women's and men's
differential justice perceptions, suggesting that women's socialization within
patriarchal society produces differences between men and women, causing wom-
en to be more likely to dissociate justice from achievement. Socialization into the
cultural values of women's particular societies, on the other hand, produces
differences between women. These were not, however, as we had predicted. On
the one hand, Eastern women's higher levels of labor force participation do not
cause Eastern woman to be more desert-oriented. Instead, Eastern European
women's preference for a need-based distribution of scare resources suggests an
internalization of the socialist egalitarian values of "to each according to her/his
need." On the other hand, Western women's exposure to the dominant values of
capitalism makes them distrustful of a needs-oriented justice standard, so that
Western women are no more supportive of a needs-based distribution of resources than the men in their societies. This stands in opposition to Gilligan's results, whose empirical research centered around the responses of Western women
to hypothetical situations. It also points to the cultural bias inherent in Kohlberg's

research. After controlling for education, employment activities, and household responsibilities, gender-related differences in "compassionate" justice reasoning were nonexistent, but only in Western societies. The same does not apply in Eastern societies. This suggests that education does not bring about the emergence of universal justice perceptions, but rather the internalization of the society's cultural values whose content has a salient impact on justice perceptions.

Real-Life Distributive-Justice Situations

As we have argued, justice perceptions in real-life situations are also influenced by the rational considerations of individuals who are directly affected by the distribution of societal resources. Analyzing differences at this level gives a more realistic picture of men's and women's justice perceptions for they go beyond the gender-specific normative mandates regarding the "proper" response. Tables 12.6 through 12.9 present the estimated parameters of the structural equation models of real-life situations using the three justice factors fatalism, economic inegalitarianism, and egalitarianism, as endogenous, latent constructs for each of the four countries of analysis.[9] The tables list the exogenous variables hierarchically resulting in two models for each country.

In the first models (first three columns in each table), the same exogenous variables are used that were also used in Table 12.5. In the second models (last three columns), two additional variables are added, measuring the subjects' experiences with and perceptions of sexual discrimination. The first item ("How often have you personally experienced injustice because of your sex?") measures individuals' personal experience with sexual discrimination. The second item ("How important do you think one's sex is for success in our society?") measures individuals' awareness of sexual inequality and its effect on the equality of opportunity in the work force. In controlling for the two discrimination items, we expect the dissipation of gender differences in justice perceptions in the manner described above. Such an effect was postulated by Döbert and Nunner-Winkler (1986).

A first look at Tables 12.6 through 12.9 reveals a distinct pattern followed by most of the determinants: Whatever the direction of the determinants for egalitarianism, the same seem to be followed by the determinants for fatalism. The determinants for economic inegalitarianism, on the other hand, often go in the opposite direction. The forces that cause individuals to support a redistributing state for the achievement of a just distribution of societal resources may also cause them to turn fatalistic. This same pattern is also evidenced by the effect of gender on justice perceptions in all countries except Poland. It can only be speculated that perhaps the normative integration through strong, traditional Catholic values, which have a particularly strong effect on women, prevents women from turning fatalistic, thereby resulting in the reversal of this effect.

Table 12.6. Real-Life Justice Perceptions in the United States of America; Standardized Coefficients of Structural Equation Model[a]

	Fatalism	Economic inegalitarianism	Egalitarianism	Fatalism	Economic inegalitarianism	Egalitarianism
Sex (1 = female)	.127* (2.353)	-.192** (-3.090)	.307*** (4.658)	.044 (.841)	-.164* (-2.504)	.266*** (3.898)
Lower education	-.053 (-.525)	.384** (3.278)	.873*** (6.872)	.021 (.227)	.383** (3.212)	.852*** (6.428)
Intermediate education	-.195** (-3.218)	.427*** (5.683)	.203** (2.777)	-.122* (-2.165)	.419*** (5.506)	.195** (2.716)
Marital status	-.120 (-1.560)	-.077 (-.976)	-.285*** (-3.349)	-.126 (-1.928)	-.061 (-.764)	-.295*** (-3.505)
Household 1 (2–3 persons)	.018 (.212)	.122 (1.270)	.259* (2.523)	-.009 (-.107)	.094 (.972)	.273** (2.707)
Household 2 (more than 3 persons)	-.026 (-.254)	.030 (.260)	.194 (1.584)	-.036 (-.381)	.001 (.059)	.226 (1.893)
Age	-.003 (-.638)	-.004 (-1.583)	-.011*** (-4.589)	.002 (1.285)	-.005 (-1.922)	-.011*** (-4.568)

(continued)

Table 12.6. (Continued)

	Fatalism	Economic inegalitarianism	Egalitarianism	Fatalism	Economic inegalitarianism	Egalitarianism
Employment (1 = full- or part-time)	.037 (.559)	−.081 (−1.096)	−.125 (−1.581)	.015 (.245)	−.088 (−1.177)	−.157* (−2.034)
Personal experience with gender injustice				.127*** (4.953)	−.046 (−1.518)	.037 (1.201)
Gender as determinant of success				.126*** (4.524)	.015 (.448)	.061 (1.791)
R^2	.025	.118	.150	.085	.123	.159
Goodness of fit index (GFI)		.990		.990		
Bentler's (1989) comparative fit index (CFI)		.960		.965		
Root mean square residual (RMR)		.132		.146		
n		1254		1254		

[a] t-values in parentheses.
*$p_t \le .05$.   **$p_t \le .01$.   ***$p_t \le .001$.

Table 12.7. Real-Life Justice Perceptions in *West Germany*; Standardized Coefficients of Structural Equation Model[a]

	Fatalism	Economic inegalitarianism	Egalitarianism	Fatalism	Economic inegalitarianism	Egalitarianism
Sex (1 = female)	.205*** (4.078)	-.225*** (-3.877)	.109** (3.238)	.084 (1.614)	-.176* (-1.980)	.049 (1.361)
Lower education	.078 (-.879)	.174 (1.730)	.209*** (3.483)	-.005 (-.056)	.151 (1.533)	.293*** (4.807)
Intermediate education	-.082 (-1.281)	.161* (2.203)	.113** (2.676)	-.033 (-.521)	.139* (1.967)	.122** (2.768)
Marital status	-.072 (-1.021)	.194* (2.418)	-.027 (-.610)	-.057 (-.831)	.213** (2.718)	-.046 (-.955)
Household 1 (2–3 persons)	.006 (.077)	-.095 (-1.039)	-.023 (-.463)	.047 (.590)	-.137 (-1.527)	-.034 (-.603)
Household 2 (more than 3 persons)	-.102 (-1.090)	.030 (.282)	-.018 (-.298)	-.048 (-.519)	-.042 (-.410)	-.030 (-.465)
Age	-.010*** (-5.912)	.009*** (4.835)	-.003** (-2.592)	-.007*** (-4.406)	.0076*** (3.509)	-.002 (-1.690)

(continued)

Table 12.7. (Continued)

	Fatalism	Economic inegalitarianism	Egalitarianism	Fatalism	Economic inegalitarianism	Egalitarianism
Employment (1 = full or part-time)	-.167** (-3.129)	.089 (1.463)	-.047 (-1.386)	-.154** (-2.941)	.078 (1.311)	-.030 (-.807)
Personal experience with gender injustice				.128*** (4.770)	-.150*** (-4.857)	.013 (.680)
Gender as determinant of success				.223*** (7.709)	-.073* (-2.259)	.064** (3.222)
R^2	.071	.083	.058	.154	.124	.076
Goodness of fit index (GFI)		.989		.986		
Bentler's (1989) comparative fit index (CFI)		.958		.967		
Root mean square residual (RMR)		.186		.174		
n		1443		1443		

[a] t-values in parentheses.

* $p_t \leq .05$.   ** $p_t \leq .01$.   *** $p_t \leq .001$.

Table 12.8. Real-Life Justice Perceptions in Poland; Standardized Coefficients of Structural Equation Model[a]

	Fatalism	Economic inegalitarianism	Egalitarianism	Fatalism	Economic inegalitarianism	Egalitarianism
Sex (1 = female)	-.074 (-1.174)	-.053 (-1.369)	.101* (2.332)	-.102 (-1.619)	-.049 (-1.231)	.098* (1.975)
Lower education	.264** (2.623)	-.307*** (-4.237)	.720*** (9.138)	.307** (3.077)	-.306*** (-4.243)	.736*** (9.172)
Intermediate education	.167* (1.965)	-.151** (-2.772)	.4863*** (7.676)	.178* (2.143)	-.151** (-2.813)	.497*** (7.763)
Marital status	-.039 (-.490)	.053 (1.070)	-.003 (-.047)	-.029 (-.357)	.038 (.791)	.008 (.142)
Household 1 (2-3 persons)	.117 (.904)	-.045 (-.571)	.071 (.812)	.095 (.743)	-.039 (-.507)	.071 (.799)
Household 2 (more than 3 persons)	.117 (.844)	-.056 (-.671)	.070 (.750)	.088 (.645)	-.051 (-.624)	.074 (.781)

(continued)

Table 12.8. (Continued)

	Fatalism	Economic inegalitarianism	Egalitarianism	Fatalism	Economic inegalitarianism	Egalitarianism
Age	.000	.005**	-.001	-.001	.005**	-.001
	(.009)	(3.019)	(-.430)	(-.202)	(3.017)	(-.496)
Employment (1 = full- or part-time)	-.077	.092*	-.104*	-.078	.087*	-.100*
	(-1.103)	(2.116)	(-2.041)	(-1.150)	(2.064)	(-2.084)
Personal experience with gender injustice				.118*	-.046	.118**
				(2.197)	(-1.425)	(3.114)
Gender as determinant of success				.079*	.017	-.012
				(2.144)	(.771)	(-.047)
R^2	.022	.090	.197	.043	.095	.208
Goodness of fit index (GFI)		.980		.990		
Bentler's (1989) comparative fit index (CFI)		.965		.985		
Root mean square residual (RMR)		.177		.117		
n		1003		1003		

[a] t-values in parentheses.

*$p_t \leq .05$.   **$p_t \leq .01$.   ***$p_t \leq .001$.

Table 12.9. Real-Life Justice Perceptions in *Russia*; Standardized Coefficients of Structural Equation Model[a]

	Fatalism	Economic inegalitarianism	Egalitarianism	Fatalism	Economic inegalitarianism	Egalitarianism
Sex (1 = female)	.136 (1.768)	−.094 (−1.436)	.206*** (3.452)	.082 (1.022)	−.055 (−.822)	.205*** (3.331)
Lower education	.170 (1.186)	−.222 (−1.816)	.461*** (4.103)	.218 (1.496)	−.164 (−1.354)	.469*** (4.043)
Intermediate education	.069 (.799)	.061 (.840)	.243*** (3.621)	.128 (1.462)	.067 (.916)	.223** (3.223)
Marital status	.046 (.405)	−.098 (−1.032)	−.193* (−2.255)	.086 (.750)	−.072 (−.751)	−.169 (−1.898)
Household 1 (2–3 persons)	.159 (1.078)	.201 (1.606)	.147 (1.310)	.183 (1.245)	.187 (1.525)	.143 (1.257)
Household 2 (more than 3 persons)	.240 (1.559)	.085 (.652)	.201 (1.722)	.236 (1.533)	.074 (.584)	.186 (1.564)

(continued)

Table 12.9. (*Continued*)

	Fatalism	Economic inegalitarianism	Egalitarianism	Fatalism	Economic inegalitarianism	Egalitarianism
Age	-.001	.001	.009***	-.001	-.001	.009***
	(-.309)	(.172)	(3.606)	(-.345)	(-.256)	(3.430)
Employment	-.167	.036	.127	-.069	.050	.117
(1 = full- or part-time)	(-1.381)	(.467)	(1.829)	(-.754)	(.654)	(1.638)
Personal experience with gender injustice				.149**	-.078	-.032
				(3.027)	(-1.901)	(-.846)
Gender as determinant of success				.113*	.039	-.018
				(2.269)	(.945)	(-.481)
R^2	.022	.033	.103	.041	.040	.108
Goodness of fit index (GFI)		.989		.989		
Bentler's (1989) comparative fit index (CFI)		.952		.976		
Root mean square residual (RMR)		.181		.171		
n		894		894		

[a] *t*-values in parentheses.

*$p_t \leq .05$.   **$p_t \leq .01$.   ***$p_t \leq .001$.

Before controlling for individual perceptions of sexual discrimination, we see that, in all countries except Germany, the highest percentage of explained variation is offered by the determinants for egalitarianism, accounting for between 10 and 20 percent of the variation. It is interesting to note that most of the explained variation is captured by the sex variable: Regressions of egalitarianism on gender only (not shown here), explain 33 percent in the United States, 29 percent in Western Germany, and 21 and 16 percent in Poland and Russia, respectively. In the complete models, sex is a highly significant determinant of egalitarianism in all countries except Poland, where it is weakly significant. This seems to confirm Gilligan's thesis that views on granting equal regard for all individuals' needs constitute a moral perception for which men and women differ the most from one another. The fact that the effect for economic inegalitarianism is significant only for the United States and Western Germany comes as no surprise. The transformation process experienced by former socialist countries has resulted in a greater acceptance of the ideology of a liberal economy in addition to the continued commitment to the socialist ideology of egalitarianism. Thus, we do not expect to find much variation in the professed beliefs of Eastern European men and women with regard to inegalitarianism. This assumption is supported in that the variation coefficients for the three items making up the factor for economic inegalitarianism are lowest for Poland and Russia (not shown here).[10] Whereas in Russia, the belief in economic inegalitarianism appears to be rather diffusely distributed (Table 12.9), in Poland education appears to be the strongest determinant of economic inegalitarianism, especially supported by the intelligentsia with higher educational credentials (Table 12.8).

In the former socialist countries, gender does not have an effect on fatalistic perceptions of justice.[11] In fact, very little of the variation is accounted for by all the determinants taken together. In Poland, fatalism appears to be embraced by individuals with lower and intermediate levels of education, a countertendency to the progressive and rational considerations of the inegalitarian intelligentsia. On the other hand, gender is significantly related to fatalism in the two Western capitalist societies. Western women are significantly more likely to have a fatalistic attitude toward the distribution of societal resources than Western men. Women appear to perceive fatalism as an alternative to egalitarianism, since both are positive.

We hypothesized that women who believe that there is no way to alleviate perceived sexual inequality may take on a fatalistic attitude, feeling that they would be discriminated against no matter how societal resources are distributed. Women living in welfare-oriented societies, such as Germany, have beliefs that allow them to perceive the alterability of their situation through state interventionism. We predicted that these women support state-guided distributional measures in the hopes of alleviating sexual inequality, causing them to identify with egalitarianism. To test for this effect, the two variables measuring perceived discrimination were added to the model. This resulted in an enormous increase in explained variation for economic inegalitarianism, and a moderate increase for egalitarianism for the Western German model. In Western Germany, this addition resulted in the disappearance of the sex effect on both fatalism and egalitarianism. This leads to the conclusion that women's awareness of their discriminatory position in Western Germany gives rise to their identification with these two justice perceptions. The negative significant effect of gender on inegalitarianism weakens, but does not completely disappear. In the United States we observe a similar tendency for fatalism, but not for egalitarianism. Our hypothesis that the minimal state ideology existing in the United States blurs the possibility of calling upon the state for the redistribution of societal resources as a viable option to alleviate sexual inequality seems to be confirmed. This explains the nonsignificant effect of sexual discrimination on egalitarianism. In this, American women tend to support egalitarianism independent of their perceptions of sexual discrimination. This support would then be determined by normative factors.

Although the inclusion of perceived discrimination in the Eastern European models does not result in a notable additional explained variation, this is not completely unexpected. The complete models reveal a significant main effect of perceived sexual discrimination on fatalism in the former socialist countries and on egalitarianism in Poland. These effects do not, however, alter the effects of gender on the various factors measuring justice perceptions. Feminism and sexual equality were never topics of concern in socialist societies per se, or were at most of marginal concern, subsumed under the class struggle of the proletariat. Therefore, it is not surprising that perceived discrimination has no effect on women's justice sentiments in these countries.

DISCUSSION

In this study, we attempted to dissipate the illusion of the caring, but unjust woman. We analyzed the concept of women's special concern for the needs of others and its possible implications for "feminine" justice perceptions. We utilized the approaches taken by moral psychologists Lawrence Kohlberg and Carol Gilligan as well as by social justice research done in the field of social psychology as the theoretical framework to test for the effect of the normative order radiated through gender role socialization and through cultural values on gender differences in preferences for justice principles. We posited that for hypothetical moral dilemmas, women will support a needs-oriented resource distribution. In societal-level distribution situations in which women are directly affected, normative explanations would lead us to predict that women prefer egalitarianism. Patriarchal culture also socializes women to be helpless, so that women's preference for fatalism could be the product of normative forces as well.

The works of Döbert and Nunner-Winkler (1986) provided insight into the idea that justice perceptions may be guided by rational considerations as well. This concept was the impetus for formulating an alternative explanation for gender differences in justice perceptions. We retraced concepts arising from the field of comparative social justice research according to which justice norm preferences are shaped both by the society's normative and cultural background, as well as by rational considerations. We argued that the normative and rational forces that work to shape justice perceptions are often opposing forces. If the rational considerations of individuals are able to rise above the normative forces, then this should lead to a questioning of prevailing justice ideologies. Taking a real-life approach, we tested for the possibility that women's awareness of sexual inequality will affect their preferences for distribution norms. We hypothesized that a real-life approach would allow us to test whether women's preferences for egalitarianism reflect rational behavior, since the interests of women are directly dependent upon a redistributing state. Engendering a justice perception based on distributional fatalism could also reflect rational considerations in situations in which the normative constraints of "cultural values" prevent women from perceiving the state as a medium to alleviate perceived sexual discrimination. In both cases, we predicted that gender differences in justice perceptions would disappear after introducing items measuring gender injustice into the models of analysis. At the same time we posited that in different societies there are different ideologies at work, although all share in preserving the values of patriarchal culture (Connell 1992). We predicted that the various normative and cultural backgrounds of societies guide the direction of rational considerations. It is for this reason that a comparative analysis is of particular relevance.

Our analysis confirmed many of our predictions. The results for hypothetical moral dilemmas suggest that women's socialization into patriarchal culture causes women to spurn distributive measures based on competitive or achievement-oriented values. Here there are no significant differences between Western and Eastern European women since women living in both Eastern European and Western nations tend to reject desert as the basis of the distribution of scarce resources. Furthermore, there is a tendency for Western women to be less favorable toward a needs-based distribution of resources. Although we predicted the opposite based on Western European women's lower levels of labor force participation, we may still assume that these preferences reflect the normative force of liberal democratic ideologies. Western women's exposure to the values of capitalism appears to lead them away from favoring need as a distribution norm. At the same time, Eastern European women appear to have internalized the socialist ideals of "to each according to his/her need" evident in their support for a needs-based distribution of scarce resources.

In the second part of our analysis, we attempted to discover whether the normative considerations that guide women's distribution norm preferences in hypothetical moral situations, continue to shape preferences when women's own rational interests are at stake. There we saw that in controlling for perceptions of gender injustice, German women's preferences for egalitarianism and distributional fatalism disappeared. In this, we concluded that German women's justice perceptions are indeed affected by rational considerations. In the United States, the same is true, but only for fatalism, since the minimal-state ideology in the United States channels awareness of sexual discrimination into women's frustration and away from seeking support from the state (egalitarianism). In both cases it seems that the normative considerations that guided women's behavior in hypothetical moral dilemmas ceased to be of importance as soon as women's own interests were involved. Western women are able to seek a rational, "justifiable alternative" (Döbert and Nunner-Winkler 1986) to the individualistic conceptions of justice in capitalist societies when faced with the discrimination of their gender.

The Eastern European models also revealed women's preference for egalitarianism. Preference differences between men and women did not disappear after controlling for the gender injustice items. This could be the result of one of two explanations. It could be that the normative forces guiding women's distribution preferences in hypothetical moral dilemmas translate into similar preferences at this level as well because the "justifiable alternatives" based on rational considerations have been destroyed by socialist rhetoric of sexual equality.[12] This does not, however, rule out the possibility that there is another self-interested basis that the two gender injustice items fail to capture. One possibility would be that Eastern European women feel that they will be increasingly discriminated against within the framework of the new system. Measuring this possibility lies outside the context of this paper and is the basis of possible future research. Similarly, we found that in the United States, preference differences between men and women with regard to egalitarianism did not dissipate after controlling for the gender injustice items. American women's preferences for egalitarianism are shaped by normative forces. This would mean that egalitarianism stands more for an ideal than for a rational way to redistribute societal resources in women's favor. On the other hand, the gender injustice items are not significant main effects either, which must lead us to the previously stated conclusion that American women who perceive sexual discrimination feel they have no way to turn to change this situation.

The results offered by this study give insight into the complexity of gender-related differences in justice perceptions. We hope to have proven that explanations that rest on socialization alone or on the idea of some innate or acquired "feminine" mode of moral reasoning is at best simplistic. Our comparative analysis of both Eastern European and Western nations shows that there are important differences between women. These differences are brought about by women's regard for or disregard of their own interests. They are also brought about by the normative and cultural backgrounds of the societies in which women live, which guide the direction of women's rationally shaped justice perceptions.

NOTES

1. An earlier version of this chapter was presented at the Fourth International Social Justice Conference, held in Trier, Germany, July 1–4, 1993.

2. See Walker (1991) for a review of research on gender-specific differences in moral judgment using Kohlbergian methods of measurement for which this is not the case.

3. Murphy and Gilligan refer to the two moralities as *postconventional formal* (PCF) and *postconventional contextual* (PCC). Whereas PCF "derives solutions to all moral problems from concepts like the social contract or natural rights," PCC describes a "commitment for which one bears personal responsibility and which leaves the possibility of alternate formulations" (1980:83).

4. Because of the sometimes contradictory nature of normative and rational influences, some authors describe individuals as perceiving social justice with a *split consciousness* (Kluegel and Smith 1986; see also Chapter 9 in this volume).

5. We use the word *patriarchy* in a similar sense that Tuttle offers, namely as "the universal political structure which privileges men at the expense of women") (1986:242). All societies are patriarchies, evident in the concentration of power in men's hands, the exclusion of women from public life, the asymmetrical social expectation concerning domestic responsibilities, and other characteristics revealing women's disadvantaged position as a group. Nevertheless, as Walby (1990) accurately points out, there are important differences not only between, but also within societies, in the privileges allotted to women and the different forms of gender inequality may change over time.

6. Maximum-likelihood estimates were used for all structural equation models presented in this study (PROC CALIS of SAS).

7. The indisputable stronghold of the Catholic Church in Poland becomes particularly obvious in the success of its crusade for the "right to life" despite the fact that Poland has one of the highest abortion rates in the industrialized world (Heinen 1992).

8. Since similar commonalities did not arise in the second part of the analysis, where we look at real-life justice situations, we refrained from using the dummy variable, Region, and present four separate tables of results instead.

9. In Table 12.3, the aggregate measurement model for all four countries is given. Though they were estimated, we do not report the measurement models for each country here.

10. If economic inegalitarianism is regressed on sex only, only 15 percent is explained for Poland and 5 percent for Russia, but 23 percent both for the United States and Western Germany (not shown here).

11. Gender explains only 1 percent of fatalism in Poland and 7 percent in Russia (not shown here).

12. Women's awareness of sexual discrimination is much lower in Eastern European countries, thereby making it an insignificant factor for women's justice perceptions. Based on our sample, mean discrimination values for women are 2.11 and 1.87 in the United States and Western Germany, respectively, differing significantly from 1.31 for Poland and 1.57 for Russia. For gender as determinant of success, we find 2.40 and 2.60 for the United States and Western Germany, but 1.82 and 1.73 for Poland and Russia.

APPENDIX

Methods of the International
Social Justice Project

Duane Alwin and Bernd Wegener

The International Social Justice Project (ISJP), and the resulting 1991 survey were developed over a period of several years, with the planning beginning as early as 1987 (by David Mason and Witold Morawski), and the formulation of the "working principles" in 1989 (see the Preface to this volume). The importance to the project participants of high standards of methodology is reflected in that statement of principles, as well as in the summary documentation for the project, which accompanies the codebook of the merged ISJP dataset (Alwin et al. 1993), and also in a number of detailed national project documentations (e.g., Kleebaur and Wegener 1991). Because the full documentation and questionnaire are too long to reproduce here, in this section we briefly describe the methods employed in the development of the ISJP dataset.

The methodological characteristics of the thirteen surveys are summarized in Table A.1 (adapted from Alwin et al. 1993:6), which displays important information on the survey organization conducting the study in each country, the languages involved, the age range of the populations studied, methods of sampling, the mode of interviewing, field dates, average interview length, types of interviewers, completion rates, and sample sizes for each country. In the following we give somewhat more depth to this information, providing a firmer basis for interpreting the nature of the methods employed.

WORKING PRINCIPLES

The ISJP working principles were developed to ensure that high standards of methodology would be followed by all participating nations. These principles were developed on the basis of an adaptation of a similar document from the International Social Survey Programme (ISSP), a consortium of annual social attitude surveys conducted in several countries (see Davis and Jowell 1989).

Table A.1. ISJP: Technical Feature of the Surveys[a]

Country	Organization	Language	Sample	Ages	Field dates	Mean length of interview (minutes)	Mode	Int. type	Completion/ response rate (%)	Cases (N)
Bulgaria	Academy of Sciences	Bulgarian	Household	18+	6/1–7/15	60	Face-to-face	RI	86.0/90.3	1405
Czechoslovakia	STEM	Czech, Slovakian	Address list	18+	6/26–7/14	70	Face-to-face	PI	82.7/ —	1181
East Germany	ZUMA/INFAS	German	Household	18+	4/1–6/15	78	Face-to-face	PI	62.5/70.7	1019
West Germany	ZUMA/INFAS	German	Household	18+	4/1–6/15	65	Face-to-face	PI	63.0/70.5	1837
Estonia	Saar Poll	Estonian, Russian	Household	18+	2/14–3/9	60	Face-to-face	PI	93.2/ —	1000
Great Britain	RSGB	English	Household	18+	5/3–7/17	—	Face-to-face	PI	66.1/71.1	1319
Hungary	TARKI	Hungarian	Address list	18+	7/17–7/30	65	Face-to-face	PI	74.1/ —	1000
Japan	—	Japanese	Electoral list	20+	7/17–9/17	65	Face-to-face	RI	51.8/ —	777
Netherlands	SRF	Dutch	Telepanel	18+	5/31–6/11	45	Computer self-administered	—	66.1/70.2	1783
Poland	ISS	Polish	Household	18+	6/20–7/2	—	Face-to-face	PI	79.0/88.0	1542
Russia	VCIOM	Russian	List of inhabitants	16+	10/20–11/25	75	Face-to-face	PI	76.3/ —	1734
Slovenia	ISS	Slovene	List of inhabitants	18+	6/1–8/28	—	Face-to-face	—	91.1/95.0	1375
United States	ISR/SRC	English	RDD Telephone	18+	3/10–7/20	52	Telephone	48 PI	68.1/71.7	1414

[a] Interviewers (Int. type) are classified as: RI, from research staff; PI, professional trained-interviewers. All field dates are in 1991, except Estonia (in 1992). RDD, random digit dialing.

The essential components to the working principles were that each national participant would adhere to the following methodological standards:

1. Field a common questionnaire, replicated exactly in each country, except for translations, using identical questionnaires with questions in identical order; country-specific questions were to be allowed only if they were placed at the very end of the interview.
2. Use an agreed-upon national probability sample design, with known probabilities of selection, yielding a minimum of 1.000 respondents.
3. Use a questionnaire, translated from an agreed-upon English-language questionnaire, with nonliteral translations—that is, culturally equivalent questions rather than literal questions—to be the exception and indicated in the documentation.

Although there are variations across countries in adherence to these principles, in the main the resulting data gathering closely followed these guidelines. Further information can be obtained in the summary documentation and codebook (Alwin et al. 1993). While these working principles reflect standards that were not always completely achieved, we can be comforted to some extent by Kish's (1987) reminder that virtually all elements of research design in the social sciences represent a set of compromises rather than the comprehensive adherence to ideal rules.

QUESTIONNAIRE DEVELOPMENT

The development of the ISJP questionnaire was undertaken in four stages. First, a very broad array of questions was solicited from project participants, according to the conceptual domain of interest (i.e, social, political, and economic domains), and these were put into a machine-readable form for dissemination and discussion in plenary meetings. Second, a draft of the questionnaire was developed by a subcommittee for translation and pretesting in the fall of 1990. Third, a plenary meeting in early 1991 formulated the basic content to the final questionnaire, including allowance for country-specific content at the end of the interview. In the fourth and final stage of questionnaire development, a subcommittee worked through electronic communication to finalize an English-language draft of the questionnaire, which was then given to each participating group for translation and additional pretesting.

MEASUREMENT

Comparative survey research requires that methods of measurement achieve a high level of functional equivalence of measurement cross-nationally. The standard approach to implementing such equivalence of measurement is to rely on a literal as opposed to a conceptual replication of questions (see Alwin, Braun, Harkness, and Scott 1994). The assumption is that the sameness of procedures, within the limitations of translation, will provide comparable measures across national contexts. This approach is problematic for a number of reasons (Galtung 1982), but there are a number of procedures commonly used for dealing with the equivalence of translation, notably the use of back-translation to the source language questionnaire. This method was recommended to the ISJP participants and followed in most of the participating countries (see also Chapter 1).

SAMPLING METHODS

The construction of a representative sample in each country was seen as an extremely important requirement of this study, with an emphasis on documentation of:

1. the sampling strategy and procedures, particularly the sampling frames at each stage of selection;
2. the selection procedures, including probabilities of selection at each stage;
3. other special design features affecting the representativeness of the sample.

In some cases the national studies used a sample of households, and the documentation includes information about how respondents were sampled within households. Also, the documentation provides information regarding any over- or undersampling done in certain geographical areas. For example, in East Germany, oversampling was called for because information regarding the first sample stage (voting districts) was, in 1991, less established than in the West.

Although, as stipulated by the working principles, it was desirable to use probability methods in constructing the sample, in fact the approaches to sampling in the ISJP surveys varied to a certain extent (see Alwin et al. 1993). Table A.1 indicates the organization conducting the surveys, the nature of the first-stage sampling frame, and the age range of the target sample. In some cases quota methods were used in an effort to attempt to ensure representativeness of the sample, and in most of these cases replacement methods were applied if sample addresses could not be contacted. Most national teams provided weight variables that adjust for differences in household size and differences in response rates by population subclasses.

MODE OF INTERVIEWING

Most national surveys used face-to-face interviewers, which was the agreed-on mode of interviewing. Primarily because of financial reasons, however, there were two exceptions: In the United States interviews were conducted by telephone, and in the Netherlands interviews were self-administered via computer. The study documentation clarifies, to the extent possible, the nature of questionnaire administration, if it departs from the standard face-to-face interview. Where possible, details were provided regarding the personnel used as interviewers, the number of interviewers (see Table A.1), how interviewers were trained, how the interviewing assignments were made, the average number of interviews conducted by interviewers, and whether callbacks were made and the number of callbacks (see Alwin et al. 1993).

COMPLETION RATES

One of the most important measures of data quality refers to the relative success of the survey in obtaining completed interviews from the target sample. The information given in Table A.1 includes the final number of cases obtained for each country, along with a completion rate for each survey in the ISJP. The completion rate is here defined as the final analyzable sample size divided by the net sample (the latter being defined as the total number of issued addresses/households/telephone numbers minus the cases out of the sample because of ineligibility). This is different from the response rate, which sometimes takes into account only contacted households. The study documentation provides whatever details are available regarding the dispensation of the sampled cases, so that in most cases both a "response rate" and "completion rate" could be computed.

Obviously, it is not possible to compute such measures of data quality without being able to distinguish the sources of target sample attrition. Where such information on the dispensation of the target sample is absent or insufficient, these measures of data quality are unknown and can only be estimated. Moreover, where quota methods and sampling with replacement are used, the tabulation of these quantities must be undertaken with great care. Completion rates in such cases can be reported only if certain assumptions are made about how elements in the target sample are counted, that is, the number of cases in the target sample should include the counts of both initial and replacement samples. Moreover, where these methods are used, the distinction between the target sample and net sample is typically not maintained, so a completion rate cannot always be accurately computed. Within these limitations, we have tried to report completion rates for the various surveys as accurately as possible (Alwin et al. 1993:10–26).

DOMAINS OF MEASUREMENT

The ISJP survey covered several domains of content. These can be briefly summarized in the following categories.

Current Life Situation.   Home ownership, past and present employment, occupation, job characteristics (firm size and supervisory status on the job), schooling, educational certification and vocational training, marital status, spouse's schooling, educational certification and vocational training, spouse's employment and occupation.

Household Justice.   Household division of labor and perceptions of fairness.

Economic and Social Beliefs.   Social class self-placement, beliefs about the poor (prevalence, future prevalence, and reasons for poverty), beliefs about the rich (prevalence, future prevalence, and reasons for wealth), personal experiences of injustice, beliefs about income differences, beliefs about factors that have and should have an influence in level of pay.

Political.   Beliefs about the role of government in shaping income inequality, satisfaction with domains of life (including government, community, job standard of living, income, family life, life as a whole).

Economic.   Income sources, total family income, perceptions of family need, job income, perceptions of job income deserved, perceptions of economic well-being compared to other people (other people in general, people with the same level of education, people in similar jobs), income estimates of managing director of a corporation and a factory worker (both actual and just income perceptions), perceptions of income inequality.

Micropolitical.   Political participation, political party identification, political efficacy, self-assessed liberal/conservatism, perceptions of equality of opportunity and rewards for effort, need, and intelligence, perceptions of the fairest way to allocate wealth and income.

Social Justice (Micro- and Macrojustice).   Perceptions of justice of social arrangements, beliefs about factors contributing to personal social standing, beliefs about government ownership of industries and utilities, preference for socialism, postmaterialism.

Background.   Father's employment and occupation, respondent's work history in terms of first and previous to present job, unemployment times, religious preference and activity, citizenship, voting, ethnicity.

CODING OCCUPATIONS AND EDUCATION

In the project, particular care was taken to define social status positions in a way to make them comparable across countries. Occupations are of fundamental importance in this respect. Apart from location in the hierarchy of a firm or organization (supervisory status), four types of information were used to assess occupational position.

First, regarding all types of jobs that were addressed in the questionnaire (R's present, first, and previous job, father's and spouse's job, etc.), it was asked into which type of *Berufsstellung* or occupational level a job would fall. *Berufsstellungen*, deriving originally from the German census classification, order occupational positions according to the levels of responsibility exercised in a job and according to the educational requirements for a job. To our knowledge, the ISJP is the first project in which this type of classification was used in an international context. We believe that in spite the fact that the system of *Berufsstellungen* is genuine to the German system, it serves particularly well for comparing occupational levels across countries.

When asked for *Berufsstellungen* the respondent is first required to sort his or her job (or any job he or she is asked for) into one of the following seven categories:

A. Self-employed farmer
B. Self-employed professional
C. Self-employed in business or trade
D. Employee in nonmanual occupation (government) or employee in nonmanual occupation (nongovernment)
E. Employee in manual occupation
F. On-training scheme or volunteer worker
G. Agricultural cooperative (only in former Czechoslovakia)

For each selected category A to E, a list of subcategories is shown for the respondent to choose from (Alwin et al. 1993: Appendix B: English-Language Version of the German *Berufsstellungen*):

A. Self-employed farmer
   10   a small farm (up to 50 acres)
   11   a medium farm (50–249 acres)
   12   a large farm (250–749 acres)
   13   a very large farm (750 acres or more)
   14   farmer in agricultural association
   15   farmer, working alone or with family members (Russia only)
   16   farmer, having employees who are not family members (Russia only)
   17   supervisor, agrarian (Hungary only)
B. Self-employed professional (for example, a doctor or lawyer in own practice)
   20   works alone
   21   one other employee
   22   2–9 employees
   23   10 employees or more

C. Self-employed in business or trade
    30   works alone
    31   one other employee
    32   2–9 employees
    33   10–49 employees
    34   50 employees or more
    36   other self-employed in business or trade
    37   member of a production association
    40   helps out/assists in family business

D. Employee in nonmanual occupation government (Codes 50–53 appear on
    the *Berufsstellungen* variables only in the East German, West German, and
    Russian subsets of the ISJP data)
    50   Civil servant (*Beamter*) doing routine clerical tasks (for example,
         shorthand typist, counter clerk, cashier, receptionist, shop assistant)
    51   Civil servant (*Beamter*) having some self-directed responsibilities (for
         example, laboratory technician, draftsman)
    52   Civil servant (*Beamter*) self-directed, but working under the su-
         pervision of other (for example research officer, secondary school
         teacher) or having limited supervisory responsibility for other white-
         collar employees (for example, head clerk, secondary school head of
         department)
    53   Civil servant (*Beamter*) mainly self-directed; or mainly involved in
         management and policymaking (for example, head of department or
         division, university lecturer, school principal, diplomat, military offi-
         cer, judge)
    Employee in nonmanual occupation (nongovernment)
    60   doing routine clerical tasks (for example, shorthand typist, counter
         clerk, cashier, receptionist, shop assistant)
    61   having some self-directed responsibilities (for example, laboratory
         technician, draftsman)
    62   self-directed, but working under the supervision of others (for example,
         supervisory responsibility for other white-collar employees (for exam-
         ple, head clerk, secondary school head of department)
    63   mainly self-directed; or mainly involved in management and poli-
         cymaking (for example, head of department or division, university
         lecturer, school principal, diplomat, military officer, judge)
    64   armed forces, nonofficer only
    65   country-specific nonmanual other

E. Employee in manual occupation
    70   laborer (for example, furniture remover)
    71   semiskilled worker (for example, assembly-line worker)
    72   qualified craftsman (for example, motor mechanic, carpenter)
    73   supervisor or foreman of manual workers

As a second means of assessing occupation, respondents were asked to describe what they do in their job (or any other job), i.e., what their occupational activity in production or service is. Subsequently, these descriptions were coded into the three-digit unit group level of the International Standard Classification of Occupations (ISCO) of the International Labour Office (1968). This scheme is internationally widely used, and it could be assumed that in most of the participating countries some familiarity with the scheme existed. Use of the 1968 version of ISCO was imposed, though at the time of the survey, an improved version, ISCO 1988, was already available (International Labour Office 1990). In comparison to ISCO 1968, ISCO 1988 attempts to classify occupations into a near-hierarchical order; it also includes a number of new jobs that were nonexistent at the time of the 1968 release. However, as the ISCO 1988 scheme had by 1991 been published only in English, French, and Spanish, a preliminary German version being also available, it was decided to make the 1968 version mandatory, not the 1988 version. Otherwise, non-English-speaking countries would have had to translate ISCO job titles and job descriptions into their own languages first in order to being able to code according to ISCO 1988. Also, it had to be taken into account that various scales of occupational prestige are still tied to the ISCO 1968 codes. In some of the participating countries (Germany, United Kingdom, United States, Slovenia), however, both types of ISCO codings were performed, and are both included in the international dataset (see Alwin et al. 1993:Appendix C, for a summary of ISCO 1968 codes).

From the three-digit ISCO 1968 codes, occupational prestige scores were created. This is the third type of information used. We relied on the work of Donald Treiman (1977), who has proposed a standard international occupational prestige scale, deriving this scale from prestige studies in sixty countries. It should be noted, however, that this scale is now almost twenty years old, and that voices raising criticism as to the validity of the scale as a status measure have steadily increased. But the Treiman scale is still the only available prestige scale to date claiming to be cross-nationally functional (see Wegener 1992).

As an alternative, however, a second occupational prestige scale has been added to the dataset, the so-called magnitude prestige scale or MPS (Wegener 1988). The development of this scale is based on extensive material from surveys in Germany, using the technique of bi-modal magnitude estimation that was borrowed from psychophysics. While this scale has the advantage of being newer compared to Treiman's scale, and also of having been well tested in status attainment modeling, little is known about how well it serves in an international comparison (see Alwin et al. 1993:Appendix E, for Treiman and MPS scores).

The fourth type of strategy in dealing with occupational information in the dataset is by construction class categories. We base this strategy on the Goldthorpe class scheme (Goldthorpe 1987); for each job asked in the questionnaire, a Goldthorpe class position has been assigned. The project has taken new routes in constructing these class variables. While it has become customary in some camps to construct Goldthorpe classes exclusively based on information on occupational activities in terms of ISCO, the present study takes the hierarchy of *Berufsstellungen* as the central criterion, using ISCO codes only when this is required for assigning specific occupations to one of the Goldthorpe classes. As a "project within the project," the British team in particular must be credited for developing this novel classification scheme for Goldthorpe classes. In the codebook (Alwin et al. 1993:Appendix F), the algorithm and SPSS-recode commands for constructing Goldthorpe classes with the ISJP data are reported. An extended report by Gordon Marshall, Carole Burgoyne, and Adam Swift (Marshall et al. 1992) can be requested from Gordon Marshall (e-mail: gmarsh@vax.oxford.ac.uk).

Next to occupation, education, and the training a person received is what is important for determining that person's social position, but here also comparability is a chronic problem. Not only do the educational institutions in different countries differ, but in particular also the linkages between the school systems and the occupational systems differ such that returns to education in terms of status gains vary between countries. Basing comparisons, therefore, on simply counting the years of schooling received is not a viable option. While no perfect and once-and-for-all solution for comparative research seems to exist, in the ISJP it was decided we rely on recent works by the CASMIN project (Comparative Analysis of Social Mobility in Industrial Nations), which was explicitly set up to explore the possibilities of comparative analyses of stratification and social mobility. CASMIN derived an "education scale" consisting of eight hierarchically ordered levels obtained by a combination of two dimensions: (1) a hierarchy of levels of formal schooling and (2) a distinction between formal schooling and vocational training (König et al. 1988). The following eight educational levels are thus obtained, coded into seven categories:

1. Level 1a: Less than general (primary) formal education
2. Level 1b: General (primary) formal education
3. Level 1c: General (primary) formal education and basic vocational training
4. Level 2a,b: Medium vocational training (2a) and medium formal education (2b)
5. Level 3a: Secondary formal education (*Abitur, Maturitas*)
6. Level 3b: Lower tertiary (vocational) training
7. Level 3c: Higher tertiary (vocational) training (diploma, doctorate).

DATA DISSEMINATION

Data, including codebook and extensive documentation (as in Alwin et al. 1993), from this project may be obtained from either the Inter-University Consortium for Political and Social Research (ICPSR), Institute for Social Research, University of Michigan, Ann Arbor MI 48103-1248, or from the Zentralarchiv für Empirische Sozialforschung, Universität zu Köln, Postfach 410 960, 50869 Cologne.

References

Abercrombie, Nicholas and Bryan S. Turner. 1978. *The Dominant Ideology Thesis. British Journal of Sociology* 29:149–70.

Abercrombie, Nicholas, Steven Hill, and Bryan S. Turner. 1980. *The Dominant Ideology Thesis.* London: Allen & Unwin.

Abercrombie, Nicholas, Stephen Hill, and Bryan S. Turner. 1986. *Sovereign Individuals of Capitalism.* London: Unwin Hyman.

Abercrombie, Nicholas, Stephen Hill, and Bryan S. Turner. 1990. *Dominant Ideologies.* London: Unwin Hyman.

Adams, J. S. 1965. "Inequity in Social Exchange." Pp. 267–99 in *Advances in Experimental Social Psychology,* Vol. 2, edited by Leonard Berkowitz. New York: Academic.

Adler, Frank. 1991a. "Soziale Umbrüche." Pp. 174–218 in *Das Ende eines Experiments: Umbruch in der DDR und deutsche Einheit,* edited by Rolf Reißig and Gert-Joachim Glaeßner. Berlin: Dietz.

Adler, Frank. 1991b. "Ansätze zur Rekonstruktion der Sozialstruktur des DDR-Realsozialismus." *Berliner Journal für Soziologie* 2:157–75.

Ajzen, Icek and Martin Fishbein. 1980. *Understanding Attitudes and Predicting Social Behavior.* Englewood Cliffs, NJ: Prentice-Hall.

Alber, Jens. 1982. *Vom Armenhaus zum Wohlfahrtsstaat. Analysen zur Entwicklung der Sozialversicherungen in Westeuropa.* Frankfurt: Campus Verlag.

Alexander, Jeffrey. 1987. *Twenty Lectures: Sociological Theory Since World War II.* New York: Columbia University Press.

Alexander, Karl L., Bruce K. Eckland, and Larry J. Griffin. 1975. "The Wisconsin Model of Socio-Economic Achievement: A Replication." *American Journal of Sociology* 81:324–42.

Alves, Wayne M. 1982. "Modelling Distributive Justice Judgments." Pp. 205–35 in *Measuring Social Judgments: The Factorial Survey Approach,* edited by Peter H. Rossi and S. L. Nock. Beverly Hills, CA: Sage.

Alves, Wayne M. and Peter H. Rossi. 1978. "Who Should Get What? Fairness Judgments of the Distribution of Earnings." *American Journal of Sociology* 84:541–64.

Alwin, Duane F. 1987. "Distributive Justice and Satisfaction with Material Well-Being." *American Sociological Review* 52:83–95.

Alwin, Duane F. 1992a. "Equity Theory." Pp. 563–75 in *Encyclopedia of Sociology,* edited by Edgar F. Borgatta and Marie L. Borgatta. New York: Macmillan.

Alwin, Duane F. 1992b. "Scales of Justice: Empirical Evidence for Theories of Justice Evaluation." Unpublished paper. Institute for Social Research, University of Michigan, Ann Arbor.

Alwin, Duane F. 1994. "Life Cycles, Cohorts, and Perceptions of Economic Well-Being." Paper presented at the 13th World Congress of Sociology, Bielefeld, Germany, July.

Alwin, Duane F., Michael Braun, Janet Harkness, and Jacqueline Scott. 1994. "Measurement in Multi-National Surveys." Pp. 26–39 in *Trends and Perspectives in Empirical Social Research,* edited by Ingwer Berg and Peter Mohler. Berlin and New York: de Gruyter.

Alwin, Duane F., Ronald L. Cohen, and Theodore M. Newcomb. 1991. *Political Attitudes Over the Life Span. The Bennington Women After Fifty Years.* Madison: University of Wisconsin Press.

Alwin, Duane F., Ludmilla Khakhulina, Piet Hermkens, Voyko Antoncic, and Wil Arts. 1992. "Comparative Referential Structures, System Legitimacy, and Justice Sentiments." Paper presented at the 87th annual meeting of the American Sociological Association, Pittsburgh, Pennsylvania, August 20–24.

Alwin, Duane F., David M. Klingel, and Merilynn Dielman. 1993. *International Social Justice Project: Documentation and Codebook.* Ann Arbor: Institute for Social Research, University of Michigan.

Anderson, Charles H. 1974. *The Political Economy of Social Class.* Englewood Cliffs, NJ: Prentice-Hall.

Andrews, Frank M., J. N. Morgan, and J. A. Souquist. 1973. *Multiple Classification Analysis.* Ann Arbor: University of Michigan Press.

Apter, David. 1964. *Ideology and Discontent.* New York: Free Press.

Archer, Margaret S. 1988. *Culture and Agency. The Place of Culture in Social Theory.* Cambridge: Cambridge University Press.

Arts, W., P. Hermkens, and P. van Wijck. 1991. "Income and the Idea of Justice: Principles, Judgments and Their Framing." *Journal of Economic Psychology* 12:121–40.

Arts, W., P. Hermkens, and P. van Wijck. 1992. *The Capricious Respondent: The Framing of Justice Principles and Judgements Revisited.* Working Papers International Survey on Social Justice, no. 5, Butler University, Indianapolis.

Arts, W. and R. van der Veen. 1992. "Sociological Approaches to Distributive and Procedural Justice." Pp. 143–76 in *Justice: Interdisciplinary Perspectives,* edited by Klaus R. Scherer. Cambridge: Cambridge University Press.

Ashford, Douglas E. 1986. *The Emergence of the Welfare States.* Oxford: Basil Blackwell.

Atkinson, John W. 1964. *An Introduction to Motivation.* New York: Van Nostrand.

Bandura, Albert. 1979. *Sozial-kognitive Lerntheorie.* Stuttgart: Klett-Cotta.

Barnes, Samuel H., Max Kaase, et al. 1979. *Political Action: Mass Participation in Five Western Democracies.* Beverly Hills, CA: Sage.

Barry, Brian. 1989a. *A Treatise on Social Justice,* Vol. 1: *Theories of Justice.* Hemel Hempstedt: Harvester-Wheatsheaf.

Barry, Brian. 1989b. *Theories of Justice.* Berkeley: University of California Press.

Batygin, G. S. 1989. "'Virtue'" against Interests: Notes on the Reflection of Distributive Relations in Mass Consciousness." Pp. 170–86 in *New Directions in Soviet Social Thought,* edited by Murray Yanowitch. Armonk, NY: M. E. Sharpe.

Becker, Gary S. 1964. *Human Capital. A Theoretical and Empirical Analysis with Special Reference to Education.* Chicago: University of Chicago Press.

Bell, John and Erik Schokkaert. 1992. "Interdisciplinary Theory and Research on Justice." Pp. 237–53 in *Justice: Interdisciplinary Perspectives,* edited by Klaus R. Scherer. Cambridge: Cambridge University Press.

Bellmann, L. 1992. "Entlohnung in den neuen Bundesländern. Strukturelle Determinanten der Einkommensunterschiede aus den Daten des Arbeitsmarktmonitors." *Mitteilung aus der Arbeitsmarkt- und Berufsforschung 25*:27–31.

Bendix, Reinhard. 1970. "Tradition and Modernity Reconsidered." Pp. 36–54 in *Embattled Reason*, edited by Reinhard Bendix. New York: Oxford.

Benhabib, S. 1992. "The Generalized and the Concrete Other." Pp. 267–302 in *Ethics: A Feminist Reader*, edited by E. Frazer, J. Hornsby, and S. Lovibond. Cambridge: Basil Blackwell.

Bentler, Peter M. 1989. *EQS Structural Equation Program Manual*. Los Angeles, CA: BMDP Statistical Software.

Benton, A. A. 1971. "Productivity, Distributive Justice and Bargaining Among Children." *Journal of Personality and Social Psychology 18*:68–78.

Berger, J., M. H. Fisek, R. Z. Norman, and D. G. Wagner. 1985. "Formation of Reward Expectations in Status Situations." Pp. 215–61 in *Status, Rewards, and Influence*, edited by J. Berger and M. Zelditch. San Francisco: Jossey-Bass.

Berger, J., M. Zelditch, B. Anderson, and B. P. Cohen. 1972. "Structural Aspects of Distributive Justice: A Status Value Formulation." Pp. 1119–46 in *Sociological Theories in Progress*, Vol. 2, edited by J. Berger, M. Zelditch, and B. Anderson. Boston: Houghton-Mifflin.

Bergson, Abram. 1989. *Planning and Performance in Socialist Economics: The USSR and Eastern Europe*. Boston: Unwin Hyman.

Berk, Richard A. 1983. "An Introduction to Sample Selection Bias in Sociological Data." *American Sociological Review 48*:386–98.

Berk, Richard A. and Subhash C. Ray. 1982. "Selection Bias in Sociological Data." *Social Science Research 11*:352–98.

Bernard, J. 1981. *The Female World*. New York: Free Press.

Bierhoff, Hans W., E. Buck, and R. Klein. 1986. "Social Context and Perceived Justice." Pp. 165–85 in *Justice in Social Relations*, edited by H. W. Bierhoff, R. L. Cohen, and J. Greenberg. New York: Plenum.

Binzen, Peter. 1970. *Whitetown USA*. New York: Vintage.

Blaschke, D., F. Buttler, W. Karr, et al. 1992. "Der Arbeitsmarkt in den neuen Ländern. Zwischenbilanz und Herausforderungen." *Mitteilung aus der Arbeitsmarkt-und Berufsforschung 25*:119–35.

Blau, Peter M. 1964. *Exchange and Power in Social Life*. New York: Wiley.

Blau, Peter M. 1971. "Justice in Social Exchange." Pp. 56–68 in *Institutions and Social Exchange: The Sociologies of Talcott Parsons and George C. Homans*, edited by H. Turk and R. L. Simpson. New York: Bobbs-Merrill.

Bobo, Lawrence, and James R. Kluegel. 1993. "Opposition to Race-Targeting: Self-Interest, Stratification Ideology, or Racial Attitudes?" *American Sociological Review 58*:443–64.

Bollen, Kenneth A. 1989. *Structural Equations with Latent Variables*. New York: Wiley.

Bond, Michael Harris (ed.). 1988 *The Cross-Cultural Challenge to Social Psychology*. Newbury Park, CA: Sage.

Boudon, Raymond. 1986. "The Logic of Relative Frustration." Pp. 171–96 in *Rational Choice*, edited by Jon Elster. Oxford: Basil Blackwell.

Braun, Michael, Jacqueline Scott, and Duane F. Alwin. 1992. "Economic Necessity or Self-Actualization? Attitudes Towards Women's Labor-Force Participation in the East and West." *European Sociological Review 10*:29–47.

Brickman, Philip, Robert Folger, Erica Goode, and Y. Yaacov Schul. 1981. "Microjustice and Macrojustice." Pp. 173–204 in *The Justice Motive in Social Behavior*, edited by Melvin J. Lerner and Sally C. Lerner. New York: Plenum.

Brinkmann, Christian, Knut Emmerich, Volkmar Gottsleben, et al. 1992. "Arbeitsmarktpolitik in den neuen Bundesländern. Braucht der ostdeutsche Arbeitsmarkt arbeitsmarktpolitische Sonderregelungen?" *WSI Mitteilungen 45*:420–30.

Broughton, John. 1983. "Women's Rationality and Men's Virtues: A Critique of Gender Dualism in Gilligan's Theory of Moral Development." *Social Research 50*:597–642.

Buchanan, Allen E. 1982. *Marx and Justice: The Radical Critique of Liberalism.* Totowa, NJ: Rowman and Littlefield.

Burgoyne, C., A. Swift, and Gordon Marshall. 1993. "Inconsistency in Beliefs about Distributive Justice: A Cautionary Note." *Journal for the Theory of Social Behaviour 23*:328–42.

Bürklin, Wilhelm. 1992. "Die Struktur politischer Konfliktlinien im vereinten Deutschland: Eine Nation—zwei getrennte politische Kulturen?" *Christiana Albertina 34*:15–32.

Byrne, Barbara. 1989. *A Primer of LISREL.* New York, Springer-Verlag.

Calvin, Jean. 1984. *Unterricht in der christlichen Religion. Institutio christianae religionis.* Edited by Otto Weber. Neukirchen-Vluyn: Neukirchener Verlag.

Carmines, Edward G. and S. P. McIver. 1981. "Analyzing Models with Unobserved Variables: Analysis of Covariance Structures." Pp 65–115 in *Social Measurement: Current Issues*, edited by George W. Bohrnstedt and Edgar F. Borgata. Beverly Hills, CA: Sage.

Carnap, Rudolf. 1954. *Testability and Meaning.* New Haven, CT: Yale University Press.

Carroll, Glenn R. and Karl Ulrich Mayer. 1986. "Job Shift Patterns in the Federal Republic of Germany: The Effects of Social Class, Industrial Sector, and Organizational Size." *American Sociological Review 51*:323–41.

Castles, Francis G. 1978. *The Social Democratic Image of Society.* London: Routledge and Kegan Paul.

Central Intelligence Agency. 1991. *World Factbook 1991.* Washington, DC: Author.

Central Intelligence Agency. 1992. *World Factbook 1992.* Washington, DC: Author.

Cheal, O. J. 1979. "Hegemony, Ideology and Contradictory Consciousness." *Sociological Quarterly 39*:752–66.

Chodorow, Nancy. 1974. *The Reproduction of Mothering: Psychoanalysis and the Sociology of Gender.* Berkeley: University of California Press.

Cichomski, Bogdan. 1992. "Legitimation of Social Orders and Socioeconomic Position of the Individual as Factors in the Perception of Justice in Twelve Nations." Paper presented at the "International Social Justice Project" Conference, Ann Arbor, Michigan, August.

Clarke, Harold D. 1991. "Measuring Value Change in Western Industrialized Societies: The Impact of Unemployment." *American Political Science Review 85*:905–20.

Clarke, Harold D. and Allan Kornberg. 1989. "Public Reactions to Economic Performance and Political Support in Contemporary Liberal Democracies: The Case of Canada." Pp. 253–82 in *Economic Decline and Political Change*, edited by H. D. Clarke, M. C. Stewart, and G. Zuk. Pittsburgh: University of Pittsburgh Press.

Cohen, Joshua. 1993. "Moral Pluralism and Political Consensus." Pp. 270–91 in *The Idea of Democracy*, edited by David Copp, Jean Hampton, and John Roemer. Cambridge: Cambridge University Press.

Cohen, Ronald L. (ed.). 1986. *Justice: Views from the Social Sciences.* New York: Plenum.

Connell, R. W. 1992. "Postmodern Patriarchy: Sexual Politics and Contemporary Cultural Change." Paper presented at the 87th Annual Meeting of the American Sociological Association, Pittsburgh, August 20–24.

Connors, Walter. 1991 *The Accidental Proletariat.* Princeton, NJ: Princeton University Press.

Converse, Philip. 1964. "The Nature of Belief Systems in Mass Publics." Pp. 206–61 in *Ideology and Discontent,* edited by David Apter. New York: Free Press.

Coughlin, Richard. M. 1980. *Ideology, Public Opinion and Welfare Policy.* Berkeley, CA: Institute of International Studies.

Csepeli, György. 1991. "J. Erdelyi, a Fascist Poet and His Sources of Inspiration. Poetry and National Socialism in Hungary." Pp. 257–67 in *Fascism and European Literature,* edited by S. Larsen, B. Sandberg, and R. Speirs. Bern: Peter Lang.

Csepeli, György and Antal Örkény. 1992a. "From Unjust Equality to Just Inequality." *New Hungarian Quarterly 33*:71–77.

Csepeli, György and Antal Örkény. 1992b. *Ideology and Political Beliefs in Hungary: The Twilight of State Socialism.* London and New York: Pinter.

Dahrendorf, Ralf. 1965. *Gesellschaft und Demokratie in Deutschland.* München: Piper.

Dahrendorf, Ralf. 1969. "The Service Class." Pp. 140–50 in *Industrial Man,* edited by Tom Burns. Harmondsworth: Penguin.

Dahrendorf, Ralf. 1971. *Die Idee des Gerechten im Denken von Karl Marx.* Hannover: Verlag für Literatur und Zeitgeschehen.

Dahrendorf, Ralf. 1974. *Pfade aus Utopia.* München: Piper.

Dahrendorf, Ralf. 1979. *Life Chances.* University of Chicago Press.

Davis, James A. and Roger Jewell. 1989. "Measuring National Differences. An Introduction to the International Social Survey Programme." Pp. 1–13 in *British Social Attitudes: Special International Report,* edited by Roger Jewell et al. Aldershot: Gower.

Davis, Kingsley. 1948. *Human Society.* New York: Macmillan.

Davis, Kingsley and Wilbert E. Moore. 1945. "Some Principles of Stratification." *American Sociological Review 10*:242–49.

Deaux, K. 1976. *The Behavior of Women and Men.* Monterey, CA: Brooks & Cole.

Della Fave, L. Richard. 1980. "The Meek Shall Not Inherit the Earth." *American Sociological Review 45*:955–71.

Della Fave, L. Richard. 1986a. "The Dialectics of Legitimation and Counternorms." *Sociological Perspectives 29*:435–60.

Della Fave, L. Richard. 1986b. "Toward an Explication of the Legitimation Process." *Social Forces 65*:476–500.

Deppermann, Karl. 1961. *Der hallesche Pietismus und der preussische Staat unter Friedrich III. (I.).* Göttingen: Vandenhoeck & Ruprecht.

Deutsch, Morton. 1975. "Equity, Equality, and Need: What Determines Which Value Will Be Used as the Basis of Distributive Justice?" *Journal of Social Issues 31*:137–49.

Deutsch, Morton. 1985. *Distributive Justice: A Social-Psychological Perspective.* New Haven, CT: Yale University Press.

DiQuattro, Arthur. 1986. "Political Studies and Justice." Pp. 85–116 in *Justice,* edited by Ronald L. Cohen. New York: Plenum.

Döbert, Rainer and Gertrud Nunner-Winkler. 1986. "Wertwandel und Moral." Pp. 289–321 in *Gesellschaftlicher Zwang und moralische Autonomie,* edited by Hans Bertram. Frankfurt: Suhrkamp.

Dornstein, Miriam. 1991. *Conceptions of Fair Pay. Theoretical Perspectives and Empirical Research*. New York: Praeger.

Douglas, Mary. 1982. *In the Active Voice*. London: Routledge & Kegan Paul.

Douglas, Mary and Aaron Wildavsky. 1982: *Risk and Culture*. Berkeley: University of California Press.

Duch, Raymond M. 1993. "Tolerating Economic Reform: Popular Support for Transition to a Free Market in the Former Soviet Union." *American Political Science Review* 87:590–608.

Dunn, John. 1980. *Political Obligation In its Historical Context*. Cambridge: Cambridge University Press.

Durkheim, Emile. 1983. *Über den Selbstmord*. Frankfurt: Suhrkamp.

Edelman, Murray. 1971. *Politics as Symbolic Action*. New York: Academic.

Eisenstadt, S. N. and Ora Ahimeir. 1985. *The Welfare State and Its Aftermath*. London: Croom Helm.

Eiser, J. Richard. 1986. *Social Psychology—Attitudes, Cognition and Social Behaviour*. Cambridge: Cambridge University Press.

Eiser, J. Richard and J. van der Pligt. 1988., *Attitudes and Decisions*. London: Routledge.

Eley, Geoff. 1986. *From Unification to Nazism: Reinterpreting the German Past*. Boston: Allen & Unwin.

Elliott, Euel and Rose-Marie Zuk. 1989. "The Structure of Public Economic Evaluations: The United States, 1976–84." Pp. 173–94 in *Economic Decline and Political Change*, edited by H. D. Clarke, M. C. Stewart, and G. Zuk. Pittsburgh: University of Pittsburgh Press.

Elster, Jon. 1989a. *The Cement of Society*. Cambridge, Cambridge University Press.

Elster, Jon. 1989b. *Solomonic Judgements*. Cambridge: Cambridge University Press.

Elster, Jon. 1992. *Local Justice: How Institutions Allocate Scare Goods and Necessary Burdens*. Cambridge: Cambridge University Press.

Elster, Jon. 1995. "The Empirical Study of Justice." Pp. 81–98 in *Pluralism, Justice and Equality*, edited by David Miller and Michael Walzer. Oxford University Press: Oxford.

Enders, Ulrike. 1986. "Kinder, Küche, Kombinat—Frauen in der DDR." *Aus Politik und Zeitgeschichte B6–7*(86):26–37.

Erikson, Robert and John H. Goldthorpe. 1992. *The Constant Flux*. Oxford: Clarendon.

Erikson, Robert, Norman Luttbeg, and Kent L. Tedin. 1991. *American Public Opinion: Its Origins, Content and Impact*. New York: Macmillan.

Esping-Andersen, Gøsta. 1990. *The Three Worlds of Welfare Capitalism*. Cambridge, UK: Polity.

Estlund, David. 1989. "The Persistent Puzzle of the Minority Democrat." *American Philosophical Quarterly* 16:143–51.

Europa Publications. 1993. *Europa World Yearbook 1993*. London.

Evans, M. D. R., Jonathon Kelley, and Tamas Kolosi. 1992. "Images of Class, Public Perceptions in Hungary and Australia." *American Sociological Review* 57:461–82.

Faludi, Susan. 1991. *Backlash: The Undeclared War Against American Women*. New York: Crown.

Feagin, Joe R. 1975. *Subordinating the Poor*. Englewood Cliffs, NJ: Prentice Hall.

Feather, Norman T. 1974. "Explanations of Poverty in Australian and American Samples: The Person, Society and Fate." *Australian Journal of Psychology* 26:199–216.

Fenwick, R. and J. Olson. 1986. "Support for Worker Participation: Attitudes among Union and Non-Union Workers." *American Sociological Review* 51:505–22.

Ferge, Zs. 1986. *Fejezetek a Magyar Szegenypolitika Tortenetebol (Chapters from the History of Hungarian Social Policy).* Budapest: Magveto.

Finifter, Ada and Ellen Mickiewicz. 1992. "Redefining the Political System of the USSR: Mass Support for Political Change." *American Political Science Review* 86:857–74.

Fiske, Susan T. and Shelley E. Taylor. 1991. *Social Cognition.* New York: McGraw-Hill.

Flanagan, O. and K. Jackson. 1987. "Justice, Care and Gender: The Kohlberg-Gilligan Debate Revisited." *Ethics* 97:622–37.

Flora, Peter. 1986. *Growth to Limits,* Vol. 2. Berlin: Walter de Gruyter.

Flora, Peter and Arnold J. Heidenheimer (eds.). 1981. *The Development of Welfare States in Europe and America.* New Brunswick, NJ: Transaction.

Flora, Peter and Arnold J. Heidenheimer. 1987. *The Development of the Welfare States in Europe and America.* New Brunswick, NJ: Transaction.

Freud, Sigmund. 1925 [1964]. "Some Psychical Consequences of the Anatomical Distinction Between the Sexes." Pp. 243–58 in *Standard Edition of the Complete Psychological Works,* Vol. 19. London: Hogarth Press and Institute of Psycho-Analysis.

Frick, J., P. Krause, and J. Schwarze. 1991. "Haushalts- und Erwerbseinkommen in der DDR." *Kölner Zeitschrift für Soziologie und Sozialpsychologie* 43:334–43.

Fuchs, Dieter, Hans-Dieter Klingemann, and Carolin Schöbel. 1991. "Perspektiven der politischen Kultur im vereinigten Deutschland. Eine empirische Studie." *Aus Politik und Zeitgeschichte* B32(91):35–46.

Furnham, Adrian. 1983. "Attributions for Affluence." *Personality and Individual Differences* 4:31–40.

Furnham, Adrian and Alan Lewis. 1986. *The Economic Mind.* New York: St. Martins.

Galston, William. 1991. *Liberal Purposes.* Cambridge: Cambridge University Press.

Galtung, Johan. 1982. "On the Meaning of 'Nation' as a Variable." Pp. 17–34 in *International Comparative Research. Problems of Theory, Methodology, and Organization in Eastern and Western Europe,* edited by Manfred Niessen and Jules Peschar. New York: Pergamon.

Ganzeboom, Harry B. G., Peter M. De Graaf, and Donald J. Treiman. 1992. "A Standard International Socio-Economic Index of Occupations." *Social Science Research* 21:1–56.

Gaus, Günther. 1983. *Wo Deutschland liegt. Eine Ortsbestimmung.* Hamburg: Hoffmann & Campe.

Geiger, Theodor. [1932] 1972. *Die soziale Schichtung des deutschen Volkes.* Darmstadt: Wissenschaftliche Buchgesellschaft.

Geißler, Rainer. 1991. "Transformationsprozesse in der Sozialstruktur der neuen Bundesländer." *Berliner Journal für Soziologie* 1:177–94.

Gilligan, Caroll. 1982. *In a Different Voice. Psychological Theory and Women's Development.* Cambridge, MA: Harvard University Press.

Gilligan, Carol. 1991. "Moralische Orientierung und moralische Entwicklung." Pp. 112–46 in *Weibliche Moral,* edited by Gertrud Nunner-Winkler. Frankfurt: Campus Verlag.

Glaeßner, Gert-Joachim. 1977. *Herrschaft durch Kader: Leitung der Gesellschaft und Kaderpolitik in der DDR.* Opladen: Westdeutscher Verlag.

Golding, Peter and Susan Middleton. 1982. *Images of Welfare.* Oxford: Martin Robertson.

Goldthorpe, John H. 1987. *Social Mobility and Class Structure in Great Britain,* 2nd ed. Oxford: Clarendon.

Goldthorpe, John H., David Lockwood, Frank Bechhofer, and Jennifer Platt. 1968. *The Affluent Worker: Industrial Attitudes and Behaviour.* Cambridge: Cambridge University Press.

Greenberg, Jerald and Ronald L. Cohen (eds.). 1982. *Equity and Justice in Social Behavior.* New York: Academic.

Gross, Jonathan and Steve Rayner. 1985. *Measuring Culture.* New York: Columbia University Press.

Gurr, T. R. 1991. "America as a Model for the World? A Skeptical View." *PS: Political Science 24*:664–65.

Haan, Norma. 1978. "Two Moralities in Action Contexts: Relationships to Thought, Ego Regulation, and Development." *Journal of Personality and Social Psychology 36*:286–303.

Habermas, Jurgen. 1975. *Legitimation Crisis.* Translated by T. McCarthy. Boston: Beacon.

Habich, Rainer, Michael Häder, P. Krause, and E. Priller. 1991. "Die Entwicklung des subjektiven Wohlbefindens vom Januar bis zum Herbst 1990 in der DDR und Ostdeutschland." Pp. 332–56 in *Lebenslagen im Wandel: Basisdaten und -analysen zur Entwicklung in den Neuen Bundesländern,* edited by Projektgruppe "Das Sozioökonomische Panel." Frankfurt: Campus Verlag.

Habich, Rainer, Detlef Landua, W. Seifert, and A. Spellerberg. 1991. ""Ein unbekanntes Land": Objektive Lebensbedingungen und subjektives Wohlbefinden in Ostdeutschland." *Aus Politik und Zeitgeschichte, B32*(91):13–33.

Hahn, Jeffrey W. 1993. "Public Opinion Research in the Soviet Union: Problems and Possibilities." Pp. 37–47 in *Public Opinion and Regime Change,* edited by Arthur H. Miller, William M. Reisinger, and Vicki L. Hesli. Boulder, CO: Westview.

Halle, David. 1984. *America's Working Man.* Chicago: University of Chicago Press.

Haller, Max. 1989. "Die Klassenstruktur im sozialen Bewußtsein. Ergebnisse vergleichender Umfrageforschung zu Ungleichheitsvorstellungen." Pp. 447–69 in *Kultur und Gesellschaft. Verhandlungen des 24. Deutschen Soziologentages,* edited by Max Haller, H.-J. Hoffmann-Nowotny, and Wolfgang Zapf. Frankfurt: Campus Verlag.

Hamilton, V. Lee and Joseph Sanders. 1992. *Everyday Justice.* New Haven, CT: Yale University Press.

Hampton, James. 1982. "Giving the Grid, Group Dimensions an Operational Definition." Pp. 64–82 in *Essays in the Sociology of Perception,* edited by Mary Douglas. London: Routledge & Kegan Paul.

Heider, Fritz. 1958. *The Psychology of Interpersonal Relations.* New York: Wiley.

Heinen, J. 1992. "The Polish Democracy Is a Masculine Democracy." *Women's Studies International Forum 15*:129–38.

Hempel, Carl G. 1965. "Fundamentals of taxonomy." Pp. 137–54 in *Aspects of Scientific Explanation and Other Essays in the Philosophy of Science,* edited by Carl G. Hempel. New York: Free Press.

Hempel, Carl and Paul Oppenheim. 1948. "Studies in the Logic of Explanation." *Philosophy of Science 15*:135–75.

Herf, Jeffrey. 1984. *Reactionary Modernism.* New York: Cambridge.

Herz, Thomas A. 1990. "Die Dienstklasse. Eine empirische Analyse ihrer demographischen, kulturellen und politischen Identität." Pp. 231–52 in *Lebenslagen, Lebensläufe, Lebensstile,* Soziale Welt Sonderband 7, edited by Peter A. Berger and Stefan Hradil. Göttingen: Otto Schwartz.

Hill, Claude. 1964. *Puritanism and Revolution*. New York: Schocken.

Hinrichs, Carl. 1941. *Friedrich Wilhelm I. König von Preussen*. Hamburg: Hanseatische Verlagsanstalt.

Hochschild, Jennifer L. 1981. *What's Fair? American Beliefs About Distributive Justice*. Cambridge, MA: Harvard University Press.

Hofstede, Geert. 1984. *Culture's Consequences*. Beverly Hills, CA: Sage.

Hogsnes, Geir. 1989. "Wage Bargaining and Norms of Fairness—A Theoretical Framework for Analysing the Norwegian Wage Formation." *Acta Sociologica* 32:339–57.

Holton, Robert J. and Bryan S. Turner. 1986. *Talcott Parsons on Economy and Society*. London: Routledge & Kegan Paul.

Homans, George C. 1974. *Social Behavior: Its Elementary Forms*, 2nd ed. New York: Harcourt Brace Jovanovich.

Houghton, John W. 1991. *Culture and Currency: Cultural Bias in Monetary Theory and Policy*. Boulder, CO: Westview.

Huber, Joan and William H. Form. 1973. *Income and Ideology*. New York: Free Press.

Huinink, Johannes and Karl Ulrich Mayer. 1993. "Lebensverläufe im Wandel der DDR-Gesellschaft." Pp. 151–71 in *Der Zusammenbruch der DDR*, edited by Hans Joas and Martin Kohli. Frankfurt: Suhrkamp.

Huntington, Samuel. 1991. "Democracy's Third Wave." *Journal of Democracy* 2:12–34.

Hye, Kyung Lee. 1987. "The Japanese Welfare State in Transition." Pp. 243–63 in *Modern Welfare States*, edited by Robert Friedman, Neil Gilbert, and Moshe Sherer. New York: New York University Press.

Hyman, Richard and Ian Brough. 1975. *Social Values and Industrial Relations*. Oxford: Basil Blackwell.

Inglehart, Ronald. 1977. *The Silent Revolution. Changing Values and Political Styles Among Western Publics*. Princeton, NJ: University Press.

Inglehart, Ronald. 1979. "Value Priorities and Socioeconomic Change." Pp. 305–42 in *Political Action: Mass Participation in Five Western Democracies*, Samuel Barnes, Max Kaase, et al. Beverly Hills: Sage.

Inglehart, Ronald. 1990. *Culture Shift in Advanced Industrial Society*. Princeton, NJ: Princeton University Press.

Institute for Public Policy Research. 1993. *Social Justice in a Changing World*. London: IPPR.

International Labour Office. 1968. *International Standard Classification of Occupations (ISCO)*, rev. ed. Geneva: ILO.

Iyengar, Shanto. 1990. "Framing Responsibility for Political Issues: The Case of Poverty." *Political Behavior* 12:19–40.

Jancar, W. 1985. "Women in the Opposition in Poland and Czechoslovakia." Pp. 31–46 in *Women, State, and Party in Eastern Europe*, edited by Sharon Wolchik and Alfred Meyer. Durham, NC: Duke University Press.

Jansson, Bruce S. 1988. *The Reluctant Welfare State*. Belmont, CA: Wadsworth.

Jasso, Guillermina. 1978. "On the Justice of Earnings: A New Specification of the Justice Evaluation Function." *American Journal of Sociology* 83:1398–1419.

Jasso, Guillermina. 1980. "A New Theory of Distributive Justice." *American Sociological Review* 45:3–32.

Jasso, Guillermina. 1983. "Social Consequences of the Sense of Distributive Justice: Small-Group Applications." Pp. 243–94 in *Equity Theory. Psychological and Socio-*

logical Perspectives, edited by David M. Messick and Karen S. Cook. New York: Praeger.

Jasso, Guillermina. 1990. "Methods for the Empirical and Theoretical Analysis of Comparison Processes." Pp. 369–419 in *Sociological Methodology*, edited by C. C. Clogg. Washington, DC: ASA.

Jasso, Guillermina. 1993. "Choice and Emotion in Comparison Theory." *Rationality and Society* 5:231–74.

Jasso, Guillermina and Peter H. Rossi. 1977. "Distributive Justice and Earned Income." *American Sociological Review* 42:639–51.

Jennings, M. Kent. 1991. "Thinking about Social Injustice." *Political Psychology* 12:187–204.

Jones, Lancaster F. and Jonathon Kelley. 1984. "Decomposing Differences Between Groups." *Sociological Methods and Research* 12:323–34.

Jöreskog, Karl G. and Dag Sörbom. 1985. *LISREL VI: Analysis of Linear Structural Relationships by Maximum Likelihood, Instrumental Variables, and Least Squares.* Uppsala: University of Uppsala.

Jöreskog, Karl G. and Dag Sörbom. 1988. LISREL 7. *A Guide to the Program and Applications*, 2nd ed. Chicago: SPSS Inc.

Kahn, A., V. O'Leary, J. E. Krulewitz, and H. Lamm. 1980. "Equity and Equality: Male and Female Means to a Just End." *Basic and Applied Psychology* 1:173–97.

Kahneman, D., J. L. Knetsch, and R. Thaler. 1986. "Fairness as a Constraint on Profit Seeking: Entitlements in the Market." *American Economic Review* 76:728–41.

Kalberg, Stephen. 1987. "The Opinion and Expansion of "Kulturpessimismus": The Relationship between Public and Private Sphere in Early Twentieth Century Germany." *Sociological Theory* 5:150–64.

Karniol, R. and D. T. Miller. 1981. "Morality and the Development of Conceptions of Justice." Pp. 91–129 *The Justice Motive in Social Behavior*, edited by Melvin J. Lerner and Sally C. Lerner. New York: Plenum.

Kelley, Jonathon and M. D. R. Evans. 1993. "The Legitimation of Inequality: Occupational Earnings in Nine Nations." *American Journal of Sociology* 99:75–125.

Kerckhoff, Alan C. 1989. "On the Social Psychology of Social Mobility Processes." *Social Forces* 68:17–25.

Kidder, L. H., M. A. Fagan, and E. S. Cohn. 1981. "Giving and Receiving: Social Justice in Close Relationships." Pp. 153–78 in *The Justice Motive in Social Behavior*, edited by Melvin J. Lerner and Sally C. Lerner. New York: Plenum.

Kiewiet, D. R. 1983. *Macroeconomics and Micropolitics*. Chicago: University of Chicago Press.

Kinder, Donald and David Sears. 1985. "Public Opinion and Political Action." Pp. 659–742 in *The Handbook of Social Psychology*, 3rd ed., Vol. 2, edited by Gardner Lindzey and Elliot Aronson. Reading, MA: Addison-Wesley.

Kish, Leslie. 1987. *Statistical Design for Research*. New York: Wiley.

Kleebaur, Sabine and Bernd Wegener. 1991. *Dokumentation. International Social Justice Project: Arbeitsgruppe für die Bundesrepublik Deutschland.* ISJP Arbeitsbericht 7 (German Research Report 7), Heidelberg.

Kluegel, James R. 1988. "Economic Problems and Socioeconomic Beliefs and Attitudes." *Research in Social Strratification and Mobility* 7:273–302.

Kluegel, James R. 1989. "Perceptions of Justice in the U.S.: Split Consciousness Among the

American Public." Paper presented at the Conference on Perception of Social Justice in East and West, Dubrovnik.

Kluegel, James R. and Eliot R. Smith. 1981. "Beliefs about Stratification." *Annual Review of Sociology* 7:29–56.

Kluegel, James R. and Eliot R. Smith. 1986. *Beliefs About Inequality: American Views of What Is and Ought to Be*. Hawthorne, NY: Aldine de Gruyter.

Kohlberg, Lawrence. 1973. "Continuities in Childhood and Adult Moral Development Revisited." Pp. 198–244 in *Life-Span Developmental Psychology: Personality and Socialization*, edited by Paul B. Baltes and K. W. Schaie. New York: Academic.

Kohlberg, Lawrence. 1981. "The Future of Liberalism As the Dominant Ideology of the Western World." Pp. 231–42 in *Essays on Moral Development: The Philosophy of Moral Development*, edited by Lawrence Kohlberg. San Francisco: Harper & Row.

Kohlberg, Lawrence. 1982. "A Reply to Owen Flanagan and Some Comments on the Puka-Goodpaster Exchange." *Ethics* 92:513–28.

Kohlberg, Lawrence. 1984. *Essays on Moral Development: The Psychology of Moral Development*, Vol. 2. *Moral Stages and the Life Cycle*. San Francisco, CA: Harper & Row.

Kohlberg, Lawrence and R. Kramer. 1969. "Continuities and Discontinuities in Child and Adult Moral Reasoning." *Human Development* 12:93–120.

Kohlberg, Lawrence, C. Levine, and A. Hewer. 1983. *Moral Stages: A Current Formulation and a Response to Critics*. Basel: Karger.

Kohn, Melvin L. 1989a. "Cross-National Research as an Analytic Strategy." Pp. 77–103 in *Cross-National Research in Sociology*, edited by Melvin L. Kohn. Newbury Park, CA: Sage.

Kohn, Melvin L. (ed.). 1989b. *Cross-National Research in Sociology*. London: Sage.

Kolosi, Tamas, Zs. Papp, Cs. Pal, and J. Bara. 1980. *Retaghelyzet-retegtudat* (*Social Status and Social Consciousness*). Budapest: Kossuth.

König, Wolfgang, Paul Lüttinger, and Walter Müller. 1988. "A Comparative Analysis of the Development and Structure of Educational Systems." CASMIN Project, Institut für Sozialwissenschaften, Universität Mannheim.

Korte, Karl-Rudolf. 1990. "Die Folgen der Einheit. Zur politisch-kulturellen Lage der Nation." *Aus Politik und Zeitgeschichte, Beilage zur Wochenzeitung Das Parlament* B27(90):29–38.

Kuechler, Manfred. 1987. "The Utility of Surveys for Cross-National Research." *Social Science Research* 16:229–44.

Kuhn, Thomas S. 1970. *The Structure of Scientific Revolutions. International Encyclopedia of Unified Science*, II, 2, 2nd ed. Chicago: University of Chicago Press.

Kurz, Karin. 1989. *Klassenbildung und soziale Mobilität in der Bundesrepublik Deutschland: Überlegungen zu einem Klassifikationsschema*. Ph.D. thesis, Department of Sociology, University of Mannheim.

Lakatós, Imre. 1970. "Falsification and the Methodology of Research Programmes." Pp. 91–196 in *Criticism and the Growth of Knowledge*, edited by Imre Lakatós and Alan Musgrave. Cambridge: University of Cambridge Press.

Lane, Robert E. 1962. *Political Ideology: Why the American Common Man Beliefs What He Does*. New York: Free Press.

Lane, Robert E. 1986. "Market Justice, Political Justice." *American Political Science Review* 80:383–402.

Lerner, Melvin J. 1975. "The Justice Motive in Social Behavior: An Introduction." *Journal of Social Issues 31*:1–20.

Lerner, Melvin J. 1977. "The Justice Motive: Some Hypotheses as to Its Origins and Forms." *Journal of Personality 45*:1–52.

Lerner, Melvin J. 1980. *The Belief in a Just World*. New York: Plenum.

Lerner, Melvin J. and Linda A. Whitehead. 1980. "Verfahrensgerechtigkeit aus der Sicht der Gerechtigkeitsmotiv-Theorie." Pp. 251–99 in *Gerechtigkeit und soziale Interaktion. Experimentelle und theoretische Beiträge aus der psychologischen Forschung*, edited by Gerold Mikula. Bern: Huber.

Leventhal, G. S. 1976. "Fairness in Social Relations." Pp. 211–39 in *Contemporary Topics in Social Psychology*, edited by J. Thibaut, J. T. Spence and R. C. Carson. Morristown, NJ: General Learning Press.

Leventhal, G. S. and D. Anderson. 1970. "Self-Interest and the Maintenance of Equity." *Journal of Personality and Social Psychology 15*:57–62.

Leventhal, G. S., J. Koruza, and W. R. Frye. 1980. "Beyond Fairness: A Theory of Allocation Preferences." Pp. 167–218 in *Justice and Social Interaction*, edited by Gerold Mikula. New York: Springer Verlag.

Leventhal, G. S. and D. W. Lane. 1970. "Sex, Age, and Equity Behavior." *Journal of Personality and Social Psychology 15*:312–16.

Lewis, Michael. 1978. *The Culture of Inequality*. Amherst: University of Massachusetts Press.

Lindenberg, S. 1992. "An Extended Theory of Institutions and Contractual Discipline." *Journal of Institutional and Theoretical Economics 148*:125–54.

Lockwood, David. 1964. "Social Integration and System Integration." Pp. 370–83 in Social Change: Explorations, Diagnoses and Conjectures, edited by G. K. Zollschan and W. Hirsch. New York: Wiley.

Lockwood, David. 1992. *Solidarity and Schism*. Cambridge: Cambridge University Press.

Ludz, Peter Christian. 1968. *Parteielite im Wandel: Funktionsaufbau, Sozialstruktur und Ideologie der SED-Führung*. Opladen: Westdeutscher Verlag.

Luther, Martin. [1523] 1900. "Von weltlicher Obrigkeit, wie weit man ihr Gehorsam schuldig ist." Pp. 229–81 in *D. Martin Luthers Werke. Kritische Gesamtausgabe*, Vol. 11. Weimar: HBN.

Luther, Martin. [1525] 1908a. "Ein Sendbrief von dem harten Büchlein wider die Bauern." Pp. 375–401 in *D. Martin Luthers Werke. Kritische Gesamtausgabe*, Vol. 11. Weimar: HBN.

Luther, Martin. [1525] 1908b. "Wider die räberischen und morderischen Rotten der Bauern." Pp. 344–61 in *D. Martin Luthers Werke. Kritische Gesamtausgabe*, Vol. 11. Weimar: HBN.

Major, B. and J. B. Adams. 1983. "Role of Gender, Interpersonal Orientation, and Self-Presentation in Distributive-Justice Behavior." *Journal of Personality and Social Psychology 45*:598–608.

Mann, Michael. 1970. "The Social Cohesion of Liberal Democracy." *American Sociological Review 35*:423–39.

Mann, Michael. 1973. *Consciousness and Action Among the Western Working Class*. London: Macmillan.

Mannheim, Karl. 1928. "Das Problem der Generationen." *Kölner Vierteljahreshefte für Soziologie 7*:309–21.

Marer, Paul. 1993. "Economic Transformation in Central and Eastern Europe." Pp. 53–98 in *Making Markets: Economic Transformation in Eastern Europe and the Post-Soviet States*, edited by Shafiqul Islam and Michael Mandelbaum. New York: Council on Foreign Relations Press.

Markovsky, B. 1988. "Anchoring Justice." *Social Psychology Quarterly 51*:213–24.

Marshall, Gordon. 1982. *In Search of the Spirit of Capitalism: An Essay on Max Weber's Protestant Ethic Thesis.* New York: Columbia University Press.

Marshall, Gordon and Adam Swift. 1993. "Social Class and Social Justice." *British Journal of Sociology 44*:187–211.

Marshall, Gordon, Carole Bourgoyne, and Adam Swift. 1992. "Constructing the Class Variables for the Project." Working paper of the International Project on Popular Perceptions of Social Justice (January).

Marx, Karl. [1845/46] 1968. "Die deutsche Ideologie, I. Teil." Pp. 341–417 in *Karl Marx. Die Frühschriften*, edited by Siegfried Landshut. Stuttgart: Kröner.

Mason, David S. 1985. *Public Opinion and Political Change in Poland.* Cambridge: Cambridge University Press.

Mason, David S., D. N. Nelson, and B. M. Szklarski. 1991. "Apathy and the Birth of Democracy: The Polish Struggle." *East European Politics and Societies 5*:205–35.

Mason, David S. and Svetlana Sydorenko. 1992. "Perestroika, Social Justice, and Public Opinion." Pp. 70–91 in *Ideology and System Change in the USSR and East Europe*, edited by Michael Urban. New York: St. Martin's.

Mayer, Karl Ulrich. 1992a. "Wiedervereinigung, soziale Kontrolle und Generationen. Elemente einer Transformationstheorie." Studienbrief der Fernuniversität Hagen.

Mayer, Karl Ulrich. 1992b. "Transition to Post Communism. The Socio-Economic Transformation of East Germany." Unpublished report, Max-Planck Institut für Bildungsforschung.

Medvedev, Roy. 1977. "Socialism, Justice and Democracy." Pp. 7–24 in *The Just Society*, edited by Ken Coates and Fred Singleton. Spokesman.

Meier, Arthur. 1990. "The Social Imperative: Contradictions of Socialist State Technological Policy." *International Sociology 5*:27–38.

Miller, Arthur H., Vicki Hesli, and William Reisinger. 1993. "Comparing Citizen and Elite Attitudes Toward a Market Economy in Russia, Ukraine and Lithuania." Paper presented at the 1993 convention of the American Association for the Advancement of Slavic Studies, Honolulu.

Miller, Arthur H., William M. Reisinger, and Vicki L. Hesli (eds.). 1993. *Public Opinion and Regime Change.* Boulder, CO: Westview.

Miller, David 1976. *Social Justice.* Oxford: Oxford University Press.

Miller, David. 1991. "Review Article: Recent Theories of Social Justice." *British Journal of Political Science 21*:371–91.

Miller, David. 1992. "Distributive Justice: What the People Think." *Ethics 102*:555–93.

Miller, David. 1994. "Review of K. R. Scherer (ed.), *Justice: Interdisciplinary Perspectives.*" *Social Justice Research 7*:167–88.

Mincer, J. 1974. *Schooling, Experience, and Earnings.* New York: Praeger.

Moeller, Bernd. 1987. *Geschichte des Christentums in Grundzügen.* Göttingen: Vandenhoeck & Ruprecht.

Moeller, Bernd. 1988. *Deutschland im Zeitalter der Reformation.* Deutsche Geschichte, Vol. 4. Göttingen: Vandenhoeck & Ruprecht.

Mommsen, Wolfgang J. 1981. *The Emergence of the Welfare State in Britain and Germany*. London: Croom Helm.

Moore, B., Jr. 1978. *Injustice. The Social Basis of Obedience and Revolt*. London: MacMillan.

Morrison, C. 1984. "Income Distribution in East European and Western Countries." *Journal of Comparative Economics* 8:120–38.

Mosse, George. 1964. *The Crisis of German Ideology*. New York: Grosset & Dunlap.

Mühlen, Karl-Heinz zur. 1986. "Arbeit IV. Reformation und Orthodoxie." Pp. 635–39 in *Theologische Realenzyklopädie*, Vol. 3, 2nd ed. Berlin: de Gruyter.

Mulhall, Stephen and Adam Swift. 1992. *Liberals and Communitarians*. Oxford: Basil Blackwell.

Müller, Hans-Peter. 1992. "Durkheims Vision einer "gerechten" Gesellschaft." *Zeitschrift für Rechtssoziologie* 1:16–43.

Murphy, John M. and Carol Gilligan. 1980. "Moral Development in Late Adolescence and Adulthood: A Critique and Reconstruction of Kohlberg's Theory." *Human Development* 23:77–104.

Nails, D. 1991. "Sozialwissenschaftlicher Sexismus: Carol Gilligans Fehlvermessung des Menschen." Pp. 101–8 in *Weibliche Moral*, edited by Gertrud Nunner-Winkler. Frankfurt: Campus Verlag.

Nichols, Theo and Peter Armstrong. 1976. *Workers Divided*. Glasgow: Fontana/Collins.

Nielson, K. 1979. "Radical Egalitarian Justice: Justice as Equality." *Social Theory and Practice* 5:209–26.

Nilson, Linda. 1981. "Reconsidering Ideological Lines: Beliefs About Poverty in America." *Sociological Quarterly* 22:531–48.

Noll, Heinz-Herbert. 1992a. "Soziale Schichtung: Niedrigere Einstufung der Ostdeutschen." *Informationsdienst Soziale Indikatoren* 7:1–6.

Noll, Heinz-Herbert. 1992b. "Zur Legitimität sozialer Ungleichheit in Deutschland: Subjektive Wahrnehmungen und Bewertungen." Pp. 1–20 in *Blickpunkt Gesellschaft 2. Einstellungen und Verhalten der Bundesbürger in Ost und West*, edited by Peter Mohler and Wolfgang Bandilla. Opladen: Westdeutscher Verlag.

Norden, Gilbert. 1985. *Einkommensgerechtigkeit. Was darunter verstanden wird*. Wien: Böhlaus.

Nozick, Robert. 1974. *Anarchy, State and Utopia*. New York: Basic Books.

Offe, Claus. 1976. *Industry and Inequality*. New York: St. Martin's.

Olsson, Anders S. 1989. *The Swedish Wage Negotiation System*. Uppsala: University of Uppsala Press.

Ossowski, Stanislaw. 1963. *Class Structure in the Social Consciousness*. New York: Free Press.

Oyen, E. (ed.). 1990. *Comparative Methodology, Theory and Practice*. London: Sage.

Page, Robert Y. and John T. Young. 1989. "Public Opinion and the Welfare State: The United States in Comparative Perspective." *Political Science Quarterly* 104:59–89.

Pakulski, Jan. 1990. "Poland: Ideology, Legitimacy, Political Domination." Pp. 38–64 in *Dominant Ideologies*, edited by Nicholas Ambercrombie, Stephen Hill, and Bryan S. Turner. London: Unwin Hyman

Parkin, Frank. 1971. *Class, Inequality and Political Order*. New York: Praeger.

Parkin, Frank. 1979. *Marxism and Class Theory: A Bourgeois Critique*. London: Tavistock.

Parsons, Talcott. 1937. *The Structure of Social Action*. New York: Free Press.

Parsons, Talcott. 1951. *The Social System*. New York: Free Press.

Parsons, Talcott. 1970. "Equality and Inequality in Modern Society, or Social Stratification revisited." Pp. 13–72 in *Social Stratification: Research and Theory for the 1970s*, edited by E. O. Laumann. Indianapolis, IN: Bobbs-Merrill.

Parsons, Talcott. 1971. *The System of Modern Societies*. Englewood Cliffs, NJ: Prentice Hall.

Phares, E. Jerry. 1976. *Locus of Control in Personality*. Morristown, NJ: General Learning.

Piaget, Jean. 1965. *The Moral Judgement of the Child*. New York: Free Press.

Pizzorno, Alessandro. 1991. "On the Individualistic Theory of Social Order." Pp. 209–34 in *Social Theory for a Changing Society*, edited by Pierre Bourdieu and James S. Coleman. Boulder: Westview.

Polish General Social Survey. 1992. *Codebook 1992*. Warsaw: Institute for Social Studies, University of Warsaw.

Pollack, Detlef. 1990. "Das Ende einer Organisationsgesellschaft. Systemtheoretische überlegungen zum gesellschaftlichen Umbruch in der DDR." *Zeitschrift für Soziologie* *19*:292–307.

Pollitt, K. 1992. "Are Women Morally Superior to Men? Debunking "Difference" Feminism." *Nation* 255:799ff.

Poulantzas, Nicos. 1974. *Politische Macht und gesellschaftliche Klassen*. Frankfurt: Athenäum.

Przeworski, Adam and Henry Teune. 1970. *The Logic of Comparative Social Inquiry*. Malabar, FL: Robert E. Krieger.

Pye, L. W. 1971. "The Legitimacy Crisis." In *Crises and Sequences in Political Development*, edited by L. Binder et al. Princeton, NJ: Princeton University Press.

Ragin, C. C. 1987. *The Comparative Method*, Berkeley: University of California Press.

Ramsey, Frank P. 1965. "Theories." Pp. 212–36 in *The Foundations of Mathematics and other Logical Essays*, edited by R. B. Braithwaite. London: Routledge & Kegan Paul.

Rawls, John. 1971. *A Theory of Justice*. Cambridge, MA: Harvard University Press.

Rawls, John. 1993. *Political Liberalism*. New York: Columbia University Press.

Reis, Harry T. 1984. "The Multidimensionality of Justice." Pp. 25–61 in *The Sense of Injustice*, edited by R. Folger. New York: Plenum.

Reis, Harry T. 1986. "Levels of Interest in the Study of Interpersonal Justice." Pp. 187–210 in *Justice in Social Relations*, edited by H. W. Bierhoff, R. L. Cohen, and J. Greenberg. New York: Plenum.

Renner, Karl. 1953. *Wandlungen der modernen Gesellschaft*. Wien: Verlag der Wiener Volksbuch handlung.

Retherford, Robert D. and Minja Kim Choe. 1993., *Statistical Models for Causal Analysis*. Chichester: Wiley.

Rimlinger, Gaston V. 1971. *Welfare Policy and Industrialization in Europe, America and Russia*. New York: Wiley.

Ringer, Fritz. 1969. *The Decline of the German Mandarins*. Cambridge, MA: Harvard University Press.

Ritzman, Rosemary, L. and Donald Tomaskovic-Devey. 1992. "Life Chances and Support for Equality and Equity As Normative and Counternormative Distribution Rules." *Social Forces 70*:745–63.

Robinson, V. R. and W. Davis. 1990. "Explaining Perceptions and Evaluations of Gender Inequality in Four Countries: Austria, West Germany, Great Britain, and the United States." Unpublished manuscript.

Rokeach, Milton. 1976. *Beliefs, Attitudes and Values*. San Francisco: Jossey-Bass.

Rokkan, Stein. 1974. "Dimensions of State Formation and Nation Building." Pp. 562–600 in *The Formation of National States in Western Europe*, edited by Charles Tilly. Princeton, NJ: Princeton University Press.

Rorty, Richard. 1990 "The Priority of Democracy to Philosophy." Pp. 279–302 in *Reading Rorty*, edited by Alan R. Malachowski. Oxford: Basil Blackwell.

Rorty, Richard. 1991. "The Priority of Democracy to Philosophy." Pp. 175–96 in *Objectivism, Relativism, and Truth*, edited by Richard Rorty. Cambridge: Cambridge University Press.

Rose, Richard. 1992. "Toward a Civil Economy." *Journal of Democracy 3*:13–26.

Rosenbaum, M. 1991. *Frauenarbeit und Frauenalltag in der Sowjetunion*. Münster: Verlag Westfälisches Dampfboot.

Rotter, Julian B. 1966. "Generalized Expectancies for Internal Versus External Control of Reinforcement." *Psychological Monographs 80*:1–28.

Runciman, William G. 1966. *Relative Deprivation and Social Justice. A Study of Attitudes to Social Inequality in Twentieth-Century England*. London: Routledge & Kegan Paul.

Rutkevich, M. N. 1987. "Socialist Justice." *Soviet Sociology* 26:52–66.

Sampson, Edward E. 1975. "On Justice as Equality." *Journal of Social Issues 31*:45–64.

Sassoon, Anne Showstack. 1987. *Gramsci's Politics*. Minneapolis: University of Minnesota Press.

Scheffler, Samuel. 1992. "Responsibility, Reactive Attitudes, and Liberalism in Philosophy and Politics." *Philosophy and Public Affairs 21*:299–323.

Scherer, Klaus R. 1992. "Issues in the Study of Justice." Pp. 1–14 in *Justice: Interdisciplinary Perspectives*, edited by Klaus R. Scherer. Cambridge: Cambridge University Press.

Schlozman, Kay L. and Sidney Verba. 1979. *Injury to Insult*. Cambridge, MA: Harvard University Press.

Schmitter, Philippe. 1988. "The Consolidation of Political Democracy in Southern Europe." Unpublished manuscript. Stanford University, Stanford, CA.

Schokkaert, Erik. 1992. "The Economics of Distributive Justice, Welfare and Freedom." Pp. 65–113 in *Justice: Interdisciplinary Perspectives*, edited by Klaus R. Scherer. Cambridge: Cambridge University Press.

Schupp, Jürgen and Gert Wagner. 1991. "Basisdaten für die Beschreibung und Analyse des sozio-ökonomischen Wandels der DDR." *Kölner Zeitschrift für Soziologie und Sozialpsychologie 43*:322–33.

Schwarz, Rudolph. 1978. "Luthers Lehre von den drei Ständen und die drei Dimensionen der Ethik." *Luther Jahrbuch 45*:15–23.

Schwarze, J. 1991a. "Ausbildung und Einkommen von Männern. Einkommensfunktions schätzungen für die ehemalige DDR und die Bundesrepublik Deutschland." *Mitteilung aus der Arbeitsmarkt- und Berufsforschung 24*:63–69.

Schwarze, J. 1991b. "Einkommensverläufe in der DDR von 1989 bis 1990. Unbeobachtete Heterogenität und erste Auswirkungen der marktwirtschaftlichen Orientierung." Pp. 188–212 in *Lebenslagen im Wandel: Zur Einkommensdynamik in Deutschland seit 1984*, edited by U. Rendtel and Gert Wagner. Frankfurt: Campus Verlag.

Schwinger, Thomas. 1980a. "Just Allocation of Goods, Decisions among Three Principles." Pp. 95–125 in *Justice and Social Interaction*, edited by Gerold Mikula. New York: Springer-Verlag.

Schwinger, Thomas. 1980b. "Gerechte Güter-Verteilungen. Entscheidungen zwischen drei Prinzipien." Pp. 107–40 in *Gerechtigkeit und soziale Interaktion. Experimentelle und theoretische Beiträge aus der psychologischen Forschung*, edited by Gerold Mikula. Bern: Huber.

Sennett, Richard and Jonathan Cobb. 1973. *The Hidden Injuries of Class*. New York: Vintage.

Sewell, William H., Archibald O. Haller, and George W. Ohlendorf. 1970. "The Educational and Early Occupational Status Attainment Process: A Replication and Revision." *American Sociological Review* 35:1014–27.

Shepelak, Norma J. and Duane F. Alwin. 1986. "Beliefs about Inequality and Perceptions of Distributive Justice." *American Sociological Review* 51:30–46.

Shklar, Judith. 1992. *Faces of Injustice*. New Haven, CT: Yale University Press.

Shlapentokh, Vladimir. 1986. *Soviet Public Opinion and Ideology*. New York: Praeger.

Siemienska, R. 1985. "Women, Work, and Gender Equality." Pp. 31–46 in *Women, State, and Party in Eastern Europe*, edited by Sharon Wolchik and Alfred Meyer. Durham, NC: Duke University Press.

Skidmore, William L. 1984. *Sociology's Models of Man*. New York: Gordon & Breach.

Smelser, Neil J. 1985. "Evaluating the Model of Structural Differentiation in Relation to Educational Change in the Nineteenth Century." Pp. 113–29 in *Neofunctionalism*, edited by Jeffrey Alexander. Beverly Hills, CA: Sage.

Smith, Tom W. 1989. "Inequality and Welfare." Pp. 59–86 in *British Social Attitudes: Special International Report*, edited by Roger Jowell, Sharon Witherspon, and Lindsay Brook. Aldershot: Gower.

Sneed, Joseph. 1971. *The Logical Structure of Mathematical Physics*. Dordrecht: Reidel.

Sørensen, Aage B. and Nancy B. Tuma. 1981. "Labor Market Structures and Job Mobility." *Research in Social Stratification and Mobility* 1:67–94.

Stegmüller, Wolfgang. 1973. *Probleme und Resultate der Wissenschaftstheorie und Analytischen Philosophie. Vol. 2*. Berlin: Springer Verlag.

Stephan, H. and E. Wiedemann. 1990. "Lohnstruktur und Lohndifferenzierung in der DDR. Ergebnisse der Lohndatenerfassung vom September 1988." *Mitteilung aus der Arbeitsmarkt- und Berufsforschung* 23:550–62.

Stern, Fritz. 1961. *The Politics of Cultural Despair: A Study in the Rise of the Germanic Ideology*. Berkeley: University of California Press.

Stevens, S. S. 1975. *Psychophysics. Introduction to Its Perceptual, Neural, and Social Prospects*. New York: Wiley.

Szydlik, Marc. 1992. "Arbeitseinkommen in der Deutschen Demokratischen Republik und der Bundesrepublik Deutschland." *Kölner Zeitschrift für Soziologie und Sozialpsychologie* 44:292–314.

Tauber, I. 1986. *A Hatranyos Tarsadalmi Helyzet es a Bunozes Osszefuggesei, Kulonos Tekintettel Egyes Kisebbsegi Csoportokra (The Correlation between Social Deprivation and Criminality: Focus on Minority Groups)*. Budapest: Tankoynvkiado.

Taylor-Gooby, Peter. 1989. "The Role of the State." Pp. 35–58 in *British Social Attitudes: Special International Report*, edited by Roger Jowell, Sharon Witherspon, and Lindsay Brook. Aldershot: Gower.

Taylor-Gooby, Peter. 1991. "Ideology, Attitudes and the Future of Welfare Citizenship: Welfare State Regimes and Women's Unwaged Work." Paper presented at the conference *Quality of Citizenship*. Utrecht.

Therborn, Goran. 1980. *The Ideology of Power and the Power of Ideology.* London: Verso.

Thomas, Michael. 1991. "Wenn es konkret wird: Hat Marxistische Klassentheorie Chancen in der modernen Unübersichtlichkeit?" Pp. 395–406 in *Die Modernisierung moderner Gesellschaften. Verhandlungen des 25. Deutschen Soziologentages,* edited by Wolfgang Zapf. Frankfurt: Campus Verlag.

Thomas, William I. 1966. *On Social Organization and Social Personality,* edited by Morris Janowitz. Chicago: University of Chicago Press.

Thompson, James B. 1990. *Ideology and Modern Culture.* Oxford: Basil Blackwell.

Thompson, Michael. 1982. "A Three Dimensional Model." Pp. 31–62 in *Essays in the Sociology of Perception,* edited by Mary Douglas. London: Routledge & Kegan Paul.

Thompson, Michael, Richard Ellis, and Aaron Wildavsky. 1990. *Cultural Theory.* Boulder: Westview.

Tidmarsh, K. 1993. "Russia's Work Ethic." *Foreign Affairs* 72:67–77.

Tönnies, Ferdinand. [1935] 1979. *Gemeinschaft und Gesellschaft: Grundbegriffe der reinen Soziologie.* Darmstadt: Wissenschaftliche Buchgesellschaft.

Törnblom, Kjell Y. 1992. "The Social Psychology of Distributive Justice." Pp. 177–236 in *Justice: Interdisciplinary Perspectives,* edited by Klaus R. Scherer. Cambridge: Cambridge University Press.

Trappe, Heike. 1992. "Erwerbsverläufe von Frauen und Männern in verschiedenen historischen Phasen der DDR-Entwicklung." Pp. 172–208 in *Familie und Erwerbstätigkeit im Umbruch,* Sonderheft 148, edited by Notburga Ott und Gert Wagner. Berlin: DIW.

Treiman, Donald. 1977. *Occupational Prestige in Comparative Perspective.* New York: Wiley.

Troeltsch, Ernst. 1961. *Die Soziallehren der christlichen Kirchen und Gruppen,* Gesammelte Schriften, Bd. 1. Aalen: Scientia.

Tuttle, L. 1986. *Encyclopedia of Feminism.* New York: Facts on File.

Tversky, Amos and Daniel Kahneman. 1981. "The Framing of Decisions and the Psychology of Choice." *Science* 211:453–58.

Van Wijck, P. 1993. "On Equity and Utility." *Rationality and Society* 5:68–84.

Van Wijck, P. 1994. "Evaluating Income Distributions." *Journal of Economic Psychology* 15:173–90.

Verba, Sidney, Norman H. Nie, and Jae-on Kim. 1987. *Participation and Political Equality: A Seven Nation Comparison.* Chicago: University of Chicago Press.

Verba, Sidney, Kay Schlozman, Henry Brady, and Norman Nie. 1993. "Citizen Activity: Who Participates? What Do They Say?" *American Political Science Review* 87:303–18.

Volf, Miroslav. 1987. "Arbeit und Charisma." *Zeitschrift für evangelische Ethik* 31:411–31.

Wacker, Luise. 1922. *Die Sozial- und Wirtschaftsauffassung im Pietismus untersucht in ihrer ideellen Ausgestaltung bei Spener, in ihrer praktischen Auswirkung auf Francke.* Ph.D. dissertation, University of Heidelberg.

Wahba, M. A. 1972. "Preferences Among Alternative Forms of Equity: The Apportionment of Coalition Reward in the Males and Females." *Journal of Social Psychology* 87:107–15.

Walby, S. 1990. *Theorizing Patriarchy.* Cambridge: Basil Blackwell.

Walker, Lawrence J. 1991. "Geschlechtsunterschiede in der Entwicklung des moralischen Urteils." Pp. 109–20 in *Weibliche Moral,* edited by Gertrud Nunner-Winkler. Frankfurt: Campus Verlag.

Walster, E., E. Berscheid, and G. W. Walster. 1973. "New Directions in Equity Research." *Journal of Personality and Social Psychology,* 25:151–76.

Walster, E., G. W. Walster, and E. Berscheid. 1978. *Equity: Theory and Research*. Boston, MA: Allyn & Bacon.

Walzer, Michael. 1981. "Philosophy and Democracy." *Political Theory* 9:379–99.

Walzer, Michael. 1983. *Spheres of Justice: A Defense of Pluralism and Equality*. New York: Basic Books.

Warnke, Georgia. 1992. *Justice and Interpretation*. Oxford:, Basil Blackwell.

Watson, P. 1992. "Gender Relations, Education, and Social Change in Poland." *Gender and Education* 4:127–47.

Weatherford, M. Stephen. 1989. "Political economy and political legitimacy: the link between economic policy and political trust." Pp. 225–52 in *Economic Decline and Political Change*, edited by Harold D. Clarke, Marianne Stewart and Gary Zuk. Pittsburgh: University of Pittsburgh Press.

Weber, Max. 1948. *From Max Weber*. Edited by H. H. Gerth and C. W. Mills. London: Routledge and Kegan Paul.

Weber, Max. 1972a. *Gesammelte Aufsätze zur Religionssoziologie*. Tübingen: Siebeck-Mohr.

Weber, Max. 1972b. *Wirtschaft und Gesellschaft*, 5th ed. Tübingen: Siebeck-Mohr.

Weber, Max. 1979. *Die protestantische Ethik*. Gütersloh: Gütersloher Verlagshaus.

Wegener, Bernd. 1982. "Outline of a Structural Taxonomy of Sensory and Social Psychophysics." Pp. 1–40 in *Social Attitudes and Psychophysical Measurement*, edited by Bernd Wegener. Hillsdale, NJ: Erlbaum.

Wegener, Bernd. 1987. "The Illusion of Distributive Justice." *European Sociological Review* 3:1–13.

Wegener, Bernd. 1988. *Kritik des Prestiges*. Opladen: Westdeutscher Verlag.

Wegener, Bernd. 1991. "Relative Deprivation and Social Mobility. Structural Constraints on Distributive Justice Judgments." *European Sociological Review* 7:3–18.

Wegener, Bernd. 1992a. "Class, Mobility, and the Distributive Justice Norms." ISJP Arbeitsbericht 13 (German Project Report 13), Heidelberg.

Wegener, Bernd. 1992b. "Concepts and Measurement of Prestige." *Annual Review of Sociology* 18:253–80.

Wegener, Bernd. 1992c. "Gerechtigkeitsforschung und Legitimationsnormen." *Zeitschrift für Soziologie* 21:269–83.

Wegener, Bernd. 1994. "Soziale Gerechtigkeitsforschung: Normativ oder deskriptiv?" Öffentliche Vorlesungen, Humboldt-Universität zu Berlin.

Wegener, Bernd and Stefan Liebig. 1991. *Etatismus und Funktionalismus. Ein Vergleich dominanter Ideologien in Deutschland und den USA*. ISJP Arbeitsbericht 5 (German Research Report 5), Heidelberg.

Weidig, Rudi. 1988. *Sozialstruktur der DDR*. Berlin: Dietz.

Weiner, Bernard. 1976. *Theorien der Motivation*. Stuttgart: Klett.

Weir, Margaret, Ann Shola Orloff, and Theda Skocpol. 1988. *The Politics of Social Policy in the United States*. Princeton, NJ: Princeton University Press.

Wheaton, Blair, Bengt Muthen, Duane F. Alwin, and Gene F. Summers. 1977. Assessing Reliability and Stability in Panel Models. Pp. 84–136 in *Sociological Methodology*, edited by David R. Heise. San Francisco, Jossey-Bass.

Wilensky, Harold L. 1975. *The Welfare State and Equality*. Berkeley: University of California Press.

Wilensky, Harold L., Gregory M. Luebert, Susan Reed Hahn, and Adreinne M. Jamieson. 1985. *Comparative Social Policy*. Berkeley, CA: Institute of International Studies.

Willis, Paul. 1977. *Learning to Labor*. Westmead: Saxon House.

Wilson, Kenneth L. and Alejandro Portes. 1975. "The Educational Attainment Process: Results from a National Sample." *American Journal of Sociology* 81:343–63.

Winkler, G. 1990a. *Frauenreport '90*. Berlin: Die Wirtschaft Berlin GmbH.

Winkler, G. 1990b. *Sozialreport '90. Daten und Fakten zur Lage in der DDR*. Berlin: Die Wirtschaft Berlin GmbH.

Wolchik, S. 1985. "The Precommunist Legacy, Economic Development, Social Transformation, and Women's Roles in Eastern Europe." Pp. 31–46 in *Women, State, and Party in Eastern Europe*, edited by Sharon Wolchik and Alfred Meyer. Durham, NC: Duke University Press.

Wolchik, Sharon and Alfred Meyer (eds.). 1985. *Women, State, and Party in Eastern Europe*. Durham, NC: Duke University Press.

Wolfe, Alan. 1989. *Whose Keeper? Social Science and Moral Obligation*. Berkeley: University of California Press.

Wollheim, Richard. 1962. "A Paradox in the Theory of Democracy." Pp. 71–87 in *Philosophy, Politics and Society*, 2nd Ser., edited by Peter Laslett and W. G. Runciman. Oxford: Basil Blackwell.

Wright, Erik O. 1985. *Classes*. London: New Left Books.

Yanowitch, Murray (ed.). 1989. *New Directions in Soviet Social Thought*. Armonk, NY: M. E. Sharpe.

Zaslavskaya, Tatyana. 1986. "Social Justice and the Human Factor in Economic Development." *Kommunist* no. 13.

Index